1989

W9-CLF-743

Socrates and Aristophanes

SOCRATES

and

ARISTOPHANES

LEO STRAUSS

The University of Chicago Press

Chicago and London

The University of Chicago Press, Chicago 60637
The University of Chicago Press, Ltd., London

© 1966 by Leo Strauss
All rights reserved. Published 1966
Midway reprint 1980
Printed in the United States of America

Library of Congress Cataloging in Publication Data

Strauss, Leo.
 Socrates and Aristophanes.

 Reprint of the ed. published by Basic Books, New York.
 Includes bibliographical references and index.
  1. Aristophanes—Criticism and interpretation.
  2. Socrates. I. Title.
[PA3879.S78 1980]   882'.01   79-18391
ISBN 0-226-77691-3

Contents

Socrates and Aristophanes

I Introduction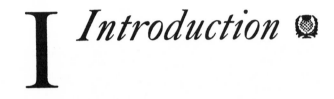

Our Great Tradition includes political philosophy and thus seems to vouch for its possibility and necessity. According to the same tradition, political philosophy was founded by Socrates.

Since Socrates did not write books or speeches, we depend entirely on other men's reports for our knowledge of the circumstances in which, or of the reasons for which, political philosophy was founded. The difficulty is increased by the fact that the reports in question are not in entire agreement with one another. Our chief sources are the dialogues of Plato, some remarks of Aristotle, Xenophon's Socratic writings, and Aristophanes' *Clouds*. Aristotle did not know Socrates' thought except through reports oral or written; Aristophanes, Xenophon, and Plato knew Socrates himself. While Xenophon and Plato were friends and admirers of Socrates, Aristophanes was not; he seems to present Socrates as a sophist in the Socratic sense of the term. As for the Platonic dialogues, their present-day use by scholars is ordinarily based on two decisions: on the distinction between genuine and spurious among those writings that the tradition has transmitted to us as genuine; and on the contention, which is partly based on the allegedly certain knowledge of the sequence in which the genuine dialogues were written, that only the early dialogues are Socratic or that they are, at any rate, more Socratic than the later ones. Whatever we might have to think of these decisions, the Platonic dialogues are admittedly not reports, but works of art; they do not permit us to distinguish incontestably between what Socrates himself thought and the thoughts that Plato merely ascribed to him. In a letter that has come down to us as Platonic, it is said, "There is not now nor will there be any writing of Plato; but those writings which are now said to be his belong to Socrates having become fair (noble) and young (new)." The Platonic dialogues "idealize" Socrates. Plato never vouches for the authenticity of his Socratic conversations. Plato is not a historian. The only historian among Socrates' contemporaries on whose writings we must rely for our knowledge of Socrates is Xenophon, who continued Thucydides' history, and who vouches for the authenticity of at least some of his Socratic conversations by introducing them with expressions like "I once heard him say." There is then at least a prima-facie case in favor of the view that the primary source for our knowledge of Socrates is the Socratic writings of Xenophon. The study of these writings may compel us to modify that suggestion, but this does not detract from its usefulness. Not a few errors regarding Socrates that are at present rather powerful would have been avoided if the value of Xenophon's testimony had not been dismissed as quickly and as rudely as it has been.

If Socrates was the founder of political philosophy, political philosophy was preceded by philosophy. Thus the question arises as to why pre-Socratic philosophy was able or compelled to dispense with political philosophy. This question is part of the very "problem of Socrates," for Socrates himself was a philosopher before he became a political philosopher. That it is necessary to consider the question regarding "the young Socrates" is shown by the fact that Plato draws our attention to this subject. The Platonic Socrates speaks on the day of his death about his youthful passion for "that wisdom which people call the inquiry regarding nature" (*Phaedo* 96ᵃ6–8). In the *Parmenides* Plato goes so far as to present the young Socrates (127ᶜ4–5, 130ᵉ1–4); this young Socrates seems indeed to be older than the young Socrates spoken about in the *Phaedo*, since the latter was simply "pre-Socratic" whereas the former had already completed the crucial turn toward the "ideas." It seems that the Socrates to whom Diotima revealed the secrets of Eros was also young; she certainly cross-examined him just as Parmenides cross-examined him. However this may be, we learn from Xenophon that Socrates was already famous or notorious as a natural philosopher before he ever raised the question of what a perfect gentleman is, i.e., a question comprising all the inquiries of the kind to which he dedicated himself entirely after his break with natural philosophy.[1] Still, the only available presentation of the "pre-Socratic" Socrates is that which we find in Aristophanes' *Clouds*.

The use of the *Clouds* for the understanding of "the young Socrates" can hardly be questioned on the ground that this work was an attack on Socrates or that Aristophanes was an enemy of Socrates, for an attack may be justified and an enemy may be fair. One may say that the Socrates presented by Plato and Xenophon agreed entirely with Aristophanes' judgment on the Socrates presented by the comic poet. Aristophanes and Socrates meet before our eyes in Plato's *Banquet* about seven years after the first performance of the *Clouds*. The occasion was a banquet at the end of which only three men were still awake and sober, two of them being Aristophanes and Socrates. At that time the three men were engaged in a friendly conversation that ended in an agreement about a subject of the greatest importance to Aristophanes, the subject of comedy and tragedy; Aristophanes agreed to a view propounded by Socrates. In the only Platonic presentation of Aristophanes, the poet appears to be very close to Socrates. From this fact we may understand the Platonic Socrates' analysis of the state of the soul at comedies. In that analysis we discern this strand. The state of the soul at comedies is a mixture of being pleased by our friends' innocuous overestimation of their wisdom and being pained by envy; that state of the soul is never free from injustice.[2] A friend's wisdom may not be as great as he thinks, and therefore he may be somewhat ridiculous; but his wisdom may be sufficiently great to give one cause for envy. This thought can hardly be adequate as an analysis of comedy as such, but it makes sense as the explanation of the comedy par excellence, the *Clouds*: Far from being an enemy of Socrates, Aristophanes was his friend, but somewhat envious of his wisdom—even of the wisdom of the young Socrates. Or, as one might also say, the primary object of the comic poet's envy was not Socrates' wisdom but his sovereign contempt for that popular applause on which the dramatic poet necessarily depends, or Socrates' perfect freedom.

Even if we had to grant that comic treatment is necessarily sympathetic treatment, we would not be compelled to assert that comic treatment does not distort. The philosopher is necessarily ridiculous in the eyes of the multitude [3] and therefore a natural subject for comedy. If for one reason or another the choice of Socrates recommended itself to Aristophanes, the poet was free to involve him in the most laughable situations into which a philosopher could fall, without necessarily bringing out the peculiarities of the individual philosopher Socrates. Yet, before one could even consider this possibility, one would have to know whether Aristophanes has no concern other than to excite his audience to laughter. According to his emphatic claim, this is not the case. He is as much concerned with saying serious things as he is with saying laughable ones. Being a poet, he is concerned with making men in the cities good and noble; being a comic poet, he is concerned with concealing vice, i.e., with depriving vice of its attraction by ridiculing it. Acting in accordance with justice he teaches things that are good for the city, or he takes the risk of saying among the Athenians what is just; but being a comic poet he can not do this except by treating the just things themselves comically. Goodness and justice fight on his side. He is indeed as much concerned with the approval of the laughers as with that of the wise.[4] But does this not imply that those who love or admire him because he makes them laugh are a class distinct from his wise lovers or admirers? We are surely entitled to assume that his presentation of Socrates also serves, and perhaps above all, the purpose of teaching justice—perhaps of defending justice against Socrates' attack on it by presenting Socrates as ridiculous. This would be compatible with Aristophanes' not being an enemy of Socrates; we recall that the Platonic Socrates defends the cause of justice against Thrasymachos without ever being Thrasymachos' enemy and while becoming his friend in the process.[5]

The problem of Socrates as we have sketched it, which includes that of the young Socrates, can only be preparatory to "the problem of Socrates" as stated by Nietzsche: The question of what Socrates stood for inevitably becomes the question of the worth of what Socrates stood for. In other words, the return to the origins of the Great Tradition has become necessary because of the radical questioning of that tradition, a questioning that may be said to culminate in Nietzsche's attack on Socrates or on Plato. Nietzsche began this attack in his first book, *The Birth of Tragedy*. He disowned that work to some extent in later years. Nevertheless, his earliest statement remains his broadest statement of "the problem of Socrates"; and if one reads it in the light of his later corrections, one grasps those features of his youthful statement that he maintained till the end of his career, in spite of some vacillations.[6]

Nietzsche faced Socrates as "the single turning point and vortex of so-called world history" within the context of his concern with "the science of aesthetics." This science as he understood it is both metaphysical and physiologic-psychological; it is "natural science"; according to the suggestions of *Beyond Good and Evil*, it belongs to the context of a historical physiopsychology. Nietzsche's concern is not merely theoretical; he is concerned with the future of Germany or the future of Europe—a human future that must surpass the highest that man has ever achieved before. The peak of man hitherto is that manner of life that found its expression in Greek tragedy or, more precisely, in Aeschylean tragedy. The "tragic" understanding of the world was rejected or destroyed by Socrates, who therefore is "the most questionable phenomenon of antiquity," a man of more than human size: a demigod. Socrates is the first theoretical man, the incarnation of the spirit of science, radically unartistic or a-music: "In the person of Socrates the belief in the comprehensibility of nature and in the universal healing power of knowledge has first come to light." He is the prototype of the rationalist and therefore of the optimist, for optimism is not merely the belief that the world is the best possible world, but also the belief that the world can become the best of all imaginable worlds, or that the evils that belong to the best possible world can be rendered harmless by knowledge: thinking can not only fully understand being, but can even correct it; life can be guided by science; the living gods of myth can be replaced by a *deus ex machina*, i.e., the forces of nature as known and used in the service of "higher egoism." Rationalism is optimism, since it is the belief that reason's power is unlimited and essentially beneficent or that science can solve all riddles and loosen all chains. Rationalism is optimism, since the belief in causes depends on the belief in ends,[7] or since rationalism presupposes the belief in the initial or final supremacy of the good. The full and ultimate consequences of the change effected or represented by Socrates appear only in the contemporary West: in the belief in universal enlightenment and therewith in the earthly happiness of all within a universal state, in utilitarianism, liberalism, democracy, pacificism, and socialism. Both these consequences and the insight into the essential limitation of science have shaken "Socratic culture" to its foundation: "The time of Socratic man has gone." There is then hope for a future beyond the peak of pre-Socratic culture, for a philosophy of the future that is no longer merely theoretical, but knowingly based on acts of the will or on decisions, and for a new kind of politics that includes as a matter of course "the merciless annihilation of everything degenerating and parasitical." Nietzsche himself has said that in order to understand a philosopher one acts soundly by first raising the question of the moral or political meaning of his metaphysical assertions.[8] Hence it would seem that his attack on Socrates must be understood primarily as a political attack.

Whatever one might have to think of Nietzsche's passionate and extreme attack on the Great Tradition, he points out at least one fact that justifies some doubts of that tradition. It is part of the tradition to combine the highest veneration for Socrates with the highest admiration for the tragedy of Sophocles,[9] for the tradition believes in the harmony between the true and the beautiful, between science and art. Yet, according to the tradition, Socrates accords less with Sophocles than with Euripides.

The profound kinship between Socrates and Euripides—as distinguished from Sophocles and especially Aeschylus—was sensed clearly by Aristophanes, who justly presented Socrates as "the first and foremost sophist" by looking at him in the light of "the good old time" of the Marathon fighters, or as one of the symptoms of "a degenerate culture." Aristophanes' political posture seems to foreshadow Nietzsche's political posture. Yet, whereas Aristophanes presents the young Socrates, Nietzsche's attack is directed against the Platonic Socrates: Nietzsche, whose *The Birth of Tragedy* is almost silent about comedy, uses Aristophanes' critique of the young Socrates as if it had been meant as a critique of the Platonic Socrates. He seems to imply that Aristophanes would have attacked the Socrates who defended justice and piety on the same ground on which he attacks the Socrates who assailed justice or piety, or that the Platonic Socrates is as remote from the Marathon fighters as is Aristophanes' Socrates.

II *The Clouds*

Aristophanes presents Socrates as saying and doing many laughable things; he makes him a laughingstock. Yet he does the same to all of his characters, at least to all of his important characters, regardless of whether they stand for the new ways or for the old. The old-fashioned is no less laughable, no less unreasonable, than the newfangled. Following this thought to its conclusion, one might say that Aristophanes celebrates everywhere the triumph of unreason or madness.[1] Yet he surely does nothing of this kind in the *Clouds*. While his laughable Lysistrate, for instance, is victorious, his laughable Socrates is defeated: A former disciple burns down Socrates' schoolhouse, and it is only by a lucky or laughable accident that Socrates and his disciples do not perish in the flames. Socrates had been responsible for the victory of Unjust Speech over Just Speech, and he had asserted that "Zeus is not." Surely, making that assertion was a capital crime; what happens to him is too little for someone who has committed a capital crime, but it is the utmost that could befall him in a comedy. One thus becomes inclined to believe that Aristophanes expresses his judgments by the outcome of his plays; he approves of those designs that he presents as successful, whereas he disapproves of those that he presents as failures. Even if we could regard this criterion as established and could therefore be certain that Aristophanes disapproved of Socrates' ways, we could not yet be certain that in his view Socrates deserves his fate on account of his opinions. But is it possible to accept this criterion? Did Aristophanes approve of the revolt of his Peisthetairos against the gods, or of the expulsion by his Chremylos of that sensible woman, Poverty? Are we then reduced to finding the poet's judgments in what he says in his own name in the parabaseis? But are these sayings not as much parts of the comedies as the curses of his Kleon?

11

The action that leads to Socrates' downfall is started not by Socrates but by Strepsiades. In accordance with this the *Clouds* begins with a soliloquy by Strepsiades. Strepsiades moans. All Aristophanean comedies open with moanings or complaints. But in contradistinction to the other comedies, the *Clouds* does not end in gaiety. After having given inarticulate expression to his discomfort, Strepsiades calls on Zeus the King: Whether Zeus is the king will become a question for him before long. He speaks to himself because he has no one to talk to; his son, Pheidippides, to whom he would like to talk, is fast asleep. It is still dark. He yearns for the day, for light—in the literal sense. His servants too are asleep. Strepsiades is willing to follow the majority, but he can not find sleep because he has great worries. He speaks of these worries within the recesses of his house while it is still dark. They are caused by the war, which has put an end to the good old times. The war is of some concern to him. We note in advance that the war is of no concern whatever to Socrates. Even to Strepsiades the war is a minor worry compared with the debts that he has incurred through his son, who is passionately given to horsemanship. The sleepless Strepsiades tries to bring order into his accounts. But the same son who, by spending his life in the dream world of horses and racing, has caused the disorder in his father's accounts, prevents his father from reducing those accounts to order by speaking of horses in his dreams. The son had unintentionally disturbed the sleep of his father. Now the father unintentionally disturbs the sleep of his son. Yet the son, who does not worry about the debts, again falls asleep. Continuing his soliloquy Strepsiades traces his worries to their root, to his marriage. He curses the matchmaker who induced him to marry Pheidippides' mother; he is not aware that he thus indirectly curses his beloved son himself. Strepsiades, the simple and rude rustic who lived well and in easy circumstances in the country, married the fine, spoiled, and lascivious niece of an urban patrician, a woman who demanded too much from him in every respect, inciting him to expenses beyond his habits or means and thus setting the model for their son and even for the servants. Their son—whose very name expresses the coming together of the incompatible ingredients to which he owes his being—has inherited the extravagant tastes of his mother and her line and thus ruined his father. Strepsiades now needs his son's help in order to escape the troubles in which his son has involved him. He awakens his son as gently as he can. But the gentleness is not only due to calculation; he loves his son from his heart, just as his son loves him—which, however, does not mean that there are no limits to the father's and the son's love.

Worrying or thinking for a whole night Strepsiades has discovered—not without divine help—a single and amazing path of salvation. But he is no longer young and nimble enough to take it; Pheidippides must take it. The son swears to him by Dionysos that he will do whatever his father asks him. The son would have preferred Poseidon and the father Demeter; Dionysos is as it were the second choice of either; Dionysos supplies the ground on which they can meet. The father draws his son's attention to a little house close by, the "think-tank" of certain wise souls or ghosts. Strepsiades is not sure of their names; but Pheidippides, who has nothing but contempt for those pale-faced boasters, knows that their chiefs are Socrates and Chairephon. When his father asks him to change his whole way of life, to abandon his horsemanship and to become a companion or pupil of Socrates, he absolutely refuses; he breaks his oath without the slightest hesitation, for by complying with his father's request he would disgrace himself in the eyes of his fellow horsemen. Thereupon Strepsiades threatens to throw him out of his house. Pheidippides—who is sure that his mother's relations will not leave him without horses and surer still that his father will not throw him out of his house—declares that he will not pay any attention to his father. Strepsiades no longer has any choice; he is compelled to try to become Socrates' pupil himself. He makes the attempt only after having prayed to the gods.

Socrates' downfall is brought about by Strepsiades. At the beginning of the play he does not even know Socrates' name, whereas his son, the sophisticated horseman, knows it as a matter of course. The men of the upper class know of Socrates, but they have no use for him; they despise him as a particularly ridiculous sort of pauper. The men of the lower class have no use for him and do not even know of him. Only men who are between the two classes can become interested in Socrates and therefore conceivably bring about his ruin. Differently stated, Socrates' corrupting influence can affect only a small part of the population. Through his marriage Strepsiades is a man between the upper and the lower class. From hearsay he knows, or almost knows, that Socrates belongs to a bunch of wise souls who persuade people that heaven is a stove and men are charcoals, while they teach people for money how one can win arguments regardless of whether one upholds a just or an unjust cause, and especially, which is much more difficult, an unjust cause. It seems that the wise souls transmit the persuasive teaching regarding heaven and man without charge, perhaps because it is useless by itself. Strepsiades understands that teaching literally: According to him, Socrates does not teach that heaven is *like* a stove and men are *like* charcoals, but that heaven *is* a stove and men *are* charcoals. At any rate, since Socrates teaches such strange things about heaven and man, it is not strange that he should be able to teach one how to defraud one's creditors of the last penny. Strepsiades wishes his son to become Socrates' pupil so that he will learn how to defraud their creditors: He wishes to corrupt his son; his own corruption precedes his acquaintance with Socrates and induces him to seek that acquaintance.

It takes considerable time before Strepsiades meets Socrates. Strepsiades knocks at the door of the "think-tank" with rustic force, thus making a thought miscarry, as he learns from a pupil who comes to the door. When he inquires about the thing that miscarried, the pupil tells him that this may be divulged only to disciples. Yet Strepsiades' mere assertion that he has come in order to be a disciple is sufficient for the pupil to disclose to him this and other secrets. Socrates' secrecy measures seem to be defective. On the other hand, hardly anything that the pupil says to Strepsiades —in contradistinction to what Socrates himself will say to him before long —would ever have caused any serious harm to Socrates. In accordance with this, the pupil's reply to Strepsiades' question regarding the identity of the miscarried thought or affair does not clearly reveal any miscarriage: Could the pupil be less stupid than he appears? [2] He replies that Socrates had just asked Chairephon how long a flea's jump is in terms of a flea's feet and that the area covered by a flea's foot was being measured in a most clever manner; did Strepsiades' undelicate knocking prevent the measuring of the distance covered by the flea's jump? Strepsiades' admiration for the feat induces the pupil to tell him of another one. Chairephon had asked Socrates whether in his view gnats hum through their mouths or their behinds: This question is even more subtle than the first, since the answer to it requires knowledge of the intestines of living gnats—i.e., of something that is not only very small and subtle but invisible as well. Strepsiades' admiration increases in proportion: Men who know their way in the intestines of gnats can easily defraud human creditors. The pupil can now afford to tell Strepsiades of a mishap that occurred to Socrates when he was studying the ways and revolutions of the moon—a mishap ridiculous in the eyes of Strepsiades and of most men, but not necessarily in those of Socrates' pupils. Strepsiades is, however, not deterred; perhaps he is even reassured. Perhaps equally ridiculous, but surely more successful, was Socrates' attempt to supply his starving group with a frugal dinner by cleverly executing an act of petty theft while pretending to do geometry. Strepsiades is enthusiastic about this feat.[3] It has dawned on him by now that Socrates is not merely one among the many wise souls who inhabit the "think-tank," but their chief; now Strepsiades can no longer restrain his desire to come face to face with Socrates and successfully urges the pupil to open the door so that he can enter. He is amazed by the sight of the pupils, the victims of an inhuman asceticism—they are not even permitted to breathe fresh air for any length of time. Strepsiades hears about astronomy and geometry; but he, a man of the soil, does not have the slightest interest in astronomy, although the art of defrauding one's creditors mysteriously depends on knowledge of heaven, of the heavenly bodies and their motions. He becomes at once keenly interested in the arts of measuring and mapping the earth or the land, which affect him in his capacity as patriotic citizen: Socrates and his pupils lack that motive in their studies.

Strepsiades has just pronounced a grave warning of the Spartan danger when he becomes aware of a man aloft who proves to be Socrates. For Socrates, Strepsiades and the Spartan danger are equally contemptible because they are both ephemeral. Nevertheless, he deigns to explain his strange position to Strepsiades by saying that he looks at the sun from all sides, which Strepsiades takes to mean that he looks down on the gods. Socrates does not protest. He corrects Strepsiades' impression by indirection, only after he has heard why Strepsiades came. Strepsiades is not shocked by Socrates' apparent contempt for the gods, but merely curious why he does not do this from the earth. Socrates replies that one can not discover the things aloft except by having airy thoughts as distinguished from earthy ones. Strepsiades does not quite follow, but he does not care; he has come with serious business that calls for earthy thinking because it must be transacted on the earth, to which Socrates must now willy-nilly descend. Strepsiades explains to Socrates why he is in need of the art of speaking, without saying anything about his son or his life in general. As far as Socrates knows, Strepsiades is a passionate horseman and may be a man without family; he forms his judgment about Strepsiades—about whether or not he should accept him as a pupil—on the basis of insufficient data. Strepsiades is willing to swear by the gods, as he declares spontaneously, that he will pay for the instruction whatever Socrates demands; he is not in the habit of paying cash, let alone in advance. Strepsiades must have been quite surprised to observe that Socrates does not tell his price; Socrates is interested only in Strepsiades' declaration that he will swear by the gods to pay whatever Socrates demands of him. In the first place, Socrates does not believe in oaths of this kind; if he considered the peculiarity of Strepsiades' case at all, he must be even less willing than usual to believe in oaths of this kind, for Strepsiades has said that he wishes to learn the speech or reasoning that does not pay anything. But above all it is all-important for a would-be pupil of Socrates to be eager to know what the divine things are in truth or, in other words, by which gods a sensible man would conceivably swear. For it goes without saying that Socrates is not an atheist; the gods by whom he swears are the Clouds. Perhaps these goddesses can not be called upon to watch over the payment of debts or to avenge perjury. Strepsiades, perhaps relieved that Socrates has not asked for exorbitant pay or, in fact, for any pay at all—in Strepsiades' present condition any pay would be exorbitant—expresses the utmost desire to converse with the Clouds. Thereupon Socrates solemnly initiates Strepsiades, who apprehends the worst but submits to the procedure, since Socrates assures him that there is no danger and that without the initiation and the ensuing appearance of the Clouds he will never become a clever speaker. Has Socrates abandoned his contempt for Strepsiades as an ephemeral? Or does this contempt live side by side with a zealous concern that his fellow mortals, however unpromising, acquire sound opinions about the gods? Socrates pronounces a solemn prayer to the Lord Air, to Ether, and, above all, to the Ladies Clouds, that the latter should appear to Strepsiades. Compared with this prayer, the one that Strepsiades addressed to the ordinary gods before he knocked at Socrates' door is likely to have been most perfunctory.

The Clouds respond to Socrates' pious call by a song announcing their approach. These virgin goddesses have left their father, Okeanos—i.e., the origin of all gods, if not of all beings—and are on their way toward the land of the virgin goddess Athena, a land most praiseworthy for the beauty-loving and Music piety with which it worships the heavenly gods as well as the nether ones. Socrates is the Prometheus of the *Clouds:* Bringing light to others he has no forethought of himself. The goddesses whom Socrates worships seem to care more for Athens than does their worshiper. Socrates responds to their song piously, but Strepsiades does so ludicrously, so that Socrates must rebuke him for behaving like the mocking comedians. Yet Strepsiades is bewildered rather than frivolous. From the outset he must have expected to witness extraordinary things when coming to Socrates, for he knew in advance that only extraordinary things could save him from his creditors. He was not surprised to learn that he could not become a clever speaker, and thus able to defraud his creditors, unless heaven is a stove and men are charcoals; he was still less surprised that he could not achieve his end unless he became intimately acquainted with the Clouds, who are goddesses. Yet, to hear this asserted by Socrates is one thing, and to hear and see those goddesses themselves is another. But whatever may be true of Strepsiades, whose credulity is very great because of his nature, his upbringing, and his desperate situation, those listeners or readers of Aristophanes who take the poet at his word when he says that he is not satisfied with making them laugh by all means and at all costs must wonder why acquaintance with the Clouds is indispensable for men who wish to become clever speakers or, in other words, what kind of gods the Clouds are.

Strepsiades needs to be reassured that the voices he has heard belong to goddesses and that the clouds, i.e., things that he has hitherto regarded as mere clouds, are goddesses. Socrates gives him this reassurance by an emphatic assertion and adds that the Clouds favor the indolent with powers such as those of understanding, of speaking cleverly, and of talking marvels or miracles; to some extent he now ascribes to the Clouds the effects that he had previously ascribed to the air. Strepsiades, who himself already feels some of the effect of the Clouds as Socrates has described it, is eager to see the goddesses clearly. We may observe here that what he had occasion to admire (and not merely to marvel at) since he knocked at Socrates' door were speeches, songs, or reports of sights, rather than sights. Even now it is more difficult for him than for Socrates to see the Clouds entering. He is understandably perplexed by the difference between the Clouds that he sees and what he has hitherto thought them to be. Socrates traces Strepsiades' previous error regarding the Clouds to his ignorance of the fact that the Clouds support all kinds of more or less mad sophisticates and high-class swindlers, who in return praise their benefactresses with songs and other Music things. This statement does not perplex Strepsiades, but it perplexes us. After all, Socrates himself is the devotee par excellence of the Clouds: Does Socrates claim to be Music, and is he a boaster? One thing seems to be clear: Aristophanes' Socrates claims that he and men like Aristophanes belong to the same species although, as will appear presently, to different subspecies. Strepsiades is not troubled by this difficulty; he applies Socrates' statement to the poets alone, who themselves acknowledge that for praising the Clouds they receive from them an abundance of the most delicate dishes; Socrates agrees, adding that this reward seems to be fair. As is indicated by Socrates' and his pupil's looks—to say nothing of the pupil's report of last night's dinner—Socrates, in contradistinction to the poets, does not praise the Clouds for the sake of good living. In other words, the species of favorites of the Clouds consists of a starving and a nonstarving part. What causes Strepsiades the greatest difficulty is understanding what has happened to the clouds so that they look, as the beings around him look, like mortal women; for those beings that have now come to full sight do not look like deathless women (although Socrates says that they are goddesses) or like clouds (although Socrates says that they are clouds); clouds surely are not mortal women, nor do they look like them, but rather like outspread flocks of wool. To put it as bluntly as Strepsiades does, clouds do not have noses; whereas the beings that now surround Strepsiades and Socrates, and that look like mortal women, do have noses. We shall not speculate on the right by which Strepsiades regards noses as clear proofs of femininity. It is more important to realize that to state the difficulty as Strepsiades states it means to solve it, for who has not seen clouds with noses, e.g., clouds that look like beasts with noses? As Socrates explains, the clouds can become everything they wish. They can take every shape they wish; they can imitate everything they see; they reveal the nature of everything they see by taking its shape and hence, in particular, they mock laughable men by exaggerating their shape (i.e., they are in particular the models for comic poets). They put together marvelous shapes that are not seen elsewhere, like the shapes of centaurs. It is the quasi-omnipotence [4] of the clouds that proves that they are divine. In brief, the Clouds are the goddesses of imitation and therefore the natural teachers of all imitative or likeness-making arts, and hence in particular of the art of speaking. Even Strepsiades is now convinced that the clouds are goddesses and in fact queens of the whole, and he greets them accordingly.

The Clouds in their turn greet Strepsiades and above all Socrates, whom they praise while teasing him; they declare that they favor him more than any other contemporary prattler about the things aloft with the exception of Prodikos. While they favor Prodikos because of his wisdom and judgment, they favor Socrates because of his arrogant deportment in the streets, his asceticism, and the solemn airs he puts on because of his intimacy with the Clouds. (The Socrates of the *Clouds* is then not a mere representative of a type.[5]) They ask him what he desires because they wish to supply him with it, but he is so self-sufficient that he does not even stop to reply. What he wants from the Clouds they have already granted him: Strepsiades has been duly impressed by them. Hence he now proclaims to Strepsiades that the Clouds alone are goddesses, and that everything else is idle talk. The Clouds listen to this proclamation in silence. Strepsiades is understandably surprised: Is Earth not a goddess? Above all, is the Olympian Zeus not a god? The all-daring Socrates, who came to sight at first as studying but not revering the sun, does not leave any doubt in Strepsiades' mind: Zeus, far from being a god, does not even exist. But this is manifestly absurd: If Zeus does not exist, who makes it rain? The Clouds, of course: Have you ever seen it rain without clouds? What is true of rain is true *mutatis mutandis* of fear-inspiring thunder; thunder is no threat. But the Clouds may be that without which there can be neither rain nor thunder; this does not prove that they are the cause of rain or thunder, or that they are not moved or compelled to rain or to thunder by something else or somebody else—by Zeus. Thus driven to the wall by Strepsiades, who fights valiantly for the life of Zeus, Socrates—who otherwise would have left matters at the divinity of the Clouds alone—admits that there is something higher than the Clouds, but he absolutely denies that the something higher is Zeus; it is the ethereal vortex. Strepsiades has no difficulty in understanding this contention: Zeus, who was hitherto the king, has been dethroned by Vortex, who is now the king, just as Zeus himself once dethroned Kronos; but Strepsiades still wants proof. Socrates supplies him with that proof by illustrating the genesis of thunder with an example taken from Strepsiades himself—from his gastric troubles after overeating on a holiday. The homely example does its work. Strepsiades' understanding has remarkably increased: He does not say that thunder is the same as the sounds accompanying diarrhea, but (cf. also 165) that it is like them. Still, the similarity is great; it deprives the things aloft of all their awesome glamour. Socrates debunks the things aloft (rumor has it that he held heaven to be a stove), perhaps in order to debunk justice. For one apparently overwhelming difficulty remains: Lightning bolts are thought to be the work of Zeus, who strikes perjurers with them. Yet Socrates easily takes away Strepsiades' fear, partly through expressing his utter contempt for the old-fashioned old man who believes such things: More temples and oaks holy to Zeus are struck by lightning than are perjurers. In the case of rain and thunder, Zeus has been replaced by the Clouds and Air; in the case of the punishment of perjury, Zeus has not been replaced by anybody or anything: There is no divine punishment for perjury or for any other crime. Socrates calls Strepsiades old-fashioned: The debunking of things aloft is inseparable from the debunking of antiquity, which clothes them with awe-inspiring splendor. Nothing is left for Strepsiades except to ask Socrates for an explanation of lightning in terms of air and clouds. Once this explanation is given and confirmed by Strepsiades himself, who remembers at the right moment another holiday experience that he had, he is fit to be addressed by the Clouds. He is promised that he will be blessed and famous, provided he possesses a good memory, is given to thinking, and dedicates himself with the utmost zeal to study by leading a hard life, abstaining from gymnastics, and preferring victory in action, in counsel, and in fighting with the tongue to everything else; sexual abstinence is tacitly included among the requirements. Strepsiades gives us all the assurances one could wish for regarding his frugality, endurance, and continence; his way of life (as distinguished from that of his son) has always been akin to that of Socrates and his pupils. We must wait and see whether his memory and thinking suffice. Socrates concludes the initiation of Strepsiades by asking him no longer to recognize any other gods except those that Socrates and his companions recognize, namely Chaos, the Clouds, and the tongue. The Clouds do not protest. Strepsiades promises that he will not talk to the other gods even if he meets them, or offer sacrifices or any other honoring gifts to them. He could not go further; he does not see the difference between ignoring the gods or denying their kingship or power and denying that they are. Socrates has no opportunity to correct him; for before he can say anything the Clouds, who are perfectly satisfied with Strepsiades' promise, step in with a request addressed to Strepsiades that he tell them confidently what he wants them to do for him: He will obtain what he desires if he honors and admires the Clouds—they do not say if he honors and admires no other gods except the Clouds—and if he attempts to be clever. Strepsiades replies that he does not want more than to be the very best speaker in Greece. The goddesses easily promise him that henceforth he will be among the most successful speakers in the Athenian Assembly. But his ambition does not run so high; he is content to be able to defraud any creditors, Athenian or stranger, however clever. The Clouds grant him that power, if possible, with still greater ease. Strepsiades is intoxicated with joy: In order to become known as the cleverest rogue, he is willing to undergo any hardship, however extreme, if not death itself; he almost forgets the end for the means. After promising him that he will forever lead the most enviable life in their company—they do not stoop to mention that he will have a "reputation for being the cleverest rogue"—the Clouds hand him over to Socrates, who is to start teaching him and thus to test his intelligence. They seem to have forgotten that Strepsiades' success does not depend entirely on his worshiping the Clouds, on his continence, and on his eagerness. In fact, they have merely been silent on the fourth condition, lest he change his mind. They are clever—how else could they teach men to speak cleverly?

Socrates says that the Clouds are the only goddesses (365). He also seems to address Air and Ether as gods (264–65), but he does not call them gods. He demands of Strepsiades that he recognize as gods only Chaos, the Clouds, and the tongue (423–24).[6] If we understand by "gods" superhuman beings that think, will, and speak, the Clouds are for Socrates the only gods. If we say that only thinking and willing beings can be called superhuman, we must say that according to Socrates the highest (air, ether) is subhuman, and only the Clouds are superhuman. Differently stated, whereas Ether or Air, like Poseidon (85), also originates bad things, the Clouds are responsible only for the greatest benefits to man. One may also say that the Clouds, being the only gods, are admittedly "smoke" (320, 330); whereas the other gods are not admittedly but in fact "smoke." Surely no one can deny that the *Clouds* is the only extant Aristophanean play in which the chorus, consisting of the Clouds, is simply superior to the actors proper. Yet why are the Clouds female gods? Socrates explains their appearing in the shape of mortal women by saying that they have just seen a notoriously effeminate Athenian and hence have become women. Yet, long before they appeared, Socrates knew that they are female (252–53). These divine virgins inspire the poets and other music men. They take the place of the Muses, the virgin daughters of Zeus. Socrates can not recognize the Muses; for if, as he asserts, Zeus does not exist, his daughters can not exist. Zeus is replaced by Vortex, or rather by Air and Ether. The relation of the Clouds to Ether or Air is similar to the relation of the Muses to Zeus: They themselves call Ether their father (569–70). They surely "belong" to the Air.[7] The Clouds are the natural Muses,[8] and Socrates is the priest of the natural Muses. If the imitative arts are a kind of wisdom, they must be akin to the *archai*. The Clouds derive immediately from the originating beginnings of all things and at the same time conceal them, for by imitating things they claim to be the things in question; they are by nature deceiving. They reveal the nature of things by concealing it and vice versa, just as rhetoric does. They are the goddesses of imitation: There would be no human art of imitation if there were no natural imitation, if imitation were not rooted in nature. The Clouds are *the* natural imitators [9] that are aloft or akin to the highest. This is the reason why they are the sole gods for Socrates as a man who teaches rhetoric on the basis of *physiologia*, i.e., who teaches both rhetoric and *physiologia*.

Socrates tries to discern Strepsiades' manner or nature, for he knows that different pupils need different approaches, and he has already seen that he must use novel devices in the case of Strepsiades. He asks Strepsiades point-blank whether he has a good memory and capacity for learning. This however is not the only or the worst ineptitude that he commits. The most astonishing thing is that he tests Strepsiades after he has initiated him: He has disclosed to him the most shocking innovations regarding the gods before finding out whether Strepsiades is able to live with them. It seems that in Socrates' view excellence of memory and understanding is less urgent than continence and endurance, as well as exposure to his goddesses.[10] We must also not overlook the fact that he tests Strepsiades only after the Clouds have asked him to do so. Left to himself, he might not have thought of it; the Clouds are more aware of the importance of the natural differences among men in regard to memory and intelligence than is Socrates. Strepsiades' answers to Socrates' questions about his memory and intelligence are not encouraging. It appears that his present nature is inadequate for achieving wisdom; he will have to acquire a different nature. Nevertheless, Socrates intends to pose him a question regarding the things aloft; but his response is most silly. Yet, when Socrates asks him what he would do if someone beat him, he gives an answer with which Socrates does not find fault, although it reads like a prophecy of what Strepsiades will do in the case of a pupil of Socrates (1322–23), and even of Socrates himself. But Aristophanes' Socrates has no power of divination, no *daimonion*. Accordingly, he solemnly prepares Strepsiades by a second initiation for going indoors, as it were into a fear-inspiring cave, where Socrates will instruct him in the utmost privacy, without any witnesses. We have been made witnesses to the revelation of holy or unholy mysteries that we would never have expected. But we shall never know what is now going to happen between the master and his new yet old pupil.

While Socrates and Strepsiades have their private meeting, the Clouds address the audience. More precisely, in the whole first section of the parabasis the poet himself addresses the audience, speaking through the leading Cloud in his own name and using the first person. This is another feature peculiar to the *Clouds*. After what we have observed about the nature of the Clouds, we are not altogether surprised that Aristophanes himself should almost appear as a member of the chorus of Clouds, but not as a member of the chorus of Acharnians, knights, birds, and so on. In contradistinction to the Clouds worshiper Socrates, Aristophanes is a Cloud; without knowing it Socrates looks up to Aristophanes. Yet Aristophanes does not speak of himself as a Cloud or as a pupil of the Clouds; he traces his breeding to Dionysos. Like the Clouds and unlike Socrates, he recognizes the gods recognized by the city. Nor does he claim to be a virgin; he even says that he is no longer a virgin. He rebukes the audience for the bad reception it gave to the *Clouds* at an earlier presentation. He regards this comedy as his wisest and the one that cost him more work than any other; he has composed it with special care for the wise part of the audience. He never raises such a claim for any other of his comedies. He compares the *Clouds* to the chaste virgin Elektra because it is, according to his claim, free from all vulgarity. But we must not forget that the particular decency of the *Clouds* is required by Socratic continence. Eager to receive the prize for the *Clouds* this time, Aristophanes softens his rebuke of the Athenians by reminding them of the good reception they gave to an earlier comedy of his. As Elektra looked for her brother Orestes because his lock of hair showed her that he was alive and near, the *Clouds* looks for wise spectators because there are unmistakable signs that will show Aristophanes that wise spectators are alive and near. He reminds his audience of his excellence as a poet: In contrast to his rivals he always figures out most cleverly novel conceits; he courageously attacked Kleon in the heyday of his strength, while sparing him decently after he was down; he also avoids vulgarity in all other respects; he does not claim here explicitly that he is a teacher of the just things. In the epirrhema the Clouds speak for themselves as goddesses. Their concern differs strikingly from that of Aristophanes; they are concerned not with the success of the play but with what we would not hesitate to call greater things. They rebuke the audience, i.e., the city of Athens, for its neglect of them. They benefit the city more than any other god, and yet they do not receive any worship whatever from Athens, a city famous for its piety. They thus tacitly, but only tacitly, explain why Socrates is their favorite: Socrates is the only Athenian who worships the Clouds and only the Clouds. Among their benefits they mention above all the warnings that they gave through thunder, rain, and lightning—together with sun and moon, or through their influence on sun and moon—before the Athenians foolishly elected Kleon as general, whom they and the other gods hate; they now add a piece of advice as to how the city can get rid of Kleon even now. They almost say that not Zeus but they make rain, thunder, and so on. They continue their theme in the antepirrhema, in which they rebuke the Athenians in the name of the Moon for their neglect of this goddess, likewise a great benefactor of Athens, and yet now in danger at the hands of the other gods as a consequence of the Athenians' carelessness regarding the lunar calendar. It appears that while the Clouds form part of the pantheon and hence know that above all Zeus exists, they have particularly close relations with the Moon and Sun, i.e., with beings that are in a way as important to Socrates as the Clouds themselves. How little the Clouds agree with Socrates regarding the gods they show most clearly in the two strophes that form part of the parabasis and in which these goddesses call on eight gods. They mention five gods by name (Zeus, Ether, Apollon, Athena, and Dionysos) and three not by name (Poseidon, Sun, and Artemis).[11] In each strophe the Clouds speak once of a god as "ours"; they call Ether "our father" (in the entrance song they spoke of Okeanos as their father, while saying nothing about the god Ether) and Athena "our goddess." In the first case they speak of themselves as Clouds, and in the second case they speak of themselves as Athenians: They are anxious to be adopted by the city of Athens; they wish to find a residence on earth.[12] This is important for understanding the action of the *Clouds*. For the same reason it is important to observe that when the Clouds have the first opportunity to address the city of Athens, they are completely silent about their relations with Socrates. An equally unqualified silence about Socrates is observed by Aristophanes when he speaks in his own name in the *Clouds*. Let us also note that the only goddesses called upon by the Clouds are virgins, and the only god praised by them for his universal beneficence is Ether.

Socrates and shortly afterward Strepsiades return to the light. Socrates is disgusted by Strepsiades' stupidity. Whatever he may have tried to teach him indoors, he has failed completely. Nevertheless, he is still willing to continue teaching him; but now, outdoors, he will teach him things that he has never been taught before in any way. This gives us an inkling of what Socrates had tried to teach Strepsiades indoors; he had not tried to teach him there any of the things that he is about to teach him now, namely poetics, grammar, and rhetoric. Curiosity or pedantry compels us to note the three more or less trifling changes in the conduct of master and pupil before and after the indoor session, in the hope that the *post hoc* may be a *propter hoc*. Socrates now calls Strepsiades for the first time by his name; Strepsiades now uses lewd language for the first time, at least since he knocked at Socrates' door; the oaths of the two men before and after the *privatissimum* differ remarkably. Socrates' first utterance after his reappearance and before Strepsiades' reappearance is the oath "By Respiration, by the Chaos, by the Air"; the three terms seem to refer to different aspects of one and the same thing, the air.[13] Shortly afterward (667) Strepsiades swears "by the Air." No one had ever sworn by the air (or by the ether) before. What air thus gains, the Clouds lose. It is true that no one ever swears "by the Clouds" (perhaps they are too obviously changeable to swear by). However, prior to the indoor session both Socrates and Strepsiades speak of the Clouds as goddesses and address them as goddesses; but after that event, which thus appears to be of decisive importance, Socrates never speaks of them at all, to say nothing of addressing them, and Strepsiades addresses them as "clouds" and no longer as goddesses (793, 1452, 1462). Socrates now swears "by the Graces" (773), whose place the Clouds might seem to have taken in the outdoor teaching preceding the *privatissimum*; and Strepsiades now swears "by the Mist" (814), i.e., by what the Clouds are in truth (330). Prior to his indoor instruction he had called the Clouds "queens of the whole," while afterward he calls Fraud "queen of the whole" (357, 1150). In accordance with this Strepsiades describes Socrates after the indoor meeting as "the Melian" (830). But whatever Socrates may think of the Clouds and may have taught Strepsiades about them, the Clouds have a life of their own, a will of their own: They insist on their being goddesses (804, 1121). It is not as easy to get rid of the spirits that one has conjured up as Socrates thinks. However this may be, in the *Clouds*, and only in the *Clouds*, an important part of the action takes place during the parabasis, while the purport of this action is never reported to the audience: [14] We are compelled to guess, or to put two and two together. It seems that just as in the parabasis the Clouds were silent as to Socrates, during the parabasis Socrates debunked the Clouds.

The outdoor teaching following the indoor session is to be devoted in the first place to meters, verse, and rhythms. Strepsiades is unable and unwilling to learn about meters and rhythms; he wishes to learn nothing except the Unjust Speech. Socrates explains to him that before he can learn the Unjust Speech he must learn about the correct use of words; the introduction to poetry proper is silently dropped, and thus the final catastrophe is decisively prepared. Strepsiades makes at least an effort to follow Socrates' instruction on the correct use of words—an instruction that is paradoxical yet easy to grasp, although perhaps even in Socrates' view rather useless. Socrates turns next to teaching Strepsiades injustice or, more generally, to teaching him how to think about his own affairs (as distinguished from divine affairs or the affairs aloft mentioned earlier); it seems that this part of the instruction is preparatory, at least in the case of Strepsiades, to exposure to the Unjust Speech itself. In accordance with the severe—not to say pious—requirements of Socratic instruction, Strepsiades must undergo his training in deliberation while in a position that calls for the utmost endurance; he therefore deliberates about how he can survive his present discomfort, rather than how he can defraud his creditors. Socrates is very patient with him; this master of endurance and continence fails to understand why one can not concentrate, and even sleep, while exposed to a whole army of fleas. After much prodding by Socrates, Strepsiades produces the conceit that he can postpone his payments to his creditors indefinitely by getting hold of the moon with the help of a witch and putting the moon into a box like a mirror. After Strepsiades has enlightened Socrates about the connection, apparently unknown to him, between the lunar calendar and the legal dates of payment of interest, Socrates is satisfied with Strepsiades' conceit—perhaps because Strepsiades has remembered, if dimly, a certain similarity between the moon and the mirror.[15] Yet Socrates is now eager to call Strepsiades down from heaven to earth by reminding him of his need to win lawsuits: Less astronomy (even magic astronomy) and more forensic rhetoric is what you need; you imitate me too much, in the wrong manner; you caricature me [Strepsiades as the pupil of Aristophanes' Socrates is a caricature of a caricature]; for instance, how can you do away with a written charge that you are delinquent in paying an exorbitant sum of money? Strepsiades replies that he would privately burn the text of the accusation by using a burning glass, i.e., the sun. Socrates is highly pleased with this elegant conceit; he is now much more pleased with Strepsiades than ever before. All the more striking is the immediate sequel. Strepsiades' reply, in spite of its excellence, was still too physical and insufficiently rhetorical. Socrates asks him therefore how he would avoid losing a lawsuit if he needed witnesses but had none; i.e., what he would do in a situation in which only a clever tongue and no heavenly body could help. Strepsiades replies that he would run away and hang himself before his case came up in court, for people who are dead can not be sued. Thereupon, contrary to all reasonable expectations and acting with the utmost brutality, Socrates severs his relations with Strepsiades at once. He refuses to continue his instruction on the ground that Strepsiades forgets at once whatever he has learned. In fact, Strepsiades is unable to remember what he had been taught at the beginning of the instruction following the *privatissimum*. But we are left wondering why Strepsiades' proposal that he might get rid of his difficulties by hanging himself proves poor memory or contradicts anything that he has learned from Socrates at any time, and especially at the beginning of the outdoor instruction. Perhaps Strepsiades learned from Socrates while we were not witnesses to the instruction that suicide must not be chosen under any circumstances, or at least not on account of money or the lack of money. At any rate, what Strepsiades forgot must have been of the utmost importance in Socrates' view if his reaction to Strepsiades' proposal is not to remain a wholly inexplicable act. For the fact that Strepsiades has a poor memory and is stupid was well known to Socrates for quite some time; his realization of these defects had caused him to turn in despair from the indoor instruction to the outdoor instruction. But while he spoke of these defects in the positive when he interrupted the indoor instruction, he speaks of them in the superlative when he interrupts the outdoor instruction and thus terminates the instruction altogether (629, 790).[16]

Socrates has expelled Strepsiades from his school. The old man is in despair. Not having learned to speak cleverly, he will be ruined by his creditors; he will be finished. This disaster will, however, have one great advantage. Completely impoverished and discredited and unable to earn a living by blackmailing the pauper Socrates, Strepsiades will leave Socrates alone and Socrates' "think-tank" activity will continue undisturbed. The Socrates-Strepsiades incident will have what one may not unjustly call a happy ending. That incident ends differently because Strepsiades in his despair turns to the Clouds for advice. The Clouds' interest would not have been served if the relations between Socrates and Strepsiades were to have found an altogether unspectacular or unsensational ending in Socrates' ordering Strepsiades off his premises. The advice that the Clouds give to Strepsiades is decisive, at least to the extent that it renders possible a continuation of the Socrates-Strepsiades incident. If hitherto it was Strepsiades who was primarily responsible for that incident, from now on the responsibility rests with the Clouds.

The Clouds advise Strepsiades, in case he has a grown-up son, to send him to Socrates' school to learn in his stead. They inspire him with a firmness toward his son that he hitherto lacked. When Strepsiades has left in order to fetch Pheidippides, the Clouds who, being goddesses, can not have been unaware of Socrates' cooling toward them, remind him that they are the only gods, to whom he owes the greatest benefits. They urge him to take the utmost advantage of Strepsiades' present state of mind quickly, while the opportunity lasts. Strepsiades must now perform the formidable task of compelling Pheidippides to enter Socrates' school, for the young man's tastes, as distinguished from his own, have nothing whatever in common with Socrates'. His last word to Pheidippides before he left him had been to the effect that he would expel him from the house. When he still finds him in the house, he pretends to execute that threat. Pheidippides thinks that his father has gone mad: Never in his life has he seen him so firm. His amazement and his concern for his father's sanity increase when Strepsiades ridicules him for believing, like a little child who, as such, holds the most old-fashioned views, in the existence of Zeus. He discloses to Pheidippides under the seal of secrecy—Socrates had not taken such a precaution, at least not out-doors—that Zeus has been expelled by Vortex: Socrates and Chairephon say so. The denial of Zeus's kingship must be kept a secret, we may suppose, for otherwise the men in the know can not cheat the others by means of oaths. As we might have expected, Strepsiades does not say a word to his son about the Clouds, and in particular about their divinity. While he says the most revolting things about the gods, he is very indignant when Pheidippides expresses in his old vein his contempt for Socrates and Chairephon—men who, in Strepsiades' view, excel in intelligence and thrift, while Pheidippides is stupid and a wastrel. Strepsiades is of course not oblivious of the fact that Pheidippides and Socrates have something in common (843, 803) that he himself lacks: Pheidippides can learn; he can learn something useful from Socrates. When Pheidippides doubts this, his father tells him that from Socrates he can learn self-knowledge and all other worthwhile things, for instance, the correct use of words. Pheidippides becomes ever more certain that his father is mad. But on observing that his father has returned from Socrates' school without his coat and shoes, he becomes concerned also about what is left of the family fortune and agrees to go to Socrates with his father, although not without uttering a dire warning: He has not yet lost his common power of divination. His father makes it somewhat easier for him to bite into the sour apple by suggesting that he may do more or less what he likes with the money that they will keep or acquire through the art that he is going to learn from Socrates: The squalor and disgrace of the company of Socrates and his like is only a brief interlude between long periods of horsemanship. This prospect does not at all lighten Pheidippides' gloom. Socrates can hardly ever have accepted a more unwilling pupil or one more prejudiced against him. He is too self-sufficient to be at all angered by Pheidippides' rudeness to him; he merely rebukes the silly young man for his bad enunciation. Strepsiades assures Socrates that Pheidippides has a natural fitness for learning the art of speaking; as a small child he already showed great talent for the arts, including the imitative arts: Do teach him now, above everything else, the

Unjust Speech: Socrates merely replies that Pheidippides will receive his instruction directly from the Just Speech and the Unjust Speech themselves, in the absence of Socrates. Socrates does not teach injustice; he merely exposes his pupils to the exchange between Justice and Injustice. He has no influence on that exchange and hence no responsibility for it. One must listen to the two Speeches (and in fact to all speeches) and can not prescribe to them where they should lead and which of them should be victorious; they have a life of their own, like the Clouds.

Pheidippides receives his instruction from the two Speeches without having undergone a test or an initiation. His listening to the two Speeches is the only instruction he receives that is presented to the audience. He must have had further instruction, for later on he proves to have learned from Socrates some things that he did not learn from the two Speeches; his testing may have preceded his severe indoor instruction. The Clouds preside over the debate of the two Speeches, and thus reveal themselves as more responsible for the debate or more akin to it than Socrates; they call both Speeches their "friends." As they imitate everything, they enjoy everything; they both praise the other gods with pleasure and listen with pleasure to Socrates' rejection of the other gods. They are as irresponsible, as insubstantial, as the clouds. The debate consists of two parts. The first part is entirely spontaneous, i.e., not regulated by the Clouds; the two Speeches hurl at each other almost nothing but insults and provocations. Each of them tries to lay hold on Pheidippides; only when they are about to come to blows do the Clouds feel compelled to intervene. Through their insults the Speeches reveal the character of each of them. The Just Speech is old-fashioned; the Unjust Speech is bold. (Their relation resembles that of Sparta and Athens in Thucydides.) The Just Speech pronounces the just things (as Aristophanes claims to do); accordingly he is indifferent to popular applause (like Socrates and unlike Aristophanes): he insults the audience. The Unjust Speech is popular and appeals to the audience as wise (as Aristophanes did to some extent in his own name in the parabasis); when called shameless, ribald, a pederast, and a parricide by the Just Speech, he accepts these epithets as terms of praise. While the Just Speech is now reduced to beggary in Athens, the Unjust Speech, who was formerly a beggar pretending to be a king in disguise, now thrives in Athens. This being the case, and the two Speeches contending with each other for a prize as comedies do, the Unjust Speech is doomed to win. After calling the contestants to order, the Clouds ask each of them to state the case for the kind of education for which he stands, the ancient and the novel respectively. Certain of his superiority, the Unjust Speech spontaneously grants precedence to his rival: He will refute the Just Speech on the very basis of the latter's premises, as he had already done before to some extent. For in the single piece of reasoning that occurs in the first half of the debate, the following exchange took place. The Unjust Speech asserted that Right does not even exist (just as Socrates had asserted that Zeus does not even exist); the Just Speech asserted that Right is with the gods (i.e., not with men, especially not with the contemporary Athenians). The Unjust Speech rejoined that Zeus could not have fettered his father with impunity if Right were with the gods; the Just Speech was thus reduced to silence concealed or mitigated by insults. Both Speeches argued on the premise that Zeus exists, and that one must live according to Zeus's will. But whereas the Just Speech implied that men should do what Zeus tells them to do, the Unjust Speech asserted that men should or may do what Zeus does. As a consequence of his defeat, the Just Speech is completely silent about Zeus's or other gods' being the support of Right in the rest of the debate.

In his long discourse the Just Speech, the defender of decency, recalls with nostalgia the olden times when he throve and moderation was respected. Boys were seen and not heard; they were well behaved and bred to continence and endurance; they learned the traditional music and poetry; deviations were severely punished. Love of men for boys was part of the custom, but that love was free from all frivolity and incontinence. When he speaks of the chastity both demanded and practiced in the ancient times, the Just Speech goes into such details as to make one fear that his abhorrence of unchastity is not altogether chaste. That the boys were well trained in gymnastics goes without saying. This kind of education, now ridiculed as old-fashioned, bred the men who fought at Marathon; whereas the kind of education favored by the Unjust Speech breeds effeminates. By choosing the side of the Just Speech, Pheidippides will come to loathe the market place, to be filled with anger when mocked, not to be rude to his parents, especially his father, not to have relations with dancing girls, and above all to respect older men—in a word, to be filled with reverence or sense of shame. Accordingly, the Just Speech speaks here, in the central part of his exposition, much more of what Pheidippides should abstain from or not do than of what he should do, not to say enjoy. In the third and last part of his speech the Just Speech confronts Pheidippides still more clearly with a choice that he will have to make: Will he become a glib busybody or shyster who spends his time in the market place and at the law courts, thus becoming pale-faced (like Socrates and his companions) and oversexed (unlike Socrates and his companions); or will he become a noble youth who spends his days in the gymnasium, blessed with all signs of a healthy and continent body? The Just Speech does not speak here of health of the soul; in fact, he never mentions the soul—agreeing in this with Socrates, who also never mentions the soul, if for different reasons (he replaces soul by air)—whereas the Unjust Speech does mention it.[17] The Clouds praise the Just Speech for the moderation inherent in his speech; they also praise the bliss of the men of old. Nevertheless—accustomed as they are to assimilate themselves to everything and everyone—they also praise the Unjust Speech and encourage him to try to refute the Just Speech.

The Unjust Speech recommends the new education in the first place by refuting the alternative to it. Whereas the remarks with which he had accompanied or interrupted the Just Speech were spontaneous, the remarks that the Just Speech makes on the occasion of the Unjust Speech are elicited by questions addressed to him by the Unjust Speech: The Unjust Speech is an *elenchos* of the Just Speech; the Unjust Speech argues *ad hominem*. The Unjust Speech is called the Weaker Speech because he undertakes the apparently hopeless task of opposing law and penal justice, i.e., what is generally held to be strongest. He subverts the laws and justice by raising the question regarding their foundations. The Just Speech objected, among other things, to warm baths, on the ground that they make a man cowardly. But that human son of Zeus who was the bravest and bore the greatest toils was admittedly Herakles, and Heraklean baths are warm baths; hence the case against warm baths collapses: Warm baths and a life of toil are compatible. Both the Just Speech and the Unjust Speech start from the premise that the conduct of a son of Zeus like Herakles is a model for ordinary mortals. Secondly, the Just Speech had strongly disapproved of spending one's time in the market place, i.e., of speaking in assemblies; but Homer has presented Nestor and all his other wise men precisely as good at speaking in assemblies. Both Speeches start from the premise that the most ancient poet is the best guide toward virtue, since the good is the old; both Speeches base their assertions on poetry. Lastly, the Just Speech had praised moderation, the opposite of *hybris* on the one hand and of dissoluteness on the other. To dispose first of moderation in the latter sense, it deprives one of the pleasures of love both of boys and women, as well as of the pleasures of gambling, eating, drinking, and laughing—in brief, of everything that makes life worth living. As for moderation in the first sense, it ruins life itself. A man can not help committing crimes under the compulsion of nature.[18] He may be caught; he will be hurt and even destroyed if he is unable to defend himself by speech, i.e., to render weak the laws and justice. Only with the help of the Unjust Speech will he be able to justify any crime he commits —especially in the sphere of *eros*—by referring to the example of Zeus: How can a weak mortal be expected to resist *eros* if the all-powerful Zeus is unable to do so? The gods can not reasonably have forbidden men to do what gods and men are by nature compelled to do; [19] let us obey the gods' will, not by doing what they tell us to do (or what they are held to tell us to do), but by doing what they do. Only in the company of the Unjust Speech will Pheidippides be able to enjoy what his nature prompts him to enjoy—to jump, to laugh, to regard nothing as shameful. While the Just Speech upheld the law by being silent on nature, the Unjust Speech appeals from law to nature. The Just Speech has nothing to reply except that by leading a dissolute life Pheidippides will become infamous, but when the Unjust Speech compels him to admit that the most famous orators and tragic poets and even the majority of the audience are infamous, the Just Speech concedes his defeat and deserts to the opposite camp. A way of life that is supported neither by the gods, nor by the orators and tragic poets, nor by the majority is indefensible. Or, to exaggerate considerably for the purpose of clarity, Right, being neither with the gods nor with men, exists only as *logos*, but that *logos* proves to lack *logos*. Yet the Clouds fail to applaud the discourse of the Unjust Speech, while they had applauded that of the Just Speech.

While the debate between the two Speeches that culminates in the complete defeat of the Just Speech is a part of the Socratic instruction, the way of life recommended by the Unjust Speech can not possibly be mistaken for the Socratic way of life; the life of sensual pleasures is wholly alien to Socrates, who is continent in every respect, and in particular in the respect of money, the indispensable condition of reckless dedication to sensual pleasure of any refinement. Contrary to popular rumor he does not teach "for money." He could easily have become rich by demanding money for teaching the art of speaking (876), but he does not have the slightest interest in gain, although his goddesses advise him to take advantage of his pupils; that those of his pupils who are not themselves beggars show him their gratitude by making gifts to him (we do not know whether the gifts are of money) is another matter.[20] Socrates' continence reminds us of the recommendations of the Just Speech, but it differs radically from them because he despises gymnastics and, above all, because he lacks moderation in the deeper sense of the term. He is a man of *hybris* over against the gods and the law; he does not shrink from transgressions like denying the existence of the gods and petty theft. If we may make use of a Xenophontic distinction, he possesses continence, but not that moderation which consists of piety and justice. Like the Unjust Speech, he is characterized by daring and cleverness (wisdom); continence and endurance, as distinguished from moderation, are required for the study of the things aloft. Above all, Socrates' way of life differs from the ways recommended by the two Speeches because the latter are based on the premise, vouched for by the poets, that the gods lead a life of bliss, whereas Socrates holds that the gods do not even exist; even if they did exist, he would not have taken them as his model because of their childishness as shown by their indifference to learning. In the Socratic scheme the debate between the Speeches is only a stage in the ascent toward the right life: The Unjust Speech is, as it were, the self-destruction of justice as supported by the gods. The Socratic way of life is supported neither by the gods, nor by the orators and tragic poets, nor by the majority. (In this respect it agrees with the way of life praised by the Just Speech, as that way of life came to sight under the impact of the attack by the Unjust Speech.) Therefore it is indefensible from the point of view of Aristophanes. Aristophanes pronounces the just things like the Just Speech; he exhorts to a life of sensual pleasure and of laughter like the Unjust Speech.[21] The two parts of Aristophanes' work are not simply in harmony. Perhaps this is the chief lesson to be drawn from the debate between the two Speeches.

After the triumph of the Unjust Speech Socrates gives Strepsiades an opportunity to reconsider his decision to make Pheidippides a pupil of Socrates, but that triumph merely strengthens Strepsiades' resolve: Pheidippides' instruction must be continued, in particular he must be instructed in "the major affairs." Even prior to the debate Strepsiades had been eager that Pheidippides learn to contradict "all just things," but there is a remarkable difference between favoring all kinds of dishonesty and accepting that surrender to all kinds of sensual pleasures which won out in the debate. Pheidippides, however, is altogether unimpressed by the debate; he loathes Socrates and all his works as much as before, and he again expresses his belief that his father will regret his decision. In beginning his instruction of Pheidippides by exposing him to the debate between the two Speeches, Socrates has failed to put his best foot forward; he has made another blunder. Pheidippides can not have been repelled by the Unjust

Speech's praise of the gay life, but he must have been repelled by his assertion that the gay life is incompatible with those healthy outdoor looks the lack of which was Pheidippides' major objection to the Socratics. In other words, the defeat of the Just Speech is also a defeat of gymnastics, and there is a kinship between gymnastics and horsemanship. On the basis of his experience and that of his comrades, the premise of the debate—that a life of sensual pleasure and a life of upper-class bodily exertion are incompatible—must have appeared to him to be patently wrong and to smell of the "think-tank" rather than of the race track. Going one step further in this direction, we would see the Pheidippides who is not yet converted to Socrates as a living proof that the Aristophanean combination of pronouncing the just things and praising the pleasures of the senses is in accordance with nature.

The indoor instruction of Pheidippides is as much concealed from us as is that of his father. According to Strepsiades' desire, that instruction will also deal with "the major things"; Socrates takes this to mean that Pheidippides is to become an able sophist. The screen concealing Pheidippides' instruction by Socrates himself is the second parabasis. The Clouds reassert their divinity more powerfully than ever. They announce to the audience of mortals the reward that each judge will receive if he awards the prize, as in justice he must, to the chorus of the *Clouds*, as well as the ways in which each will be punished if he does not give the Clouds their honor: Everyone depends for the proper amount and time of rain entirely on the Clouds; the Clouds no longer even allude to any other god. They now speak only in the future tense. They do not remind the audience, as they did in the first parabasis, of past benefits owed to the Clouds, for those benefits had been granted to the city; whereas now the goddesses speak of the rewards (and punishments) in store for the individuals: Individuals are going to vote for or against the *Clouds*. The Clouds exert themselves to the utmost to bring about the success of the *Clouds*, which introduces them for the first time as goddesses to the city of Athens. Their appeal amounts to an attempt to bribe the judges, who are under oath; but this is not simply an unjust act if we grant that it is just for the Athenians to honor the Clouds, and the Clouds by their appeal with teeth in it merely correct an injustice. This, however, implies that in particular ancient Athens, the Athens of Marathon, in which not a single man even dreamed of worshiping the Clouds, was unjust in the highest degree; or that the sympathy between the Clouds and the Unjust Speech, the defender of the new, is necessary or just. The Clouds themselves make clear that they are wholly powerless in Egypt—in the country of the most ancient antiquity and of excessive piety.

The parabasis must be thought to last as long as Pheidippides' indoor instruction; the time that each of these two simultaneous events takes is measured by units of different length. While Pheidippides was exposed to the hardship of Socratic training and, indeed, because of this exposure, Strepsiades looked forward in a relaxed mood to the day when his payments would become due. Pheidippides' study, at least to the extent to which it is indispensable for Strepsiades' practical purposes, is now completed. The father calls for his son at the "think-tank," making a gift to Socrates and receiving in turn his son, who is now more than sufficiently equipped to perform his filial duty. The good relations between Socrates and Strepsiades are fully restored; in fact, never before were those relations as good as they are now. Strepsiades is exuberant. Pheidippides' very looks show that he has become, as Socrates had promised, a clever sophist. And, what is most surprising, although it does not surprise his father, he is completely free from resentment about the company in which he has had to live and the ordeal he has had to undergo: He is a completely changed man, not only in his looks and skills. By giving his father a specimen of his newly acquired legal reasoning, he relieves him of any apprehension, however small, that might have lingered on. He gives him a sense of complete security due to a sense of superiority to his fellow citizens such as he had never enjoyed before; at least since the day preceding his wedding Strepsiades' spirits had never been so high as they are now. He indulges his *hybris* without any fear. The present scene is the only one in which we see father and son in perfect harmony. They had always loved one another, but hitherto their tastes and interests had always differed widely; by having become perfectly reconciled to Socrates, Pheidippides has become perfectly reconciled with his father. The alleged corruptor of the young has not merely enabled the son to perform his filial duty for the first time in his life; he has established perfect harmony between son and father. May this blessed moment last. It is fittingly the moment when the happy and proud father is going to feast his son.

While the feasting goes on, the first creditor appears and calls for Strepsiades. Strepsiades comes out—his name has been called; he is the debtor, not Pheidippides. But we must also not forget that the superlatively trained Pheidippides must not be disturbed in his feasting or in his resting from the toils of study when Strepsiades' modest training is more than sufficient for handling the situation—we shall use Pheidippides when we go to court—and Strepsiades can not deny himself the pleasure of getting back at the man who has caused him sleepless nights. Strepsiades' arguing with the creditor can not well be described as legal reasoning. Without any need, from mere *hybris*, he makes public the most terrible things that he has learned in the "think-tank." When the creditor reminds him that he has sworn by the gods to pay his debt to him, Strepsiades laughs at him for his simplicity in believing in oaths by the gods and makes it as clear to him as he can that the men who know have no obligation whatever to the ignorant: For the same reason for which Strepsiades paid what was not legally his debt to Socrates, he does not pay his legal debts to his ignorant creditors. His success in chasing away the first creditor emboldens him to treat a second creditor with still greater insolence than the first. That he deals at all with the second creditor is in itself remarkable since not he, but Pheidippides, is the debtor in this case. Strepsiades, who had originally been wholly indifferent to all studies except those dealing with the earth or the land, now makes the fullest use of his knowledge of heaven and the sea for his earthy ends. We had occasion to observe the formation of this vicious habit during his stay with Socrates. Now he asks his son's creditor whether the water coming down at each rain is always new, or the same water that was previously drawn upward by the sun—in other words, whether the total amount of water ever increases. The creditor does not know and does not care and thus loses, according to Strepsiades' principle, every claim to his money. It seems that his principle, according to which the knowers have no obligation toward the ignorant, arises from the generally accepted principle according to which madmen have lesser rights than the sane. The poor creditor asks Strepsiades to pay at least the interest that is owed to him. Continuing the theme on which he had touched in his question, Strepsiades forces the creditor by a cross-examination that foreshadows the procedure of the Platonic Socrates, to admit that as it would be unjust that the sea increase despite the influx of rivers, it would be still more unjust that money should increase merely by virtue of the flux of time. He chases the second creditor away with still greater insults than the first. The impression that his insolence is increasing is apparently contradicted by the fact that the argument he uses with the first creditor and in which he appeals to the public is blasphemous, whereas the argument he uses with the second creditor and in which he does not appeal to the public is not blasphemous; but whereas in the first argument he merely denies that he owes money and does not explicitly attack the laws, in the second argument he attacks the law that permits the taking of interest.

After witnessing Strepsiades' conduct toward the creditors, the Clouds begin to have dire forebodings regarding the old man, who is as reckless as a lover. One can not but admire their good sense. Strepsiades must have been warned by the Socratics to keep certain things secret from everyone except pupils (104, 824), but this warning certainly was not given with the required force. In addition, every word of caution was rendered nugatory by Socrates' promise that Pheidippides would win every lawsuit even if a thousand witnesses were to testify against him and none for him. Strepsiades was thus led to think that he possessed a protection superior to that afforded by the helmet of Hades. Above all, Socrates' own arrogant deportment toward the ephemerals must have filled Strepsiades with utter contempt for those who had not studied with Socrates; when he addresses the audience as "stones, number, sheep," one can not help suspecting that he uses the master's own words. Using hindsight, we are certain that the reckless old man is bound to ruin Socrates, and that it is high time for the Clouds, after the scene with the creditors, to think of dissociating themselves from Socrates. Yet they do nothing of the kind. They do indeed now disapprove of Strepsiades' dishonesty, or at any rate of its manner or degree, and they predict that on this very day some evil will suddenly befall him. One may say that they announce Strepsiades' speedy punishment, but they do not announce that they will punish him. In accordance with this, they do not know what kind of evil is in store for him, but they have an inkling of its probable source. Strepsiades' principle, according to which those who know have no obligation to the ignorant, permits of the refinement that those who know more have only small obligations to those who know less—a refinement that weakens the obligations of Pheidippides to Strepsiades. The same principle frees the Clouds from all responsibility for Strepsiades' dishonesty that is admittedly based on that principle: However much the Clouds, by encouraging him to become Socrates' pupil, may have encouraged his desire to get rid of his debts by foul means, they did not teach him that principle; and, in addition, they are the knowers par excellence, compared with whom Strepsiades is simply an ignoramus. The Clouds do not expect that Strepsiades will be punished by the law courts for his conduct toward the creditors, for they know as well as Socrates that Pheidippides can defeat anyone with his newly acquired skill. But what is true of Pheidippides is still truer of Socrates: Socrates is beyond the reach of the law. The only one in danger is Strepsiades, and the source of his danger is no other being than his son.

The Clouds have barely pronounced their forebodings when we hear Strepsiades screaming. He is being beaten by his son. The Clouds' cautious prediction has come true. Strepsiades calls on his kinsmen, rather than on his fellow citizens as such, for help against his son; he as it were returns to his kinsmen from whom he had been alienated by his marriage, by his son, and finally by Socrates. Now he comes to his senses: He asks his son in the presence of witnesses who did not witness the indoor beating whether he beats his father; for indoor beating can as little be proven to a court of law as criminal indoor instruction if the culprit does not confess. Pheidippides impudently admits the deed; the next step of the outraged father will be to accuse his son formally before a court of law (494–96). Yet, if there is any truth in what Socrates and the Clouds asserted and Strepsiades believes as to Pheidippides' forensic competence, Strepsiades will not receive satisfaction by taking that next step. The fact that he prepares it shows how much he has been shaken. His flight to the public has put a stop to the father-beating, and so he can begin to remember that turning to the court is of no use. For the time being he hurls savage insults at his son, which remind us of the insults hurled by the Just Speech at the Unjust Speech, and to which Pheidippides replies with the calm, and in the vein, of the Unjust Speech. Strepsiades, who had remembered his kinsmen for the first time, seems now to remember justice for the first time. Yet with the verbal discharge the worst is over; the evil that had befallen him so suddenly has spent itself. Pheidippides returns to the offensive by declaring that he will prove that he has beaten his father in justice. Strepsiades' hearing of a proof and his forgetting entirely about his beating, even about his present pains, are practically simultaneous: So much of a theoretical man has he become, or at least of an admirer of his son's skill, for which the old man now claims to deserve full credit. By all means he must hear the proof. Pheidippides asks him to choose which of the two Speeches he likes as the basis or the means of the proof. Strepsiades does not understand the question. It is hard to believe that he should have forgotten the two Speeches called the Just Speech and the Unjust Speech. To his outcry "two speeches indeed" Pheidippides replies "the stronger or the weaker," whereupon the father rejoins in effect that one could prove the justice of father-beating of course only on the basis of or by means of the Unjust Speech. Accordingly, Pheidippides' claim that he can prove the justice of father-beating through both Speeches must be dismissed as sheer boasting; certainly Pheidippides drops his offer immediately. Yet we must consider that Pheidippides is cleverer and better trained than his father. Perhaps Pheidippides drops the matter because he sees that his father does not follow him; perhaps the stronger and the weaker speech that he has in mind are not the Just and the Unjust Speech. In the first place, how could one possibly establish the justice of father-beating on the basis of the Just Speech, given the fact that father-beating everywhere contradicts the law, and the Just Speech regards the law as sacred? Only through the transformation of the Just Speech into the Unjust Speech or the self-destruction of the Just Speech, which is identical with the genesis of the Unjust Speech, could Pheidippides possibly prove his assertion. In other words, if the Just Speech is taken strictly by itself as stating what the gods tell men to do, it can not be used to establish the justice of beating, or fettering, one's father (904–6); in order to establish it, one must make the questionable *metabasis* from "do what the gods tell you to do" to "do what the gods do." Above all, there must be a pair of speeches different from the pair consisting of the Just and Unjust Speeches, for the following reason. The Unjust Speech is the justification of the unqualified surrender to one's own sensual pleasures; it is therefore not the speech justifying the Socratic way of life of extreme continence and endurance. The latter speech finds a partial expression in what we have hitherto called Strepsiades' principle: The man who possesses knowledge has no obligation to the ignorant, but only to the others who know. In other words, the Unjust Speech establishes his recommendations—and therefore in particular the justice of father-beating—on the basis of the stories of the gods or on the basis of the poets whereas, as we shall see, Pheidippides establishes the justice of father-beating by "physical" arguments. "Stronger and weaker speech" may mean both "the Just and the Unjust Speech" and "poetic and physical speech."

The Clouds have undergone a change similar to that which Strepsiades has undergone. These friends of speeches—to say nothing of their calculations—are no longer concerned with the evil that Strepsiades is resolved to do to his creditors, or with the evil that he has suffered at the hands of his son. They are eager to hear the discussion of father-beating or, rather, Strepsiades' rejoinder to Pheidippides' proof; they seem to have a bias in favor of Strepsiades because they are opposed to father-beating, perhaps because these daughters of Okeanos have an old grudge against Zeus's beating of his father. Yet they are not going to help Strepsiades; perhaps they can help (apart from giving or withholding rain) only by giving advice of a nontechnical nature—like the advice to send Pheidippides to Socrates' school. Strepsiades must defeat Pheidippides with the means at his disposal. In the first place, they wish Strepsiades to tell them (rather than the audience) the beginning of the discord between father and son, for that fight had begun indoors, where neither the goddesses nor the audience could observe it (1354, 1361). We recall that father and son had entered the house in perfect, unheard-of harmony. While they were feasting, Strepsiades tells the Clouds, he asked his son to take the lyre and to sing a certain song of Simonides. Pheidippides straightway refused to follow the old-fashioned habit of singing while drinking; one can not, of course, literally drink and sing at the same time.[22] Furthermore, he said that Simonides is a bad poet. At this point Strepsiades began to be angry. Then he asked his son to recite something from Aeschylus; again straightway Pheidippides expressed his loathing for Aeschylus. Strepsiades' anger increased. The disagreement between father and son regarding the old poets naturally led up to the father-beating and to the disagreement regarding father-beating—so close is the connection between veneration for antiquity and deference to old men. Strepsiades could still control his anger, and in order to preserve the hard-won harmony between father and son he went so far as to propose to Pheidippides that he recite something from the more recent poets. Thereupon the spirited Pheidippides recited straightway a passage from Euripides that describes an act of incest between a brother and sister born of the same mother. This was too much for Strepsiades to bear: He hurled insults at his son, the son replied in kind, and finally beat his father. Strepsiades, who had been willing to swallow, not to say propose, the most shameless dishonesties and the most impudent blasphemies, will not stand for incest; a line must be drawn somewhere. Yet, what induced Pheidippides to beat his father was not necessarily any enthusiasm for incest, but merely indignation about Strepsiades' failure to admire Euripides' art. There is nevertheless an obvious connection between incest and father-beating; both crimes destroy the family. However this may be, owing to Pheidippides' action, the issue is now no longer incest, but father-beating. Strepsiades states the case against this crime in powerful terms, for the ludicrous examples that he gives of his paternal care for Pheidippides (there was apparently no maternal care) and of his son's unfilial conduct can easily be translated or retranslated by everyone into the most moving plea or description. The Clouds do not think, however, that the case is settled. They wish to hear Pheidippides' proof of the justice of father-beating, although they realize that if the proof is strong, fathers face a dim prospect; if the Clouds had a bias against father-beating to begin with, they do not have it any more. Strepsiades' report of the indoor dissension may have made them realize the connection between the case for fathers or old men and the case for antiquity; and they knew all along that the case for antiquity must be defeated, or at least weakened, if the city of Athens is to adopt new divinities.

Pheidippides is thoroughly pleased with the opportunity given to him, first by his father and then by the Clouds, of attacking the old established laws. He looks back with contempt at the time when he was merely an inarticulate horseman. Contrary to our expectation he will never again return to his former way of life, even after he has retrieved the family fortunes; he has lost all taste for horsemanship. His perfect satisfaction with his newly acquired skill and power has not made him oblivious of the fact that it was his very father who, by forcing him to go to Socrates' school, made him the man he now is and therefore enabled him to show that it is just for him to beat his father. Strepsiades, however, who is still licking his wounds, looks back with regret to the happy days when his son was nothing but a horseman and bankrupted him; a healthy body is more important than healthy finances. For the first time he regrets that he ended Pheidippides' former way of life. But he is still very far even from dreaming of turning against Socrates, for, after all, it is still an open question, as the Clouds themselves have made clear, whether father-beating is not just; and if Strepsiades did not know from childhood, he surely learned from Socrates that something may cause one severe bodily pain and yet be good. Pheidippides begins his plea by asking his father whether he beat him while he was a child. Strepsiades replies that he did it out of good will toward him; Pheidippides draws the conclusion that if he beat his father out of good will toward him, he acted justly. He surely always loved his father and still loves him, the love having been strengthened in the meantime by gratitude to him for having compelled him to become a competent speaker. The previous reasoning presupposes indeed that there is equality between father and son; this presupposition is established by the fact that both father and son are equally born free. Yet equality in freedom does not exclude inequality in other respects; fathers are supposed to be superior to their children in wisdom. But if it is wisdom that gives a man the right to beat another, a grown-up son who, by virtue of having completed the Socratic training, is wiser than his father (who was unable to complete that training) may beat his unwise old father. This conclusion obviously contradicts the law as it is in force everywhere. One must then question the law. As Pheidippides takes for granted and Strepsiades does not contest, all law is of human origin; it is the work of a man like you and me, who succeeded in persuading the ancients by speech, i.e., who did not impose, for instance, the law forbidding father-beating by virtue of a preceding law or authority. Hence nothing prevents Pheidippides, by persuading his contemporaries, from establishing a new law permitting father-beating. This could be understood to mean that both the old law and the new have the same status, that they are both laws merely by virtue of persuasion, agreement, or convention. This, however, is by no means the case: Father-beating is a common practice of cocks and all other beasts, i.e., it is according to nature; for beasts do not have any conventions. Strepsiades objects to this reasoning on the ground that it would compel Pheidippides to imitate cocks also in other respects, for instance, to eat excrement and to sleep on a perch. Pheidippides calmly replies that these things are not of the same kind as father-beating, nor does Socrates think that they are. He does not even stop to show why they differ so profoundly from father-beating: Not all beasts eat excrement and sleep on perches, to say nothing of the fact that Pheidippides had not set up cocks, or other birds, as the models of man in every respect. We may also note that Pheidippides makes a distinction between what is and what Socrates thinks: He does not swear in the words of his teacher. Strepsiades has only one argument left: If I am right, you may beat your son; whereas if you are right, your son will beat you. Pheidippides replies that he may not have a son. (We note that neither Socrates nor anyone else in the "think-tank" seems to have children; the society of the "think-tank" seems to be an all-male society and hence without the prospect of progeny.) Strepsiades is completely refuted. Without knowing it, he had granted the right of father-beating before Pheidippides' return from school, when he had been brought to admit the supreme right of the knowers. Addressing his contemporaries in the audience, he generously admits that his son has proven to his satisfaction that sons justly punish their fathers if the fathers do unjust things; tacitly and even unconsciously he makes a distinction between bestial and human father-beating. Harmony between father and son has been restored. Being beaten by his son has ceased to be an evil for Strepsiades; he admits that it is a good thing if it is properly done. The Clouds' dire foreboding has come to naught if Pheidippides beat his father properly, i.e., for an unjust act. Strepsiades was beaten because he failed to admire Euripides; he now seems to grant that he did wrong in not praising Euripides. His failure to praise Euripides was due to Euripides' failure to condemn incest; he now seems to grant that it is wrong to condemn incest. Does he in fact grant this, or has he merely forgotten this divisive issue that led to the father-beating because of the pain of the beating and joy over the restored harmony? Or must we assume that by granting the justice of father-beating on the ground advanced by Pheidippides one has already granted the justice of incest?

Pheidippides is not yet satisfied. Something urges him to take a further step. Strepsiades is understandably alarmed. Pheidippides reassures him that what he is going to say will perhaps not be displeasing to his father. Strepsiades is curious to hear it. Pheidippides declares that he will beat his mother too. He expects his father to be pleased by the prospect of this act of perfect retribution. However one may look at it, there was something shocking in what he did to his father, who had suffered all the agonies of the insolvent creditor for the sake of his spendthrift son, and who had then conferred on him the supreme benefit—admittedly surpassing in value all the horses in the world—of the Socratic art. Now, however, she who had been the first cause of all his father's misery will receive her deserved punishment without Strepsiades' having to lift a finger, at the hands of her spoiled darling, the major instrument with which she had tormented her infinitely patient husband. But what seems to be the consummation of filial kindness is nothing but repulsive to Strepsiades. Far from being pleased, he is shocked as he never was before. He who had granted the justice of father-beating absolutely denies the justice of mother-beating. We know the reason for this seeming lack of consistency: The issue of incest, which had led to the father-beating, reasserts itself; if a son can lawfully beat his mother, why should it be unlawful for him to commit incest with his mother? After all, the Weaker Speech (1444–45), by which Pheidippides had established the right of father-beating, viz., the argument taken from the universal practice of the beasts, obviously justifies incest between son and mother as well. No love is lost between Strepsiades and his wife, but incest destroys the basis of what was always dearest to him except when it brought him to the precipice of bankruptcy: his relation to his son as his son and nothing but his son.[23] Pheidippides is much too sophisticated to understand his father's feelings. With his usual promptness he offers to prove the justice of mother-beating by means of the weaker speech. Strepsiades absolutely refuses even to listen to a defense of the most atrocious crime. Having come so close to the precipice, he recoils. Now he senses for the first time the badness of the Socratic training, but he knows that he has no right to blame Socrates, for Socrates did not obtrude his teaching: He himself sought it first for himself and then for his son; he has only himself to blame; he deserved his beating, for it was through him that Pheidippides learned to believe in the justice of father-beating. Yet the Strepsiades who had been exposed to Socrates and the Clouds is no longer a man who can leave matters at blaming himself. It is perhaps permitted to guess that he has this inaudible dialogue with himself: "Come to think of it—did I seek the Socratic training for Pheidippides? Of course not. The Clouds suggested it." The Clouds, who can not know that he himself had tried to become Socrates' pupil only because his son had refused to become one, throw him back on himself: You have only yourself to blame, your own dishonesty. This is true enough but does not come with the best grace from the Clouds who, knowing well what they did, had given Strepsiades, a doubly ignorant man, the greatest possible encouragement for all his wicked plans, as he reminds them. The Clouds reply to him divinely that it is their custom to encourage the lover of wicked practices until they throw him into misery so that he learns to fear the gods. Strepsiades admits that the Clouds' procedure, though wicked, is just. The Clouds do not protest: Their wickedness is in the service of justice, whereas Strepsiades' wickedness is in the service of injustice, to say nothing of the fact that they act in accordance with their nature by imitating Strepsiades to some extent. They merely tell him that he should never have thought of defrauding his creditors of their money. But is defrauding one's creditors such a monstrous crime? Does one destroy the foundations of the family by defrauding creditors who are not near kinsmen? Are there not many people who fear the gods and yet defraud their creditors? Above all, can a man of some spirit who is about to lose his last penny—for we suppose that Strepsiades has given up all thought of using Pheidippides' art—walk around with the feeling that he has only himself to blame for his disgrace? Think only of the triumph of the creditors whom he has insulted as no creditors ever were insulted, except after successful popular risings. Did the Clouds not say that the only thing that counts is to fear the gods? It is true that Strepsiades was responsible for the plan to defraud the creditors but, by Zeus, the thought of not fearing the gods had never entered his head until Socrates told him that it is ridiculous to fear the gods. What Strepsiades has to blame himself for is nothing compared with Socrates' guilt: Socrates and Chairephon have deceived him regarding the greatest matters; they have brought him and his son—a family of impeccable reputation—to the precipice of the most monstrous crime by committing the most monstrous crime; for who does not see that fear of the gods is the only solid support for the prohibition against incest? Socrates and Chairephon must be destroyed. Without the subtle suggestion of the Clouds, Strepsiades would have paid his debts and withdrawn into a still greater obscurity than the one from which he came; a suggestion by the same Clouds who advised him to send Pheidippides to Socrates induces him to resolve on the destruction of Socrates.

Strepsiades' return to piety and justice is not a return to legality. He takes the punishment of Socrates into his own hands. He can not be blamed for this, since he is certain that no law can reach this master of forensic rhetoric. Strepsiades takes it for granted that Pheidippides will join him in his punitive action; for he takes it for granted that the words of the Clouds had the same effect on his son that they had on himself, precisely because the Clouds had hitherto not given the slightest sign that they are champions of the fear of the gods. All the terrible things that his son had done and said to him are therefore forgiven; he is again his most beloved; the only culprit is Socrates. But here we see the difference between a man who has felt in his bones what the denial of the ancestral Zeus means and a man who has not felt it or, in other words, the difference between a man whose Socratic instruction was abortive and one whose Socratic instruction was complete. Pheidippides firmly refuses to wrong his teacher. His belief in the nonexistence of Zeus and the other gods is unshakable (he never believed in the divinity of the Clouds). He has nothing but contempt for his father's relapse into the archaic beliefs implying that the alleged first grounds, if not gods, are artifacts; his father had never understood the meaning of the Socratic assertion that Zeus does not even exist: In this crucial case the old man, who understood everything else too literally, failed to understand an assertion literally. Accordingly, Strepsiades no longer listens to Pheidippides. Forsaken by his son he turns to Hermes, asking him to forgive him for his insanity and to counsel him. Since his son refused to join him in his punitive action, he is no longer certain whether he ought not to bring Socrates before a court of law. We do not hear the god's reply, but Strepsiades hears him advising both against legal action (the god probably knew that the law could not reach Socrates) and against his plan to kill Socrates: Strepsiades should burn down the "think-tank." The fairness of this advice may not vouch for its high origin, but it surely agrees with it; Hermes can not be offended by a man who denies his existence. Strepsiades immediately sets out to execute this punishment on Socrates and his companions. To their frightened screams he replies with heavy sarcasm, revealing implicitly that Socrates did not take monetary advantage of Strepsiades; but speaking seriously he tells them that they are getting what they deserve for their *hybris* against the gods and for impiously inquiring regarding the Moon. Any doubts that we may have had about Strepsiades' hearing Hermes, let alone about Hermes' existence, are dispelled by the god's own appearance. He joins Strepsiades in his punitive action, encouraging Strepsiades and his slave to hit Socrates and his companions hard (yet not to kill them) for many reasons, but above all because they have wronged the gods. Socrates' daring assertion that Zeus does not exist has been refuted *ad oculos:* Even Socrates must have learned to fear the gods, i.e., he too must have fulfilled the alleged purpose of the Clouds. Yet they retain their ambiguous posture toward the end; they do not oppose Socrates' punishment, but they also do not partake in it, nor do they applaud it. Their punitive action is reserved for the unjust judges who will not grant the prize to the *Clouds.* Nor do we hear Socrates recant his blasphemies.

The *Clouds* ends with Strepsiades' greatest moment: With the assistance of a god he vindicates the gods in public. On the other hand, all his efforts to get rid of his debts have been in vain, and he has lost his son. However Strepsiades may have balanced his triumph and his defeat against each other, there can be no question that the *Clouds* ends badly for Socrates: The visible sign of his way of life, the "think-tank," has gone up in flames. Unless we assume that Aristophanes is a vulgar worshiper of success (in which case he would not have been proud of his *Clouds*), we can not infer from the unhappy ending of the play that Aristophanes unqualifiedly condemned Socrates. This inference is indeed not refuted by the fact that the man who ruined Socrates is far from being praiseworthy: A just man would never have thought of ruining Socrates because he would not have had any dealings with Socrates, and hence would never have acquired knowledge of Socrates' lack of piety and justice. The fact that Aristophanes does not unqualifiedly condemn Socrates is established by the phenomenon of the Clouds; the Clouds link Aristophanes to Socrates. Socrates is a favorite of the Clouds; Aristophanes is himself a Cloud, or at the very least he speaks as the leading Cloud. The Clouds are, if in different ways, Socrates' divinities and Aristophanes' divinities; they are as much Aristophanes' divinities as the lamenting gods are Karkinos' divinities (1261). Aristophanes and Socrates are both, as we may say provisionally, masters of the art of imitation; they belong to the same species, although to different subspecies. The difference between Socrates and Aristophanes explains why the Clouds eventually turn against Socrates. Aristophanes' disapproval of Socrates, we suspect, goes as far as, but not further than, the Clouds' disapproval of him. The Clouds claim indeed to have played a just, if wicked, game with Socrates from the beginning: They encouraged his wicked doings in order to teach him to fear the gods; they claim, as it were, to act on behalf of the gods. Yet this claim is not supported by any fact. They also claim to be the daughters of Okeanos, the origin of all gods, i.e., to belong to the same family to which all gods belong; but this claim conflicts with their claim to be the daughters of Ether, who, for all we know, can not be a descendant of Okeanos. They obviously wish to enter the rank of the gods. Their guiding objective is to be worshiped by the city of Athens. They do not wish the Athenians to cease to worship the other gods. In this respect they differ radically from Socrates. Nothing that is said or done in the play prevents us from assuming that Aristophanes shares the wish of the Clouds and that he shares to this extent Socrates' dissatisfaction with the established divine worship: The traditional pantheon must be enlarged. However this may be, all the actions of the Clouds must be understood in the light of their guiding objective. Hitherto their only worshiper in Athens is Socrates; hence they favor him and humor him: They do not mind it at all when he says the worst things of the other gods by denying their existence, although they know, or at least never deny, that the other gods exist; in other important respects too they avoid Socrates' extremism. The prospects of their being recognized by the city of Athens are very slight; Socrates has no influence in Athens beyond the small circle of his followers. The first opportunity to spread worship of the Clouds beyond that circle arises with the arrival of Strepsiades, the man between the classes; the Clouds grasp that opportunity with eager hands. If Strepsiades' plan had succeeded, their fame would have spread like his. No one can say whether in that case their ambition would have remained as moderate as they present it. Yet they come to realize that Strepsiades' folly and especially loquacity compromise everything; they must dissociate themselves from his plan. But all their efforts would have been in vain if they had quietly abandoned him; they need a spectacular end of the Strepsiades incident; Strepsiades can be depended on to tell everyone willing to listen who it was who made him truly just and pious and induced him to vindicate the gods: His bankruptcy will be rendered illustrious by the high connection of which he can boast. After Socrates has introduced the new divinities into the city, they desert him when they see how untenable or indefensible he has become, owing to the manner in which the test case has developed. At this time these versatile beings must present themselves as merely serving the worship of the other gods. While the *Clouds* ridicules Socrates, it elevates Socrates' goddesses as much as possible. From the Clouds' point of view, the end of the *Clouds* is not unhappy. If there should be a contradiction between some observations made in this paragraph and an earlier observation, one can easily solve it by tracing it to the very being of the Clouds which, after all, are self-contradictory beings. Yet for this reason it is advisable to understand Aristophanes' critique of Socrates without reference to the Clouds.

The Clouds' final action presupposes Strepsiades' dissatisfaction with Socrates. Nothing further needs to be said about Strepsiades' defects. His dissatisfaction with Socrates, however, has a respectable cause; it is due to concern with the family. The family can not be secure and flourish except by being part of the city; the family is compelled, as it were, to expand into the city by the prohibition against incest. This prohibition may owe its reasonableness to the needs of the family (or of the city); it owes its force or sacredness to divine sanctions. Strepsiades had no misgivings about the rejection of divine sanctions for oaths; on the contrary, he welcomed that rejection. Only when he sees that the same thought that liberates him from his creditors legitimates incest does he return to piety and justice. Differently stated, he had always been concerned with the city, but he did not mind transgressing the city's laws when they conflicted with his interests. His Socratic instruction brought him close to looking down on all laws; eventually he is brought to see that whoever breaks any law destroys the city as far as in him lies. Strepsiades' concern with the family is the root of his concern with the city and therefore also with the gods. Socrates, on the other hand, is wholly unconcerned with the city or the family; in this respect he agrees with the Unjust Speech. He is concerned above all with knowledge of the things aloft and, secondarily, with the art of speaking. His concern calls for an association radically different from the family, the association with his fellow students or pupils. They live by themselves; they live together, not only studying together, but also eating together; despising all ephemeral things, practicing continence and endurance to the highest degree, they form a communist society. They know of no obligation to outsiders; they recognize only the rights of those who know.[24] Socrates is aware that his small society is in need of support from the outside—a support that it receives through gifts or theft. Being an all-male society, it must replenish itself from the general population, i.e., from men who may already have formed attachments to other ignoramuses.[25] It is a society of friends and hence a society without *eros*. Only if Socrates and his pupils stemmed from oaks and rocks could his experiment be successful. This need of outside support, and not love of gain, induces him to welcome the "ephemeral" Strepsiades in spite of his contempt for all ephemerals. But Socrates has no awareness of his dependence on the city. There is only one argument of the Just Speech that the Unjust Speech does not meet: The Just Speech says to his opponent that the city feeds him. The same accusation can justly be brought against the Aristophanean Socrates, who also does not show the slightest sign of civic responsibility. He has the defect of the pure theoretician; [26] he lacks *phronesis;* he has not reflected on the conditions or the context of his own doing: he lacks self-knowledge (cf. 842). Owing to his lack of *phronesis* he can not imitate life properly; he is a-Music.[27] This lack of prudence shows itself in his whole management of the Strepsiades incident; this student of nature does not properly consider nature in its practically most important respect: the natural differences among men. He succeeds indeed in impressing Strepsiades with the Cloud worship; he would never have succeeded in becoming a public priest (359) of the Clouds. Thanks to his mastery of the art of speaking, he is indeed beyond the reach of the law, or the law qua speech is at his mercy. Nothing is sacred for him because nothing can withstand his *logos;* but he forgets the power of that *alogon* which is the basis of the family and hence of the city; he forgets the fact that he is at the mercy of force, of superior force, or that force is the *ultima ratio,* the ultimate *logos* of the city. For the very fact of the superiority of the city in regard to force, as well as the ground of this superiority—the fact that most men are above all members of their families and not of the community of knowers—can be stated by speech. That speech may be said to be the Just Speech par excellence. The Just Speech that is a character in the play is justly defeated by the Unjust Speech: The true Just Speech is the *Clouds.* The former Just Speech is based on ancestral opinions; the true Just Speech is based on knowledge of the nature of man. The true Just Speech, too, is not effective without the use of human force, but it sets that force in motion— Socrates' doctrine destroys not the city but only his "think-tank," or at most Socrates himself. He is the plaything of things—"the Clouds"—that he has in a way created but that he does not comprehend.

Socrates' downfall would have been avoided if Pheidippides had been satisfied with proving to his father the justice of father-beating and had not gone on to assert the justice of mother-beating; in other words, if he had behaved with ordinary prudence; but such prudence as he originally possessed had been expelled by the Socratic training. Yet, since the ways of imprudence or madness are infinite, his conduct is in need of further exploration. Originally he had a powerful prejudice against Socrates, and this prejudice had not been weakened, to say the least, by the debate between the two Speeches. The complete change that he underwent—his conversion by Socrates to Socrates—took place only during the indoor instruction. Hence we do not know the precise cause of his change. We do not know precisely the reasons used by Socrates against his previous notions. These reasons were not identical with those used by Socrates against Strepsiades' previous notions (cf. 478–80). For instance, Pheidippides shows no signs of ever having been initiated into the worship of the Clouds or the belief in their divinity. He merely was liberated by Socrates from belief in the gods and from respect for the law; his instruction in this respect must have been more thorough than his father's: His father did not learn that such things as father-beating and incest are by nature just. Pheidippides learned from Socrates that what he expected to achieve through horsemanship could be achieved much better by the art of speaking. Socrates treated Pheidippides differently than Strepsiades not only because Pheidippides had a better mind than his father. There is a kinship between Socrates and Strepsiades with regard to continence and endurance. There is a kinship in an entirely different respect between Socrates and Pheidippides: Pheidippides has ruined the family fortune by his dedication to horsemanship, and Socrates is a pauper for the sake of his study of the things aloft. Yet the most powerful or the most appropriate reasons would have had no effect on Pheidippides if Socrates had not first succeeded in overcoming Pheidippides' profound loathing of him by his bewitching power or charm—a charm great enough to disgust Pheidippides for the rest of his days with horsemanship and to convert him into a dedicated lover of speeches. Socrates' conversion of Pheidippides is a very great victory. This victory is concealed from the laughers by Socrates' final defeat. Once one has noticed the victory, one must wonder whether the victory or the defeat is greater; for since we do not worship "success," we must consider the implications of the fact that Pheidippides has a better nature than Strepsiades.

By failing to present to the public Pheidippides' indoor instruction, Aristophanes has failed to present to us Socrates' charm. He could not show it without ruining his comedy as comedy. He could show Socrates' charm only by its effect, as Homer showed Helen's beauty. This means that in order to understand an Aristophanean comedy, one must, considering the essence or the limitation of the comedy, transcend that limitation.

We remember how Plato presents Socrates' continence and endurance in the *Banquet*. The Aristophanean equivalent consists in presenting Socrates as ignorant of the fact that human beings can not concentrate or sleep while exposed to innumerable fleas. Aristophanes means exactly the same phenomenon as Plato. Just as one must enlarge the Platonic presentation of Socratic continence by adding to the immunity to wine and to Alkibiades' youthful bloom the immunity to fleabites, one must enlarge the Aristophanean presentation of the same subject by supplementing it with parallels of a higher order. One must transform the specific two-dimensionality of his comedy into a transcomic three-dimensionality. Transcomic does not mean tragic. The sequence of incidents in an Aristophanean comedy appears at first glance as a series of most laughable somersaults of different kinds; this is part of what I mean by its specific two-dimensionality. By thinking about each incident and the sequence of incidents one transcends that two-dimensionality. One may call the flea example the comic equivalent of Socrates' high-class continence and endurance. Of most things there are comic equivalents. Of Socrates' charm there is no comic equivalent; hence Aristophanes can not present that charm. What makes Socrates a comical subject is, on the lowest level, the fact that by his looks, his deportment, and his way of life he differs strikingly from everyone else without these differences being manifest, i.e., generally recognized, superiorities on his part; more specifically, Socrates is a comic subject because of his lack of prudence, which renders possible the Strepsiades incident. There is a story of Hegel's preferring the company of a particularly stupid man to that of others; this preference was wittily explained as due to Hegel's not understanding that man. Surely Socrates does not understand Strepsiades or see him as he is. The relation between Socrates and Strepsiades may provisionally be said to be the comic equivalent of many relations presented by Plato and Xenophon. It should be noted that Aristophanes avoids presenting any exchange between Socrates and his pupils proper; the relations within the school are not so comical as to be presentable in an Aristophanean comedy. This alone suffices to explain why he presents a large part of Socrates' instruction of Strepsiades but no part of his instruction of Pheidippides. The essence or limitation of the Aristophanean comedy may also be the reason why Pheidippides is not allowed to speak of incest between son and mother: Father-beating may be laughable, but there are crimes that are not. But there is no crime that must not be considered by him who intends to say the just things. Just as Thucydides has bound himself to the law that he remain as nearly as possible a writer of a military chronicle ("In the same summer the people of X under the generalship of Y. . . ."), Aristophanes is bound to the law that he remain as nearly as possible a writer and producer of a farce that is rich in novel conceits and satisfies an unusually quick-witted and exacting crowd.

To return to Pheidippides, what is it that urges him on to behave as he does in his conversation with his father during the feast and afterward? He has always loved his father, but that love conflicted with the inclinations he had inherited from his mother's side. Socrates freed him from these inclinations; Socrates caused the removal of every impediment to his love for his father. This is an entirely new experience for both the father and the son. Then the son realizes that the harmony between himself and his father is not complete; he wishes to make it complete. Freed from the last traces of the old-fashioned notion of filial deference, he sees himself who is wise as simply superior to his father who is not wise; he treats him as a child whom he tries to raise to his own level; he tries to transform the father-son relation into the relation of fellow knowers or into genuine friendship. Yet he is more attached to his father than to Socrates, just as his father is more attached to him than to Socrates. His father's stubbornness puts a sudden stop to his effort. He does not join him in the action against Socrates, for he has no reason whatever to be displeased with Socrates: He is captivated by the possibilities that Socrates has opened up for him. On the other hand, he does not think of coming to Socrates' aid; his attachment to Socrates does not go that far. He is not a follower of Socrates; he has not been converted by Socrates to the Socratic ways of extreme continence and endurance. He has learned from Socrates that what he believed to achieve by horsemanship can be achieved much better by the art of speaking: He has not learned to replace his end by the Socratic end. He has been converted by Socrates' charms only to the way of life recommended by the Unjust Speech. His eventual conduct toward Socrates—his neither hurting nor helping Socrates—resembles that of the Clouds and, to a higher degree, that of Aristophanes. Is he a comic equivalent of Aristophanes who, perhaps also charmed or instructed by Socrates himself, also accepts only a part of the Socratic teaching?

This question can not be dismissed on the ground that one can say with almost equal right that Pheidippides is the comic equivalent of Oidipous. The answer to our question depends decisively on whether Aristophanes can be presumed to have agreed with his Socrates regarding the gods. The fact that his Strepsiades is presented by him as not understanding the meaning of Socrates' assertion according to which Zeus does not even exist, and hence as not facing the question to which Socrates' assertion is an answer, proves that Aristophanes himself had faced it. This question is not raised in any other Aristophanean comedy with the clarity with which it is raised in the *Clouds:* The *Clouds* is Aristophanes' "wisest" comedy. In other words, no Aristophanean character is comparable to his Socrates in the decisive respect. On the other hand, all his other comedies take up at least some of the subjects that in the *Clouds* are manifestly linked to the question regarding the gods, viz., family and city, pleasure and justice, nature and convention, the ancient and the novel, the Muses, and father-beating. We must turn to the other comedies in order to see whether they supply severally or jointly the answer to the question that is not clearly answered in the *Clouds*.

III *The Other Plays*

1 *The Acharnians*

The *Acharnians* begins, like the *Clouds*, with a soliloquy by an oldish rustic who gives vent to his discomfort; but in the *Acharnians* the soliloquy takes place not indoors but in public, and it concerns matters that are not merely private but also public. Regarding the *Clouds*, one may doubt whether the oldish rustic Strepsiades or Socrates is the chief character; regarding the *Acharnians*, there can be no doubt that the oldish rustic Dikaiopolis is the chief character. Dikaiopolis has come to the Pnyx, as is his wont, very early. He is the very first to arrive, long before the Assembly begins, while the other citizens and even the magistrates, in their indifference to the concerns of the city, linger elsewhere and arrive only at the last moment. He is the only Athenian for whom the Assembly can not begin soon enough. Compelled by the war to live in town, he longs for his village where he produced everything he needed; he loathes the town where he has to buy everything. While waiting for the beginning of the Assembly he passes his time by doing a great variety of things, among them yawning and writing. At the beginning of the play we find him engaged in attempting to count the very few pleasures—exactly four—that he had in town, whereas he had there innumerable pains. He succeeds in enumerating a political pleasure, a Music pain, a Music pleasure, and another Music pain. We learn from his enumeration that he loves Aeschylus. After having mentioned his second pain he turns not to his third pleasure but to his third pain, his present pain—a pain so great and so intense that it prevents him from even completing his enumeration of his four pleasures. His present pain is connected with the war, the source of his innumerable pains. Compared with these pains, even the pains that he derived from bad poetry or music might well appear to him to have been pleasures; to say nothing of the fact that bad poetry or music, by virtue of being laughable, affords some pleasure. The political pleasure that he felt was caused by Kleon's having been heavily fined, thanks to the knights; it is possible that this event occurred in a comedy, rather than in life. Surely Dikaiopolis is as little an average rustic as Strepsiades; he is an unusually Music rustic. It is because he loves the Muses that he loathes war more than the average rustic. Loathing the war wholeheartedly, he has come to today's Assembly resolved to do everything he can in favor of peace. His private woes—in contradistinction to Strepsiades'—can not be removed except by political action, or his private pleasures can not be obtained except by benefiting the city.

Dikaiopolis finds wholly unexpected and even miraculous support. The first speaker in the Assembly, Amphitheos, and only he, has been charged by the gods to treat with the Spartans about peace; although he is an Athenian citizen he is not a human being (cf. 46 and 57), but himself an immortal. He needs the assistance of the Assembly because the magistrates have declined to supply him with funds for travel to Sparta. The gods obviously wish the Athenians to show their earnest desire for peace (without such earnestness they do not deserve peace, or there will be no genuine peace); and the clearest proof that men wish something earnestly is that they are prepared to spend money for it. Surely, the peace must be negotiated between the Athenians and the Spartans; if an immortal is to negotiate for the Athenians, he must himself be an Athenian, and he must travel to Sparta like an Athenian, i.e., he needs money for travel; but being an immortal, Amphitheos, as he says, has no travel money. The Athenians do not pay the slightest attention to the will of the gods. Against Dikaiopolis' protest, Amphitheos is silenced by the police. Dikaiopolis' pain is increased when the Assembly, far from discussing peace with Sparta, turns to alliances with barbarians against Sparta. The Athenians who had been sent to the king of Persia as ambassadors years ago have finally come back. One of them gives an account of the unheard-of things they have experienced abroad and of the efforts they have made on behalf of the city. To Dikaiopolis' disgust, the ambassador is unaware of the shocking contrast between their experiences and the simultaneous experiences of the bulk of the Athenians, between the wartime austerity in Athens and their own leisurely progress to the Persian court in the utmost comfort, being wined and dined—to say nothing of the even grander progress of the Persian king to his privy. The Athenian ambassadors introduce the Persian ambassador, the king's Eye. He has an immense eye in the midst of his forehead. It is not an Aristophanean character who understood "the king's Eye" to mean a man who is almost nothing but an eye; the poet himself presents the king's Eye as a Big Eye. The poet himself does what Strepsiades does: He understands things too literally; generally speaking, he achieves some of his comical effects by Strepsiadizing, by making himself more stupid than he is. Or, to state this from the point of view of Socrates—of a man whose fundamental defect induces him, among other things, to regard the imitation as prior to the imitated—Strepsiades is a comedian (*Clouds* 296). Dikaiopolis' strong loathing of Persian bombast and Athenian boasting, as well as of everything tending to perpetuate the war—perhaps co-operating with his ignorance of the Persian tongue and Persian gestures, and the Persian's ignorance of the Greek tongue and Greek gestures—make him certain that the whole embassy from the Persian king is a gross fraud perpetrated by the Athenian ambassadors. But so great is the Athenians' addiction to the war that Dikaiopolis' apparent unmasking of the Persian ambassadors is not even noticed by the Assembly. His patience has now reached its limit. He decides on an enormous and grand deed. He pays Amphitheos the money required for the journey to Sparta and back out of his own pocket, so that the immortal citizen can bring a truce for him alone, i.e., for him, his wife, and his children. He knows that he acts according to the will of the gods and that peace is best for the city as a whole, i.e., that his action is just; the city that prefers war to peace is unjust. He must act for the good of the city against the will of the city. Yet, since he can not force the city to make peace, the most he can do, in order to be just, is to make peace for himself alone. Amphitheos, who alone has been charged by the gods to make peace with Sparta, is to make that peace for Dikaiopolis alone (52, 131). The superhuman and the private conspire against the city.

After Amphitheos leaves, the Assembly is addressed by the Athenian ambassadors to King Sitalkes, who introduce the troops sent in support of Athens by that ally. While Dikaiopolis never believes that the Persian king would send gold to the Athenians, he is but too certain that the Thracian king has sent mercenaries for gold, at atrociously high pay, for these murderous and thievish fellows are a menace to every Athenian. Fortunately he observes, or rather invents, an omen which, by putting an end to the meeting of the Assembly, prevents a decision in favor of the Thracians' pay. As the contrast between his failure regarding the Persian embassy and his success regarding the Thracian embassy shows, fraud can not be fought by the truth, but only by fraud. The Assembly is barely dissolved when Amphitheos returns from Sparta; he has performed his mission with the speed of an immortal. Dispatch and secrecy are indispensable for the success of treason, as Machiavelli would say. Since he made the journey within such a short time, he must have netted considerable savings from his travel funds; he does not return the surplus to Dikaiopolis, who indeed does not even ask for it. It is not necesary to assume that Amphitheos is greedy for money, since he is in a great hurry because he is being pursued by some old Acharnians. Dikaiopolis does not pay attention to the dangers threatening Amphitheos. He is only interested in the treaties that Amphitheos brought back. With characteristic literalness—*spondai* means both truce and libations—and sensuality he chooses the truce that smells best and tastes best, i.e., that runs for the greatest number of years. Freed from the war, he will celebrate the rural Dionysia. Amphitheos however must run away from the Acharnians who pursue him. He is never seen or heard of again. Amphitheos' action is kept completely separate from the main action of the play; Amphitheos is a Euripidean *deus ex machina*, or rather the comic equivalent thereof. His speed is equal to his fear. He will not benefit from Dikaiopolis' truce. The only benefit that he himself derives from his philanthropic action is the possession of the travel funds.

The Acharnians do not find Amphitheos. They mistake Dikaiopolis for Amphitheos. The mistake is inevitable: Dikaiopolis and no one else celebrates the Dionysia in the country. The mistake is in fact no mistake at all, for the crime that arouses their patriotic indignation was in the first place committed by Dikaiopolis, and its fruits are enjoyed only by him. Dikaiopolis has then to face the Acharnians. Amphitheos' action proves to be only the necessary condition for Dikaiopolis' private peace, and not its sufficient condition. He must remove his private woes by private and, in addition, purely human action. The alleged crime against gods and men for which the Acharnians pursue him is treason; he has made peace for himself alone, with utter disregard of the city, by negotiating privately with the city's hated enemy; his pursuers act on behalf of the city; they embody the spirit of the city: They are old men, Marathon fighters, the most passionate haters in Athens of the Spartans, from whom they have suffered more than did any other part of the city; accordingly they hate Dikaiopolis even more than they hate Kleon. (Dikaiopolis too hates Kleon; Dikaiopolis and the Acharnians belong to the same political party; their opposition is not located on the political plane.) The Acharnians remind us of the Just Speech. Accordingly, Dikaiopolis—in spite of his name—reminds us of the Unjust Speech. Surely Dikaiopolis has in common with Strepsiades that he puts his family above the city. Yet while Strepsiades turns against the city's laws, or at least some of them, Dikaiopolis turns against the city's war; and while Strepsiades acts against the will of the gods, Dikaiopolis acts in agreement with it. Accordingly, while the *Clouds* is a playful presentation of the issue of father-beating, the *Acharnians* is a playful presentation of the much more political, grave, and explosive issue of treason; and whereas the father-beating is only partly successful, the treason is entirely successful.

Dikaiopolis is not conscious of any guilt. He has simply forgotten the city. Besides, he had the gods on his side in making peace with Sparta for himself and his family. The family is more powerfully present in the *Acharnians* than in the *Clouds;* there are no quarrels within Dikaiopolis' family. Dikaiopolis is less unerotic than Strepsiades. The Acharnians find him engaged in sacrificing and praying to Dionysos; without knowing it, he thus may gain the help of that god against the Acharnians. Dionysos is a god of sex, but not of the family; in his phallic song Dikaiopolis lovingly and jubilantly calls the god's companion adulterer and pederast, and he praises the pleasure of lying with a young slave girl in the woods. The Acharnians refuse to listen to anything Dikaiopolis might say in justification of his truce; his treason being manifest, there is nothing for them to do but to punish him with death. Realizing that the Acharnians will not permit him to say anything in favor of the Spartans, he first tries to defend his truce with the Spartans without any regard to its being a truce with the Spartans. He implies that not every private truce is defensible or decent, wholly regardless of who and of what character the enemy is; perhaps he means that in order to be decent a private truce must not be made from cowardice (from preferring slavery to fighting), or must be authorized by the gods. Dikaiopolis shows by deed that he is not a coward, yet he never justifies his action by referring to Amphitheos' commission; he never even mentions Amphitheos to the Acharnians or to anybody else: Even the Acharnians might not have believed the story. More simply, if peace is good and war is bad, it does not seem to make a difference who and of what character the enemy is. Yet can peace be better than war against an absolutely unjust enemy? Dikaiopolis is therefore driven to assert that the Spartans are not absolutely unjust, that not all injustices have been committed by the Spartans or that some injustice has been done to the Spartans. The Acharnians are still more incensed by Dikaiopolis' boldness, not to say impudence, in defending the enemy. Yet he goes still further. He almost demands that he be given the opportunity to prove the justice of his case in a court of law; he surely demands that he should be permitted to state his case with his head on the executioner's block. The Acharnians now can no longer restrain themselves. In this most desperate situation Dikaiopolis stops them by convincing them that he has as hostages for his life their very best friends, i.e., that he completely controls their sources of livelihood. Thereupon the Acharnians permit him not only to live but to say anything he pleases in favor of his Spartan friends: They who were such passionate enemies of the Spartans because of the damage the Spartans had done to their property cease to be passionate enemies of the Spartans when their passion appears to them to lead to complete destruction of their property; in other words, they who regarded the betrayal of the fatherland as a heinous crime, which they must capitally punish on the spot, would rather tolerate betrayal of the fatherland than betrayal of the sources of their livelihood (340, 290). Dikaiopolis has succeeded in convincing the fire-eating Marathon fighters that there is a higher good than the fatherland. He has stopped them and disarmed them. He could have sent them away. But he is a just man; he uses his stranglehold on them not to escape punishment for a capital crime but only to get a hearing for his side of the case. In spite or because of his victory, he is going to state the case for the Spartans with his head on the executioner's block, with the understanding that he will be executed if he does not convince the Acharnians of the justice of the Spartans. His justice—the justice of his apparent act of treason—stands or falls by the injustice of the Athenians' war against Sparta, or by the justice of the Spartans' war against Athens. It is not sufficient that the Athenians become inclined to peace because they are tired of the war; they must first come to acknowledge their war guilt; they must free themselves from their conceited patriotism. Only then can Dikaiopolis' peace be secure. But the fact that his action is just does not prove that it is legal; he settles illegally the question of whether the injustice of a city's war entitles a citizen to withdraw from that war. Still, Dikaiopolis' action against the will of the city in favor of his family succeeds because it develops into a public demonstration and thus shows a way to the city; whereas Strepsiades' action against the will of the city in favor of his family fails because it does not show a way to the city.

After they have seen that Dikaiopolis is an honest man, the Acharnians, as one might have expected, recover their open hostility to him; they are now anxious that he undergo his quasi-trial. But he is not yet ready for it. He is not yet able to speak to the Acharnians. He reveals his situation to the audience, or to us, in a soliloquy. He will not go back on his promise to speak bravely and frankly in favor of the Spartans, the enemy, but he is not eager to die. He has many fears; he knows that he is one against many, not to say against all; [1] against him the Acharnians (old rustics, Marathon fighters) and Kleon are united; he is much more exposed than Socrates. And, in contradistinction to Socrates, he is unable or unwilling to win his case by hook or by crook. He must reveal his thought on a most dangerous subject to his fellow citizens without any cleverness or disguise; he must reveal himself; he must strip. Hitherto we knew him only as an oldish rustic, if a particularly Music rustic, an Attic Hesiod, as it were. Now he reveals himself as the comic poet Aristophanes himself. In other words, Aristophanes first comes to sight as something lower than he is, in the disguise of an oldish rustic. Among the many things that Dikaiopolis admits fearing, we may then count without hesitation the danger that the *Acharnians* will not receive the first prize. Dikaiopolis' danger is so great, not only because of his justice and the unpopular character of his cause, but also because he can not use his only power—that of the comic poet— against men filled to overflowing with righteous indignation. What he needs is something that the comic poet is unable to provide: He must arouse his mortal enemies' compassion. Only by appearing as a man who is not provocative, fearless, or fear-inspiring, but most pitiable, fearful, or submissive can he who fears to die act fearlessly. Despite his immense courage, he needs, as the Acharnians see, a most clever and complete disguise, but they do not see that the disguise must not reveal his cleverness; under no circumstances must he appear to the Acharnians to be clever. Even the disguise of a rustic is no longer sufficient; he needs a still lower disguise; he must go beyond Strepsiadizing. In order to be able to endure his ordeal, he needs such a disguise as only that tragic poet who is a past master in arousing compassion can provide. However much he loves Aeschylus, he now needs the help of Euripides. Without knowing or revealing it, he, the lover of peace, who puts the household above the city, was all the time in sympathy with Euripides or the Unjust Speech (or Pheidippides), rather than with the Just Speech (or Strepsiades) or the Marathon fighter Aeschylus, who praises Ares and Lamachos, Dikaiopolis' chief antagonist.[2] Strepsiades' cause becomes publicly defensible through Socrates' art and thus destroys itself; Dikaiopolis' cause becomes publicly defensible through Euripides' art and thus preserves itself. Considerable parts of the *Acharnians* are parodies of Euripidean tragedy; but just like the other characteristics of the Aristophanean comedy, his parodies of tragedies too have their noncomic meaning. This is shown by the mere fact that each parody performs a necessary function within the particular comedy in which it occurs. Surely in the present case the parody of

Euripides indicates that Aristophanes is in need of Euripides or "depends" on him in a manner that is comically reflected in Dikaiopolis' need for Euripides.

Dikaiopolis' going to Euripides resembles Strepsiades' going to Socrates. Just as Strepsiades first meets a pupil of Socrates through whom he receives the first inkling of Socrates' wisdom, Dikaiopolis first meets a servant of Euripides through whom he receives an inkling of Euripides' wisdom; according to Euripides' servant, a man himself is his body rather than the mind (cf. *Clouds* 1275–76). But Dikaiopolis does not commit the solecism committed by Strepsiades in the corresponding scene: Although he is in much greater danger than Strepsiades, he does not pray to the gods. This difference is not sufficiently explained by the fact that Euripides is much easier of access than Socrates. Euripides' easiness of access contrasts with its alleged "impossibility" (402, 408); Dikaiopolis can easily convince Euripides that what Euripides asserts to be impossible is in fact possible, for Euripides himself is a master of rendering possible the impossible by the *deus ex machina:* Euripides himself is the *deus ex machina.* Yet, while Socrates descends to Strepsiades, Euripides does not descend: Tragedy must not mingle with comedy; tragedy can not incorporate verses from comedies, whereas comedy may—nay, must—incorporate verses from tragedy. Comedy is essentially preceded by tragedy. In contradistinction to Strepsiades, Dikaiopolis does not introduce himself by adding his father's name to his own.

Dikaiopolis asks Euripides for the rags and six other accoutrements of his most pitiable and beggarly hero, who was at the same time a clever speaker, on the ground that he needs them to save his life. Euripides grants his request without making any serious difficulty. Speaking as one clever dramatist to another, Dikaiopolis can afford to disregard entirely the dramatic illusion: The beggar's outfit is not meant to deceive the audience, but only the chorus, which, while pretending to consist of old Acharnians, must only pretend to see in him a most pitiable man in mortal danger at its hands. The comic poet can not go further in urging his audience not to take him seriously but to laugh with him about him. Yet this extreme self-depreciation is not indeed the most compassion-arousing, but the most laughable or most lowly disguise. Comedy itself is the most effective disguise of wisdom. The parody of a tragic hero in filthy rags is a still better disguise than that tragic hero himself. In other words, in pretending to take the majority of the citizens (the audience consisting chiefly of genuine "Acharnians") into his confidence against a tiny minority (the chorus consisting of the alleged Acharnians), he in fact conspires with a wise minority in the audience against the large majority.

After he has left Euripides' halls, Dikaiopolis returns to his role. Inasmuch as he is now a beggar, yet through what he says in his speech pretends to be more than a beggar, he resembles the Unjust Speech as the latter was in the good old times (*Clouds* 921–22). He trembles again at his great task: His trembling heart must speak in favor of the Spartans, with him in danger of losing his head, but at his command it ceases to tremble. The Acharnians, however, regard his hard-won intrepidity as sheer impudence. He addresses his speech not to the chorus but to the audience, and he speaks in the capacity not of a comic poet disguised as a beggar but of both a beggar and a comic poet. That is to say, his speech is not entirely jocular. He addresses the city regarding the city. He had tried to do this in the Assembly, where he appeared as a simple rustic, but there he utterly failed; he succeeds in doing it as comic poet. He apologizes for addressing the city regarding the city in a comedy: A single man can not oppose the whole city except most humbly, for there is an enormous contrast between the puniness of the individual (367) and the grandeur of the city and of that for which the city stands, the just things. Yet it may happen that the city despises the just things and that the latter thus become in their way as lowly as the comedy, or that only the comedy can safely say the just things. He warns his audience that what he is going to say will be harsh but just. It is just, not only by what it says, but also by the manner in which it says it: Dikaiopolis-Aristophanes can not be accused by Kleon of speaking ill of the city in the presence of strangers, for the *Acharnians* is performed on the Lenaian festival where only Athenians—citizens or metics—are present. His hatred of the Spartans is, of course, second to no man's, for his property too has been damaged by them (he thus denies implicitly that he is a beggar); but the Spartans are not the cause of all our evils. Above all, the Spartans are not responsible for the war. God forbid that Dikaiopolis should say that the Athenians, the city of Athens, started the war. Just as Plato's Socrates distinguishes between the unblamable laws and the blameworthy human administration of the laws, Dikaiopolis distinguishes between the unblamable city and the blameworthy human administration of the city. To mention only the main example, some silly Athenian youths had kidnaped a Megarian strumpet, whereupon the Megarians, in their anger, kidnaped two strumpets belonging to Aspasia, whereupon Perikles saw fit to vindicate the honor of that foreign female by causing his Megarian decree to be passed,

The Megarians, reduced to extremities, asked the Spartans to induce the Athenians to repeal that decree but "we"—i.e., the city—refused to repeal it. This meant war, for Sparta had to help her unjustly attacked ally, Megara, just as Athens would have helped any of her unjustly attacked allies. After having slyly appealed to an anti-Periklean prejudice, Dikaiopolis then unmistakably asserts that not Perikles but Athens, only Athens, is responsible for the war, and that the Spartans are wholly guiltless: Only because the city's war is altogether unjust is his private peace altogether just. In the Assembly he had not even hinted at the Athenians' war guilt, although one could say that Amphitheos' or the gods' action implies that the Athenians must take the initiative toward peace because the Athenians started the war. However this may be, Dikaiopolis' peace is now an accomplished fact, and he must defend it in the best publicly defensible manner. This means that his public defense does not necessarily reveal his view of the origin of the war or the true motive of his private peace.

Dikaiopolis' well-prepared speech has a resounding success: He convinces one-half of the Acharnians. It matters little that the other half is angrier than ever (his having said just things against the city makes matters not better but worse for him); for treason ceases to be treason when the city is split into two: Dikaiopolis now has powerful defenders; the Acharnians still opposed to him must now kill the other Acharnians before they can kill him. By successfully withstanding the first assault of what is in fact an alliance, he enables himself to split the alliance. The Acharnians, whom he failed to persuade but who are now seriously threatened, call Lamachos, the war spirit incarnate, to their help. Dikaiopolis would be lost if Lamachos and the hostile half of the Acharnians were to join forces. He can not possibly win Lamachos over to his side; he must therefore try to arouse enmity between the Acharnians and Lamachos. He must deny a common ground to the Acharnians and Lamachos; he must find a common ground between the Acharnians and himself. There is no common ground between him and the still-hostile Acharnians regarding the responsibility for the war. He therefore buries his accusation of the city in silence and worse than silence. Instead he takes issue with Lamachos' accusing him of being a beggar. He who had not hesitated when it suited him to describe himself as a beggar (497) can not now be a beggar (and still less a comic poet), for Acharnians have nothing in common with beggars. He now describes himself as a respectable citizen—just a plain citizen like all other plain citizens, a citizen soldier, and no brass like Lamachos. The only defense left to Lamachos [3] is that he and his like were duly elected to their high position by the *demos*, which amounts to saying that by blaming Lamachos and the like one blames the *demos*. Dikaiopolis can not meet this defense, but he turns the tables by emphasizing the fact that having been elected by the *demos* does not mean living like the *demos* and therewith truly belonging to the *demos*. While his appeal to anti-Periklean resentment had been only partly successful, his appeal to anti-brass resentment is entirely successful, for the large majority does not belong to the brass. When he suggests that he made his private peace not because of Athens' war guilt but because of his indignation over the privileges enjoyed by these war profiteers—prior to the war they were good-for-nothings and beggars; during the war they are given lucrative assignments behind the fighting lines—and the suffering of the common people—in peace hardworking honest citizens, during the war grayhaired, underpaid, and underfed fighters bossed around by fellows who could be their sons—all Acharnians come over to his side. Even Lamachos' indication that Dikaiopolis' argument is an attack on democracy is of no avail to him, for democracy means—does it not?—that everything should be for the *demos*. The justice of the war remains controversial; the unjust distribution of the burdens of the war is an unbeatable argument: Even those Acharnians who, from hatred of the Spartans or simple patriotism, could not bear to hear of Athens' war guilt, are won over by the appeal to their envy. No one trained by Socrates could have done better than, or even as well as, Dikaiopolis. Armed with Euripides' devices and political shrewdness one can overcome the superior force of the city much better than with the support of the Clouds and of Socrates' forensic rhetoric.

Lamachos leaves, declaring that he will go on waging war with the Spartans and all their allies at all times, in all places, with all branches of the armed services, and with all might. Dikaiopolis, however, invites all foreign enemies of the city to come to trade with him, i.e., to sell him their merchandise, but not with Lamachos. This is quite surprising, not because beggars do not have the wherewithal to buy (for we know already that Dikaiopolis is not a beggar), but since, as he made clear in his initial soliloquy, a major reason why he loathed life in town and therefore longed for peace was precisely that in town he had to buy everything, whereas in the country or in peace he did not buy anything. A yet greater surprise is about to come. The chorus tells us that Dikaiopolis is victorious in the debate and that he persuades the *demos* regarding his truce. This action of the *demos*, and it alone, makes his peace secure. We expect the next step to be the formal transformation of his private truce into a public truce. This precisely had been his initial desire: to have peace, public peace, so that he can stop buying things. Now he has overcome all obstacles to the fulfillment of his heart's desire. But now he has ceased to desire at all "public peace and no buying." Dikaiopolis turns away not only from the badly managed city but from the city simply. This striking change can not be explained by the fact that he alone has borne the cost of the private truce, for the converted *demos* will gladly reimburse him. We are compelled to explain the self-contradiction by the fact that he plays a variety of roles (Music rustic, comic poet, comic poet disguised as a beggar, beggar, plain citizen soldier); the two incompatible positions regarding buying belong to different roles. This compels us indeed to wonder who is the true Dikaiopolis, or who is Dikaiopolis himself. There can be no doubt as to Dikaiopolis' playing a variety of roles; at least one of these roles was assumed by him openly, if in the privacy of Euripides' house, before our eyes. With a comparatively slight exaggeration one may say that in the *Acharnians*, in contrast to the *Clouds*, everything takes place in the open; for Dikaiopolis' action, in contrast to Strepsiades' (or Socrates'), requires the support of the public: To defraud one's creditors (as distinguished from the canceling of debts through legal or revolutionary action) is not publicly defensible, whereas peacemaking is. Accordingly, there is no action during the parabasis of the *Acharnians*, whereas in the *Clouds* both Strepsiades' and Pheidippides' indoor instruction takes place during the parabaseis. For in the *Acharnians*, in contrast to the *Clouds*, the action is completed prior to the parabasis: Dikaiopolis has achieved all that he wants; he is no longer in any danger and is therefore no longer in need of any disguise or concealment; after the parabasis, and only then, can he show himself, i.e., his true motive in making his private peace. Accordingly, the action of the *Clouds* is almost completely separated from the action of the audience; the only action that is expected from the audience of the *Clouds* will follow the conclusion of the play, namely, the awarding or not awarding of the prize to the play as play. In the *Acharnians*, however, the action of the play depends decisively on the action of the audience, for Dikaiopolis needs the support of the audience for the security of his private peace: The destruction of the dramatic illusion (as in the open assumption by Dikaiopolis of a dramatic role) is part of the dramatic illusion. This is connected with the fact that in the Acharnians the chief actor is the comic poet himself.

As we have already stated, the parabasis of the *Acharnians* has a very different function from the parabasis of the *Clouds*. In the *Clouds* no one except the chorus of Clouds speaks for Aristophanes. In the *Acharnians*, however, Dikaiopolis speaks for Aristophanes (377–79, 502–3), and the chorus of Acharnians are Dikaiopolis' deadly enemies. They must first be converted by Dikaiopolis to his cause before they can speak, as they must in the parabasis, on behalf of the poet. That conversion was consummated immediately before the parabasis. After having stripped, i.e., ceased to pretend that they are old Acharnians, the chorus chants the praises of Aristophanes' excellence. This praise has become necessary because he has been calumniated by Kleon as a man who treats the city comically and insults the *demos*. His reply shows that Kleon's action had some foundation. He makes the chorus assert on his behalf that he has done great service to the Athenians by combating their vanity or boastfulness and thus preventing their being fooled by the flatteries of foreigners. Boastfulness is a vice that comedy hits and hurts more directly than any other vice.[4] Comedy would be powerless against righteous indignation if righteous indignation were not always on the verge of turning into boastfulness. Aristophanes also taught the Athenians to treat their subject cities justly. Therefore these foreigners now come to Athens full of eagerness to see that most excellent poet who had dared to say the just things among the Athenians. The poet shows by deed that one way of debunking boasters is to outboast them. His boasting reaches its peak when he makes the chorus assert that the fame of the poet's daring reached the very king of Persia—the center of the greatest pomp and pompousness—who thereupon predicted the Athenians' victory in the war on the ground that they possess not only the superior navy but also this poet who, by rebuking them as severely as he does, proves to be the best adviser. The poet thus tacitly suggests that the Persian king will not ally himself with Sparta, that Athens' prospects in the war are excellent, and hence that it would be foolish for the city to make peace now. Aristophanes' excellence is also the reason why the Spartans are anxious for a peace through which they would get hold of the poet. The Spartans show silently what the king of Persia showed by speech: The man most important for Athens' well-being is Aristophanes. The poet tacitly warns his fellow citizens against making peace with Sparta under the condition mentioned, i.e., the only one under which peace can be obtained now, for they need him badly because he treats the just things comically. The poet has given two most powerful reasons why he does not attempt to transform his private peace into a public peace. Comical treatment of the just things is necessary to the extent to which the city does not tolerate the blame of its injustice; the only safe treatment of this dangerous subject is a comical one. In other words, the noncomical teaching of the just things is in danger of becoming boastful. In addition, the poet will lead the Athenians to bliss by teaching the best things: He teaches the best things by his comical treatment of the just things (like his comical treatment of the rights and wrongs of the origin of the Peloponnesian War in the *Acharnians*). The best things are then not simply the just things. Nevertheless, both the good and the just are Aristophanes' allies, while his enemy is Kleon above everything and everyone else—Kleon who is both bad and unjust (664), whom the Acharnians had hated from the beginning, and whom they now hate even more.

In the parabasis proper of the *Clouds*, Aristophanes rebukes the Athenians, i.e., the city (525–26), in his own name. In the corresponding part of the *Acharnians* he limits himself to replying to those who rebuked him; if he rebukes anyone there, it is Kleon. This is in accordance with all that went before (515–16), especially with the fact that in his role as Dikaipolis he has won the city over to his side. He leaves the rebuke of the city in the parabasis of the *Acharnians* to the Acharnians speaking of their own concern as distinguished from the poet's concern. He thus brings out the profound difference between himself and the Acharnians [5] and therefore also between his understanding of his peace and the Acharnians' understanding of it. As he has made abundantly clear, the city is much more in need of him than he is of the city. The Acharnians too have great merit about the city, but through services in the past: They are old citizens and nothing else; they are the very men who fought at Marathon two generations ago. Hence they are useless to the city now and are treated accordingly by the city. Whereas Dikaiopolis can take care of himself, the Acharnians depend on the city. Whereas Dikaiopolis only played the beggar, the Acharnians are truly beggars. The true character of the Acharnians thus revealed to them and by them explains their action against Dikaiopolis. It also explains why they, and not Dikaiopolis, blame the city: The city neglects its best citizens, i.e., its oldest citizens. Their very Muse is Acharnian and nothing but Acharnian; it is not Aristophanes' Muse. Her effect reminds them of what goes on in the kitchen when a most savory meat is prepared. They propose a law to prevent old, slow, decrepit men like themselves from being at the mercy of young, clever, and glib speakers in the law courts: Old men ought to plead only against old men and young men against young; that is to say, those by nature weaker should be protected by the law against those who are by nature stronger; the law should establish equality, not by disregarding natural inequality, but by considering it. The Acharnians obviously do not care whether what they say about their decrepitude detracts from the glory of Dikaiopolis' victory: Their fight against Dikaiopolis was their last fight; their indignation was weakened throughout by their old age; they could be persuaded because they were not angry young men.

The second half of the play (719–end) shows how Dikaiopolis uses his victory or his peace; it reveals the end for which he has sought that peace. His first act is to open a market in front of his house in the country in order to trade with the enemies of the city. In accordance with the ambiguity of his truce, the market is both his private market and the market place, the *agora*. He surely acts as a sovereign. The first man who attends the market is a Megarian who is anxious to sell his two little girls; both father and daughters are starving as a consequence of the war, of Pericles' Megarian decree. Since no one will buy the poor girls, their father tries to sell them as little pigs for use in the mysteries; in order to be sold and thus to survive, the children are told by their father to behave like young pigs, and they obey him. Yet Dikaiopolis is incredulous; what he senses of the merchandise contained in a sack does not feel like pigs. But since the girls utter the sounds of young pigs, and since the Greek word for young pig has an obscene ambiguity, Dikaiopolis buys the girls as young pigs from their father in exchange for some salt and garlic, i.e., for things that in peacetime were exported by the Megarians. The war brings it about that the little daughters, to say nothing of his wife and mother, are less valuable to the Megarian than some salt and garlic; yet, while the young girls are sold as young pigs to Dikaiopolis, they will be fed and otherwise treated like poor girls by him, whereas they would surely starve to death if they stayed with their parents in Megara. The bargain is then not as beastly as it appears at first sight. Dikaiopolis is in his way, as his name so clearly indicates, a just man. But his justice is not free from ambiguity. The Megarian speaks of his children, his wife, and his city; Dikaiopolis does not speak of his children, his wife, and his city: He buys the Megarian's young pigs for himself alone; he uses his private market for his most private end. The bargain is consummated, thanks to the abstraction from what is revealed by sight and touch, as distinguished from hearing and words. This goes much beyond Dikaiopolis' tasting and smelling the *spondai*. Nor ought we to overlook the connection between the ambiguity of Dikaiopolis' truce, which is private and yet also in a sense public, and the ambiguity of the word publicly or decently designating a young pig and obscenely the female organ. The bargain is barely concluded when an informer arrives who tries to confiscate the merchandise imported by an enemy alien; for, lest we forget, Athens is still at war with Megara. But Dikaiopolis has him driven away by his market inspectors without any difficulty; he does not even take the trouble to explain to him that he and his farm are no longer at war.

The exhausted old Acharnians are now reduced to the status of mere spectators. They call Dikaiopolis blessed, with a view to the fact that he gathers the fruits of his peace while sitting in the market. Freed from the evils of war, he spends his time in the market, in the *agora*, like the products of the new education blamed by the Just Speech and praised by the Unjust Speech. But the market in which he sits, being his private market, is far superior to the market place proper; the unpleasant and hateworthy fellows who disgrace the *agora* are not admitted to Dikaiopolis' market. The central [6] type of man that is excluded from Dikaiopolis' market consists of bad poets and musicians.

The second visitor to Dikaiopolis' market is a Theban accompanied by a servant and bad flute players whose music reminds Dikaiopolis of the noise made by wasps. The Thebans are not starved. The Theban has come to sell birds, fish, and many other kinds of beasts. He never calls Dikaiopolis by name, as the Megarian had done (823; cf. 959). Dikaiopolis is particularly thrilled by a certain kind of fish that, he says, is particularly welcome to comical choruses; but he does not promise that delicacy to the present chorus. In this scene both Dikaiopolis and the foreigner are silent about their families and cities; the increased "privacy" is a function of the transition from little girls to food. All equivalents that Dikaiopolis can offer in exchange for the Theban's merchandise are to be found abundantly in Thebes, except informers. Accordingly, an informer who tries to seize the enemy-alien merchandise is seized by Dikaiopolis, properly wrapped, and handed over to the Theban. Since what the Theban brought is so much more valuable to Dikaiopolis than what the Megarian brought, the Theban receives a much greater reward, not just salt and garlic, but a live informer, an outstanding informer or, which is the same thing, an informer adorned with a resounding name composed of Victory and Command. Or should we say that Dikaiopolis procures a luxurious dinner for himself by deception, just as Socrates procures a poor dinner for himself and his companions by petty theft? The chorus accompanies Dikaiopolis' action against the informer with hearty approval, which leads to a dialogue between the chorus and Dikaiopolis. The dialogue deals exclusively with the wrapping, transportation, and use (especially domestic use, for clearly he can no longer be of public use) of the informer; the dialogue is silent about the delicacies that Dikaiopolis received from the Theban: They are for the use of Dikaiopolis, not of the chorus. The progress in the revelation of Dikaiopolis' end is underlined by the fact that the chorus addresses the Theban, while it had not addressed the Megarian. The Theban and the Megarian are the only foreigners who come to Dikaiopolis' market (the Spartans do not come); they may be said to surround Dikaiopolis just as the Persians and Thracians surround the Athenian Assembly: The play moves from the world of boasting and savage barbarians (and their Athenian equivalents) to the world of peaceful Greek merchants of delicacies (and their Athenian customers).

We now come to the peak of Dikaiopolis' triumph. His chief antagonist, the war-loving Lamachos, sends his servant to Dikaiopolis to buy from him some of the enemy-alien delicacies. Dikaiopolis absolutely refuses to comply with that request: Lamachos must not have any share in the peace; Dikaiopolis has bought the delicacies for himself. This action of Dikaiopolis induces the Acharnians to draw the attention of the whole city to Dikaiopolis' supreme wisdom: Thanks to his peace he has good things of all kinds in abundance to sell; all good things come to him by themselves. This is only what one would expect: Peace brings all good things and war all evils. The Acharnians forswear all communion with War without any consideration for its justice or expediency. They wish that some *eros* would unite them with the beautiful woman Reconciliation, the playmate of Aphrodite and the Graces. While still conscious of their old age, they feel rejuvenated. The last flicker of their martial ardor had led them to persecute Dikaiopolis; thanks to their reconciliation with Dikaiopolis they now experience the last flicker of their amorous ardor; the *eros* for which they long, however, resembles a painted *eros*.

Next appears a herald, calling upon the people to celebrate the festival of the Pitchers according to ancestral custom by engaging in a drinking contest. This is no longer a merely private affair of Dikaiopolis', although he is the only Athenian who can celebrate the festival in peace. He in his turn calls upon his people to speed up the cooking and roasting of the things that he has bought from the Theban and to hand him the tools so that he can prepare his favorite dish. There follows again a dialogue between the chorus and Dikaiopolis. The Acharnians now express their admiration or envy not only of Dikaiopolis' wisdom, and in particular of his mastery of the arts of cooking and gourmandise, but above all of his present feasting, in which they do not participate: He uses his delicate skills only to take care of himself. They have learned to prefer to the city not only the necessities of life (326 ff.) but also the pleasant things as such. In return Dikaiopolis does not promise them more than that they will be spectators of the products of his art.

The fifth visitor is a farmer who is in a miserable state because the Boiotians (from one of whom Dikaiopolis had bought his delicacies) have taken away his oxen, his chief support. Dikaiopolis is the only man who can supply him with a cure for his ills, by giving him a small drop of his private peace. The apparent farmer Dikaiopolis does not have an ounce of compassion for this genuine farmer, as little as he has for the Acharnians; he treats him almost as badly as he had treated Lamachos: He "just is not in public service"; by making his private peace he has become in every respect a private man, a man living by himself for himself; he cures only himself; he does not give any part, however small, of his peace and its pleasures to anyone. Even the Acharnians now become aware of the un-qualified selfishness of Dikaiopolis, who does not pay any attention to what they say about him and is concerned with nothing but the prepara-tion of his delicious dinner for his own enjoyment alone. They tell him to his face that he will starve them to death; he does not even take the trouble to reply. Next comes a man sent by a bridegroom to get some small part of Dikaiopolis' peace in exchange for meat from the wedding meal, for he wishes to enjoy the pleasures of love instead of having to go to war. Dikaiopolis again refuses to help: He would not barter away or sell any part of his peace for any equivalent. Hitherto we could think that he would not give away any part of his peace to anyone without equiv-alent, or that he would not sell any part of it to such lovers of war as Lamachos; now we see that he is merciless in preserving his monopoly of peace (it is somewhat more literally a monopoly than the "monopoly of violence"). Yet he is not quite so bad. A bridesmaid who has come with the groom's man asks him for help in the name of the bride. He sends the bride a bit of his peace so that she will not be deprived of sexual pleasures in spite of the war, for being a woman she ought not to suffer for the war. Dikaiopolis' selfishness is then qualified only by compassion for lovesick women. This is cold comfort to the Acharnians, who remain speechless now as on no other comparable occasion.

The last scene opens with the successive arrivals of two messages, one sent by the generals to Lamachos to the effect that he should proceed forthwith to the frontier in order to prevent Boiotian marauders from entering Attica, the other sent by the priest of Dionysos to Dikaiopolis to

the effect that he should proceed forthwith to the public banquet in celebration of the holiday: Everything, including dancing girls and other girls,
is waiting for him; the only thing missing among the enumerated attractions is wine. While the war-loving Lamachos is most unhappy that he
can not celebrate the festival, Dikaiopolis is most happy: Everything has
gone exceedingly well for him. Each of the two antagonists prepares himself for his contest, the one for the contest with the enemy of Athens, the
other for a drinking contest. Each gives the appropriate commands to his
slave; Dikaiopolis' commands are parodies of Lamachos' commands; Lamachos thrice protests against Dikaiopolis' insolent mockery; he even
threatens Dikaiopolis with criminal prosecution for cowardice or desertion. The leader of the chorus reveals the state of mind of the Marathon
fighters, who are so much older than Dikaiopolis, by addressing only
Lamachos with the observation that Lamachos goes away to freeze and be
on guard, while the old (1129–30) husband and father Dikaiopolis is going away to drink and to sleep with a most attractive girl; he thus also
underlines the shift that is taking place toward the end of the play from
the pleasures of food to those of drink and sex,[7] from pleasures that have
no necessary relation to the pleasures of other human beings to pleasures
that in different ways do have such a relation. From what we noted regarding Dikaiopolis' unpromising conduct, we are prepared for the fact
that the chorus as a whole now calls on Zeus to destroy a poet who on an
earlier occasion had failed to give the chorus a dinner. From the specifications of the chorus' curse we learn that that wicked poet Antimachos
(whose name would fit Dikaiopolis as well) was a horseman. Yet nothing
untoward can happen to Dikaiopolis in spite of the chorus' curse, which is
based on some sound divination; the man in fact afflicted is Lamachos, as
a tragic messenger now fittingly announces. For while the chorus chanted,
Lamachos has fought with the enemy and Dikaiopolis has won the prize
in the drinking contest. Lamachos now returns wounded, or at any rate
disabled, and in pain, sure that he is about to die; whereas Dikaiopolis
returns with a young girl on each side who by caressing him according to
his specifications increases his desire to the highest point: The hero of war
and the hero of peace reveal themselves almost literally as opposed to each
other like death and life. The chorus celebrates Dikaiopolis' victory and
carries him to the judges of the comedies, while he constantly reminds
everyone that he has won the drinking contest and thus suggests that he
should also be given the prize in the contest regarding the comedies; he
reveals himself again as none other than the comic poet himself. But the

chorus hears nothing from him about the dinner that he, being a just man, had never promised them.

The meaning of the *Acharnians* is indicated by Dikaiopolis' name: He is *the* just citizen, even *the* just city. Yet the most patriotic citizens, the Marathon fighters, persecute him as a most unjust citizen, as worse even than Kleon. No one can seriously maintain that Dikaiopolis proves his justice, his superiority to all others in justice, by refuting his persecutors, by pronouncing the just things; for the arguments by which he converts the Acharnians are not even comical equivalents of the just things, they are parodies of demagogic oratory. His injustice is shown by the use he makes of his rhetorical victory: By that victory he secures his private peace in order to enjoy it strictly for himself; he betrays not only the city but even his family in order to enjoy by himself the pleasures of the senses. When praising him in the second half of the play the Acharnians speak only of his strictly private bliss, as distinguished from any services he has rendered to others, to say nothing of the city. He acts along the lines of the Unjust Speech. He "makes use of nature" in complete disregard of the law. His "return to nature" must be properly understood. Whereas the alleged motive for his longing for peace was the necessity to buy things when living in town while in peacetime his land alone brought him every-thing he needed, his true motive is the impossibility of buying in wartime the delicacies produced by the enemy cities (36, 976); and he makes full use of every art that enhances his pleasures (1015–17). His use of art and imports makes him only a more perfect follower of the Unjust Speech. In order to see how this most unjust man can be, by virtue of his injustice, the justest of men, one must consider what he does to his opponents, the Acharnians. While he made them help him in securing his private peace, he does not give them any share in it or in its fruits. They do not derive any advantage from his action, just as they did not derive any advantage from persecuting him for his treason; except that by persecuting him they satisfied their impotent desire for revenge on the Spartans, or rather they believed that they acted as good citizens. But they also believe that they acted as good citizens by taking his side or by becoming his bodyguard. Still, while prior to their conversion they were full of hate and fear-inspir-ing, afterward they are objects of compassion: Through Dikaiopolis' ac-tion they cease to be boasters; they honestly admit their poverty and decrepitude. Whereas through that action Dikaiopolis becomes better off, the Acharnians become not indeed better off through it but better (650), gentler, juster. This must not for one moment obscure the fact that he tames them for his own interest alone, or that he treats them as, according to them, the young orators who make them ridiculous treat them (679–80); although in his case the old men do not realize their becoming ridiculous (442–44). If justice in the highest sense consists in making one's fellow citizens better men, and if boasting is the root of all evil, Dikaiopolis deserves his name. In other words, he is just because he does what the just city does—the just city too takes care only of itself, or does not meddle with other cities—as distinguished from what the city tells its members to do; he is entire and not merely a part; he is no longer a citizen. More precisely, in contrast to the Acharnians, who depend on the city but are no longer useful to the city, Dikaiopolis, who can take care of himself and takes care only of himself, is by the manner in which he takes care only of himself—i.e., by merely enjoying himself to the highest degree, by doing what his nature compels him to do—the greatest benefactor of the city; for who can doubt that the comic poet enjoyed himself to the highest degree in conceiving and elaborating his comedies? Yet this enjoyment necessarily communicates itself. Comedy, whose mother is laughter, gives birth to laughter. The comic poet's enjoyment is essentially social, although it is not simply political; it is akin in different ways to the enjoyment deriving from wine and from sex, rather than to the enjoyment deriving from food, however delicious. The enjoyments to which Dikaiopolis eventually turns are, apart from what they are in themselves, the comical equivalent of the enjoyment from comedies. By exciting the desire for these enjoyments of the senses, he makes his fellow citizens gay, desirous of living, hence desirous of peace (a common good), just. (Whether peace is expedient now is an entirely different question.) If this proves that he himself is just, it proves that his justice does not require the sacrifice of his life (cf. 357). To state it crudely, "tragedy dissolves life, but comedy makes it firm." [8]

The ways of life of both Dikaiopolis and Socrates differ from the ways of life recommended by both the Just Speech and the Unjust Speech. Superficially the two former seem to be located between the two latter; in truth the two former belong to a different plane, to a higher plane, than the two latter. The Socratic way of life is simply unpolitical, whereas Dikaiopolis', transcending the city, benefits the city. Socrates fails to help rustics against the city; he can not take on the guise of a rustic; he can not bridge the gulf between himself and the rustics; his arrogance prevents him from taking on humble disguises. Socrates is continence incarnate; Dikaiopolis is the opposite. Yet Dikaiopolis' incontinence remains within the limits of normality;[9] nor does he foster father-beating or incest.

No one can overhear the simple message that the *Acharnians* conveyed to every contemporary Athenian: Make peace as soon as it is expedient; put an end to that senseless slaughter and destruction as soon as it is feasible; this is not the Persian War. But one must add at once that this simple message is only a small part of the message of the play. The least that one would have to demand, if the Aristophanean comedy is to be understood in the light of its simple messages, is that these messages be understood in the poet's own terms. He asserts that he both teaches what is best for the city and especially the just things, and he makes his audience laugh. The question arises whether the serious and the ridiculous merely exist side by side or whether they are woven together, and, in the latter case, which of the two ingredients is predominant. The peculiar greatness of the Aristophanean comedy consists in its being the total comedy; the ridiculous is all-pervasive; the serious appears only in the guise of the ridiculous; the serious is integrated into the ridiculous. He frequently destroys the dramatic illusion, for the destruction of the dramatic illusion is ridiculous and may heighten the comical effect; yet he never destroys or even impairs the comical illusion. In the *Acharnians* he castigates the injustice or folly of the war by presenting especially Lamachos as ridiculous and as ridiculously defeated. Yet how can one present the defeat of the unjust by ridiculous means without making ridiculous the victory of the just man and the victorious just man himself? How can one present the just man without destroying the totally comical character of the comedy? Aristophanes solves the difficulty by presenting the victory of the just, or the movement from the ridiculous of injustice toward justice as a movement toward a ridiculous of a different kind. The victorious just man enjoys all sensual pleasures; he enjoys them frankly; he gives his enjoyment a frank, a wholly uninhibited expression; he says (and does) in public things that can not be said (and done) in public with propriety; he behaves ridiculously. He castigates injustice (Kleon, Perikles, and so on) by the use of gossip or slander; he praises justice with the help of obscenity; and he defeats the greatest powers that counteract these kinds of *aischrologia* by two other kinds, by the parody of tragedy and by blasphemy. *Aischrologia* of these four kinds is used by him in accordance with the requirements of the plot, which is in itself ridiculous because of its striking impossibility. For instance, the plot of the *Clouds* calls much more for blasphemy than for parody of tragedy and obscenity, whereas the opposite is obviously true of the *Acharnians*. Of the simple serious message one can say that it exists side by side with the ridiculous, but the full and sophisticated message is heard only if one takes the ridiculous as if it were serious, i.e., if one imitates the comic poet.

2 The Knights

The complaints with which this play opens are uttered in a dialogue between two servants. The soliloquies with which the *Clouds* and the *Acharnians* begin are uttered by the men who initiate the action of these plays. Can we infer from this that the action of the *Knights* requires for its initiation the co-operation of the two servants whom we hear at the beginning? Those servants are in fact the generals Demosthenes and Nikias, and their master is Demos. Demos has recently bought another slave, the Paphlagonian, in fact Kleon, who within a very short time has acquired full power over the other slaves and indeed over Demos' whole household. This intruder and upstart makes life for Demosthenes and Nikias utterly miserable. They curse him and lament their fate. Yet the active and manly Demosthenes soon gets tired of moaning and crying and suggests that they look out for something that will put an end to their tribulations. But no saving thought occurs to either of them; Nikias lacks the daring, and Demosthenes still lacks the inspiration. Although he is helpless for the time being, Demosthenes is not so helpless as to be unable to persuade Nikias to bring forth a proposal. Nikias in his fright so arranges things that Demosthenes is the one who pronounces Nikias' dangerous proposal that they desert to the enemy (for we are in the midst of the war). One could also say that Nikias brings forth in a cowardly, sophisticated, Euripidean manner the cowardly proposal that they should desert. Demosthenes rejects it, not because it is cowardly, but because he does not like Euripides and, above all, because the proposal is too risky for their skins. Thereupon Nikias proposes that they prostrate themselves before the image of some god. Demosthenes is amazed to find that Nikias truly believes in gods and asks him for some proof of the existence of gods. Nikias is convinced of the existence of gods by the fact that he is hated by the gods. Demosthenes admits that Nikias has a point but, as he shows by deed, he does not think that prostration before the image of some god would do them any good: If the gods hate Nikias, Nikias and his comrades can not reasonably hope to be helped by the gods; they must look for help elsewhere. Demosthenes proposes that they should explain their predicament to the spectators; as far as the spectators are concerned, there is at least some hope that they do not hate the two fellow slaves. Nikias, realizing that the spectators might be no less pleased by his and Demosthenes' troubles than are the gods, agrees. By explaining to the audience the situation as it exists prior to the action of the play, Demosthenes acts in effect as the spokesman for the poet (cf. 228, 233): Demosthenes is more of an orator, more fertile in clever conceits than Nikias.

According to Demosthenes, their master Demos is an ill-tempered, half-deaf old man, and the recently bought Paphlagonian is a most malicious rogue who flatters and bribes the master most cleverly and successfully with exclusive regard to his own benefit. He does not permit any other slave to come near the master; he thus can deprive his fellow slaves of their rewards: He usurped the glory of Demosthenes' great victory over the Spartans at Pylos; he calumniates to the master his fellow slaves, who are punished severely and degradingly at his bidding. One of the devices by which Kleon rules Demos is to make the master mad and stupid by oracles. While Demosthenes is far from being pleased with Demos, he hates Kleon: The punishments that Demos inflicts are considerably lighter than the punishments with which Kleon threatens.

By addressing the audience, Demosthenes may have succeeded in winning its sympathy, and this would not be a small success; but he knows that he can not expect to receive advice from the audience. He therefore repeats his exhortation to Nikias that they deliberate which way and toward whom to turn. Nikias can not do better than to repeat his proposal that they desert. Demosthenes repeats his refutation of this proposal by going into details: Like Zeus, for example (cf. *Wasps* 620), Kleon oversees or watches everything; they could not escape him and his punishments. Nikias does not repeat his second proposal, the proposal that they turn to the gods; he now proposes that they die. Demosthenes is willing to die, provided they do it in a most manly manner. Nikias proposes that they follow the model of the most manly Themistokles, who committed suicide by drinking the blood of a bull. When he hears of drinking, Demosthenes takes hope; he is willing to drink, not indeed bull's blood, but unmixed wine: He transforms the means for dying into a means for living; by drinking wine he might become inspired and thus discover a way out. The sober

Nikias can not believe that drunkenness is conducive to sound deliberation. It is much more difficult for Demosthenes to convince Nikias of the virtues of wine-drinking than to persuade him to steal some wine for him while the Paphlagonian is asleep through drink. Having had his fill of excellent wine, Demosthenes has his inspiration; the plan that occurs to him is not his but the spirit's; the wine inspires him to consult the oracles with which Kleon holds Demos enthralled. At his command Nikias steals these oracles from the sleeping Kleon; improving on Demosthenes' command he brings him that holy oracle which Kleon guards with the greatest care. Demosthenes reads the oracle while continuing to drink. He soon discovers that the oracle points the way to Kleon's destruction. Acting on the advice conveyed by the oracle, Demosthenes will destroy Kleon's power.

It appears then that the action of the *Knights* could not have been initiated without the co-operation of Demosthenes and Nikias. To say the least, without the suggestive presence of Nikias' piety (his belief in oracles), Demosthenes would not have been inspired with the thought of exploiting the belief in oracles for the liberation of Athens. This is not to deny that the agreement (such as it is) between Demosthenes and Nikias regarding the use of the oracle could not have been achieved except through Demosthenes' becoming drunk: The sober Demosthenes could not have reached an agreement with the sober Nikias.[10] Demosthenes' decision to drink wine and thus to bring his thought or life to its highest pitch in its turn takes the place of Nikias' proposal that they destroy their lives; this proposal in its turn takes the place of Nikias' earlier proposal that they turn to the gods—a proposal that Demosthenes had rejected because he doubted the existence of the gods. It is the same Nikias who believes that the gods exist on the ground that they hate him and who proposes suicide as a way out of an apparently hopeless situation; since the gods hate him, he can not, like Dikaiopolis, love his life, his soul (*Acharnians* 357). The connection between these two proposals of Nikias throws light, if insufficient light, on the darkest occurrence in the *Clouds*. We recall that Socrates puts a sudden and unexplained stop to his instruction of Strepsiades when this pupil had just proposed to commit suicide in order to get out of an apparently hopeless situation; it appeared that Strepsiades could not have made that proposal unless he had forgotten a lesson given to him by Socrates during the indoor instruction (see above, pp. 26–27). Could suicide be the consequence of the belief in gods as beings necessarily inimical to man? For regardless of whether gods are the work of man's fear or of his love of beauty—of his longing for never-aging and never-perishing thinking beings of indescribable splendor—they impair man's self-esteem. Certain it is that while Nikias proposes, prior to Demosthenes' address to the audience, first that they desert and then that they turn to the gods, after that address he proposes first that they desert and then that they commit suicide: He replaces turning to the gods by suicide, or he treats turning to the gods and suicide as interchangeable. But let us return to Kleon's oracle.

If we can trust Demosthenes—for we do not hear the full text of the oracle—the oracle speaks of four men who rule Athens in succession. All four men are sellers of something. The order seems to be one of descent or degradation. The leather seller Kleon is the third. He will be driven out and replaced by a sausage seller. The sausage seller will be the last seller to rule Athens: Can we hope that with the expulsion of Kleon and the short-lived rule of the sausage seller, the nonsellers, i.e., the gentlemen, will again rule Athens, i.e., that the golden age that preceded the age of the sellers' rule will return? Be this as it may, like punitive Zeus, Kleon is the third in a series of rulers, and like Zeus he lives in fear of his possible successor (Aeschylus *Prometheus* 957–59). Or, as even the austere Thucydides seems to hint, Kleon is the comical equivalent of Perikles. The pious and inactive Nikias draws at once this despondent conclusion: Where can we find that sausage seller whom the oracle meant? Demosthenes replies: We must seek him. This unbelieving man does not know that the oracle makes it unnecessary for them to do any seeking: A sausage seller just passes by as if by divine ordination. What is still more marvelous, the sausage seller who suddenly appears at exactly the right moment will prove to be the very sausage seller who succeeds in ousting Kleon. The two generals call him to them so that he can hear of the bliss in store for him. Since someone has to go into the house in order to watch Kleon, whose premature appearance might spoil the fulfillment of the oracle, and since Nikias is in the habit of doing such errands for Demosthenes, he asks Demosthenes to inform the sausage seller of the oracle of the god. Demosthenes performs this task with the proper solemnity. The poor fellow is sensible enough to believe that he is being ridiculed when Demosthenes greets him as the one about to become, as the oracle in Demosthenes' hand pronounces, the absolute ruler of Athens, of the Athenian empire, and of the Greater Athenian empire of the imminent future. He sensibly wonders how he, a sausage seller, can become, let alone a ruler of the world, merely a man of standing, an *hombre*. Demosthenes replies that precisely because he is a low-class fellow he will rise to the greatest height in Athens. The sausage seller modestly declares himself to be unworthy of great power.

Demosthenes is dumbfounded by this sign of decency: "You do not mean to say that you stem from gentle folk?" "By the gods, I stem from low-class people." Demosthenes is reassured: If the sausage seller were ever so slightly decent, he would be unable to tackle Kleon. The sausage seller, who obviously has no inkling with how little breeding present-day Athens is governed, points out to Demosthenes the very defective character of his education: He knows nothing of the things of the Muses. He lacks the education belonging to either the Just Speech or the Unjust Speech of the *Clouds*. Demosthenes assures him that the less he knows the better: Leading the *demos*, far from any longer requiring a music education and an honorable character, requires ignorance and rascality. The sausage seller can now no longer avoid listening to the oracle. From both Demosthenes' introductory statement and the text of the oracle that he now quotes in part, it becomes clear that the oracle is not as simple and perspicuous as Demosthenes has led us to believe; for instance, one needs Demosthenes' considerable ingenuity in order to see that the blood-drinking serpent of which the oracle speaks signifies a sausage. Above all, the oracle as quoted says nothing about the fact that the rascality of the sausage seller is required for the overcoming of the rascal Kleon. When the sausage seller can not deny that the oracle as interpreted by Demosthenes flatters him, he expresses doubt of his ability to take care of the *demos*. Demosthenes silences him by showing that, quite apart from the oracle, the art and the vulgarity that the demagogue needs do not differ from the art and the vulgarity that the sausage seller already possesses fully. The sausage seller is now willing at least to take up the fight against Kleon, but he needs allies in that fight. These allies, Demosthenes assures him, will be the knights and the better people in general, to say nothing of Demosthenes himself and the god. Since the sausage seller is obviously afraid of the coming fight, Demosthenes gives him the further assurance that Kleon will not look as terrifying as usual: From fear of Kleon no craftsman has dared to make a mask resembling him closely, but since the spectators are clever, they will recognize Kleon. (Demosthenes proves again that he is the spokesman for the poet.) At this moment—at exactly the right moment—Nikias announces the approach of the formidable Paphlagonian.

Before turning to the action proper, let us consider the plan that originated in Demosthenes, not without Nikias' assistance. Kleon exercises quasi-tyrannical rule in Athens. He owes that power not to any merit but to his shameless demagoguery and brutality. He is feared by everyone, but he is hated above all by the better people. They are by themselves unable to deprive him of his power. They need a demagogue still lower and meaner than Kleon who can out-Kleon him (cf. 328–32). It is in the light of this need felt by the knights and their comrades that Demosthenes interprets Kleon's oracle and uses it against Kleon. The better people do not run any risk in adopting this policy: The lowliest of the lowly or— this is the same in the view of the better people—the lowest of the low will always remain dependent on the better people; he is a safe instrument in their able hands.[11] This conceit may be described in the language of Spinoza as an eternal verity. We have observed in our time how the Prussian knights attempted to get rid of the demagogues of the Weimar Republic—of the rule of "the November criminals"—by using Hitler; the cleverest among them viewed Hitler as Demosthenes views the sausage seller. Yet their attempt was not inspired by an oracle. Or, more precisely, in the *Knights* the initiative is entirely with the better people: Demosthenes has to emancipate the sausage seller from his modesty by appealing to his modesty; the sausage seller is told by his betters and the god that he ought to act impudently, in a low-class manner, for his own good as well as for the good of the city; he does not follow his own impulses as Kleon does. In his humble way the sausage seller is just. But so is Demosthenes, as appears especially if one compares his action with that of Dikaiopolis. It is true that the oracle predicts (and thus sanctions) his action, i.e., his use of the oracle, as little as Amphitheos' divine mission in the *Acharnians* includes any reference to Dikaiopolis' action, i.e., his financing of Amphitheos' journey to Sparta; but Dikaiopolis uses his journey and its result for his private benefit alone. Demosthenes' action is juster than Dikaiopolis' action also for this reason: Amphitheos' speedy journey to Sparta and back, as well as the ensuing strictly private peace of Dikaiopolis, is much more incredible than the availability of writings that claim to be oracles and the ensuing expulsion of one demagogue by another.

Kleon appears. He smells that a conspiracy is afoot, a conspiracy against the *demos;* for in his view any conspiracy against his power is by this very fact a conspiracy against the *demos.* However despicable he may be, one can not deny that he possesses some political judgment; the dissatisfaction of his enemies with the rule of sellers is dissatisfaction with the rule of people belonging to the *demos.* The sausage seller recoils from Kleon, who is at his most terrifying. Demosthenes is compelled to ask the knights to come to the rescue of the sausage seller. These youngish men who form the chorus of the play arrive at once, eager to fight Kleon and to destroy him. Kleon in his turn calls on the old men who form the chief law court, reminding them of the monetary benefits that he has bestowed on them by fair means or foul, yet no one comes to his help. Those on whom he calls are probably in the theater, enjoying the *Knights;* Demosthenes, we recall, had made sure of the good will of the audience. In the view of the knights, Kleon is justly deserted by everyone because of his injustice. In his despair Kleon tries to win over the very knights, his bitterest enemies, by claiming that he is being attacked because of the benefits that he was about to confer on them; they merely laugh at this shameless and pitiable last-minute attempt to appease them. He would be lost if the contest of blows were not replaced by a contest in shouting. This is done at the suggestion of the sausage seller, who thus reveals again that he is not deprived of all generous feelings, or that in his view the control over Demos will not go to the victor in a brawl in which Demos himself does not participate. As could be expected, Kleon accepts the proposal with pleasure; he immediately begins the new contest by accusing his opponent—of whom he knows nothing except that he is a low-class fellow—of betraying the city to the enemies with which she is at war. The sausage seller, with the support of Demosthenes, counters by charging Kleon with the embezzlement of public funds. In the ensuing exchange of threats, as well as of both accusations and boasts of thefts, perjuries and other illegal actions, Kleon has a slight edge over the sausage seller—which confirms the chorus' view of him, but also rekindles their fear of him and thus increases their anger at him. Their angry outburst at him is, to say the least, not inferior to anything that the vile sausage seller has achieved hitherto. But when the sausage seller turns to reviling Kleon for the dishonesty that he practiced in his leather trade, Kleon cannot repay him in the same coin because he knows nothing of the sausage seller or his trade. Here is the first clear victory for the sausage seller. The knights become convinced to their great satisfaction that the sausage seller surpasses Kleon in shamelessness and crookedness and hence will oust him. They show us to what extremes political hatred can drive men. Rejecting with angry contempt the very basis of their own claim to public respectability, they urge the sausage seller to show, by defeating Kleon in the contest for the crown of impudence, vulgarity, and crookedness, that breeding and moderation are meaningless things. They themselves do not show a trace of moderation. (When the sausage seller misses a chance for a vicious retort, they make up for it.) They do not for a moment pause to consider that precisely if their estimate of the sausage seller is sound, his rule will be worse for Athens and for them than Kleon's. Their recklessness is not justified by the oracle. Perhaps it is justified by their trust in Demosthenes' dexterity.

Surer of the knights' approval than he was before, the sausage seller now has the initiative. He refuses to permit Kleon to have the first word. His eagerness to speak is not sufficiently explained by the upper-class support on which he can count; he must have some faith in his ability to speak. Kleon, who is proud of his oratory, which is inspired by his drinking unmixed wine, traces his opponent's self-confidence to some success that he has had as a low-class accuser against a helpless man by dint of the utmost exertion and continence. The sausage seller is indeed certain of his power as a speaker without the support of wine. He boasts that he needs only a hearty meal including soup in order to be superior to Kleon in outshouting the orators and in terrifying Nikias. Kleon and Demosthenes, in contradistinction to the sausage seller and Nikias (cf. 87–88), enjoy the drinking of unmixed wine; but while the sausage seller agrees with Nikias regarding temperance, he differs from him in his daring or manliness. His boast makes his upper-class allies wonder whether he, the low-class offspring of low-class people, deserves their trust since he is likely to think of nothing but his own interest (358–60). But this doubt lasts only for a moment. They give their whole attention to the contest of foul insults between Kleon and the sausage seller, which sways to and fro and in which the sausage seller now has an edge over Kleon. They surely have never heard a greater display of shamelessness. They encourage the sausage seller to give Kleon, who in their view is at bottom a coward, the knockout blow. But Kleon does not give up; he is sure of the support of the Council or of the *demos*. The chorus sees in Kleon's pertinacity merely another sign of that shamelessness of which Kleon himself is not ashamed to boast.

The sausage seller now tries to prove his superiority in shamelessness by boasting of his upbringing among the dregs of the populace. While a boy he was already an accomplished thief and perjurer. An orator who observed his cleverness prophesied that he would become a ruler of the *demos*. This prediction, based as it was on the observation of our sausage seller's nature, as well as on knowledge of Athenian politics, could seem to be a much better guarantee of his successor than the oracle which, apart from all other ambiguities, did not point to this sausage seller in particular. Another difference between the two predictions may be even more important. Our sausage seller has heard of the oracle only now through Demosthenes, whereas he knew the orator's prediction from his childhood. Yet that prediction did not have the slightest effect on him; it did not stir this clever and unscrupulous scoundrel out of his easygoing and low-class life; it did not make him ambitious. He bore without murmuring and apparently even enjoyed his way of life. The reason is obvious: He did not believe in that prediction (cf. 426, 212); he was too modest to believe in it. Or, as we might also say, he is a petty rogue and vulgar fellow; knowing this, he knows his place; he knows that he justly belongs in the gutter in which he lives, and hence he defers to his betters. Nor is he the one who is filled with ferocious hatred of Kleon; he attacks Kleon out of respect for his betters. The obscurity in which he lives explains why Kleon, who of course knows the oracle concerning the sausage seller, does not feel at all threatened by our sausage seller. Kleon is unable to compete with him in vileness of upbringing; the shift from Kleon's rule to that of the sausage seller would manifestly bring about Athens' utmost degradation. Yet he can do no more than threaten that he will shake land and sea, like Poseidon (431; cf. 409), and thus defeat the sausage seller. To what straits he is reduced he shows by accusing the poor fellow of having robbed the city of an enormous amount of money, without specifying the amount involved and the place or other circumstances of the crime (435–36; cf. 280–81). The sausage seller's obscurity or namelessness proves to be an asset. He replies by accusing Kleon of a crime of the same kind, while specifying the amount involved and the place of the crime. It was a stab in the dark; but by a piece of good luck he has caught Kleon, who immediately relents, offering the sausage seller a cut if he will keep quiet. The knights have no doubt that that son of the gutter will gladly take the bribe, but to our great amazement he does not respond: He is exclusively concerned with gratifying his betters by winning the contest in insults, or rather in accusations; in his unbelievably vulgar way he is as superior to money as Perikles (cf. 472–74). The contest ends in a draw. But having rivaled Kleon in calumniating, he can be thought to have achieved a glorious victory. This is surely the opinion of the chorus, who had described the sausage seller earlier with enthusiasm as a greater knave than Kleon (328–29) but who praise him now, full of joy beyond words, as most excellent in flesh and soul and as the savior of the city and of themselves, the cream of the city. No wonder that immediately thereafter the sausage seller breaks all records by accusing Kleon of having entered into secret negotiations with the Spartans about the prisoners of Pylos with a view to his own advantage. Kleon's countercharge that his enemies are engaged not in one conspiracy but in many, one of them with the Persian king and with the Boiotians, is a very poor second compared with the sausage seller's master stroke. Yet Kleon will bring his charge before the Council, to which he proceeds in the greatest rage and at the greatest speed. The sausage seller is urged by his betters to follow him there. He does this after having left behind with them the tools of his trade, but of course not his mean attire. They remind him of the feats that he has achieved in his boyhood as a thief and perjurer in his customary haunts: They expect him to act before the Council according to their mind.

We are not permitted to witness the proceedings before the Council, since they take place during the parabasis; for the action of the play must go on during the parabasis since it can not be completed until shortly before the end of the play. The parabasis of the *Knights* is remarkably irenic. Neither the poet nor the knights who form the chorus rebuke the city of Athens, nor do either of them boast of their merits or make demands on the city: Being engaged in a life and death struggle with the monstrous Kleon, they need all the good will they can get. In the parabasis proper the knights speak on behalf of the poet; this is in obvious agreement with Demosthenes' having acted as the poet's spokesman from the beginning of the play. As goes without saying, the knights' alliance with the poet differs profoundly from their alliance with the sausage seller; while the poet's power of foul invective is not inferior to that of the sausage seller, the sausage seller does not hate Kleon. The knights explain why Aristophanes, in contradistinction to the ancient comic poets, is the first who easily succeeded in inducing the knights to address the theater on his behalf; he hates the same men as they do, especially Kleon, and he dares to say the just things. The novel comedy of Aristophanes defends the ancient polity, the polity antedating the rule of the four sellers. The knights explain then —and this they do at the request of the poet—to that part of the audience that is interested in this kind of thing, why he so long deferred coming forward with comedies in his own name. According to the poet, presenting comedies is the most difficult work of all, and, besides, the Athenians are by nature singularly change-loving; he held back with his work known to be his lest he too soon become too old in the eyes of the public. To justify Aristophanes' conduct, the chorus speaks of three other comic poets who did not act as wisely as he did and, by implication, of his superiority to them as a comic poet. Two of these comic poets show clearly by their fate how bad it is for a comic poet to become an old comic poet. The author of the *Knights*, in contradistinction not only to those two comic poets but also to his incarnation as Dikaiopolis, is still young: The young author of a novel kind of comedy wishes to remain young as long as possible, for he wishes to show a way toward the restoration of the ancient, which is a rejuvenation. The knights too are young (731).

Speaking for themselves the knights praise their fathers who, everywhere victorious, adorned the city and—unlike the men now pre-eminent in Athens—did not demand extraordinary honors as a reward for doing their duty. The knights nobly abstain from speaking of their own merits; they fight for the city and the gods of the land without any thought of rewards. They ask only that when peace comes they not be envied for their knightly looks. They do praise their horses, as it were their gods, and in particular the youngest ones, with special regard to the horses' recent feat near Corinth; it is not the knights' fault that, as a follower of Kleon himself stated, the Corinthian enemy ascribed the feat of the horses not to the horses but to the knights themselves. In the first strophe that forms part of the parabasis, the young horsemen—for all we know some of them may have been companions of our Pheidippides—pray to Poseidon, the son of Kronos, as the god who is at present (because of the recent victories of the navy and of the cavalry) dearer to the Athenians than any other god. They beseech him to come to their chorus. In the second strophe they pray to Athena, the protectress of their most holy land, which surpasses all others in war, poets, and power. They beseech her to come to them, together with their helper Nike, so that they may defeat both the comic poet's rivals and Kleon. The difference between Poseidon and Athena reminds us of the difference between the knights and the poet.

In the *Clouds* there was a powerful reason why we should not hear of the action that took place during the parabasis, i.e., Socrates' indoor instruction. In the *Knights* the sausage seller, who returns victorious from the Council meeting, gives a precise report of the important event that took place during the parabasis. He gives his report to the knights, who had been fearing for him—like maidens who fear for the beloved man who goes out to do battle for them with the enemy—and who now are not only relieved to see him back safe but are nobly overjoyed with his victory. Their noble welcome contrasts with his artless and crude report, but also with their own earlier utterances. Two reasons account for this change in the conduct of the knights. In the first place they had just acted as the spokesmen for the poet, and the cause of the poet is not simply identical with the cause of the knights. Above all, the prospect of Kleon's imminent defeat makes his well-bred enemies gentler; the knights are certainly much less savage in the second half of the play than they were in the first. As the sausage seller reports, Kleon had succeeded in arousing the Council to the highest pitch of anger against the conspiracies of the knights: He had not even alluded to the utterly insignificant sausage seller. The sausage seller realized that his early education in shamelessness would not suffice for performing the task that his betters had assigned him; he called on all divinities of shamelessness for help. He knew better than to attempt to refute Kleon's charges. He did not even pretend, as Kleon still pretended, that the members of the Council are concerned with the well-being of the city, or at least with the preservation of the established regime. He appealed to each Council member's private advantage. He shouted to the Council the good news that sprats, which since the beginning of the war had been in short supply, had just become available at an unheard-of low price: No one yet knows of this most fortunate event, except the members of the Council; they must keep it secret until they have made their buy, and they must act fast; first come first served. They immediately forget all the public dangers. Kleon could not dare to question the truth of the sausage seller's announcement, let alone remind the Council of the public danger, without becoming utterly unpopular. He moves that on account of the happy event one hundred oxen be sacrificed to Athena. The Council approves the motion. The sausage seller has no choice except to out-Kleon Kleon by moving that two hundred oxen be sacrificed to Athena and in addition one thousand goats be vowed to Artemis. In his utmost perplexity Kleon now performs an about-face never surpassed by any earlier or later politician. Acting on the maxim that it is better to abandon one's policy than one's power, he suddenly turns from violently opposing all peace negotiations with Sparta to urging such negotiations: Let us make peace with Sparta now, and you will have still cheaper sprats tomorrow and ever after. But the members of the Council are much more interested in inexpensive sprats today than in peace and still cheaper sprats tomorrow. The Council meeting ends in a hurry. The sausage seller rushes to the market in order to buy for practically nothing all available seasonings for the sprats and to give the seasonings away to the Council members, who are, of course, immensely grateful to the man who not only brought them the good news about the cheap sprats but in addition gave them the seasonings gratis.

The knights barely have time to praise their ally, who in their view has shown again that he surpasses the rascally Kleon in rascalities—they no longer call the sausage seller rascal—and to warn him that the fight with Kleon is not yet over: The sausage seller has won two skirmishes; the decisive battle is yet to come. Kleon himself reappears. As is his wont, he is filled with rage and sputters the direst threats, but now he swears with unusual frequency. His rage is now directed solely against the sausage seller; he does not say a word against the knights. It has taken him a long time to see that he is threatened, not by the knights or Demosthenes, but by the sausage seller. The sausage seller unintendingly reveals his superiority—one is tempted to say his natural superiority—to Kleon by the manner in which he responds to his opponent's threats. He is indeed as good as Kleon, or better, at threatening; but while Kleon is genuinely savage and full of hate (as were the knights), the sausage seller only plays the savage; he does not lose his ease and good nature while shouting the most terrible things. The exchange of threats leads inevitably to Kleon's threatening to drag his enemy before the *demos*, who will punish him for what he has done to Kleon. But even Kleon's ultimate and most powerful threat does not frighten the sausage seller, who is sure that he can defeat Kleon in the sovereign Assembly as he has defeated him in the street brawl as well as before the Council. Kleon boasts that he has the *demos* in his pocket. To this boast the sausage seller does not at first reply in kind; at first he merely replies: "How strongly you believe that the *demos* belongs to you." He lacks Kleon's *hybris* with respect to the *demos*, because he simply belongs to the *demos* or is simply a child of the *demos;* whereas Kleon despises the *demos*, the sausage seller has a filial respect for it (cf. 725). He who is deferential to Demosthenes and the knights is still more deferential to the *demos*. For the same reason he despises Kleon, who boasts of the cleverness with which he controls the *demos;* he replies to this boast by saying that his behind is as good as the whole of Kleon in cajoling and fooling the *demos*, but he knows that the *demos* can not be fooled "all of the time" (cf. 1121–30). Still, if the sausage seller looks forward with great confidence to the contest to be decided by the *demos*, we can not but tremble. He has proved his superiority to Kleon in the use of foul language and of calumnies, as well as in appealing to the private interest of the members of the Council. But will he be superior to Kleon in taking care of the public interest, be it only the public interest as the *demos* understands it at any given time? After all he completely lacks political experience. Besides, will Kleon, the recognized leader of the *demos*, not be its spokesman? Both difficulties are overcome, not by the sausage seller, but by the poet, who has so arranged things that the *demos* has taken on the shape of Demos, the master of a household, an individual who as such does not need a spokesman, and whose private interest completely takes the place of the public interest. As a consequence of the personification of the *demos* Kleon is, just like Demosthenes, a slave of the *demos*, whereas the sausage seller is, or proves to be, a son of the house, and the knights simply do not "belong."

All of the action that could be observed by the audience had taken place in front of Demos' house. Demos is inside and knows nothing of the action of the play. He appears for the first time when the two opponents shout for him to come out. Kleon complains that he is being beaten by the sausage seller and the knights because he is in love with Demos. Demos does not pay any attention to the knights, but asks the sausage seller who he is. From the outset he is confronted with the choice not between Kleon and the knights but between Kleon and another plebeian. The sausage seller replies that he too is in love with Demos and wishes to do him well and that many gentlemen share his feeling, but that he and they are prevented by Kleon from benefiting Demos, and ultimately by Demos himself who, although an old man, behaves with the perverseness typical of beloved boys in preferring the basest lovers—sellers and craftsmen—to the respectable ones. He speaks as if he had become oblivious of his low-class origin and trade. His stricture on the low pursuits is not likely to have endeared him to Demos; still less could his rebuke of Demos' conduct toward his lovers do so. On the other hand, when Kleon called himself a lover of Demos, he meant that he was perfectly satisfied with Demos as he is or acts, or that he did not wish Demos to be changed a whit. Kleon goes beyond this. He explicitly defends Demos' amorous preference by saying that Kleon, and not the so-called respectable lovers, is the benefactor of Demos: It was Kleon who captured the Spartans at Pylos. The sausage seller asserts that Kleon's feat does not differ from an act of theft that the sausage seller committed on his way from his shop. This reply is good to the extent that it reveals to Demos the low origin of Kleon's enemy. Otherwise it is, to say the least, quite insufficient to discredit Kleon's claim in the eyes of Demos. Therefore, when Kleon asks Demos to hold an Assembly at once to decide the contest between his two lovers, and the sausage seller opposes Kleon's request by demanding that the decision not be made in the Pnyx, Demos decides in favor of Kleon's proposal. The sausage seller regards his cause as lost: Demos is amenable to reason only when he is in his house, i.e., when he acts with a private man's prudence in handling his own affairs. The knights do not share the sausage seller's despondency, but they do not deny that Kleon in the Assembly is the most formidable enemy. They warn the sausage seller of Kleon's Promethean resourcefulness; they no longer incite him to use the maximum of shamelessness and vulgarity. The contest in front of Demos is, if not of greater dignity, at least of greater gravity than the two preceding contests.

Kleon opens the decisive contest by praying to Athena that he be rewarded or punished in accordance with his merits or demerits in relation to the Athenian *demos*. The sausage seller does not pray, nor does he ask for any reward, but he expresses his willingness to undergo the most terrible and degrading human punishments if he does not love Demos and cherish him. Kleon begins to prove his love of Demos by telling the benefits that, as councilor, he bestowed on Demos in utter disregard of the well-being of any private citizen: Kleon can not for his life see Demos as a private citizen, as a human individual. Just the opposite is true of the sausage seller; for him, what Kleon calls private citizens are merely other human individuals like Demos himself; as he claims, it is the easiest thing in the world to rob other individuals for the benefit of Demos. He at once gives Demos a proof of his caring for him as a human being: He supplies him with a cushion so that he can sit comfortably on the hard stones of the Pnyx. Demos is greatly pleased with the sausage seller's act of kindness and wonders whether his benefactor is not a descendant of the tyrannicide Harmodios, whose memory is so dear to the *demos*, i.e., whether he is not of respectable descent: Courtesy to an old man is not the sign of a ruffian; he asks him who he is. Before the sausage seller can reply to his question, Kleon starts his counterattack by belittling the sausage seller's good deed, but he forgets to continue the enumeration of his own merits in relation to Demos. Unable to deny that the sausage seller was kind to Demos, he boasts that he himself is a good fighter for the *demos*. In the sausage seller's view, Kleon's contempt for small acts of kindness and his boasting of his fighting for the *demos* prove only his lack of compassion, which shows itself clearly in his preventing peace with Sparta and thus prolonging unnecessarily the misery in which Demos, who in peace lives comfortably in the country, lives in town. In other words, Kleon, like other politicians or "boasters," sees nothing but the *polis*, which is in a sense superhuman, and does not see the simple, unpretentious human beings who form the largest part of the *polis*. Kleon of course claims that he imposes this hardship on Demos for the sake of Demos' empire and pay; while Kleon provides Demos with the political goods (money and empire), the sausage seller provides him with what one may call the natural goods (783–85, 805–7, 868–74, 881–86). When the sausage seller asserts that Kleon's warlike and imperialist policy is a mere fraud that serves no other purpose but to keep Kleon in power, the demagogue replies that his merits surpass those of the very founder of the Athenian empire, Themistokles. Having provoked Kleon to go to such lengths, having replied in particular that Themistokles preserved the old things and added new ones, i.e., having alluded to Kleon's destruction of the old, the sausage seller has no difficulty in eliciting the first indication of Demos' dissatisfaction with Kleon. He uses this opportunity to tell Demos what he should think of Kleon. Kleon thereupon attempts to accuse the sausage seller of the theft of public funds; the sausage seller easily defeats this attempt by a reply in kind. The knights can not restrain their joy over the first victory of the sausage seller before Demos himself; they prophesy to the sausage seller that if he continues along the road that he has taken, he will become the greatest of the Greeks —the sole ruler of Athens and her empire, comparable to Poseidon (840; cf. 431), the knights' god, and very rich to boot. Joyful in their anticipation of Kleon's final defeat, they forget that the sausage seller was meant to be baser than Kleon and acceptable only as a tool to be used by the better people for getting rid of Kleon.

Kleon, addressing the knights and swearing by Poseidon, calls their joy premature: His power is secure as long as anything remains of the shields taken at Pylos. Those shields, as the sausage seller accuses Kleon to Demos, are to be used by the leather-selling youths who conspire against Demos; the conspirators are not, as Kleon does not tire of asserting, the gentlemanly youths. Demos, who has been trained well by Kleon in believing in conspiracies, immediately believes the sausage seller's story and turns more strongly against Kleon than ever before. Having defeated Kleon on his favorite ground, the sausage seller makes the next move on his own favorite ground by asking that leather seller whether he has ever given leather to Demos for his shoes. Kleon is reduced to silence. Demos replies to the question with an emphatic No, strengthened by an oath. Thereupon the sausage seller gives Demos the pair of shoes that he himself is wearing—shoes that he had to buy. Demos declares him now to be the man who to his knowledge has acquired the greatest merit about the *demos* and is more benevolent than anyone else to the city and to the toes: Demos agrees with the sausage seller that benefiting the city means in the last analysis benefiting the bodies of the citizens. Kleon is shocked by this low understanding of politics; he points to what he has done to raise the moral level of the city by suppressing catamites. The sausage seller replies that Kleon took this action merely from envy: The catamites are potential orators.[12] Aristophanes' Kleon is as much as Thucydides' Kleon (III 38) an enemy of speeches. Whereas the sausage seller only lacks both the ancient and the modern education, Kleon is opposed to both kinds of education. But to return with the sausage seller to the main issue, he now accuses Kleon of never having supplied Demos with the clothing befitting an old man in winter (we are in the midst of winter) and straightway gives Demos his own coat. Thereupon Demos declares that the sausage seller does not indeed surpass Themistokles, but equals him in wisdom and inventiveness. When Kleon bitterly complains about the monkey tricks with which the sausage seller harasses him, his opponent replies that he uses the very tricks by which Kleon himself acquired his power and preserved it; he only goes to the end of the road and thus beats Kleon at his own game (cf. 50–4). Kleon has no choice but to give Demos his own overcoat. Demos however is repelled by the stench of hide that the leather seller's overcoat exudes. The sausage seller reminds Demos—in this case the true *demos*, i.e., the audience—of still graver impairments of public health for which Kleon was responsible. Demos entirely agrees with the sausage seller. When Kleon calls the sausage seller a scoundrel for disconcerting him with buffooneries, his opponent replies that he does what he does because the goddess has commanded him to defeat Kleon by false pretenses or boasts: The modest sausage seller plays the boaster from modesty, from deference to his betters and, ultimately, to the gods. Kleon does not notice that the sausage seller refers to the oracle. But having seen by now that all his past benefactions to Demos are of no avail, he promises Demos future benefits; he even promises to make him a young man by pulling out his gray hairs. The sausage seller who, among other things, knows better than Kleon what genuine rejuvenation means, counters Kleon's promises of future benefits by present gifts (904–10). Kleon is now completely helpless; he threatens the poor sausage seller with monetary burdens and with fines that would ruin the wealthiest man. The sausage seller does not threaten Kleon with anything; he merely wishes him the worst. He is sure that everything will work out well by itself. We remember that he never did anything to bear out the prediction which he had received as a boy that he would rule the *demos* (425–26). His wish regarding Kleon is fulfilled, although not literally, at once. Demos, agreeing with the sausage seller's literal wish, praising him as a citizen of singular goodness to the many, deprives Kleon of his power. Kleon, probably remembering the oracle, warns Demos that his successor will be worse than he was; he does not even dream that the sausage seller could become his successor. Yet the discovery with the sausage seller's help of another fraud perpetrated by Kleon on Demos suffices to induce the master to appoint the sausage seller as his steward, i.e., to make the sausage seller the successor to Kleon; he deprives Kleon of the ring of office and gives it to the sausage seller.

Kleon, who knows that he will be deprived of his power by a certain sausage seller but does not know or remember that his present opponent is a sausage seller, is certain that Demos' decision is not the end of the story. Yet he is cowed; he senses more strongly than before his dependence on Demos: He addresses him now as master. After all, the ring is now on the sausage seller's finger. Having seen that neither his past benefits nor his promises of future benefits help him, he turns to the divine promises, to the oracles in his possession. The sausage seller would be unable to defeat him if he could not meet him on that ground too; he too claims to possess oracles. This does not do away with the fact that Kleon has now regained the initiative; the sausage seller follows in Kleon's footsteps more slavishly or literally than before; he uses the very expressions first used by Kleon (960–72; cf. 996–97). Above all, the sausage seller is unable to compete with Kleon's claim that according to his oracles Demos will rule not only —as according to Kleon's policy—all Greeks (797) but rather—along the lines of Demosthenes' promise to the sausage seller (169–74)—every land. While the two rivals leave in order to fetch their oracles, the knights welcome the day when Kleon will have perished, while admitting that Athens owes to him some ambiguous blessings—blessings that are in agreement with the education peculiar to him or his swinish taste in music. It would appear—and this would be entirely in the spirit of the oracle as interpreted by both Demosthenes and Kleon—that Kleon's education, however low, was still superior to the sausage seller's (cf. 986–87, 1235–36).

Kleon claims that the oracles in his possession stem from Bakis, while the sausage seller claims that the oracles in his possession stem from Bakis' older (and hence better) brother. It almost goes without saying that while Bakis speaks of Pylos, Bakis' older brother is silent about Pylos. It is perhaps more important to observe that the sausage seller, in contradistinction to Kleon, uses obscene language.[13] It is surely most important that both sets of oracles make a distinction between Athens and Demos; yet while Kleon assigns to Demos the central place among the themes of his oracle, the sausage seller does not. Since Kleon had asserted that his oracle promised Demos universal rule, Demos wishes to hear from both rivals the oracle that predicts that he will become an eagle in the clouds. Yet Kleon, who is much more concerned with his rule in Athens than with Demos' rule over the whole earth, quotes to him an Apollinic oracle that, according to his interpretation, urges Demos to preserve Kleon's rule.

Demos does not understand the oracle as quoted by Kleon, and the sausage seller asserts that that oracle in fact warns Demos against Kleon. He then quotes one of his own oracles which, according to his interpretation, is another warning addressed to Demos against Kleon, and which appeals at once to Demos. Kleon is not nimble enough to contest that interpretation. He therefore quotes another of his oracles which, while alluding to the navy, according to his interpretation recommends him to Demos; Demos again fails to understand the oracle, and the sausage seller again interprets the oracle as being directed against Kleon's rule. Neither of the two rivals has hitherto complied with Demos' wish that they recite to him the oracle that predicts a splendid future for him; this failure was primarily due to Kleon's preoccupation with his own fate. Now the sausage seller goes so far as to speak in oracular language of Demos' lack of good counsel. This induces Kleon to quote an oracle dealing with Pylos: Pylos proves that Demos, following Kleon's advice, was excellently counseled. But this oracle has the same fate as his two preceding oracles. The sausage seller then turns to an oracle about the navy (without the navy no Pylos), an oracle that Demos is very eager to hear, since he is worried about how his sailors will get their pay; but that oracle too proves to be above all a warning against Kleon and, more particularly, against his unjust policy toward Athens' allies. While forbidding injustice, the oracle does not show how the necessity leading to injustice can be overcome; the sausage seller promises to overcome it. This time Demos had difficulty in understanding the sausage seller's oracle, but Kleon was unable to use this opportunity for questioning the sausage seller's interpretation of the oracle. The sausage seller exploits Kleon's helplessness by quoting another oracle; this time Kleon does contest the sausage seller's interpretation. Yet this fact merely underlines the sausage seller's general superiority on Kleon's favorite ground: Although much less familiar than Kleon with the use of oracles, he has learned much faster and better than Kleon how to interpret them to Demos' satisfaction. He will soon prove to be not inferior to Kleon in inventing oracles. After Kleon's oracles supporting his rule have been thoroughly discredited, he turns to fulfilling Demos' wish to hear the oracle predicting him a splendid future: Demos will become an eagle and king of the whole earth. An oracle of the sausage seller adds to the rule over the whole earth rule over the Red Sea and a judgeship in Ekbatana. He as it were suggests that if Athens must expand she should expand toward the East, rather than toward the West (cf. 174). These oracles dealing with universal rule are not even pretended to be quoted but are obviously made up by the two antagonists as they go; these oracles possess even less authority than Kleon's oracles supporting his rule. Kleon finally tells of a dream in which Athena seemed to him to pour wealth and health over the *demos;* the sausage seller in his turn had a dream in which Athena seemed to him to pour ambrosia over Demos' head and a fluid of an opposite character over Kleon's. The sausage seller's dream brings Demos back to the issue before him: He gives himself over to the sausage seller—to a man without any education—as an educator, for his re-education. Demos does not long for universal empire any more. His dream of universal empire was sustained by oracles. For a long time Kleon had succeeded in controlling Demos by means of the oracles in his possession and by preventing Demos from hearing other oracles or other men's interpretations of his own oracles (cf. 58–61). This defect in Demos' education is cured in the oracles scene, which taught him that every oracle—whether of Bakis or of Apollon or of anybody else—can be matched by an oracle of the opposite purport and that the same oracle can easily be interpreted to predict opposite things. This is not to deny that Demos' rejection of Kleon is supported by the oracles as interpreted by the sausage seller, although not exclusively by them. Yet Demos' surrender to the sausage seller's guidance and surely his newly arisen desire for re-education have no oracular support whatever. We must also remember that regarding the only subject concerning which Demos spontaneously desired information during the oracles scene—how his sailors and soldiers will get their pay (1065–79)—the oracles were silent.

One does not appreciate the oracles scene properly if one does not remember that the whole action of the *Knights* was triggered by an oracle or a certain interpretation of an oracle. But that oracle or interpretation can not be properly appreciated before one knows the outcome of the action.

Kleon makes a last effort to ingratiate himself with Demos, who is cured of his dream of empire, by offering to take care of his daily needs. He has now thoroughly learned what the sausage seller knew from the very beginning, namely, to treat Demos as an individual, as a human being. Hence the two rivals now engage in a contest regarding the dishes that would be most pleasing to Demos. How important this issue is in the eyes of Demos can be seen from the fact that he tacitly revokes his decision in favor of the sausage seller by declaring that his decision will depend on which of the two rivals will feed him best. The third and last round of the popularity contest will be decided by Demos' belly alone; we have done for good with political

100 Socrates and Aristophanes

and sacred considerations. While the rivals prepare their offerings to Demos indoors, the knights, who had been completely silent during the oracles scene, address Demos for the first time. Thanks to the sausage seller they have become completely reconciled to Demos, and they are sure that the sausage seller will win the final round as he has won all previous rounds. They flatter Demos by praising him as the tyrant ruler over all men, while deploring that he is an easy prey to all flatterers. Demos replies that they are the fools if they regard him as a fool; he does not mind the appearance of being fooled by his stewards; he uses those thieves for his well-considered purposes and gives them at last what they deserve. All the while he is greatly annoyed because he has to wait so long for the culinary delights for which Kleon and the sausage seller had whetted his appetite. This annoyance is compensated by the pleasure that he derives from observing the rivalry between his two lovers, who by now have come back, in gratifying him. While they compete in making him comfortable, Kleon reminds him of what he has done for him at Pylos and the sausage seller of what Athena has done and is doing for him. Kleon has no choice but to follow his rival in praising the goddess. The uneducated but moderate sausage seller as it were educates Kleon, who is somewhat less uneducated but full of *hybris*, in piety. Or, if Kleon might have had some head start in displaying piety (cf. 763, 1091–92), the sausage seller now has overtaken him. But the contest will not be decided on the ground of piety, for the climax is reached when the sausage seller cheats Kleon of the merit of having prepared a most delicious dish for Demos' enjoyment in as exact an imitation as possible of the manner in which Kleon cheated Demosthenes of the merit of having reduced the Spartans at Pylos. When Demos, full of admiration for the sausage seller's feat, asks him how he had thought of it, he piously traces the feat to Athena, although the trick that he uses against Kleon merely repeats a trick that as a boy he had used on the market (cf. 1193–98 with 417–20). He thus shows his superiority not only to Kleon, who before now had always claimed for himself the whole merit of the victory at Pylos, but also to Demosthenes, who had traced the conceit of consulting Kleon's oracles for the purpose of destroying him to the spirit of wine (1203, 108; cf. 903). Demos now acts exactly as he had done after Pylos: He gives the whole credit for his gratification not to the cook but to him who served him the dish. Kleon admits for the first time that he is in danger of being surpassed in impudence by his rival (1206; cf. 409). This sets the stage for the sausage seller's final move in the contest. He asks Demos to decide now which of the two rivals is the better man in regard to Demos and especially to his belly by comparing the contents of the baskets of the two. The sausage seller's basket proves to be empty and Kleon's to be full of good things. Not without the sausage seller's assistance, Demos thus realizes that while the sausage seller has given everything he had to his dear little daddy, Kleon, that slave in need of whipping, has cheated his master of the largest share. Kleon protests that he had stolen in the interest of the city, i.e., he denies the identity of the city and the *demos*. Demos can not permit this distinction. He commands Kleon to return the garland that Demos had given him formerly, so that he can crown the sausage seller with it.

Kleon knew quite well that this fate would overtake him sooner or later, for he knew his oracles. But one of his oracles makes him certain that the fateful moment has not yet come: His rival can not be the individual designated by the oracle as his conqueror and successor. This does not mean that in his view the oracle designates his successor by name, for he does not know his rival's name. His certainty that the sausage seller is not his successor is based on his certainty that the oracle designates as his successor a man of a certain kind and that his rival is not a man of that kind. Less oracularly, he knows that his successor will belong to a certain kind of sausage seller, but his rival seems to him to be of a type higher than any sausage seller (cf. 1235–44): He knows that his successor will be a greater rogue than he himself (949–50), but he has sensed as well as we did that his rival does not meet this condition (cf. 1252). The sausage seller on his part contends that the oracle designates him very clearly by name. This contention is not borne out by the text of the oracle, or by the only interpretation of the oracle of which we know (197–210). Kleon proceeds to cross-examine his rival in order to prove to him, and above all to Demos, that this individual does not meet the requirements laid down by the oracle. To his horror Kleon learns that his rival had no education whatever as a child except in vulgarity and impudence—the sausage seller now conceals the fact that he has some knowledge of letters (189)—and that when grown up he exercised the trade of a sausage seller and occasionally took the passive part in homosexual relations (1242; cf. schol. on 428). Only one very tenuous hope remains for Kleon. The oracle designates as his successor a man who sells sausages at the gates of the city and not in the market place. When Kleon learns that his rival sells his sausages at the gates he knows that his end has come, for he firmly believes in his oracle, i.e., in his interpretation of the oracle. As a matter of fact, the oracle does not say anything about the gates of the city as distinguished from the market. Kleon's interpretation is reasonable—given the fact that according to the oracle his successor will be less respectable than he himself—if we assume that a sausage seller plying his trade at the gates will be still less respectable than a man who sells his merchandise in the market place: The beardless sophisticates who exude the novel education spend their time in the market place (1373–81), and is not the novel education from a certain point of view better than no education at all? Yet, however sound Kleon may be as an interpreter of oracles, he is no match for the sausage seller as a user of oracles. He claimed that he is designated in the oracle by name. As he discloses after Kleon is ruined beyond hope of repair, his name is Agorakritos; his name points to the market, not to the gates of the city. That is to say, the oracle as interpreted by Kleon rules out our sausage seller, as Kleon has contended, or is in favor of Kleon's continuing in office for the time being. Kleon is a victim not simply of his belief in his oracles or in his interpretation of his oracles, but more immediately of the sausage seller's lie about his status: With an amazing cleverness he has divined Kleon's interpretation of the oracle and lied accordingly. The right kind of clever lies are better than oracles, however cleverly interpreted. The sausage seller's lie can not be detected as long as the detection might do him harm, because he is wholly unknown to everyone present; he derives the greatest advantage from his being a nobody. He did gamble. No wonder that he gives the prize of victory to Zeus.

The sausage seller's use of Kleon's oracle dispels the last doubt as to his now being eager to take Kleon's place. This seems to conflict with his modesty, not to say humility. This difficulty is underlined by a brief scene in which Demosthenes appears again after a long lapse of time. He has completely lost his feeling of being superior to the sausage seller. He approaches him with the request to remember that he has become a man of standing thanks to him and to give him a lucrative job. The sausage seller does not even reply. It would be wrong to say that Demosthenes is as much cheated by the sausage seller of his victory over Kleon as he was by Kleon of his victory over the Spartans, for, as we have seen, the victory over Kleon was entirely the work of the sausage seller alone. The impious Demosthenes is defeated by the sausage seller just as the impious Socrates is defeated by Strepsiades. More precisely, as will soon become clear, the impious Demosthenes is defeated by unforeseeable Chance, just as the impious Socrates is defeated by the unforeseen effect on Strepsiades of the conclusion regarding incest from the Socratic teaching about the gods. Far from being a tool of Demosthenes, the knights, or the better people generally, the sausage seller proves to be the loving son of Demos: He is now eager to rule because he has seen that he is better fitted to take care of his old father than any of the mercenary slaves (Kleon, Demosthenes, Nikias, and so on) on whom Demos had hitherto to depend. He acts as if, having been exposed as an infant, he has now recognized his father and been recognized by his father, who repents of his mistake.

While the sausage seller begins to take care of Demos indoors, we are entertained by the second parabasis. The second parabasis surely is not as irenic as the first; the reason why the knights were irenic in the first parabasis has been disposed of by Kleon's ruin. On the other hand, the second parabasis abstains even more than the first from pleading for, or praising, the knights or the poet; but this abstention is likely to have different reasons in the two cases. Nor is there a strong link between the subjects of the second parabasis and the action of the play. One might find a tenuous link between the last round of the contest for Demos' favor and the two strophes that lampoon men notorious for being famished or voracious. The antepirrhema describes a rebellion of the triremes against the imperialism in a western direction as advocated by the lamp seller Hyperbolos. Shall we say then that the second parabasis is more revealing by what it does not say than by what it says? Having understood the bearing of the brief and ominous reappearance of Demosthenes, we believe that we understand why the knights should now be almost completely silent about themselves—only at the beginning (1266) do they allude to horsemen—and simply silent about the action of the play. In the epirrhema they assert the propriety of blaming wicked people, yet the man whom they blame is blamed not because he is wicked—although he is wicked through and through—but for a different reason: Even the worst wickedness—a wickedness surpassing that of Kleon—is not as bad as the quality of Ariphrades, a corrupter of music and poetry who is unsayably obscene. (Aristophanes manages to say how obscene he is.) Did the knights change their minds as to what the worst thing is? Neither in the second parabasis nor afterward do they say anything about Kleon and hence against him.

During the second parabasis the sausage seller has transformed Demos completely. From old and ugly he has made him young and beautiful; [14] he has restored him to the state in which he was in the olden times, in the times preceding the rule not only of the sellers but even of Perikles, nay, of Themistokles; he has restored him to the state in which he was in pre-democratic Athens: After his restoration he looks like one of the Athenian nobles of the olden times; [15] he has restored him to the shape that he had at Marathon, when he defended his sacred land against the barbarian invaders and had not yet begun to dream of empire. The knights hail him indeed as king of the Greeks, but the sausage seller, who knows better, refrains from doing so. Athens had been decaying more and more; she had been aging more and more; the better citizens were longing with ever-increasing despair and fury for the good old times, for the restoration of the ancestral polity, i.e., for the rejuvenation of Athens. The rejuvenation of Athens requires that the *demos* be rejuvenated, i.e., brought back to its ancient deference to the better people. But is this possible? [16] If the decay of Athens is due not to mere mistakes but to the aging of the *demos*, the *demos* must be literally rejuvenated. The *demos* rejuvenates itself literally by the passing away of its older members and by the coming in of new members, like a river. This is obviously not the longed-for rejuvenation. The literal rejuvenation is possible only if the *demos* is personified: A being like Demos can be rejuvenated literally, as is proven by the feat of Medea; a human being (as distinguished from a being that is a conflation of human beings) can be rejuvenated by magic, or rather by a god-like action like the one now performed by the sausage seller. Demos' rejuvenation is prepared by the fact that even in his old age he behaved like a boy who is wooed by lovers (737); he behaved as if he were still young and beautiful. Demos never grew up; he always remained in need of tutelage. This much is clear: The longing for the good old times can not be satisfied by political action. The nonpolitical action for which it calls must proceed from the invention of marvelous conceits (1322), i.e., from altogether novel conceits. In this way the Aristophanean comedy becomes completely reconciled with the city. Such a reconciliation is necessary because what is politically healthy is the old or ancestral, whereas the boast of comedy, and especially of Aristophanean comedy, is the novelty of its conceits; [17] in other words, the bringing back of Marathonian Athens, which the sausage seller has apparently achieved, renders impossible not only Socrates and all his works but the Aristophanean comedy as well. Yet now we see that there is a secret bond between the young Aristophanes' novel comedy, which aspires to the restoration of the ancient regime, and the young sausage seller's rejuvenating action, an action that requires more than the beating of one's father; it requires that he be cooked.

Demos reappears, having become young and beautiful and overflowing with gratitude to his rejuvenator. The two men have a dialogue that lasts until the end of the play. The chorus, which in all other plays has the last word or almost the last word, is silent in the last seventy-four lines of the *Knights:* The knights have become as irrelevant as Demosthenes; the city is entirely in the hands of Demos and his rejuvenator, who is now as much Demos' father as he was his child.[18] Demos, who always was in tutelage, will remain in tutelage. The sausage seller tells the grateful Demos that if he knew the extent of the change that he has undergone thanks to the rejuvenation, he would regard him as a god. Since thereupon he lets him know the extent of that change, we are entitled to expect that Demos will regard the sausage seller as a god and treat him accordingly: The sausage seller will become the absolute ruler of Demos. He lets Demos know the extent of the change that he has undergone by reminding him of the grave mistakes he used to commit and by inducing him to state the outlines of his future conduct. It appears that there is no question whatever of scuttling the navy, although there is complete silence about the empire or panhellenic rule. Demos also declares, agreeing therein entirely with the Just Speech, that from now on unbearded youths will not be permitted to spend their time in the market, sophisticating and politicking: Demos will compel them to go hunting. As a reward for his good intentions the sausage seller supplies Demos with a healthy boy for his use, thus confirming Demos' restoration to his ancient state. He next supplies him with a young woman, the Thirty Years' Truce, for his enjoyment, asking him to take her and to go to the fields: With the return of peace the individual called Demos can return to the country life for which he had longed. To this extent the fate of Demos reminds us of the fate of Dikaiopolis. Yet the sausage seller may mean more than this. The rejuvenation of the *demos* means transforming the corrupt, predominantly urban *demos*, which is in a constant state of political excitement, into the predominantly rural *demos* of the olden times, when the tillers of the soil minded each his own business, leaving the government in the hands of their betters.[19] If we remember how the sausage seller treated Demosthenes when this distinguished man made his last appearance, we will be inclined to go even further and view the sausage seller's action in the light of the first action that Plato's perfect ruler performs after he has acquired power: Plato's perfect ruler too begins his rule by sending the *demos* "into the fields." We shall surely recognize in the sausage seller a super-Peisistratos.[20] The last of the hero's three final actions consists in meting out proper punishment to Kleon. As we ought to have expected, it is not harsh. Kleon is condemned to sell sausages at the gates of the city—sausages containing a mixture not only of the flesh of dogs and donkeys but of other parts of dogs and donkeys as well—while exchanging insults with the strumpets who ply their trade there.

At first glance it seems that the happy ending of the play is the fulfillment of an oracle, just as the happy ending of the *Acharnians* may seem to be ultimately due to the action of the divine Amphitheos. Closer inspection shows that the end of the play, which is indeed the final outcome of Demosthenes' view of Kleon's oracle, is at variance with the spirit of that oracle, i.e., with that oracle as interpreted by both Demosthenes and Kleon.[21] The oracle led us to expect that Kleon would be defeated and succeeded by a man still more despicable than he. More generally stated, the oracle seemed to predict an ever-increasing decay of Athens. We are in no position to say whether the oracle in fact had this misanthropic character, since we hear only a small part of it literally quoted, and that part does not bear out the misanthropic interpretation. But perhaps one can say that the agreement between men so different from one another as Demosthenes and Kleon regarding its interpretation puts that interpretation beyond any doubt. Apart from this, the misanthropic interpretation of the oracle, which in a way governs the whole action of the play, is in agreement with the only teaching regarding the gods that is adumbrated within the play, namely, Nikias' proof of the existence of the gods. This is not to deny that there are also philanthropic oracles, but the oracles quoted in the *Knights* just do not happen to predict Demos' glorious future. Yet whatever the god or the oracle may have intended, the sanguine, active, and unbelieving Demosthenes transforms the doom into a policy. He does this in the first place by giving the oracle a rational interpretation: Since Kleon has enthralled the *demos* through his shamelessness, he can be defeated only by someone surpassing him in shamelessness. Besides, he foresees the effect of the apparent fulfillment of the oracle on Demos and Kleon, who believe in oracles. Not the oracle but a human promise is fulfilled. But even Demosthenes' hope falls far short of the outcome. This is owing to the fact, in no way foreseen by either the oracle or Demosthenes, that the particular sausage seller who happened to pass by when Demosthenes was looking for a sausage seller proved to be quite an extraordinary man.

That sausage seller proves to be not only not worse than Kleon but better than all earlier statesmen: He proves to be a godlike man. While this ending is at variance with the oracle and Demosthenes' plan, it is however not altogether unexpected. As the action proceeds, the character of the sausage seller reveals itself as altogether different from what we had been led to believe: The lowest of the low proves to be the born ruler, the natural ruler in the most exacting sense of the term. At the beginning he seems to be a fellow whom a decent man would not touch with a ten-foot pole and would use only in a desperate situation; eventually the un-savory means becomes a resplendent end, a man who is justified in look-ing down even on Demosthenes. As the action proceeds, it becomes clear that while he utterly lacks breeding or while his manners surpass those of Kleon in shamelessness and vulgarity, he possesses the virtues of both Demosthenes and Nikias while he is free from the vices of either. If it is permitted to illustrate what seems to be a purely comic situation by a tragic situation, the sausage seller is superior to Demosthenes and Nikias in the same way in which Shakespeare's Julius Caesar is superior to Brutus and Cassius. More than this: As a man who truly deserves to rule, he is not eager to rule; he is less than any one else in the play a busybody and, at any rate, in this respect altogether just. He does possess the unenviable qualities through which Kleon surpasses the gentlemen Demosthenes and Nikias, but he uses these qualities for an altogether decent purpose, first deferring to the judgment of his betters and then guided by his own understanding (cf. *Lysistrate* 1109). In other words, the lowest possible breeding is more than adequate for coming to power in a democracy. The sausage seller is more capable than anyone else of gratifying Demos' whims, but he gratifies them only in order to make him receptive to what is by nature good for him. He is enabled to surpass Demosthenes, Nikias, and Kleon because he alone, this peculiar child of the lowest *demos*, "by nature loves the *demos*" (cf. *Clouds* 1187); he has compassion with the *demos*. However indecently he may have behaved in his boyhood and after he has grown up, prior to the play or within the play, he has never acted improperly or contemptuously toward the *demos*. The natural ruler of the city and hence in particular of the *demos* must above everything else be a lover or friend of the *demos*, and such love is most likely to come from a child of the *demos*. The sausage seller abolishes the extreme democ-racy out of love for the *demos* from which he stems: Everything for the *demos* and by the authority of the *demos*, but nothing through the *demos*. We are thus led to think that the best regime consists of the *demos* and its best child, who acts as its father, in other words, that the best regime is not in need of an upper class, a class of gentlemen. Aristophanes' ex-periment is diametrically opposed to Aristotle's experiment in the two last books of the *Politics*, where we find a best regime without any *demos*, consisting only of gentlemen; but it foreshadows to some extent Plato's city of pigs.

If the sausage seller is a most desirable ruler, we must revise our notion according to which education and gentlemanship are prerequisites for decent rulership. The sausage seller, to repeat, lacks both the ancient education praised by the Just Speech and the novel education praised by the Unjust Speech. Yet he possesses all the virtues required for ruling well. This means that his virtue is altogether by nature.[22] He has the root of the matter in himself. From this it follows that education and gentlemanship are not as important, not to say all important, as is generally thought, especially by the gentlemen.[23] For Demosthenes it goes without saying that a man of lowly status, origin, and upbringing can not but be a low character: Decency comes from decent upbringing, upper class or perhaps rural; it can not arise in the dregs of the urban populace. Demosthenes is a very clever man, but he is refuted by the action of the play; he is shown not to have given sufficient thought to the character and conditions of virtue and vice. It is no longer necessary to speak of his political blindness: How can he have any trust in the sausage seller's gratitude to him and his like if the sausage seller is as thoroughly rotten as Demosthenes believes him to be? Yet the mere fact that he himself is a slave (of the *demos*) should be sufficient to enlighten him. At the beginning the sausage seller regards himself as a petty rogue and most vulgar fellow and believes that he therefore justly lives in the gutter; that is to say, from the point of view of the gentlemen he possesses self-knowledge, just as the gentlemen possess self-knowledge. But as we see in retrospect, both the sausage seller and the gentlemen lack self-knowledge; at the end of the play the sausage seller has acquired self-knowledge; whether Demosthenes has acquired it, one can not say. The only evidence that the better people possess of the sausage seller's crookedness is what he himself told them of his boyish pranks (cf. 483–84).

The *Knights* can be said to be Aristophanes' most political play; it is the only play without gods, poets, and women (and children). We are therefore not surprised that it should reveal the natural ruler of the city. By showing that that ruler is a man without any education, it reveals the relation between the city and education, or the gulf separating the city from the sphere of the Muses. That gulf, like some others, can be bridged. Yet the bridge proves that there is a gulf. Let us compare the action of the *Knights* with that of the *Acharnians*, in which the poet himself, thinly disguised, is the hero. Dikaiopolis succeeds in swaying the *demos* (*Acharnians* 626), but the *demos* there is in fact only a part of the *demos:* the old Acharnians. Dikaiopolis shows by his whole conduct that he does not love the *demos*. The pleasures that he enjoys and conjures are indeed, in contradistinction to Socrates' pleasures, communicable to many, not to say to all, but he is not primarily concerned with communicating them.[24]

In other words, Dikaiopolis' action is of questionable justice, while the sausage seller's is not. In accordance with this, not the sausage seller, but Demosthenes and the Knights are from the beginning the poet's spokesmen in the *Knights*. With a view to all this we are compelled to retract our sanguine suggestion that in the *Knights* the Aristophanean comedy becomes completely reconciled with the city: In the good city, the city rejuvenated by the natural ruler, not only Socrates but Aristophanes as well would be impossible.

The Aristophanean comedies are sometimes compared to fairy tales. By a fairy tale one probably means the story of the fulfillment of a perfectly just wish—a fulfillment that is impossible but presented as having taken place and that is exhilarating but not ridiculous. The *Knights* comes closer than any other Aristophanean comedy to being a fairy tale in this sense. The sausage seller, to say nothing of the other actors and the chorus, does and says as many laughable things as any other Aristophanean hero, but all or almost all of those things are deliberate parodies of Kleon's deeds and speeches. He acts ridiculously on purpose. He himself is not ridiculous. This becomes clear particularly at the end of the play. However ridiculous a sausage seller in rags, using foul language and playing monkey tricks, may be, once he has revealed himself fully as the natural ruler, the rags and everything going with them have fallen off, and he is clothed in greater splendor than Demos having become young and beautiful. There "the right of nature shines forth" (cf. *Gorgias* 484ᵃ 6-ᵇ1), burying with disgrace everything concealing and denying it. Nothing is more revealing than his dismissing Demosthenes without a word. Viewed in the light of the ending, the natural ruler's having been a sausage seller seems to be like the disguise of a fairy-tale prince. Yet, like a true fairy-tale prince, the natural ruler of the *Knights* was a true sausage seller who did not know that he is something better, who did not claim to be something better and did not wish to be something better. In a word, he is in no sense a boaster. From the point of view of very crude people—and Aristophanes is, to say the least, never oblivious of their point of view—every man who claims to be distinguished or to excel is a man who "wishes to be something special" or is a boaster and hence ridiculous. From that point of view Socrates and Aristophanes are, of course, boasters. The sausage seller's neither claiming nor wishing to be "something special" is an important part of his charm. Perhaps we are also bidden to think that the true ruler is less open to ridicule within the compass of comedy—of a kind of work primarily addressed to crowds—than poets and philosophers.

One must also consider the fact that the plan that triggers the action of the *Knights*—Demosthenes' conceit to use Kleon's oracles for his destruction—is much more reasonable and hence much less ridiculous than Strepsiades' plan to get rid of his debts with the help of Socratic rhetoric and Dikaiopolis' plan to live in peace by financing Amphitheos' journey to Sparta and back. But the happy ending of the *Knights* is not in accordance with Demosthenes' plan. Strepsiades' turning to Socrates and Dikaiopolis' availing himself of Amphitheos are perfectly rational compared with the coincidence that a sausage seller, and this particular sausage seller, turns up just at the moment when Demosthenes has read Kleon's oracles. The natural ruler comes to power through a more than improbable act of Chance: Only such an act of Chance can bring the natural ruler to power, precisely because the natural ruler must be a child of the lowest *demos*, hence must live in the utmost obscurity, and must be perfectly free from ambition or can become a ruler only by being compelled to become it. It is above all for this reason that the sausage seller is the comic equivalent of Julius Caesar. This is to say nothing of the fact that the happy ending of the *Knights* requires the rejuvenation of Demos and therefore the personification of the *demos*. The action of the *Knights* partakes no less than that of the other plays of the ridiculous character of the impossible. Nothing remains then than to leave matters at the reasonable wish that the city be ruled by the well-bred or the gentlemen.[25]

The personification of the *demos* differs from the personification of the clouds and the two Speeches because what the clouds and the two Speeches stand for are parts of man, while Demos is a conflation of many human beings into one human being; while the Clouds and the two Speeches can talk, Demos not only talks but also eats and sleeps. The two Speeches are between the Clouds and Demos, since only the Clouds are goddesses; Demos, whom all men fear like a tyrant, who is so eager to be served and flattered, who fattens his servants in order to devour them (1111–20, 1131–40), is even less of a god than the two Speeches. Yet Kleon, who pretends to be Zeuslike, depends absolutely on Demos. Through the personification of the *demos* the city becomes a household. The reduction of the city to the household has two different reasons. The first is indicated by the word "fraternity": All fellow citizens ought to be like brothers. Besides, Demos' return to the country is a return from the sphere of boasting to that of the enjoyment (and procuring) of the natural goods, to the "economic" life (805–9), comparable to Dikaiopolis' action. The sausage seller's action parodies, and is prepared by, Kleon's action, which consisted in making political activity ever more an economic activity: The *demos* lived on the pay that it received for attending the Assembly and the law courts. But just as Dikaiopolis' private peace is not public peace, i.e., peace pure and simple, the sausage seller does not return to the country; the economic life is not possible without political life; the *demos* is not identical with the city (273–74, 811–12, 1005–10). The fundamental political predicament is disposed of in the *Knights* by the absorption of the individuals into the individual called Demos, as well as by the absence of women (and children). Aristophanes will experiment with the diametrically opposed solution in the *Assembly of Women.*

3 The Wasps

This play begins, just as the *Knights*, with a dialogue between two slaves. Yet whereas in the *Knights* the slaves are in fact generals, in the *Wasps* the slaves are literally slaves. Accordingly, the dialogue opening the *Knights* leads up to the design that animates the action of the play, whereas the dialogue opening the *Wasps* is a consequence of the design already in the process of execution—a design the conception of which was entirely the work of the slaves' master, Bdelykleon ("the loather of Kleon"), the son of Philokleon. What is at stake in the *Knights* is the fate of the two slaves, or rather of a newly bought slave (Kleon); whereas what is at stake in the *Wasps* is the fate of the master, or rather of the master's father. It is characteristic of the plan of Bdelykleon, as distinguished from the plans of Dikaiopolis and Strepsiades, that it can not be executed without the help of slaves.

It is still dark. The two slaves—Sosias and Xanthias—are on guard duty. Xanthias has fallen asleep and is awakened by Sosias, who also has slept for a while. They are sleepy because they have drunk wine. It seems that Xanthias is more sleepy than Sosias, perhaps because he has drunk more than Sosias. They tell each other the dreams that they had just had. The work that they have to perform resembles that of hoplites (359–64). Accordingly their dreams are like the dreams of citizens; they dream each in his way of the affairs of the city; each in his way dreams of himself as of a citizen (41, 44, 51). While in the *Knights* the slaves are in truth political men, in the *Wasps* the slaves are political men in their dreams. Xanthias had dreamed of a powerful eagle sweeping down on the market place, seizing a shield, and carrying it aloft into heaven, and then that Kleonymos, a notorious coward, had thrown it away. According to Sosias this means that Kleonymos has thrown away his shield not only on earth and on sea but in heaven as well (cf. *Peace* 1186). Xanthias, accepting Sosias'

112

interpretation, regards his dream as a bad omen which Sosias denies, swearing by the gods. Yet Xanthias, who has, as it seems, a higher notion of bravery than his companion, is not satisfied; to throw away one's weapons (of defense or of offense) is a grave matter. The discussion of Xanthias' dream (15–27) forms the center of the opening scene (1–53). Sosias' dream concerns the whole ship of state; its subjects are a pernicious measure intended by Kleon, one of Kleon's lackeys, and Alkibiades' lisp; his dream is more political than Xanthias'; Sosias too is worried by his dream. Yet, according to Xanthias' interpretation, which Sosias accepts, the dream proves to be a good omen, thanks to Alkibiades' intervention in the dream, for thus the dream bodes ill for Kleon and his adherents. The fact that one of the two dreams recounted at the beginning of the play, the less political dream, proves to be a dubious omen, while the more political dream proves to be a good omen, forebodes the outcome of the play which, while politically most satisfactory, will not be altogether satisfactory.

The preceding observations must suffice for explaining why Xanthias, rather than Sosias, addresses the audience in order to inform it about the situation as it exists at the beginning of the play. This "prologue" is distinguished from the corresponding parts of the *Knights*, in which Demosthenes addresses the audience (35–70), by the fact that it does not form a part of the action but deals in the first place, if briefly, with the play as play.[26] He asks the audience not to expect something very grand surpassing its capacity (like the *Clouds*), or on the other hand a crude comedy such as another abuse of Euripides, to say nothing of Kleon (like the *Acharnians* or the *Knights*). We may then expect to hear a play the ending of which is neither as happy as that of the *Acharnians* and the *Knights* nor as unhappy as that of the *Clouds*. Yet the mere names of the chief characters of the *Wasps* warn us against taking too seriously the poet's promise that the play will avoid the crudely comic. Correspondingly we are warned not to take too seriously the promise that the *Wasps* will not surpass the capacity of the audience, i.e., of its vast majority, those who laugh without being or becoming wise. The *Wasps*, as well as any other Aristophanean comedy, is a combination of crude comedy and something surpassing the capacity of the audience, of something very low and something very high. Xanthias outlines a happy medium to which Aristophanes does not even aspire. What he tells us about the subject of the play can be summarized as follows. The slaves' master has commanded them to watch all exits from the house lest his father, whom he has locked up indoors, leave the house. The reason is that Philokleon suffers from an uncanny disease which no one in the audience is likely to guess. Two men seem to guess that Philokleon suffers from love of dice or from love of drinking respectively; both are wrong; in particular he can not suffer from love of drinking, since this is a disease of decent men. A third man suggests that Philokleon suffers from love of sacrificing or from love of hospitality. Xanthias does not deny that Philokleon suffers from love of sacrificing, but denies that he suffers from love of hospitality. After the audience has failed completely (or almost completely) to guess Philokleon's disease, Xanthias discloses to it that he suffers from the love of sitting in judgment as a heliast; in fact he is quite obsessed with that love. He appears in court as early as Dikaiopolis in the Assembly, although for a very different reason, for he is an ill-tempered man; in this regard he resembles old Demos, but he differs from him because he is eager to inflict the greatest possible punishment (cf. *Knights* 67–70). The son strongly disapproves of his father's misanthropic disease. He has tried everything to cure him of it, including purifying him by Corybantic rites, but without any success. Nothing remains for the son to do but to prevent the father by force from leaving the house. This is difficult enough and altogether impossible without the help of the slaves. Xanthias concludes his address by stating to the audience the names of the father and the son; he calls the son's manner haughty and pompous.

Bdelykleon, who had been asleep on the roof of the house, awakens and warns the somewhat negligent slaves that his father is trying to escape through the chimney. He himself is compelled to push his father back by force. Philokleon next tries to open the door; Bdelykleon's prompt action deprives him of this hope too. The old man is shocked that through his forced absence from the court a defendant will escape punishment, for once when consulting the oracle at Delphi the god had told him that if any defendant escaped Philokleon, Philokleon would wither away. For him his vote as a juryman is a sword to kill with; he is a hanging judge. Xanthias is amazed by this misanthropic oracle of the evil-averting Apollon. Philokleon threatens to gnaw through the net that his besiegers have spread out in order to prevent his escape; he desists when he is reminded in a somewhat exaggerated way of the condition of his teeth (164; cf. 155 and 368–71). After all his efforts to escape by force have failed, he has recourse to guile; he tries to escape from the house in a manner resembling that in which Odysseus escaped from Polyphemos' den; he behaves like the comic equivalent of Odysseus. But he achieves nothing apart from his claiming, not entirely without success, to be another Odysseus (the hero who punished Polyphemos and the suitors) and imposing on his son the role of the cannibal Polyphemos—a son who behaves toward his father as Polyphemos intended to behave toward Odysseus, i.e., a son who is worse than a father-beater. He is forced back into the house, which is again firmly locked. Reduced to complete helplessness, he calls on his fellow jurymen and on Kleon to come to his help. But he makes still one more attempt to escape, which indeed also fails, yet, since it reveals the inexhaustible character of the old man's drive, brings it about that it is now his son who is reduced to despair. There is no respite for the besiegers, for at any moment now Philokleon's fellow jurymen—who are in the habit of calling him out when they march to the court, and who can be depended on to try to raise the siege—can arrive, and then the battle will begin in earnest; for apart from their superiority in number, each of them is armed with a sting in his back like a wasp, and when they are angered they act like wasps. This implies that while Philokleon is angry with or without provocation, his allies are angry only when provoked. There is then some hope that Bdelykleon may appease them.

Philokleon has made all told three attempts, all of which have failed, to escape by transforming himself or pretending to transform himself into another being: into smoke (144), into Odysseus (184–85; cf. 193–94), and into a sparrow (207). His allies will soon be seen to have transformed themselves with greater success into wasps.

The chorus of wasps, of old men who both in manner and looks resemble wasps, makes its entry. Wistfully remembering their youthful exploits or pranks, they try to march briskly, while very much sensing their age. Since it is still dark, they proceed with the help of lamps carried by the male children of some of them. They have been urged by Kleon, their protector, to be in court on time in order to condemn the wealthy Laches. They themselves are poor, and now, because of the war, living costs are high; all the greater is their need for the jurymen's pay, which barely provides one day's subsistence for a small family: How can they live on the days on which the courts are not in session? Whatever we may have to think of Kleon, his followers of this kind can not but arouse our compassion. Although the insufficient lighting as well as the gnawing hunger give rise to a heated exchange between one of the wasps and his son, father and son are at peace with each other. The ordinary old juryman and his son, in contradistinction to Philokleon and his son, need each other; the child would starve without his father's earning the juryman's pay, and the father would not be able to earn that pay without the help of the child carrying the lamp. When they arrive before Philokleon's house, they are surprised to see that contrary to his custom Philokleon is not yet waiting for them there; for he is always eager to sit in judgment, being the fiercest among them and the one who never has compassion. They suspect that Philokleon may be ill, since yesterday a defendant was acquitted. In the song with which they try to call him out—for he is a lover of singing,[27] although, as we recall, not a lover of drinking—they encourage him not to take that disappointment too much to heart, for today there is another opportunity to ruin another rich defendant.

Philokleon explains to the wasps that he is prevented from joining them by his son and his slaves, who are taking only a short nap, although he is as eager as always to inflict some evil. He prays Zeus to bring himself to have pity on his sufferings, either by managing his escape or by destroying him: Life without inflicting evil is not worth living. Apparently he has lost all hope of escaping by human means, even with the help of the wasps. To their question why his son prevents his attending the courts he replies that Bdelykleon does not permit him to do anything evil, but is willing to feast him sumptuously—something for which Philokleon has no liking; he enjoys not the pleasures of the body but hurting his fellow men. The wasps are wholly unable to understand this state of things: an old juryman and his son who both are not interested in the juryman's pay; they are obviously not in need of the pay; they are rich. Yet, while the father is enthusiastically in favor of the (democratic) courts, the son opposes them; hence, the wasps, having been well trained by Kleon, infer that Bdelykleon is a conspirator against the *demos*. They see that Philokleon is in need of a novel conceit in order to leave the house without his besiegers becoming aware of it; but Philokleon, who believes his inventive power to be exhausted, asks them to become inventive. Yet they are still less able than Philokleon to imitate the resourceful Odysseus. Nor is their reminding him of his warlike exploits of any help, for he is no longer young and nimble, to say nothing of the fact that now the conspirator Bdelykleon has like a tyrant liberated the slaves, armed them, and uses them against his old father.[28] Still, something must be done at once, for it is almost morning. The wasps here call Philokleon "little bee"; they know somehow that he is not a wasp. In his desperate situation Philokleon decides to attempt again the desperate measure—desperate because of the desperate condition of his teeth—of gnawing through the net that his besiegers have spread to prevent his escape, although he has some pious scruples since "net" (*diktyon*) reminds him of Diktynna (Artemis). This time he succeeds. But now he fears that his son will discover his progress before he has finished. The wasps assure him that they will take care of Bdelykleon so that he will learn not to profane the Eleusinian mysteries or to trample on the goddesses' decrees. Philokleon and the wasps are pious, while Bdelykleon is impious. At the suggestion of the wasps Philokleon tries to let himself down through a window on a rope. They promise that if the slaves posted below attempt to prevent his escape, they will call up their spiritedness and overcome the slaves; he has nothing to fear; he must boldly let himself down after having prayed to his family gods.[29] He prays to the hero Lykos—who, like him, is always pleased by the tears and lamentations of defendants, but who alone of all heroes, and surely in contradistinction to Zeus (392–93; cf. 327–28), deigns to sit at the side of the condemned—to have pity on him and help him. The pitiless Philokleon, as distinguished from any pitiless gods, is in need of help and hence in need of pity.

Philokleon's stealthy descent is discovered in the nick of time by Bdelykleon. He awakens Xanthias and commands him to beat Philokleon in order to make him ascend again. The wasps, whose sharp anger has been aroused, come forward to Philokleon's help, preparing to use their sharp stings. Yet apparently sensing their decrepitude, they send their children to fetch Kleon by telling him what is at stake; they are confronted by an enemy of their city who preaches the novel doctrine that one should not try lawsuits. Philokleon himself had already called for Kleon's help (197). But Kleon will not come to the help of the jurymen, just as the jurymen did not come to the help of Kleon in the *Knights* (255–57). However the jurymen's action in the *Knights* may have to be explained, Kleon's action in the *Wasps* can be traced to the demagogue's knowing that Bdelykleon, as distinguished from Demosthenes and the knights, is not dangerous to him, or that Philokleon, whose name is misleading, not to say a red herring, is not truly his ally. The spokesman for the poet had told us at the beginning that the *Wasps* is not devoted to the lampooning of Kleon. The *Knights* presents the political issue (Kleon's scandalous rule) in the guise of private life: The political men are presented as slaves of the householder Demos. In the *Wasps* the issue is private from the beginning: Bdelykleon is concerned with nothing but the disease peculiar to his father, a nonpolitical disease, a passion traced by Philokleon himself to the Delphic oracle. This passion, which distinguishes him from all other jurymen, makes him a halfhearted supporter of Kleon, whose accusations, calumnies, and suspicions feed his own desire to inflict harm. The issue between Bdelykleon and

Philokleon becomes political through the wasps, who march to the court at Kleon's request (242), and who are the ones who accuse Bdelykleon of antidemocratic machinations (342–45). It is for this reason that Bdelykleon is faced with a political issue despite the nonpolitical character of his primary concern.

Bdelykleon faces the wasps, bringing with him his father, who has been recaptured and is gripped firmly by Xanthias and Sosias. He urges the wasps to listen to him quietly, which they absolutely refuse to do. He tells them that he will not let his father go under any circumstances. He knows that the wasps possess dangerous stings—Xanthias only comes to know it now (420, 427; cf. 211–29)—with which they can ruin him as they have ruined Philippos, the "son" of Gorgias (cf. *Birds* 1701). They demand for the last time that he let his father go; otherwise they will attack. Philokleon urges them to attack Bdelykleon and his helpers at once and at every suitable part of their bodies. Bdelykleon, undisturbed by all these threats, calls out the rest of his slaves—their number is another proof of his not being poor—to make sure that his father will not be snatched away by the wasps and goes back to the house to make other preparations for the impending fight. His composure seems to be justified, or at least to be effective; his father again invokes the help of a hero, and the wasps complain about the misery of old age as shown by Philokleon's being held prisoner by his own slaves whom he has benefited so much. The harsh Philokleon, however, reminds the slaves of the floggings he had given them in former times. Both the wasps, who describe themselves as irascible and just, and Philokleon threaten the slaves, but the wasps do not use their stings: Philokleon does not possess a sting. The fight is started by Bdelykleon, who returns from the house armed with a stick that he gives to one of his slaves and a smoking torch that he gives to another, commanding them to drive the wasps away from the house. Their easy success against the wasps confirms Xanthias in his preconceived view, not shared by Bdelykleon, that the wasps are not dangerous. The defeated wasps accuse Bdelykleon of attempting to subvert the laws and to make himself a tyrant. He again proposes conversation and reconciliation, which they indignantly reject. Bdelykleon, who overestimates the wasps' ability or willingness to fight, begins to wonder whether it would not be better for him simply to disinterest himself in his father. But he has gone too far for that, for, as the wasps warn him, he is now known to be a conspirator against the *demos*. He vainly tries to convince them of the absurdity of the ubiquitous hunt for subversives, especially in the case of a man like

himself, who has no other concern but to free his father from his infatuation with acting as a juryman and to make him lead a decent life of genuine enjoyments. The deadlock is broken thanks to Philokleon, who has
not said a word since his son's return from the house and who now replies
to him that he prefers the meagerest trial to the richest dishes. This difference between father and son, rather than Kleon's policy and his control
of the courts, is the chief issue of the play. Bdelykleon keeps to it by replying to his father that his strange preference is due only to ingrained habit
and that, if he would only listen to what he has to say, he would show
him that he does wrong by acting as a juryman—that he is the slave of men
who hold him in contempt. Philokleon denies that he is the slave of anyone: "I rule over all." He is now no longer concerned with escaping in
order to act as a juryman that day, but with upholding his dignity by
proving that by acting as a juryman he rules over all; he is not primarily
concerned with the prevention of subversion or the safety of the democracy. He proposes that the wasps decide the issue that divides father and
son. Bdelykleon agrees and commands his slaves to let his father free.
Philokleon is so sure of the strength of his case and of the wasps being on
his side that he declares that, if he is defeated in the argument, he will
commit suicide. Although to be alive without judging and condemning is
for him not worthwhile, his infatuation with judging and condemning
does not go so far that he would continue indulging his habit or passion
if it were proven to be foolish. Yet Bdelykleon is not so sure of his father's
willingness to commit suicide (Philokleon does not, like Nikias, regard
himself as hated by the gods) or of his reasonableness. He asks him therefore which penalty he is prepared to undergo if he does not abide by the
decision of the wasps. (In framing this question he has some difficulty in
remembering a legal term.) It is safe to say that in that case Philokleon
will be prevented by force from ever again attending the courts and that
the wasps will cease to take any interest in him. In the words of Philokleon, in that case he will never again receive his juryman's pay.

Father and son are now about to engage in a debate as to whether the
jurymen are the rulers of all or the slaves of the demagogues. The wasps
remind their fellow juryman of what is at stake in the debate: The old
citizens will be laughed at everywhere, their whole dignity will be lost, if
Bdelykleon wins; in order to defend the cause of the old men, Philokleon
must say something new. While the chorus exhorts the father, the son
prepares to make written notes of what the old man is going to say; not
only his memory of legal terms but his memory simply does not seem to

be very good. In this respect at any rate he reminds us of Strepsiades, while his father-beating reminds us of Pheidippides. He surely puts the family above the city as much as do Strepsiades and Dikaiopolis.

Philokleon sets out to prove that the juryman's rule is not inferior to any kingly rule, especially if one considers the fact that the juryman is old and poor. He speaks of the juryman in general, not of himself in particular; for instance, the typical juryman, as described by him, is poor and does not always condemn. In fact, as he will state at the end of his speech, the juryman's power is not inferior in any respect to that of Zeus. All men in fear of accusation—and who is not in fear of accusation in Athens?—flatter him in order to appease his anger. There is no humiliation to which the defendants, however rich and powerful, will not submit in order to be acquitted. By hook or by crook they avoid the appearance of being in any respect superior to the juryman; they try to divert him by telling him fabulous or amusing stories or by making jokes; they try to soften him by making their children's tears appeal to his compassion; they supplicate him like a god. And like a god he enjoys the self-abasement, especially of the high and mighty, their begging for mercy, which is induced by his formerly having shown them mercy, and their despair when after promising mercy he does not keep the promise. The juryman's congenital or habitual wrath is appeased by his being flattered, by his being induced to laugh, and by his being moved to pity. The *Acharnians* led us to believe that comedy is insufficient for counteracting the anger and indignation of men like the Acharnians and the wasps, and that what Aristophanes can not achieve can be achieved only by Euripides. Now we must begin to wonder whether Aristophanes' moving the audience (which includes the jurymen) to laughter is not meant to continue and complete what Euripides' moving it to compassion began: to moderate their anger and indignation, which are indeed indispensable to the city.

Bdelykleon suggests to his father that he has not yet mentioned any solid benefit accruing to the jurymen from their alleged rule. Thereupon Philokleon mentions very briefly a mild sexual pleasure and then some Music pleasures that jurymen enjoy. This does not satisfy Bdelykleon. Philokleon mentions next, among other signs of their power, that Kleon and other outstanding men supply them with such comforts for their bodies as remind us of what Kleon and the sausage seller had been doing to Demos. Bdelykleon is now surer than ever that he will be victorious. Thereupon Philokleon reminds himself of an item that he had forgotten—obviously because of its strictly domestic and hence inconspicuous character—namely, the flatteries and kindnesses that the juryman receives at the hands of his daughter and wife on account of the pay that he brings home from the court. Far from being dependent for his food and drink on his son or the son's steward, he is the admired center of the family. Here again Philokleon speaks above all of the typical juryman and not of himself [30]—so far as we know, he himself does not have a wife and a daughter. The same is true of his statement that Bdelykleon fears him to the highest degree whereas he does not fear Bdelykleon at all: Bdelykleon fears the jurymen in general, but he does not fear Philokleon at all. Still, on the present occasion Philokleon describes the jurymen by a feature distinguishing him from all or most of his fellow jurymen: Most jurymen do not have well-to-do sons. Yet, since this addition only enhances the jurymen's sense of their grandeur, Philokleon's speech as a whole makes the wasps believe that they of all men live on the Isles of the Blessed and gratifies them more than any speech ever did. Philokleon enjoys his son's defeat and his apparent despair. In their way the wasps give Bdelykleon a chance to appease their anger without his having to undertake the hopelessly difficult task of refuting his father.

Bdelykleon is aware of the difficulty. He knows that it is difficult and requires a better mind than can be found among the comic poets to cure a disease that for a long time has been in the process of becoming engrained in the city. The alliance between his father and the wasps has forced him to try to cure not only his father's disease but that of the wasps as well. Since he believes that he can cure it, he makes clear by his initial statement that he is not a comic poet. He is so appalled by the difficulty of his task that even he, who hitherto has not given any sign of piety, seems to feel unable to cure the disease in question without the help of Zeus. When he calls on Zeus by saying "our father, the son of Kronos"—Zeus, the father of gods and men, who fettered his father, Kronos—his father stops him by telling him not to say father and warning Bdelykleon that he will kill him if he does not win his argument; thereupon Bdelykleon calls no longer on "our father" Zeus but on "little daddy" Philokleon. He asks him to figure out roughly the revenue of the city and the annual pay for the six thousand dikasts. On the basis of the computation by Bdelykleon, Philokleon figures out that the dikasts' pay is less than a tenth of the revenue. He is shocked by this result and wonders where the bulk of the revenue goes. Bdelykleon answers of course that it goes to the demagogues who, in addition, receive enormous bribes and gifts from the subject cities, while the jurymen receive no such bribes and gifts at all. Philokleon can not deny these things, but in his view the fact that the jurymen are short changed in these respects does not prove that they are the slaves of the demagogues. Bdelykleon proves this decisive point by contrasting the strenuous and penurious life of the jurymen with the easy life and the lucrative deals of the demagogues from whom the jurymen have to take orders. Philokleon, who was wholly unaware of those deals, begins seriously to doubt that he has a Zeuslike power. Bdelykleon rubs in the lesson by stating that, given the extent and wealth of the Athenian empire, every Athenian could live in luxury but for the demagogues who keep the people poor deliberately so that they will always obey the demagogues out of gratitude for the negligible sums that they dole out to the people. This argument, which reminds us of the argument by which Dikaiopolis defeats Lamachos and wins the approval of the Acharnians, succeeds: Philokleon is crushed. He drops the sword with which he promised to kill his son in case of the son's defeat, or himself in case of his own defeat (714; cf. 522–23 and 653–54). Bdelykleon goes on to say that even when the demagogues have come to fear the people, they do nothing but make big promises that they never keep. And he concludes that it was because of the jurymen's being fooled by the demagogues that he has locked up his father and that he is willing now, as he has always been, to grant him every wish except to act as a juryman. We note that Bdelykleon does not try to prevent other men from serving on juries who are anxious to do so not because they believe in the grandeur of that work but because they need the pay in order to survive, having no wealthy sons to support them or, in other words, that he is not concerned with abolishing or even reforming the established judicial system. He is a man who merely minds his own business.

The wasps are now in a position to pronounce judgment. They decide firmly in favor of Bdelykleon. They beseech Philokleon not to be stubborn or unreasonable but to accept the gift of that god whose presence is manifest now and here. They draw his attention to the difference between themselves and him who is blessed to have such a kind and sensible son. Bdelykleon thereupon enumerates the pleasures and comforts with which he will supply his father. Philokleon, however, remains silent and thus keeps his son worried as to whether he is not still in a state of despair. The wasps comfort him with the thought that his father may be silent because he considers his previous error and the required change of heart. They prove to be mistaken. As strongly as ever, Philokleon still prefers condemning to all pleasures and comforts. The only effect that Bdelykleon's speech had on him is that he is now willing to condemn Kleon for his embezzlements: By thus showing himself stronger than Kleon, he will at last acquire that Zeuslike power that he heretofore wrongly believed himself already to possess. Yet since he has lost the wasps' support, he can not have any hope of ever again condemning anyone. It is therefore not surprising that he accepts, after some hesitation, the compromise solution proposed by his son that he continue judging, not indeed in the public courts, but at home where there are enough servants in need of being judged. It is easy for Bdelykleon to show his father that "here" he will judge in much greater comfort than "there." The only difficulty remaining for Philokleon is that he does not know who will give him the juryman's pay when he judges at home. Bdelykleon disposes of this difficulty with two words. Philokleon is now perfectly reconciled to his fate. As appears now, what makes life worth living for him is not that his condemning is important, or that it makes him the equal of Zeus, but condemning as such. Bdelykleon's father-beating has been entirely successful. He has implicitly convinced the decrepit wasps of the justice of his act of father-beating, just as Dikaiopolis had convinced the decrepit Acharnians of the justice of his act of treason. This father-beating has received the full approval of the *demos*, since it manifestly appeared to proceed from the wise son's good will toward his foolish and nasty father in a matter of which the *demos* is competent to judge; it did not proceed from *physiologia* or manifest impiety. One may add that Bdelykleon had tried all ancestral or pious means of curing his father before he turned to using force against him (112–25).

Bdelykleon goes into the house to fetch the implements needed for the session of the court that must take place at once in order to compensate Philokleon for his long deprivation. After Bdelykleon had completed his speech, the wasps sensed the presence of a god. At that time Philokleon was still far from being reconciled to the necessity of ceasing to act as a juryman, for the god in Delphi had given him the oracle that he would wither away if any defendant escaped him (158–60, 733). Now, after it has been settled that he can continue to comply with the oracular command, Philokleon remembers that the replacement of the public court by courts at home was promised by another oracle and therewith becomes assured that he is not transgressing the will of the gods in acceding to his son's wish. When Bdelykleon returns with the implements, his father first misses only one item, the shrine of the hero Lykos, his favorite hero, but he is mistaken, for Bdelykleon had not forgotten it; he did forget another sacred thing, however, and Philokleon fetches it from the house. In the meantime it transpires that the dog Labes has stolen and gulped down a piece of Sicilian cheese and has thus become a proper subject of Philokleon's judicial activity. At the suggestion of one of the servants, another dog will act as the accuser of Labes. While the final preparations for the session of the court are under way, the excellent relationship between father and son remains unchanged, although the father becomes somewhat impatient because he is eager to condemn, and the father-beating son becomes somewhat impatient because of his father's extreme attachment to local custom, which shows itself in his apprehension that his son might have forgotten one or another of the customary implements.

Bdelykleon opens the session of the court with a novel act of divine worship. The wasps pray to the Pythian Apollon that Bdelykleon's undertaking may succeed to their benefit. Bdelykleon prays to Apollon Aguieus, the protector of the house, that he may melt his father's harsh, irascible temper and make him gentle and compassionate. The dog Kyon (from the same deme as Kleon) has charged the dog Labes (from the same deme as Laches) of having eaten the Sicilian cheese without sharing it with any other dog. Philokleon is as ill-disposed to the accuser as to the defendant, yet the utmost he can hope to achieve in the circumstances is to condemn the defendant. Kyon formally states the charge against Labes. It is easy to see an accuser as a barking dog or a barking dog as an accuser. Kyon's precise charge is to the effect that Labes has stolen the Sicilian cheese without giving him a share of it although he had asked for some. According to Philokleon, Labes' crime consists not in the act of theft but in not sharing the booty with the community, i.e., the jurymen. He ignores his son's request not to judge before hearing the defendant; he is as harsh and ill-tempered as ever. Since Labes is too frightened to speak in his defense— it is hard to see a barking dog as apologizing—Bdelykleon does it for him. He praises him as the best dog now living, a very apt ruler of many sheep, i.e., as better than the accuser and preferable to him as a commander; his services are great; he ought to be forgiven for the theft if he committed it, given his lack of Music education.[31] When Bdelykleon compares the hard life of Labes, far away from home, with the soft life of Kyon, who never leaves home, Philokleon has for the first time the unfamiliar feeling of pity for a defendant, a feeling that Bdelykleon tries to deepen by bringing in Labes' puppies, who supplicate and beguile the hanging judge. Philokleon does shed tears, but not from pity. Things look very bad for Labes. Yet, thanks to a deception practiced by Bdelykleon, his father casts his vote in favor of acquittal. When the old man realizes that he has acquitted a defendant, he faints; for, as he explains after coming to, he has a bad conscience because of having acquitted a man and fears that something untoward will be done to him by the gods; he asks them to forgive him for what he has done involuntarily and contrary to his manner. We recall the Delphic oracle. We recall also that he did not faint when it was settled that he should never again attend the sessions of the public courts. We recall finally that the deepest reason for his obsession with condemning was not his belief in the Zeuslike character of the condemner. We see now that that reason was his fear of the gods' wrath about compassion. It is this fear that made him immune to compassion and made him enjoy the infliction of evil. It is this fear that distinguishes him from the wasps, whose inspiration is purely political, not to say economic. Philokleon is not a wasp. With a view to the fact that waspishness is the opposite of gentleness, we may call Philokleon for the reason indicated a superwasp, while Bdelykleon is simply a nonwasp. The core of the action of the *Wasps* has nothing to do with the wasps but is the fight between the superwasp Philokleon and the nonwasp Bdelykleon. The question that we can not help raising after we have witnessed what seems to be Bdelykleon's complete victory over his father is whether Philokleon will ever get rid of his bad conscience or fear. Bdelykleon, who is likely to know of the oracle, tells him not to worry and reminds him of the pleasures that await him; he obviously does not understand or appreciate the old man's disturbance. Philokleon has no choice but to give in. What happens to his apprehension is concealed from us for the time being, since he follows his son into the house; it is concealed from us by the parabasis.

In the *Wasps* the parabasis occurs very late, much later proportionately than in the *Knights* and the *Clouds* and even later than in the *Acharnians*. In the *Knights* and the *Clouds* the parabasis is completed well before the end of the first half of the play. In the *Acharnians* the parabasis occurs within the second half, but it is completed long before the end of the second third. In the *Wasps*, however, the parabasis begins at about the end of the second third. The reason that the parabasis occurs so late in the *Acharnians* is that the action of that play is primarily a conflict between the chorus (the Acharnians) and the poet (the chief character), and therefore the chorus can not well speak for the poet before the Acharnians and Dikaiopolis have become completely reconciled; the parabasis follows immediately on that reconciliation, i.e., at the earliest possible time. There is no conflict between the chorus and the poet in the *Knights* and the *Clouds*. In the *Wasps* there is apparently also a conflict between the chorus and the poet, inasmuch as the wasps are on the side of Kleon and the poet is opposed to Kleon. In other words, Bdelykleon's refutation of Philokleon reminds us of Dikaiopolis' refutation of Lamachos; accordingly, one would expect that the parabasis should follow immediately on the reconciliation between the wasps and Bdelykleon. The mere fact that this expectation is disappointed shows that the reconciliation between Bdelykleon and the wasps does not have the importance of the reconciliation between Dikaiopolis and the Acharnians: Bdelykleon, that man of a haughty and pompous manner whose name is uglier than that of any other Aristophanean character, as distinguished from Dikaiopolis, is not a comic poet. The conflict between the wasps and the poet regarding policy or regarding Kleon is not a conflict between the wasps and the poet as such. As is indicated by the location of the parabasis in the *Acharnians* on the one hand and in the *Wasps* on the other, the homologue of the reconciliation between the Acharnians and Dikaiopolis, i.e., of the cure or conversion of the Acharnians, is not the reconciliation between the wasps and Bdelykleon but Philokleon's cure or conversion from his obsession with condemning. The wasps are much less important for the *Wasps* than the Acharnians are for the *Acharnians*. In the *Knights* and the *Clouds* the cure of Demos and of Strepsiades could not occur except close to the end of the play. In the *Acharnians* the part following the parabasis reveals the meaning of Dikaiopolis' private peace by showing what he did with that peace. In the *Wasps* the part following the parabasis, however, shows not what Bdelykleon does with the cure or conversion of his father (he has told us about this often enough) but what the cured or converted Philokleon does; the cure or conversion of Philokleon will prove to be less complete than the cure or conversion of the Acharnians. That is to say, Bdelykleon is not only not the comic poet; he is much less important than Philokleon.

In the parabasis proper the wasps explicitly blame the audience in the name of the poet. The poet has been wronged by the citizens although he has bestowed many benefits on them, either as in the beginning of his career by speaking like a ventriloquist through comedies presented in the name of another man, or as thereafter by holding the reins of the mouth of his own Muse. He was indeed more highly honored in Athens than anyone else without however becoming inflated or indecent or ever using his Muse as a procuress. Nor did he ever attack mere human beings, but with a kind of Heraklean anger he attempted the greatest things by fearlessly engaging that monster Kleon himself—a work in which he is still engaged. By his not accusing the citizens on this point, the poet indicates that the merits of his fight against Kleon were duly recognized by the Athenians. What he has just cause to complain about is the fate of last year's comedy, in which he attacked the forensic orators—the evil things that strangle the fathers and are especially dangerous to those who are not busybodies— while sowing the most novel conceits: The Athenians did not permit these seeds to sprout. (He means the *Clouds*.) He swears many times by Dionysos (1046; cf. *Clouds* 519) that they have never heard better verses than those of his play of last year. It is a disgrace for the Athenians not to have seen this at once. The poet does not say that the Athenians failed to appreciate the attack in the *Clouds* on the forensic orators. Fortunately, his failure with "the unnumbered myriads" in no way detracts from the regard in which he is held by the wise. He concludes with the warning that if the Athenians wish to be in the odor of cleverness, they must cherish and foster those who seek to invent something new and to say it, and must preserve those men's thoughts by locking those thoughts in coffers. Aristophanes seems to attach a greater importance to the *Clouds* than to his fight against Kleon. We have seen already that the fight against Kleon is not the core of the *Wasps*.

The rest of the parabasis of the *Wasps* deals with the wasps, just as the corresponding parts of the *Clouds*, the *Acharnians*, and the *Knights* deal respectively with the Clouds, the Acharnians, and the knights (or with beings belonging to the Clouds, the Acharnians, and the knights). The wasps, as distinguished from the Clouds and the knights, do not call on any god; in this respect, just as in many others, they resemble the Acharnians, who only call on the Acharnian Muse. The wasps sing of their youth, long since gone, when they were most pugnacious in choruses and in battles (but not in law courts), although they regard themselves as still superior in vigor to the decadent youths of the present. When they were young, they knew no fear and crushed the enemy, for they were not concerned with speaking well; they above all others were responsible for many cities' paying the tribute that younger men steal. They explain to the audience why they have the nature, i.e., the looks, of wasps. They are the true sons of Attica, autochthonous, a most manly breed who, filled with spiritedness and anger, defeated the Persians. The old Athenians' manner and way of life resembles that of wasps: They are singularly quick to anger and ill-tempered when provoked; they act in swarms; they gain their livelihood by stinging; and there are stingless drones among them.

What is most painful to them is that men who have never served in war get the pay belonging to the wasps. The only political reform they propose is that henceforth no one without stings should receive the jurymen's pay. They dispel any lingering doubt that they hold firmly to the established jury system or that their reconciliation with Bdelykleon is based on the tacit recognition of that system. (They do not pay the slightest attention to Bdelykleon's fantastic "campaign promises"; cf. 698–712.) Yet they praise themselves most highly with regard to what they did in war, especially in the war against the barbarians. Their taste is fundamentally the same as that of the Just Speech. Waspishness is best used and of course indispensable in war. Waspishness in judging is a perhaps inevitable excrescence of waspishness properly used; for it is hard to bring it about that the qualities needed by the city to hold its own against foreign enemies should not affect the conduct of fellow citizens toward one another, especially in wartime.

When Philokleon reappears, accompanied by his son, he has not lost his habitual ill-temper, but he no longer has a bad conscience for having acted against the gods' command. His old temper is admittedly due to his lack of desire to be well-treated or for the good things in general: Could he still prefer treating others ill (168, 322, 340) to being well-treated himself? He surely detests the mantle of wool woven in Ekbatana that his son forces on him and the Laconian shoes that his son compels him to put on. In contradistinction to his son, he loathes all alien things and especially everything reminding him of Sparta; in spite of his son's wish he can not, as Bdelykleon admits, look and strut in his new clothes like a somewhat effeminate rich man of fashion. While his son forces the Persian mantle on him, Philokleon swears with more than usual frequency and expresses his displeasure with the generating and raising of children; we recall that he was prepared to kill his son (653–54), and we shall soon see him waiting for his son's death (1352–54); in contradistinction to the wasps he is a most unnatural father. He is wholly unfit for the life of refined pleasures to which his son tries to educate him. After Bdelykleon has arranged that his father be properly dressed, this man of haughty and stately manners turns in the central part of this scene to preparing the old man for making stately speeches in the company of learned and clever men. Philokleon would tell myths or fables, about a mother-beating for example, whereas according to Bdelykleon one must speak on such occasions about human things as they occur in domestic life; the conversation should be, so to speak, Euripidean rather than Aeschylean (cf. *Frogs* 959–60). Philokleon could easily tell fables about domestic animals, but this is of course not what his son wants him to do. He has in mind things of grandeur that one has experienced, like having been a spectator at games in important company or, more particularly, a spectator at an athletic contest the report about which one should accompany, as wise men do, with pertinent judgments on the bodily build and the like of the contestants. Philokleon is not very good at this kind of thing. However nasty he may be, we begin to suspect that he is not simply inferior to his impeccable and even nice son, who reveals himself more and more as somewhat priggish. He asks his father next what kind of manly feats performed in his youth he would tell when drinking with men of standing from other cities, i.e., in a situation in which some boasting is practically inevitable. Bdelykleon expects his father to tell them of his hunting exploits and the like. But Philokleon has nothing of this kind to tell. One begins to wonder whether Philokleon's lack of social graces is not the result of his always having been a poor man; one begins to wonder, that is, whether Bdelykleon is not a *nouveau riche* who wishes to believe that he comes from a family of old wealth. The fifth and last part of Bdelykleon's introduction of his father to elegant society consists in teaching him how to be a banqueteer. At this stage his treatment of his father reminds one vaguely of Socrates' treatment of Strepsiades (cf. 1208–9 with *Clouds* 649, 694), but the differences between the two pairs are so manifest that nothing further need be said on this subject. Philokleon learns among other things that there is a decent way of lying down. In rehearsing a banquet scene Bdelykleon supposes one of the fellow banqueteers to be Kleon, whom he plays for his father's instruction; it could seem that Bdelykleon and Kleon belong to the same social stratum, although Bdelykleon is not (any longer) a seller. Philokleon proves to be up to Bdelykleon's standards regarding drinking songs, except perhaps that he is improperly offensive to Kleon. But he still does not wish to have anything to do with drinking (cf. 78–80): "Drinking is bad," for it leads to assault and battery and hence eventually to fines. Bdelykleon denies that one has to pay fines when one drinks in gentlemanly society; there the place of fines is taken by the telling of graceful and ingratiating jokes. Philokleon is interested in the prospect that if he does something bad, i.e., if he hurts others, he may not have to pay fines for it. He seems to be on the way from harming others by condemning them to harming others in a nonjudicial capacity without having to fear that he himself will be condemned judicially.

While Bdelykleon and his father dine and drink, the wasps, who have been silent since the parabasis, present a kind of rudimentary second parabasis. They speak no more about themselves; they are no longer of any importance as wasps. The dining of the play's heroes reminds them by contrast of the dining of some Athenian starvelings who are affiliated with Kleon. They next praise a father who has three very Music sons, the most gifted of them being Ariphrades, who had been described in the second parabasis of the *Knights* as wickeder than Kleon, as an obscene corrupter of music and poetry; he is now described as owing all his achievements to nature and none to education. Were they reminded of that father by Philokleon, the father of a son who aspires to stately things, although Bdelykleon and Ariphrades are as opposed to each other as two human beings can be, the moderate Bdelykleon's merits being due, so to speak, entirely to his education? The wasps finally state, as if they were the poet himself, using the first person singular, that while Kleon can silence him for a while, he is powerless against him. The limits of the poet's power lie elsewhere.

We hear about the banquet from one of Bdelykleon's servants, who comes back from it suffering from the beatings that the ex-dikast Philokleon had inflicted on him. Philokleon had been more affected by the wine than any of his companions and was by far the most insolent of them all. As soon as he, who hitherto had detested all good things and especially wine, had filled himself with many good things, he began to dance, jump, mock, and misbehave in other ways, i.e., to behave according to the counsels of the Unjust Speech (*Clouds* 1078). When one of his companions likened him because of his conduct to various kinds of despicable people, he outdid him by repaying him in kind, shouting loudly. The company was amused by this spectacle, except one of them, whose taste was offended by it; Philokleon made him his special target, denouncing him as someone who gives himself airs. He insulted everyone in turn by ridiculing him in a vulgar manner and by ineptly telling pointless stories. In a word, he acted like a character in a most vulgar comedy. We are not told how he acted toward his son or how his son reacted to his father's behavior; perhaps Bdelykleon was hiding in embarrassment. When Philokleon has become completely drunk he leaves for home, beating up everyone he meets on the way. When the servant sees him approach reeling, he rushes away, fearing to be beaten again. Philokleon is followed by the people whom he has insulted and who threaten to summon him into court. He chases them away, declaring that he can not even hear of lawsuits anymore. He is as vicious or malicious as ever, at least since we have known him; he is by nature malicious. But the form of his malice has radically changed; it is no longer guided by the oracle, but by wine. The fact that his transgression of the divine command had no bad consequences for him seems to have put his conscience to rest; he is no longer driven by his nature to condemn others judicially, but he is now liable to be condemned judicially himself. His son's hope that he will escape criminal prosecution by the use of gracious and ingratiating speeches seems to be disappointed because of the old man's reckless surrender to the promptings of his nature. His whole concern now is with the naked flute girl whom he has taken away from his drinking companions and whom he is eager to enjoy without any hope that his eagerness might be shared by her. As reward he offers to make her his concubine as soon as his son is dead; for the time being he can not dispose of his property, being not yet of age. His son, being ill-tempered and extremely stingy, watches his every step, since he fears that his only father might become corrupted. Philokleon has not only ceased to be eager to condemn, he has exchanged roles with his son; while remaining his son's father, he has ceased to be old; he has become rejuvenated, while his priggish son now stands revealed as an old man incapable of rejuvenation. By virtue of having been beaten by his son, he himself, who was never happy with being Bdelykleon's father, has become a young son (cf. 1297–98) who waits for his father's death; the father–son relation is reversed: The just son is worried about his naughty father's corruption. In other words, Philokleon has now become initiated (1363). His turning away from the law courts to wine and women reminds us of Dikaiopolis' corresponding turning away from war.

Bdelykleon becomes fully aware of the success of his re-education in the next scene, which consists of three parts. In the first part he takes the flute girl away from his father, justifying his action by Philokleon's extreme old age; he thus breaks the promise that he had made earlier (739–40). Yet the old man is no longer in a mood or in a position to insist on his rights. He takes his revenge by telling a story along the lines suggested to him by his son—a story of what he had seen while a spectator at an athletic contest; he does not drop names, however, and the story is pertinent to the situation. In the second part a baker woman accuses Philokleon of having beaten her and demands compensation for the damage he did by ruining her merchandise. To Bdelykleon's disapproval of his conduct and his warning that they will have a lawsuit on their hands, he replies along the lines of the instruction that he received from his son, i.e., that he will reconcile the woman by telling her clever or gracious stories.

The story that he does tell her is nothing but an insult to her, who thereupon summons him to the authorities in charge. Chairephon, who had come with her, acts as witness for her. Philokleon mocks both the woman and Chairephon, and Euripides to boot. He approaches a situation in which his hand is against everyone and everyone's hand is against him; confronted with his extreme nonconformism, even Chairephon, the constant companion of the arch nonconformist Socrates, is on the side of law and order. Even Bdelykleon is reduced to silence. In the last part of the scene Philokleon is summoned by a man who also brings his witness with him on account of outrage pure and simple. Bdelykleon urges the accuser to desist from legal action: He will pay him whatever reparation he demands. Philokleon, who joyfully confesses that he has beaten the man and thrown stones at him, intervenes by telling this victim too a story along Bdelykleon's lines—a story that adds insult to injury. Both Bdelykleon and the victim are disgusted, whereupon Philokleon tells another story of the same kind and to the same effect. Even when his son, again using force against his father, drags him into the house, he starts telling another story of the same kind.

The scene that we have just summarized seems to present the complete failure of Bdelykleon's attempt to re-educate his father; the whole scene is a single parody of the solemn Bdelykleon by his naughty father. From sheer *hybris* Philokleon has rendered nugatory Bdelykleon's promise that by making gracious and ingratiating speeches one will escape criminal prosecution for any mischief one may have done while drunk. One can not trace Bdelykleon's failure to his father-beating, for this action was entirely successful, precisely because it was performed without any Socratic support and in a spirit entirely opposed to Socrates' asceticism: Bdelykleon used force against his father in order to induce him to enjoy good living. His failure to re-educate his father reminds us indeed of Socrates' failure to re-educate Strepsiades. (Philokleon, like Strepsiades at the end of the *Clouds*, is in the opposite camp from Chairephon; Socrates is compelled to rebuke Strepsiades for his jesting and acting like the comedians—*Clouds* 296.) Both Socrates and Bdelykleon overestimate the power of education or misjudge the natures of the old men who are to be re-educated; yet Bdelykleon knew his pupil for a long time, and he does not have the excuse that he despises the ephemeral things. This man of haughty and pompous manner has too exalted a notion of education and gentlemanship (see above, pp. 107–108), just as he does not understand the importance that the oracle had for his father (see above, p. 125). The questioning of gentlemanship that is implied in the action of the *Wasps*, as it is implied in a different way in the action of the *Knights*, comes into the open in Philokleon's revulsion against the saltless pleasures of what his son regards as good society and in his parodying his son.

If Bdelykleon has failed, it does not follow that the poet disapproves of his design: It is obviously reasonable to prevent a malicious juryman from venting his malice on defendants. What then does Bdelykleon's failure mean?

If Bdelykleon has failed, the wasps are not aware of it. The reason is that they envy the fate of Philokleon, who has a soft life before him. They are indeed not quite certain whether he will take to it, since it is hard to get rid of one's nature or habits; but it is by no means impossible to change one's habits when one is exposed to other men's thoughts, as no one knows better than the wasps. While they can not yet judge of Philokleon (they have just witnessed his outrageous conduct), they do not hesitate to praise his son abundantly because of his love for his father and his wisdom; they have never seen anyone as mild and kind as he is. They do not go so far as to prove his mildness by his dragging his father into the house, although they show their approval of that act by praising the son immediately after that act. They prove Bdelykleon's mildness by the speech with which he wished to lead his father from his preoccupation with condemning to more stately things. In case of conflict—and that case has now arisen—the wasps side with Bdelykleon against Philokleon. Philokleon is completely isolated.

A servant, appropriately swearing by Dionysos—perhaps he is Xanthias, who acted as the poet's spokesman at the beginning of the play—tells the chorus or the audience of the troubles that some god has brought into the house. Under the influence of wine and the flute, Philokleon is overjoyed; he dances in the ancient manner without stopping, while he blames the present tragedians as old fogies. Having been rejuvenated he has returned to the good old times, like Demos in the *Knights*. He appears, perhaps playing Polyphemos, the solitary cannibal. He surely is no longer in need of associates in order to hurt people, as he was while he was a juryman. Earlier in the play he had imitated Odysseus and thus forced on his son the role of Polyphemos; now he has become Polyphemos (1502, 1506) without, however, transforming the much less flexible Bdelykleon into an Odysseus. He next parodies a tragic dancer. The servant does not tire of complaining about the old man's madness. Philokleon finally challenges the modern tragedians, who claim to dance well. Three tiny men appear, a trio of brothers (cf. 1275–83); they are unknown to Philokleon but identified for him by the servant. They are all poor dancers; one of them is a poor tragic poet, and they are ridiculed accordingly by Philokleon, who engages with them in a mad and modern dance. The chorus, applauding the scene, joins in the dance; dancing rapidly and madly, they all leave the stage. No one ever before had, in the act of dancing, led out a comical chorus. Philokleon suffers nothing from his accusers; he enjoys the immunity that the comic poet himself enjoys. While Bdelykleon has failed to make a gentleman out of him, Philokleon has become, thanks to his nature, far superior to what Bdelykleon aspired for him: the incarnation of an ingredient of Aristophanes' comedy, be it only its lowest ingredient.

Despite the names of the two chief characters, the issue in the *Wasps* is less Kleon or the Athenian jury system than Bdelykleon's attempt to transform his father, this entirely atypical juryman, from a man eager to inflict evil as well as not to suffer anything good (1125, 340–41) into a man eager to enjoy the good things and not eager to inflict evil. This attempt is only partly successful. Philokleon can be induced to enjoy the good things, but he can not be brought to give up inflicting evil. He can be cured of his eagerness to judge or to condemn strictly speaking, or from his longing for the greatest stateliness, or Zeuslike grandeur. He retains to the end his natural inclination to malice and mischief, his natural nastiness or bitterness. It is obvious that malice is a necessary ingredient of the Aristophanean comedy. As is shown by the example of the sausage seller, a man may indeed possess to the highest degree the powers of foul invective and of unscrupulous calumny and use them without being in any way malicious; but Aristophanes does not act, as the sausage seller does, at the behest of his betters. He claims for himself a kind of Heraklean anger (1030). In order to fight the accusers and condemners, in order to accuse the accusers and to condemn the condemners, he must reproduce within himself the spirit of accusation and condemnation before he can reproduce it in his characters. In order to fight the excrescence of waspishness, he needs a modification of that excrescence; the *Wasps* seems to teach that for this purpose that excrescence of waspishness which was, to begin with, peculiar to Philokleon must be transformed into that excrescence which is peculiar to comedy.

Aristophanes claims that the *Wasps* is a comedy that avoids both faulty extremes: It is neither vulgar nor of transcendent wisdom; it keeps to the right mean. As such it teaches the just things, and in particular it attacks the unjust Kleon, as is indicated by the very names of the two chief characters. One may say that the comedy that keeps to the mean serves the regime that keeps to the mean, the moderate regime of the time of Marathon—a regime that has no place for the Aristophanean comedy. The claim raised on behalf of the *Wasps* and the implications of that claim prove to be the comical equivalent of the claim that the Aristophanean comedy as such raises in fact. The Aristophanean comedy achieves the right mean, not by avoiding vulgarity on the one hand and transcendent wisdom on the other, but by integrating vulgarity and transcendent wisdom into a whole that can, among other things, convey the moderate political message. The Aristophanean comedy circles around the mean between vulgarity and transcendent wisdom, i.e., it avoids it while pointing toward it. It is extreme in both directions: It is too low and too high for gentlemen. Its lowest ingredient or stratum is presented in Philokleon—in his becoming as well as in his being—as distinguished from Dikaiopolis, for instance; Philokleon lacks compassion altogether, while Dikaiopolis has compassion at least for lovesick women.

4 *The Peace*

This play reminds us at once of the *Acharnians,* since the immediate objective of the chief actor in each of the two plays is peace. The *Peace* reminds us next of the *Wasps;* these two plays are the only ones that begin with a dialogue between two servants, neither of whom is responsible for the design executed in the play. In both plays the design was conceived by the servants' master. In the *Clouds,* the *Wasps,* and the *Peace* —as distinguished from the *Acharnians* and the *Knights*—the design is of purely human origin.

The servants are busy feeding a dung beetle. While servant A feeds the malodorous and voracious beast, servant B prepares the food from ass dung and similarly disgusting things and is therefore much more exposed than his companion to the stench; hence servant B does the complaining and most of the swearing; hence it is servant B who addresses the audience. In his view the particular beetle for which he prepares the food, while dirtier than a pig or dog (for it eats nothing but excrement), is in addition conceited and gives itself airs, demanding that the repulsive things that it eats be carefully and daintily prepared. By whatever god the beast may have been sent, it surely does not come from Aphrodite, or yet indeed from the Graces. Servant A suspects that some would-be clever youth in the audience will wonder what the meaning or purpose of the beetle is, and that some foreigner will reply to him that the beetle hints at the shamelessness of Kleon, the leather seller, who smells of hides. He does not tell us what he thinks of this guess. But it is safe to say that the question of the cleverish youth is wiser than the answer: The beetle has even less to do with Kleon than the dissension between Philokleon and Bdelykleon.

Servant B, who addresses the audience directly, does not answer the question of what the beetle means, i.e., at what it hints; and he explains the *logos* [32] of the play to the whole audience, which consists of parts of very different qualities: His single explanation must satisfy all these parts despite their differences. His master, he says, suffers from a novel kind of madness, a kind different from the ordinary Athenian madness. The whole day he looks heavenward and rails at Zeus, addressing Zeus himself, for the harm that he inflicts on the Greeks. Just when he has said this, he hears, and we hear, the master, who is still inside the house, complaining to Zeus, addressing Zeus himself, about what he does to the Greeks; he is sure, however, that Zeus harms the Greeks only unwittingly. Continuing to address the audience, the servant says that what they have just heard is the very evil of which he had spoken: The master's madness consists in railing at Zeus while addressing Zeus. The brief interruption of the servant's report by the master's exclamation also permits us to see a change in the master's opinion; he has come to reckon with the possibility that Zeus does not intend to harm or ruin the Greeks. That there had been a change in the master's madness, or rather a progress of it, appears from what the servant says next. At the beginning the master spoke only to himself: "How could I ever come straight to Zeus?" Even in this stage he wished to talk to Zeus, but he did not believe that one could talk to Zeus while he was on earth and Zeus in heaven. Therefore he began to think of ascending to heaven and built ladders for the purpose, but he fell down and broke his head. Finally, yesterday, he brought home an enormous dung beetle in order to ride to heaven on its back—just as Bellerophon tried to ride to heaven on the back of Pegasos. The master appears, sitting on the back of the beetle and about to ascend; he anticipates no difficulty for his extraordinary journey, except that while making it he might be exposed to the unbearably bad breath of the beetle. The servant is still more amazed by his master's insanity than he was before; he is even over-awed by it. The madness is obviously progressive. This must not blind us to the fact that in the servant's view the master's railing at Zeus or talking to Zeus, not to say praying to Zeus, was already a sign of madness. Certain it is that this talking was in vain. Yet, the servant's common sense seems to be entirely refuted, inasmuch as the certainly mad attempt to ascend to heaven on the back of a dung beetle leads to a most happy issue. Whatever may be true of the other plays, the *Peace* presents a clear case of the triumph of madness.

The servant is in no way assured of his master's sanity when he is told by him that he is undertaking his novel and daring flight in the interest of all Greece. On speaking again to his master about the latter's madness, he is told by him to speak piously and to pray with shouts, and to tell the others that they should not permit any sounds to escape from their lips or any stench from their excretions; the sounds would distract the master and the smells would attract the beetle. The servant simply disregards these commands; as if he had been commanded to be silent, and as if he had never learned about his master's intention, he says that he can not possibly be silent if his master does not tell him where he intends to fly. The master replies that he intends to fly heavenward to Zeus, in order to ask him what he plans to do in regard to the Greeks. When the servant draws his attention to the fact that Zeus might not answer his question, the master replies that in that case he will indict the god for betraying Greece to the Persians, i.e., that he will infer from Zeus' actions that he is wittingly destroying the Greeks. He surely is open to the possibility that he might have to act against Zeus, and he takes it for granted that Zeus has obligations to the Greeks. Thereupon the poet's spokesman, swearing by Dionysos, cries, "Never as long as I live." Since his protest is of no avail, he calls out his master's two little daughters, telling them that their father is about to leave them without their knowing it in order to ascend to heaven and that they should beseech him not to do it. The father explains to the girls that he must make his journey because there is no money left in the house, so that they are in danger of starving; his public-spirited action is primarily dictated by his and his family's extreme need. He explains to them further that he chose the beetle as his vehicle because, as he had learned from Esop, the beetle is the only winged being that ascended to the gods (he means without the gods' will). When the older of the girls finds it incredible that such a malodorous animal should have come to the gods, she is told that hatred of the eagle induced and enabled it to do so; besides, the beetle is preferable to any other beast for his purpose since it can live on his excrement during the journey. After having replied in equally cogent fashion to other objections raised by his daughter and having said farewell to the two girls, he asks the audience, for whose sake he claims to be undertaking his journey, to abstain from excreting lest the beetle rush downward and throw him off. (He will address the audience in the sequel more than once.) He then exhorts the beetle to rise straight to the halls of Zeus, forgetting about all mortal and earthly food, and he exhorts an individual in the Piraeus, who is excreting, to prevent the stench from reaching the beetle. The latter exhortation is necessarily laughable for the audience, but as the rider himself points out, he himself speaks in jest; only when the beetle begins to rise does he feel fear and hence cease to jest. Since he is mad or obsessed with his conceit, his jesting is somewhat surprising. Ordinarily Aristophanes' heroes are quite earnest. Strepsiades and Philokleon did jest, but they did not say that they did. Besides, while Philokleon both jests and is mad only at the end of the *Wasps*, the hero of the *Peace* both jests and is mad already at the beginning of the play.

One could say that by speaking of his jesting the master destroys the dramatic illusion even more than by addressing the audience. Continuing in the same vein, he gives an order to the machinist of the theater, who is in charge of the beetle's illusory ascent. Before addressing the machinist he had addressed himself, Zeus, the servant, the beetle, his daughters, the audience, and an individual in the Piraeus; he had received responses only from himself, the servant, and one of his daughters. According to servant A, the beetle speaks (12). The hero of the *Peace* surely addresses an unusually large variety of beings.

In the *Wasps* we hear the names of the servants whose dialogue opens the play, and the servant who explains the design of the master to the audience tells it the names of the master and of the master's father, Bdelykleon and Philokleon—these names that are so misleading. In the *Peace*, however, we do not hear the names of the servants whose dialogue opens the play, nor does the servant who explains to the audience the design of the master tell it the master's name. Can we infer from this that in the *Peace* the name of the master is the very opposite of misleading? He has no wife, for if he had one, he could not marry one of the two companions of Eirene (Peace) whom he brings home from heaven. His children are both females. This fact seems to be sufficiently explained by the opportunity it offers to the poet to make a parodic use of a verse from Euripides' *Aiolos*.[33] But, to say nothing of the *Lysistrate*, of the other male Aristophanean peacemaker, Dikaiopolis, we know with certainty only that he has female children, i.e., that he has not generated warriors (*Acharnians* 132, 244 ff., 1061–62).

The name of the master is Trygaios. He is a vinedresser. His very name reminds us of vintage. His name reminds us also of comedy, which Aristophanes likes to call "trygedy." We take it that he, like Dikaiopolis, is the comic poet in a lowly disguise. No better emblem of the Aristophanean comedy could be imagined than a flight to heaven of the thinly disguised poet on the back of a dung beetle. That comedy combines the highest and the lowest. The Philokleontic ingredient to which our attention was drawn by the last part of the *Wasps* is not as low as that indicated by the dung beetle—that disgusting beast, dirtier than a pig, which is attracted only by what our nature abhors without being in fear or in awe of it, and by what repels Aphrodite and the Graces. While the beetle hints primarily at the coprological only, it hints secondarily and above all at all other low ingredients of the Aristophanean comedy. Yet those things could not be ingredients of comedy if our nature were not also attracted by them, or at any rate by speech about them. They are repulsive by nature and by custom or convention. They are repulsive partly by nature and partly by convention. Man's nature longs for relief from the burden of convention, however indispensable and even salutary, even of ennobling convention, and therewith for return to nature. The Aristophanean comedy achieves that relief by both its lowest and its highest; the relief that it achieves by its lowest is the vehicle by which it relieves the highest in man from the burden of convention. We must add immediately that while convention is laughable in the light of nature—to say nothing of the fact that the conventions of one people (say, the Greeks) are laughable in the light of the conventions of another (cf. 289–91)—nature is laughable in the light of convention or law. Hence the Aristophanean comedy moves back and forth between the Just Speech and the Unjust Speech. Both the defeat of the unlawful or the *restitutio in integrum* of the lawful and the victory of the unlawful or the *restitutio in integrum* of the natural can be exhilarating and laughable as is shown by the *Clouds* on the one hand, and by the *Acharnians*, the *Knights*, and the *Wasps* on the other. Given the all-comprehensive character of the distinction between nature and convention, the Aristophanean comedy can indeed be said to present human life as a whole. Differently stated, comedy can achieve this work since it surpasses tragedy only by presupposing it, as is shown most simply by the parodic use that it makes of tragedy. The dung beetle is the only being that enables Trygaios to enter heaven against the will of the gods. Being the vehicle for the highest flight or being an ingredient of high art, the dung beetle is conceited and very demanding: It demands that its detestable food be carefully prepared. The beetle entered heaven originally, in the olden times (133), because of its hatred of the eagle, the bird of Zeus, which also stands, among other things, for Demos' imperial aspirations.[34] It indicates therefore the debunking by comedy of the grand, solemn, stately, and pompous, of everything excelling or high, as boasting. Comedy rises high in order to bring down the high. This would not be possible if it did not presuppose the distinction between what is truly high, high by nature, and what is high only by convention: Comedy rises to what is highest by nature in order to lower what is high only by convention.

Without misadventure Trygaios arrives on the beetle's back at the house of Zeus. He knocks at the door. Hermes who, perhaps assisted by the beetle's smell, has smelled the presence of a mortal, opens the door and pours a flood of insults about the mortal's impious daring over his ears. Trygaios does not lose his composure; he brings the god to his senses by mock humility, then softens him by telling him that he has ascended to heaven in order to bring him some meat, and finally asks him to call Zeus to the door. But the gods have departed the day before (the very day on which Trygaios brought home the beetle) for the highest part of heaven, out of anger with the Greeks (just as Trygaios had acted out of anger with Zeus). The gods wished no longer to see the Greeks fighting one another or to receive their entreaties for victory over their Greek enemies; for the Greeks, especially the Athenians, prefer to wage war against one another, although the gods have tried to make truce among them. (We remember Amphitheos' mission.) In order to punish the Greeks, the gods have handed them over to Polemos (War), to do with them as he likes. Polemos has thrown Eirene into a deep pit below; since she would therefore be within easy reach of the Greeks, he has covered her with many stones so that they can never get her out. In addition he has obtained an immense mortar in which to pound the cities. Trygaios thus learns from a god immediately after his arrival in heaven what he was so eager to find out, namely, what Zeus intends to do to the Greeks: Zeus destroys the Greeks wittingly; it is now certain that Trygaios must act against Zeus. One could also say that what he learns from Hermes is that he has no right to blame Zeus (not Zeus, but the Greeks are responsible for the ruin of Greece) and that Zeus must have heard Trygaios' quasi-supplications but did not heed them and did not wish to hear them again, perhaps because they are only the supplications of a powerless citizen who merely minds his own business (191). Which interpretation one prefers depends on whether one regards eternal war or the complete destruction of the warring parties as a fit punishment for having willed the war and its continuation.

Neither Hermes nor Trygaios speaks of Zeus' punishing the Greeks. If the Socrates of the *Clouds* had stooped to look down on such ephemeral things, he might have said that the ruin of Greece was a likely consequence of the fratricidal war; he would not have traced that ruin to Zeus. But Aristophanes is not Socrates. By making his Trygaios trace the danger to Zeus, he is enabled or compelled to make a distinction between the destruction proper, which is the work of Polemos, and the mere permission given by Zeus to Polemos.

Hermes leaves because the fear-inspiring Polemos is about to emerge from Zeus' house; Trygaios hides as well as he can. The terrible enemy of man appears with an immense mortar in his hands. He looks as terrible as Lamachos: [35] He does not look as terrible as war pure and simple; in this case, at any rate, the personification weakens the terror. Nevertheless Trygaios is frightened to the utmost. Polemos sputters dire threats against the various Greek cities—threats that Trygaios accompanies with comments partly addressed to the audience. Despite his concern with the salvation of all Greeks, he is sufficiently attached to his own so as not to mind Polemos' threats against Sparta and Megara,[36] as distinguished from those against Sicily and Athens; for some reason, Polemos' threat against Athens does not happen to be as explicit as that against the other cities. With his usual brutality, Polemos commands his helper Kydoimos (Uproar) to bring him a pestle; he learns from him that they have none, owing to the fact that both of them moved in only yesterday; he sends him therefore to Athens to fetch one. Trygaios does not see what poor humans can do to avert the danger; calling on Dionysos he wishes that Kydoimos perish on his way. But Kydoimos returns, fortunately without the Athenian pestle, i.e., Kleon, who has perished. When Trygaios hears this, he is glad and gives thanks to Athena. He had to ride to heaven in order to hear the most important political news concerning Athens. Polemos sends Kydoimos to fetch a pestle from Sparta. Trygaios, again filled with fear, addresses the audience: If anyone among you happens to have been initiated in the mysteries of Samothrake, he should now pray that Kydoimos will not return safe and sound. Trygaios himself is obviously not initiated, just as he is not initiated in the Eleusinian rites (375). But Kydoimos returns safe and sound, fortunately however without the Spartan pestle, i.e., Brasidas, who has also perished. The strange fact that the two chief cities have incurred the same loss at the same time induces Polemos to ask Kydoimos how Brasidas perished; he learns that Brasidas' campaign to the north was not truly a Spartan enterprise.[37] Just as Trygaios had praised Athena for the death of Kleon, he now praises the Dioskuroi for the death of Brasidas; he had not called on the help of either Athena or the Dioskuroi.[38] He now has hope that Polemos will not grind the cities to smithereens. Polemos does go indoors with his helper to make a pestle but, as is shown by the fact that he never returns, he does not succeed. Trygaios expresses his joy over Polemos' leaving, in words reminding us of Dikaiopolis (cf. 293 with *Acharnians* 269–70). The only thing remaining for him to do is to disinter Eirene. He calls for the help of all Greeks— of the farmers, merchants, joiners, artisans, metics, strangers, and islanders.

The deaths of Kleon and Brasidas made possible the peace between Athens and Sparta, but a further step was needed in order to bring about that peace, the peace of Nikias. Just as the loss of the pestles is the comic equivalent of the deaths of the two war leaders, the disinterring of Eirene is the comic equivalent of the conclusion of the peace treaty, or rather of the peace negotiations. Accordingly, Trygaios' tracing the ruin of Greece to Zeus—to his action or his permission—is the comic equivalent of "Socrates' " tracing it to nothing but the war itself. We have already observed that the comic equivalent of a thing is its low counterpart—for instance, Socrates' easy endurance of fleabites is the comic equivalent of his easy endurance of heat and cold, or of toil and wine. It would be more correct to say that his easy endurance of fleabites is as a matter of course included in his endurance as such but is not properly mentioned in noncomical speech. However this may be, now we see that in the light of the Aristophanean comedy, natural explanations, being explanations in terms of the nondivine and hence low (like Socrates' explanations of thunder and lightning) appear to be the comic equivalents of theological explanations. Given the reciprocity of nature and convention in regard to laughter, this also means that theological explanations are the comic equivalents of natural explanations. One is thus led to wonder whether comic equivalents par excellence or in the strictest sense occur at all outside the region within which *theologia* and *physiologia* diverge. From the point of view of the Aristophanean Socrates the answer must be in the negative. The laughable is the defective of a certain kind. Given the variety of views as to what constitutes shortcomings, a man is most clearly laughable if he pretends to have an excellence while in fact he has only the corresponding defect, i.e., if he is laughable according to his own admitted standard. Hence pretense, affectation, or boasting become the preferred theme of comedy. Now if Zeus, who claims, or on whose behalf men claim, that he is the father of gods and men, that he is most powerful and wise, and that he deserves the highest veneration, does not even exist, as Aristophanes' Socrates indeed asserts, he is the greatest example of boasting that can be imagined. His case is the most perfect case of contrast between claim and being; he is the absolute subject of comedy; the comedy par excellence is the comedy of the gods. But let us return to Aristophanes himself.

The chorus arrives in compliance with Trygaios' call. Its members put themselves under his command; they will not cease working that day until they have brought Peace, the greatest of all goddesses, to light. In contradistinction to the Acharnians, they are from the beginning on the hero's side. The only difficulty they cause Trygaios arises from it being very hard for them to stop shouting and dancing from joy about the end of the war, for they loathe war more than their old age. By their shouting they might rekindle Polemos indoors and bring Kleon to life below and thus be prevented from disinterring the goddess. The dangers threatening from Polemos on the one hand and Kleon (as distinguished from Brasidas) on the other are hard to distinguish.[39] The chorus submits, promising in addition that in the future they will no longer act as ill-tempered and harsh jurymen. They only await the command of Trygaios, whom not they but Chance, which on this occasion was friendly, has elected as their commander with full power. When he ponders how they might remove the stones that cover Eirene, Hermes appears. He insults Trygaios again for his impious daring and threatens him with destruction; Trygaios is again in no way disturbed. Hermes tells him that Zeus has made it a capital crime to be found disinterring Eirene. Trygaios admits that he is attempting the forbidden thing and accepts the punishment with perfect composure. He only desires to be initiated so that he will be happy after death, i.e., so that what was meant to be an evil will be good; but he does not pursue this quasi-suicidal theme. He asks the god not to denounce him since he had brought him meat. Hermes declares that Zeus will destroy him if he does not scream of what he has seen (Zeus has gone away to the highest place in heaven). Trygaios prays to him not to scream of what he has seen; at his request the chorus beseeches that most philanthropic and munificent god for the same favor, reminding him of the sacrifices they have brought him in the past and will bring him in the future. Trygaios' enterprise can not succeed unless the greatest possible silence is observed. Here is the basis of a possible agreement between Trygaios and Hermes, the god of thievery and everything stealthily done. In order to sway Hermes, Trygaios reveals to him a terrible and dangerous conspiracy against all gods—an enterprise comparable to Dikaiopolis' use of Amphitheos (403; cf. *Acharnians* 128). Moon and the clever rascal Sun have for a long time been conspiring against all gods to betray Greece to the barbarians, since the Greeks sacrifice to the gods whereas the barbarians sacrifice to Moon and Sun. Moon and Sun are bent on destroying all the gods and all the Greeks in order to receive the offerings from the soil of Greece to be occupied by the barbarians and thus to be the sole gods everywhere. Hermes himself has observed what he now recognizes as a sign of this conspiracy. Accordingly, Trygaios beseeches the gods to help him and his chorus in bringing Eirene to light. Since the gods depend on the Greeks, and the Greeks will be destroyed if Peace is not brought to light at once, Sun and Moon will succeed in their enterprise unless Hermes acts in the interest of Zeus but against Zeus' express prohibition. Hermes begins to see the light. But Trygaios knows that there is a tension between the common good and the private good; after all, it will be Hermes who will have to account to Zeus for his disobedience after the danger has been averted. He therefore promises Hermes that henceforth Athens will celebrate all her festivals in honor of Hermes and that he will be worshiped everywhere by Greeks to a much higher degree than ever before; he practically promises Hermes that in reward for his help he will be treated by the Greeks as if he were the sole god. He at once gives the god a golden cup. The god, thus moved to compassion, not only abstains from betraying the Greeks to Zeus, but even helps them in disinterring Eirene; Trygaios' success is now assured.

Trygaios succeeds in transgressing Zeus' prohibition with impunity by threatening Hermes, and indirectly all other gods, with a danger coming from Sun and Moon. He as it were makes a diplomatic *ad hoc* alliance with Sun and Moon against "all gods." Sun and Moon are of course also gods, but they are gods of a different kind than the gods who are peculiar to the Greeks or to whom the Greeks belong. We remember from the *Clouds* that the astronomer Socrates took Sun and Moon much more seriously than the gods and that his quasi-goddesses, the Clouds, are closer to the Moon and to the Sun than to the other gods known to the Athenians. We suggested that the Clouds are the natural Muses. Accordingly we shall distinguish Sun and Moon from Zeus and the other gods as the natural gods from the Greek gods. We call them the natural gods because they are regarded as gods by all men and not merely by the barbarians, just as on the other hand the barbarian gods simply are beings other than Sun and Moon.[40] There is no objection to counting the earth too, for instance, among the natural gods, although there is no need for it now.[41] The Clouds praise their father Ether for his universal beneficence, but surely Sun and Moon come closer to being universally beneficent than Zeus and his fellows. Trygaios is emphatically a Greek, an Athenian, but he is the first man we find in Aristophanes' work who left not only Greece but the earth. He is aware of his being a poor human (263). Hermes senses in him primarily the mortal (180; cf. 236), rather than a Greek in particular; as mere mortal he is related to Sun and Moon, rather than to the gods. One could also say that Sun and Moon are older than the Greek gods, just as there were barbarians before there were Greeks. Besides,

Sun and Moon come to sight as self-moving (hence living) beings of utmost splendor, which are visible to all men at regular intervals and thus reveal themselves to men without ever descending to earth or men's ascending to heaven. To return to Trygaios, regardless of whether or not he believes in the conspiracy, so helpful to him, of Sun and Moon against the gods, he surely does not believe that Zeus is friendly toward the Greeks; he may also remember better than we do the oracle used in the *Knights*, the Clouds being wicked if just, Nikias' theologoumenon and Philokleon's oracle. He surely acts against Zeus' will. The distinction between Zeus' will and his permission is of no importance; by permitting Polemos to do to the Greeks what he likes, Zeus has forbidden under penalty of death the disinterment of Peace. Whereas Dikaiopolis acted against the city with the support of the gods, Trygaios is compelled to act against the gods although with the support of all Greeks; accordingly Dikaiopolis brings about only his private peace, while Trygaios brings about public peace. In contradistinction to Bdelykleon, Trygaios does not merely disregard a divine prohibition, but meets it head on. If he is not completely mad, he must believe that he can escape Zeus' punishment. Seeing Hermes with his own eyes, he can not share Socrates' view according to which the gods are not. But he acts on the view that they are not greatly to be feared or that they are not very powerful. He acts as if he agreed rather with Strepsiades, who understood Socrates' denial of Zeus' being to mean that Zeus has lost his power or kingship. To exaggerate somewhat, Trygaios Strepsiadizes. It is not necessary to dwell on the difference between Strepsiades and Trygaios: Trygaios did not need Socrates in order to arrive at the view on which he acts. He surpasses Socrates in knowledge of the gods, since he has ascended to heaven.

The Greeks are no longer compelled to steal Eirene, since Trygaios has succeeded in transforming the guard into an accomplice. The chorus, who had put themselves originally under Trygaios' command, now put themselves, without asking Trygaios, under Hermes' command; they act as pious men. They ask that wisest of the gods to direct their work with an artisan's competence (426–39; cf. 357–60): Trygaios is not an artisan. Hermes is in charge of the technical operation; the deed as a whole is Trygaios'. At Trygaios' suggestion, they pray to the gods. He had not prayed before his journey; with the winning over of Hermes his posture toward the gods has naturally changed. He and the chorus wish the best to the lovers of peace and even more the worst to the lovers of war. Trygaios pours libations to Hermes, the Graces, the Horai (the sisters of

Eirene), Aphrodite, and Desire (the son of Aphrodite). Under the guidance of Hermes the work of pulling Eirene out of the pit proceeds, but not quite satisfactorily. The chorus demands that Trygaios and Hermes put their hands to the work; but Trygaios claims that he has been doing it all along. They do not make sufficient progress because some of the Greeks do not exert themselves properly, or even obstruct the work. Hermes finds fault especially with the Megarians and the Athenians. When, at the suggestion of the leader of the chorus, the farmers alone do the pulling, the work proceeds much better, and with a few more efforts on their part Eirene comes to the surface, together with her companions, Opora and Theoria.

As we have seen, there was some resistance to the liberation of Eirene, but that resistance was overcome by harder work on the part of the peace lovers: It was not overcome by speeches and surely not by a debate. In the *Peace*, much more than in the four preceding comedies, the success of the design depends decisively on deeds as distinguished from speech: on the ascent to heaven on the back of the beetle, the loss of the two pestles, Polemos' failure to make a new pestle, and the disinterring of Eirene. The only speech required for the success of the plan is Trygaios' persuasion of Hermes—a matter of about twenty verses. Trygaios attempted to argue with Zeus, and nothing would have been easier for the poet than to arrange a full debate between Trygaios and Zeus; but the attempt was abortive. The resistance to peace on the part of some Greeks could be overcome without speech because the large majority is firmly in favor of peace, and that majority is led by Trygaios and Hermes. Particularly striking is the contrast between Trygaios and Dikaiopolis; Dikaiopolis had to engage in a debate with the Acharnians and would not have succeeded in that debate without his borrowings from Euripides. While one opposite of speech is deed, another opposite of speech is silence. Surely the significance of Trygaios' action is concealed by the brevity of the speech by which he persuades Hermes.

Owing to his war-caused poverty Trygaios lacks words with which to address Eirene properly. He does find words in praise of Theoria (523–26; cf. 342 and context). Among the joys that are due to her he enumerates the songs of Sophocles and "the little verses" of Euripides; Hermes does not approve of the latter. We recall the link between Dikaiopolis and Euripides. Otherwise Hermes shares the joys of Trygaios, the chorus, and the Greeks in general about the return of peace. Some difference of feeling can be observed in the audience: While all farmers are most happy about the peace, not all artisans are; the makers of weapons prefer war to peace. It could seem that the arts as such are not as praiseworthy as agriculture. At the suggestion of Hermes, Trygaios urges the farmers—the very men who disinterred Peace (550 ff., 508, 511)—to return to the fields after having exchanged the tools of war for the tools of peace, or to turn from the works of war, even of disinterring Peace, to the works of peace proper. In their own view at any rate the farmers who, as such, are lovers of peace are therefore as such just. We recall the connection between justice and piety. The vinedresser Trygaios is of course himself one of the countrypeople who are eager to return to the fields from which they have been separated so long on account of the war. He praises both the looks of the tools of farming and the old way of life that was supplied by the goddess Eirene. The members of the chorus in their turn praise Eirene, who has been the sole benefactress of the countrypeople. They sing as if they never owed anything to Demeter or any other goddess or god. They have already called Eirene the greatest of all goddesses (308) and the most philanthropic and munificent divinity (392–94).

The overwhelming impression made by Eirene and the recollection of her past benefactions made it impossible for Hermes to receive the novel and supreme honors that Trygaios had promised him. On the other hand, while Eirene may have eclipsed entirely all other gods, no one can forget Hermes, who in addition is still present and visible: Without his help the goddess would never have come to light. In fact, as no one knows better than the farmers, Eirene had been wholly unable to come to the surface under her own power; even after her liberation she had given no sign of being at all able to move by herself. The farmers found her in the pit, but they have no doubt that she was not in the pit during all of her absence from Greece. They therefore ask Hermes as the most benevolent god where she was during that long time, perhaps in order to ask him afterward how or by whom she had been transported to wherever she was before being in the pit. Hermes does not answer the question as posed by the farmers, but he tells them how Eirene left Greece. He could simply and truthfully have said that in the meantime she had been with the gods, but this answer could easily have led to further questions that might have been awkward. We recall the difficulty in which the Just Speech became entangled when he replied to the question raised by the Unjust Speech as to where Right is by saying that Right is with the gods (*Clouds* 903–4). The farmers had heard Hermes say that Zeus had made it a capital crime to disinter Eirene. We also recall that Trygaios originally blamed Zeus for the destruction of Greece, i.e., for keeping Eirene away from Greece. In his reply to the farmers Hermes implicitly denies any guilt of any god: Not the gods, but you Attic farmers are responsible for the war; the gods, or at any rate Hermes, are responsible for the return of peace. Hermes turns the tables on his simple-minded questioners. He reverses entirely the judgment on the farmers that was implied and not merely implied in everything that went before and according to which the farmers, rather than any other class, are dedicated to peace.

In contradistinction to the titles of the four plays previously discussed, the title of the play now under discussion does not indicate the chorus. The reason for this is that the character or composition of the chorus of the *Peace* is obscure and meant to be obscure. From Trygaios' call to his helpers (292–98) one would expect the chorus to consist of farmers, artisans, merchants, and so on from all Greek cities. This expectation is confirmed to some extent by the praises and blames pronounced as they pull Eirene out of the pit (464–508). This does not prevent the poet, as is his wont, from destroying the dramatic illusion and treating the chorus as consisting of Athenian citizens only (347–56). Finally, however, it becomes clear that the chorus consists of Attic farmers only (603 ff.). This obscurity reveals, while concealing it, the difference between farmers and artisans or a certain kind of artisans. We also note that the chorus of the *Peace* acts throughout the play in a strictly ministerial fashion, much more so even than the chorus of the *Knights:* The sole contribution of the chorus of the *Peace* consists, so to speak, in nothing but bodily, nontechnical labor.

According to Hermes the loss of the goddess was caused originally by the misfortune that Phidias suffered. (Phidias had been condemned to exile for having stolen gold that he had been given as the material for a statue of Athena.) Phidias' friend Perikles, who knew the natures of the farmers, feared that he might become implicated in Phidias' fate and therefore, in order to divert their attention, arranged the passing of the Megarian decree, which led to the war; once the war had started it could not be stopped and Eirene disappeared. Hermes could easily have traced the war, as Dikaiopolis had done, to Perikles (or his Aspasia). But for the reason indicated he exculpates Perikles, who according to him acted under the duress [42] brought on by the natures of the farmers. Given the connection between Perikles and Phidias, Hermes could be thought to have exculpated Phidias as well: Were the natures of the farmers not already effective in Phidias' condemnation? Trygaios has never heard of a connection between Eirene and Phidias. The chorus however sees a connection: Eirene is beautiful to look at, and Phidias was famous as a maker of beautiful statues. As far as we could observe hitherto, Eirene, who outshines all other gods, is nothing but a statue.[48] As far as we could observe hitherto, she and her companions never speak or move, whereas their counterparts, Polemos and his companion, speak and move, i.e., are clearly living. But for the presence of Hermes it could look as if only repulsive and misanthropic gods are living beings, while the beautiful and philanthropic ones are the work of artisans—artists as distinguished from farmers. Differently stated, but for the presence of Hermes it would look as if only female divinities were beautiful and philanthropic; we remember the close connection between Eirene on the one hand and Aphrodite and the Graces on the other (456; cf. *Acharnians* 989); we also remember that Trygaios has only female children. (Just as Polemos is less terrible than war itself, Eirene is more beautiful than peace itself.) And as for Hermes, we must not forget that his becoming philanthropic was due to Trygaios' speech and gift. At any rate, Hermes seems to link the blame of the farmers with praise of Phidias.

Hermes speaks next of the damage done to Attic farmers by the Peloponnesians and to the Peloponnesian farmers by the Athenians. Trygaios and the chorus fully approve of what Athens did to the enemy farmers; they still possess something of the warlike zeal of the Acharnians in the play of that name. We may note here that while in the *Acharnians* Dikaiopolis reveals his true being ever more as the action proceeds, Trygaios, who had acted successfully against Zeus' will, becomes ever more an ordinary farmer as the action proceeds. It is in accordance with this that, in contradistinction to Dikaiopolis, Trygaios does not assert Athens' responsibility for the outbreak of the war and that when Hermes asserts it, he avoids the issue by limiting himself to expressing his amazement about the connection between Eirene and Phidias. Hermes finally shows how the rural population that had found refuge in Athens looked for guidance to the speakers who chased Eirene away whenever she tried to appeal to the Athenians. The savagery of the speakers would have had no effect but for the support of the farmers; the worst of the orators was, of course, Kleon. Trygaios urges Hermes to be silent about Kleon since he is dead and therefore no longer belongs to Athens; he does not deny Hermes' charges against Kleon. Yet he is sufficiently patriotic to desire to change the subject. Therefore he who earlier in the play had spoken to beings of every kind addresses Eirene with the question why she is silent.

He thus raises in effect the question of the manner of being of this exemplary divinity. Eirene does not reply: Is she speechless in addition to being motionless? Hermes asserts that she will not speak to the spectators because she is angry with them for what they have done to her: It is not a defect of the gods but the fault of human beings if the gods do not speak. Hermes surely imputes to Eirene the feeling toward the Athenians that the gods have toward the Greeks in general (203–9). This is not convincing: If she was as angry with the Greeks as the other gods, why was it necessary for Polemos to inter her? Polemos' action seems rather to prove what is hardly in need of proof, that Eirene can not be angry, just as it seems to prove that Eirene can move under her own power. Be this as it may, especially since Trygaios is not a spectator, he might have proposed to Hermes that Eirene should whisper to Trygaios just as Hermes had whispered to Strepsiades (*Clouds* 1478–85). He avoids some embarrassment by proposing that she should whisper to Hermes, her fellow god. Hermes asks Eirene to tell him how she feels about the Athenians. According to him Eirene whispers to him that she blames them for having turned her down three times in the Assembly when she came of herself with many truces after their success in Pylos. This, Trygaios admits, was a mistake, and he asks her for forgiveness. After Eirene has begun to speak, or rather to whisper in a manner inaudible to mortals, she can not stop, although one might say that she does not say anything: She utters only questions. According to Hermes, Eirene has asked him who was most malevolent to her in Athens and who was her friend; Trygaios only tells her or Hermes who was most benevolent to her: If she has ears to hear, she must know by now who was the greatest enemy of peace in Athens. According to Hermes Eirene has asked him further who is now the leader of the people. When Trygaios mentions the name of the individual in question (Hyperbolos), a miracle happens: Eirene turns her head away. There are things so shocking as to make even statues move their heads. In other words, it is now clear beyond a shadow of doubt that Eirene is more than a statue. Hermes explains her movement without pretending that Eirene has given him the explanation. Trygaios reassures Eirene regarding the people's choice as well as he can. The third and final request of Eirene is for information about many other things, especially about ancient things that antedate her departure from Athens, and in the first place about Sophocles. Trygaios tells her that Sophocles has become Simonides, i.e., greedy, and that what is true of Sophocles is true *mutatis mutandis* of everything: Everything has become worse since she left. The remark about Sophocles is not altogether surprising: Hermes had no objection to Trygaios' praise of Sophocles as distinguished from Euripides, and a poet liked by Hermes is likely to be a lover of gain. After we have seen or heard that Eirene is more than a statue, Hermes asks Trygaios to take Opora for his wife and to restore Theoria to the Council. As far as Trygaios is concerned, peace is more than a *restitutio in integrum;* he receives a new wife. Hermes and the overjoyed Trygaios take leave of each other. The god asks the mortal to remember him, i.e., the promise he had made to him; Trygaios does not even reply. Yet the dung beetle has disappeared —it will stay in heaven—and Trygaios does not know how to descend to the earth. At Hermes' suggestion he descends on the side of Eirene; Opora and Theoria follow him. The beautiful goddess has taken the place of the ugly dung beetle.

It is not sufficient that Eirene be brought to light and properly welcomed, or rather, she can not be properly welcomed if she is not known to be a living being. As soon as possible after this has been accomplished, the parabasis occurs. The parabasis of the *Peace*, which conceals nothing but Trygaios' descent, strikingly differs from the parabaseis of the four preceding plays. In the first place, it has no epirrhema or antepirrhema. As a consequence, the chorus of Attic farmers does not say a word about itself. This is in perfect agreement with the obscurity regarding the character and composition of the chorus, an obscurity indicated by the title of the play. The parabasis deals solely with the poet himself, with the praise of his art and the blame of his rivals and of some tragic poets, and with the chorus as chorus. Not even the audience, or the city, is praised or blamed. In none of the preceding plays were the gods as important as actors as in the *Peace*. All the more striking is the fact that no divinity—not even Eirene—is mentioned in the parabasis except the Muse (or the daughter of Zeus) thrice and the Graces once; Eirene is replaced by the Muse and the Graces: Aristophanes the poet is the sole theme of the parabasis. The emphasis is on his excellent art, rather than on his political merits: Justice (or its opposite) is not even mentioned. The parabasis does speak of the poet's fight against Kleon in the same context and vein as the parabasis of the *Wasps* does; in fact, most of the verses dealing with this subject are taken over literally from the *Wasps*. This agreement corresponds to the fact that the *Wasps* and the *Peace* are the only plays that begin with a conversation between two servants, while the design executed in the play is their master's. All the more striking are the differences between the two parabaseis; those differences confirm what we have suggested regarding the difference between the priggish Bdelykleon and Trygaios as the comic poet himself. The most important of these differences is that the parabasis of the *Peace* does not even allude to the *Clouds;* such an allusion would be superfluous in the *Peace*. Secondly, in the parabasis of the *Wasps* the poet never speaks about himself in the first person, while in the parabasis of the *Peace* he does so precisely in verses that he otherwise takes over literally from the earlier play; by acting in this manner, i.e., by silence, the poet comes closer to the *Clouds* in the *Peace* than in the *Acharnians*, the *Knights*, and the *Wasps*. Nowhere else does he speak about his looks (his baldness) as emphatically as in the parabasis of the *Peace*. As we have seen, there are more reasons than this for asserting that the comic poet himself is powerfully present in the *Peace*.

Trygaios states to the audience what is uppermost in his mind after his return from the gods: He suffers from pain in his legs, and from on high the human beings looked smaller and less evil than they do when viewed from the earth. The gods have less reason, one is tempted to infer, for being indignant and punitive than men. We remember the difficulty caused by Zeus's punishing the Greeks for their war with perpetuation of that war. When one of the servants comes out of the house and, noting without surprise that his master has come back, asks him about his experiences, he only tells him of his pain in the legs. This does not satisfy the poor fellow, who goes on to ask him whether he has seen other men roaming in the air. Trygaios has seen only a few souls of dithyrambic poets, who collected lyric preludes as they flew. This does not agree with the servant's notions, for he has heard that all men become stars in the air after death. Thereupon Trygaios assures him that this tale is true and that for instance the poet Ion of Chios [44] is now the morning star. This does not mean, of course, that there are only poets in the air—it just so happens that Trygaios met only poets—or that all stars are poets, but that the stars live like human beings (for instance, there are wealthy stars who go out to dinner). Trygaios seems to parody a poetic account of the stars. We must not forget his own tale of the conspiracy of Sun and Moon. Without telling the servant even Opora's name, he hands her over to him to lead her into the house and prepare her for the wedding bed, while he will restore Theoria to the Council. The two women are admittedly prostitutes, and since they have come from heaven there can be no doubt that there are gods who keep brothels—a fact that adversely affects the status of the gods in the eyes of the servant. On the other hand, there can be no doubt that Opora and Theoria are living beings; they are in need of food, if of the food of gods. The chorus envies the old man Trygaios for his happiness, for his rejuvenation: Not all old men have become rejuvenated through the coming of peace, and in particular not the farmers who form the chorus, as they had hoped (350–52). Peace does not beautify everybody; peace is in need of beautification: hence Eirene the goddess. In Trygaios' view it is only fair that he be treated differently from everybody else: He was the one who by his journey on the back of the beetle saved the Greeks. Only the beautifier deserves beautification. The exchange between Trygaios and the chorus detains him so that the servant can finish the preparations regarding Opora. His return reminds his master of his duty to restore Theoria to the Council, which he can easily do since the Council is present in the theater. Since she will serve the common enjoyment of the Council, or rather the enjoyment of each of its members, there is no outrageous impropriety in Trygaios' undressing her and pointing to her attractions. The gross obscenity of this scene easily makes us forget that Trygaios no longer even alludes to Sophocles and Euripides (cf. 523–32). Obscenity is as concealing as brevity of speech. After he has done his duty regarding Theoria while neglecting his bride (he never mentions her name), the chorus praises him as a good citizen—Dikaiopolis was never praised by the Acharnians as a good citizen—but he is not satisfied with this; he is satisfied when the chorus praises him as the savior of all human beings. But when the chorus goes on to say that they will always regard him as the first, second only to the gods, he himself lays claim to be less than a savior of all human beings: The chorus has proved to be unable to do justice to his merits.

The next step is to worship Eirene with prayer and sacrifice. It becomes clear that at any rate the Eirene whom Trygaios and his servant now see is a statue: She is only spoken about (923). The master accepts the servant's suggestion that they sacrifice a sheep so that the Athenians will become lamblike to one another and to their allies: Who would be so foolish as to wish that they should become lamblike to all Greeks, let alone to all men? The chorus responds in a pious mood; it never was and never will be as pious as it is now; the reason is that it anticipates the coincidence of the will of a god with the will of Chance or the presence of a deity (939–46). When the preparations for the sacrifice are completed, Trygaios and the servant pray to the goddess. Trygaios simply and nobly prays to Eirene, as the mistress of choruses and weddings, that she accept their sacrifice. The servant prays to her not to act any more like a coquette who, after having attracted a man's attention, makes herself invisible: Eirene formerly trifled with the wishes of the lovers of peace; in the servant's view she is not as philanthropic as we were led to believe. Trygaios, associating himself with the servant's prayer, asks Eirene to give the Greeks all her blessings, in particular by making them somewhat more gentle and by filling the Athenian market—not merely a private market like that of Dikaiopolis (cf. 999–1005 with *Acharnians* 729 ff. and 860 ff.) —with the delicacies of Megara and Boiotia. Then the sheep is sacrificed— not on the altar of Eirene, who abhors slaughter—by the servant according to the requirements of the art of cooking, while Trygaios proceeds according to the art of the soothsayer. The chorus praises Trygaios for his consummate wisdom and his resourceful daring, for having suffered like Odysseus, not after having destroyed a holy city, but in order to save one. Trygaios is the perfect votary of the goddess Eirene.

While Trygaios and the servant prepare the meal, Hierokles appears, an utterer of oracles, looking like a boaster and being one. Before he has said a word, Trygaios knows that he is opposed to the peace, while the servant suspects that he has been attracted by the smell of the sacrifice. When Hierokles asks first what the sacrifice is and to which god it is offered, and then demands the firstlings, master and servant pretend not to hear anything and continue with their proceedings; but Trygaios is eventually compelled to tell him that the sacrifice is for Eirene. Hierokles is shocked by their folly, by their ignorance of what the gods think and will; Trygaios is only amused by Hierokles' involuntarily ludicrous language. According to Hierokles it was against the gods' will that Eirene has now been unfettered; the war should not cease before a wolf marries a lamb. No one knows better than Trygaios that Hierokles states the truth about the will of the gods (cf. 371–72), but having measured the power behind that will, he is in no way disturbed; he limits himself to pointing out the absurdity of a wolf marrying a lamb. One could defend Hierokles against Trygaios' mockery by taking the oracle to mean that as long as the various beings retain their natures—and, in particular, as long as the Athenians remain Athenians and the Spartans remain Spartans—there will not be peace; the unfettering of Eirene is tantamount to changing the natures of things that only the gods can change and that they will change for the sake of man in their own good time; for, from the gods' point of view, men are small beings, and therefore war among men does not seem as terrible to the gods as it does to the men themselves. Trygaios must be understood to mean that while the gods beautify life and reduce its terror —even war seen as the god Polemos is not as terrible as war itself—by this very fact they increase the terror of life or make men worse than they are in themselves. Or, more simply, while it is true that as long as things possess their natures, there will be war, it is also true that the very possibility of war requires that there be long periods of peace between wars, or that the permanence of war can not possibly mean the permanence of the present war; in fact, Trygaios sees no difficulty in Athens and Sparta ruling Greece jointly, which joint rule is far from excluding a joint war against the barbarians. After having continued for a while to assert in oracular language that the peace is premature, Hierokles asks Trygaios what sort of oracle he has followed in sacrificing. Trygaios has followed the peace-loving Homer. Hierokles rejects the authority of Homer in favor of that of the Sybil and of Bakis. This does not prevent him from demanding to partake of the sacrificial meat—a demand that Trygaios regards as premature or not yet welcome to the gods; Hierokles will get his share as soon as a wolf marries a lamb. The boaster, who is soon discovered to be also a thief, is beaten by master and servant and chased away by them.

The defeat of the last attack by the enemies of peace calls for a special celebration. Hierokles' forcible departure is immediately followed by the second parabasis. The second parabasis of the *Peace* makes up for the quasi-deficiencies of the first; it consists of a strophe and an antistrophe as well as of an epirrhema and an antepirrhema; it is completely silent about the poet and even about the chorus as chorus; it is devoted to the praise of peace and country life, but it is silent about Eirene. Eirene had not been mentioned in the first parabasis either; but this was not strange, since the first parabasis did not refer at all to the theme of the play, whereas the second parabasis does. The farmers, who in fact radically disagree with Hierokles' view that the time for peace has not yet come, are proud of their military prowess and despise those Athenians who are lions at home while they run away from battles against gods or men (cf. *Wasps* 18–19). These ordinarily pious men who refer here four times to the god are not only warlike—Hermes had made them responsible for the war— but are prepared to do battle against the gods as well, presumably when the will of the gods and the will of chance do not coincide, or when they have chance on their side: The gods willed the continuation of the war and Chance willed the simultaneous death of Brasidas and Kleon.

After the farmers have had their say, the artisans appear. They appear in two groups. The first group consists of a sickle maker and a maker of jars. They are happy about the peace and the boost that it has given to their business and are therefore grateful to Trygaios; they offer to give him as many of their products as he likes. Trygaios, whom the spokesman for this group calls thrice by his name—Hierokles had never called him by name—invites the two men to partake of the wedding dinner. The second group consists of a merchant of armor, a helmet maker, a maker of spears, and a maker of crests. They are unhappy because the peace has ruined their business; their products are no longer of any use and hence of any value; Trygaios merely pokes fun at them. His conversation with the war-loving artisans is about five times as long as his conversation with the peace-loving artisans. Hierokles too possesses an art. The large majority of the artisans is in favor of war. The farmers, who had their say between the Hierokles scene and the artisans scene, while now being fervent lovers of peace, can not be regarded, as we have seen, as simply peace-loving. As for the peace-loving artisans, they love primarily their gain and not peace. The city is an association dedicated to war. The scenes revealing the posture of the actual citizens toward war and peace are followed by a scene revealing the posture of the future citizens, repre-sented by the two sons of two of Trygaios' invited guests. (The two boys remind us of Trygaios' two young girls.) Boy A, the son of Lamachos, attempts to cite warlike verses taken chiefly from Homer. Trygaios, swearing by Dionysos, stops him; he wishes him to cite poetry praising the eating of delightful food; but, having made an effort to comply with Trygaios' wish, he relapses into his war-loving habits. Trygaios chases him away and asks boy B, the son of Kleonymos, a sensible father, i.e., a notori-ous coward, to sing something different, and his desire is fulfilled. While he sends Lamachos' son away, he welcomes Kleonymos' son into his house. The exchange with the son of Lamachos is considerably more extensive than the exchange with the son of Kleonymos. Only the sons of the cowards, it seems, can be depended on to carry the torch of the con-demnation of war into the next generation. From the point of view of the city at any rate, the dedication to Eirene—as distinguished from mere exhaustion by war—is cowardice. Trygaios, the comic poet, the perfect votary of Eirene, has no pacifist illusions. Lamachos, as distinguished from Hierokles, is one of his invited guests; Trygaios is closer to Lamachos (and Kleonymos) than he is to Hierokles. After Eirene has moved her head, no one can doubt that she is a goddess, but she surely is not the highest goddess, the ruler of all gods and all men. And no one can doubt that she will make herself invisible again in the future, especially in the city of the warlike goddess Pallas Athena.[45]

Thanks to the return for the present of Eirene, i.e., of public peace, the play ends in perfect harmony between the poet and the chorus. While Dikaiopolis' private peace precluded such harmony and therefore required that the Acharnians be deprived of the dinner following the play, the chorus of the *Peace* will partake of the dinner as a matter of course: Trygaios exhorts the chorus to eat heartily, and the chorus agrees heartily with that exhortation. Thereafter Opora is brought forth for the bridal procession. In the *Peace*, as well as in the *Acharnians*, the design of the man responsible for the action of the play is fulfilled according to his heart's desire; whereas the designs of neither Demosthenes, Strepsiades, nor of Bdelykleon receive such a fulfillment: Aristophanes demonstrates *ad oculos* the supremacy of the comic poet. After the wedding old Trygaios will live with his new wife in the country as a vinedresser, indistinguishable from all other vinedressers or farmers, except for the heavenly or at any rate unusual origin or background of his wife. His conduct will not even remotely remind us of that of any artisans, let alone of Phidias or any other maker of statues of gods or of gods; he will be a simple worshiper of the gods worshiped by all Greeks. Surely in this respect he is the opposite of Socrates. Dikaiopolis, the man of the private peace and the benefactor only of himself, stands midway between Trygaios and Socrates, for Dikaiopolis knows at least that he must be concerned with peace and war, while Socrates is wholly unpolitical. In another respect, however, Trygaios stands midway between Socrates and Dikaiopolis; Trygaios' bringing about public peace, as distinguished from Dikaiopolis' bringing about private peace, requires an action against the gods that has at least a faint resemblance to Socrates' action or rather speech against the gods. While Socrates denies the existence of the gods and turns his back on the city, the comic poet in the *Acharnians* turns his back on the city but does not act against the gods, and the comic poet in the *Peace* acts in harmony with the city but against the gods. Trygaios' actions, as well as the actions of Dikaiopolis and of Socrates, are not political inasmuch as they are actions unauthorized by the city. The individual is not simply a part of the city, just as the gods are not simply the gods of the city. The individual is lower than the city, and the gods are higher than the city; the city is between the individual and the gods. But there is also a direct connection between the individuals and the gods: Not all sacrifices and prayers are public.[46] The Aristophanean comedy reproduces the connection between the highest and the lowest and thus fulfills its duty to what is between.

The Aristophanean comedy is a copy or mirror of life, inasmuch as it starts mostly from the predicaments of ordinary people. Yet it shows how the people concerned overcome, or attempt to overcome, those predicaments in a laughable, inept, fantastic manner. Starting from the common or familiar it moves through the impossible or into the impossible. Of the plays hitherto discussed, the recourse to the impossible is most glaring in the *Peace*. In this respect the *Peace* is at the opposite pole from the *Wasps*. This is in agreement with the themes of the two plays. The *Wasps* exhibits the most common, the lowest ingredient of comedy by showing how Delphi-inspired malice is transformed into the malice peculiar to comedy in the case of a man who is malicious by nature.

5 *The Birds*

This is the only Aristophanean play whose entire action takes place far from Athens. It differs from the plays hitherto discussed in that it opens with a dialogue between two Athenian citizens who present themselves as such. These two men—Euelpides (Hopeful or the son of Hopeful) and Peisthetairos (a hybrid of "persuader of his comrade" and "trustworthy comrade")—have literally turned their backs on the city. They are prompted by the desire to escape from the restlessness or busybodyness of that grand city, especially from the perpetual litigation, to a place or a city that is tranquil. They wish to become members of a tranquil city already in existence, more tranquil even than the most tranquil city known to them, but perhaps at the same time as grand as Athens: a tranquil Athens. Since they know of no such place, they wish to find out from Tereus where they might find it. Tereus had once been a human being, in fact a king married to an Athenian woman, and then he became a hoopoe, while his wife became a nightingale; he is therefore the natural link between Athenians and birds. Being now a bird, Tereus has a comprehensive view of the whole earth; he might have seen from above a quiet place hidden away in an inaccessible valley. Yet, in order to find the bird Tereus, they themselves must be guided by birds. Each of them has bought a bird from a bird seller in Athens for this purpose. At the beginning of the play we see them lost in the desolate region to which they came by following or obeying their birds (5, 7) as if they were birds of omen: While turning their backs on the city, they have not turned their backs on the gods.

In the *Acharnians*, the *Knights*, and the *Clouds*, the design is conceived within the play in the first 128 or so verses. In the *Wasps* and the *Peace*—the plays beginning with dialogues between slaves—the design had been conceived prior to the play by the slaves' masters. In the *Birds* too the design antedates the play, but it is not clear at the beginning by whom it was conceived. But if one considers the fact that in the plays hitherto discussed the individual who explains the situation as it exists at the beginning of the play—regardless of whether he explicitly addresses the audience (as Demosthenes in the *Knights*) or not (as Dikaiopolis in the *Acharnians* and Strepsiades in the *Clouds*)—is responsible for the design unless he is literally a slave, and that Euelpides fulfills this function in the *Birds* by addressing the audience, one will be inclined to assume that the design to leave Athens for a quiet place was Euelpides'. This is not to deny that Peisthetairos shows a certain ascendancy over his comrade from the beginning (56–59).

At the beginning of the play the two Athenians are in a state of despair. Their two birds—Euelpides' jackdaw, which cost one obol, and Peisthetairos' crow, which cost three obols, the equivalent of a juryman's pay (*Knights* 255)—point in opposite directions, the jackdaw pointing forward and the crow pointing backward. The two men do not know therefore which way to turn. They do not even know where they are. They have literally come to the end of all roads. Yet precisely this fact proves to mean that they have arrived at the end of their journey. The contradictory commands given by the two birds, far from refuting the wisdom of following or obeying birds, justify it; "forward" and "backward," canceling each other out, say "here." In fact, very shortly afterward both birds point to something on high, to a habitation of birds, to the habitation of the hoopoe, Tereus. At Euelpides' call, the hoopoe's servant, who is of course also a bird, appears. When he sees the two men with their birds, he takes them for bird catchers and is frightened to death. The two Athenians are no less frightened by the servant bird. Euelpides, who is the first to recover from his fright, reassures the bird by telling it that they are not human beings, but birds. Being a bird Euelpides has some difficulty in understanding how a bird can be in need of a servant; he learns from the servant bird that it was originally the human servant of Tereus. At Euelpides' request it leaves in order to call Tereus. While the two Athenians wait for Tereus, Peisthetairos, who had been more frightened than his comrade, has the impudence to accuse the latter of cowardice; Euelpides dismisses with polite contempt his comrade's pretense to bravery. Euelpides is here clearly superior to Peisthetairos.

Tereus appears. His looks amaze and amuse Euelpides, who for the time being is the only one to converse with the bird-man, since Peisthetairos has just suffered a remarkable setback at the hands of his comrade. Euelpides' questions seem to reveal to Tereus an astonishing ignorance about birds (105–7). Tereus in his turn is in no way amused by the looks of his visitors. When he asks the two men why they have come to him, Euelpides replies that since he was first a human being like them, who had debts and took no pleasure in paying them, and then he became a bird, he understands everything that man and bird understand (their coming to Tereus has a remote resemblance to Strepsiades' coming to Socrates); they hope therefore that he might be able to tell them where to find a pleasant and soft city. Tereus takes it for granted that Euelpides, who seeks a tranquil city and loathes the Athenian jury system, seeks an aristocratically ruled city, but in this he proves to be wholly mistaken. Euelpides seeks a city where one's friends invite one in the strongest terms to a marriage feast, rather than to help them when they are in distress. Peisthetairos longs for things of the same kind, but not for the same things. He would like to live in a city where a friend feels offended if one does not pay amorous attention to his son in his bloom. Euelpides is concerned with the pleasures of the table while Peisthetairos, who is much more of a political man than his comrade, is concerned with homosexual pleasures.[47]

Tereus proposes to his visitors three cities, two of them Greek, that would meet their requirements, but Euelpides rejects each of them. At this point, when his design seems to have come to nought, it suddenly occurs to him to wonder whether life with the birds would not be the best solution for them; Tereus has shown by deed that a former human being can live among the birds, and he seems to be quite satisfied with his life. Tereus can not deny that living among the birds has great advantages: no need for money and plenty of such food as is equally pleasant and good for birds and for men. In the words of Euelpides, the life of the birds is a life of newlyweds. Euelpides is about to become a simple member of the society of birds when his comrade conceives a much grander design by improving on Euelpides' conceit. The first step would be that the birds change their way of life by no longer flying in all directions restlessly, but settling down and founding a single city. Tereus, swearing by Dionysos, is all in favor of the birds' settling down; it is safe to assume that Euelpides, who has never done any flying and loves the soft life, is also in favor of it. Yet Tereus fails to see what kind of city the birds could found. In order to make him see it, Peisthetairos asks him to look in different directions, just as in a similar scene of the *Knights* Demosthenes asks the sausage seller (the natural ruler) to look in different directions.[48] Yet Peisthetairos, as distinguished from Demosthenes, asks his pupil what he has seen on looking around. Tereus has seen the clouds and the sky. He learns now from Peisthetairos that the sky, the celestial sphere, the *polos,* can be made into the city (*polis*) of the birds. One is inclined to say that the city par excellence, the city in accordance with the whole or with nature, is the city that can be founded only by the birds. By occupying and fortifying the place between the heaven (the place of the gods) and the earth (the place of men), the birds will become the rulers of both gods and men, the universal rulers. Human beings depend of course on the gods; the gods in their turn, however, depend on the smell from the sacrifices offered to them by men. That smell must pass through the yawning void that the birds alone can occupy; the birds can control that lifeline and, if they so desire, destroy the gods by Melian famine.[49] Peisthetairos compares the situation obtaining between human beings, the birds, and the gods to that obtaining between the Athenians, the Boiotians, and Delphi; the comparison is satisfactory insofar as it implies that the Athenians are the human beings par excellence, but it also has its drawback; he points out the drawback and remedies it at the same time by speaking of "us Athenians" and "us birds" (188, 191). He transforms himself into a man-bird. The bird-man Tereus is elated by the proposal. He swears in a way by the clouds among other things, but not by any of the gods who have proper names, that he is willing to found the birds' city together with Peisthetairos, provided the other birds agree. Euelpides however is silent. Peisthetairos' grand design, which will prove to be entirely successful, seems to conflict with the desire for rest, for freedom from politics, for freedom that prompted him to journey together with Euelpides to Tereus. Yet perhaps this desire was in him only a momentary whim; we have observed more than one sign of his being at bottom a political man, a busybody. Above all, he may have realized, or remembered, that one has no choice but to be either hammer or anvil, that a man can not be free unless he participates somehow in political power, and that the rule exercised by the city tends to expand as far as it can: The life of rest requires security and protection, i.e., the city, and if the security is to be complete, universal empire, rule over all men, nay, rule over all men and all gods, since a man's happiness is threatened not only by his fellow men but also and above all by the envious or whimsical gods.

Everything depends now on whether the other birds will approve of Peisthetairos' design. He asks Tereus who should set it forth to the birds, and Tereus replies that Peisthetairos should do it, since the birds have been taught by Tereus to understand Greek. The question is merely rhetorical.

At first glance it seems that only Tereus could persuade the birds. Peisthetairos' question implies, however, that he considers himself to be as capable of persuading the birds as Tereus is, and since he does not yet know that the birds understand Greek, that he considers himself to be capable of persuading the birds—or, for that matter, any beings—without using the Greek or any other human language; he regards himself as an Orpheus who can bewitch all beings.[50] He asks Tereus next to call the birds together. Tereus undertakes to do this together with his wife, the nightingale. Peisthetairos urges him not to tarry. The song with which Tereus awakens his wife and calls on her to sing of the only thing of which she can sing—their much-lamented son, Itys—reminds us of something that we might have completely forgotten, owing to the two Athenians' preoccupations: of the divine beauty of music, which points to Apollon and his choruses of gods. The beauty of the gods belongs together with such love as unites Tereus, his wife, and their son; no such love prompts the two Athenians, who have deserted their beloved ones, if they had any, without any regret. This is not to deny that Tereus' praise of the gods is somewhat strange, coming as it does immediately after he has accepted with enthusiasm Peisthetairos' proposal to destroy the gods. The nightingale's music response calls forth a raptured praise by Euelpides, who is rebuked by Peisthetairos for thus holding up the business at hand. Tereus follows up his wife's wordless call by summoning the various birds to join him in order to hear and to discuss the novel conceit of a shrewd old man who has come to them.

It takes some time until the birds assemble. Peisthetairos is already becoming somewhat impatient, but then he hears the first bird arriving. First the birds come one by one and then in clouds. Tereus identifies them for his visitors, who comment on them. When the birds have all arrived, they form the chorus; since they have never been organized before, or since they belong to different kinds, they can not make their entry in the regular fashion in which the choruses of the preceding plays did. The Athenians, who are first merely astonished by the birds, are eventually frightened by them. Their fear proves to be justified. Tereus tells the birds that he has called them together to hear a just speech, which in addition is pleasant and useful and which stems from two old men who have arrived. The leader of the chorus accuses Tereus of having committed a most heinous crime, of having transgressed the most sacred laws of gods and birds by not only speaking to human beings but even receiving them, members of that impious race which since its beginning has been the mortal enemy of the birds; the two foreigners must be executed immediately, even before any action is taken against Tereus who, after all, is no longer a human being. Peisthetairos sees himself and his comrade lost. Euelpides tells him that he alone is responsible for their disaster, for it was Peisthetairos who led him away from Athens (339–40). Peisthetairos took Euelpides with him because he needed a follower, just as Tereus when becoming a bird needed a follower (73). We thus learn that even the original plan—the plan to leave Athens for a quiet city, or perhaps the plan to find out from Tereus the location of a quiet city—stemmed from Peisthetairos' fertile and restless brain: Precisely because he loathes activity, Euelpides might have stayed forever in active Athens; his very following Peisthetairos was because of his finding it easier to give in to Peisthetairos' importunities than to resist them. The only design that was altogether Euelpides' own was that of becoming an ordinary member of the society of birds as it is and always was.

The birds arrange themselves to attack the two men, or rather to kill and devour them. Euelpides is altogether helpless, while Peisthetairos reveals himself to possess surpassing generalship. Tereus attempts to stop his fellow birds. He grants them that all men are by nature the enemies of the birds, but he asserts all the more strongly that the two men in front of them are the birds' friends by their thought. They have come to teach the birds something useful; the wise learn from enemies, rather than from friends; it is from enemies that one learns how to be cautious, how to fortify cities, and how to build a navy. The birds can not but admit the truth of this lesson: The good is obviously not one's own or the ancestral. In addition, as they now remember, they have fared well hitherto by never opposing a recommendation made by Tereus. Tereus has saved the Athenians, at least for the time being. Yet they remain on their guard; they may still have to fight and to die fighting. Euelpides wonders where they would be buried; Peisthetairos replies that they would be buried in Athens with military honors when they tell the Athenian authorities that they have fallen in battle—he assumes that they will somehow survive their deaths. Yet the danger is over. At the very least the birds are now willing to listen to what the strangers have to say.

The birds ask Tereus who their visitors are, where they come from, and with what design. That design can in their view be only an act of chance (404–12). Tereus tells them that the two strangers long for the way of life of the birds and wish to join in it. The birds wonder whether Peisthetairos, whose pre-eminence they must have divined, expects some profit from living with them—whether he thus expects to rule over his enemies or to help his friends. It seems that they have also divined what kind of a man Peisthetairos is. Or rather, they can not even imagine that any human being might simply prefer to live among birds rather than among human beings; in other words, it seems that they would be utterly unable to understand Euelpides. Tereus replies that Peisthetairos' design goes much beyond what the birds surmise, that he has in mind an unbelievable and unspeakable prosperity of the birds; to say the least, he does not make clear what advantage Peisthetairos expects to derive from his design. This is not surprising, since Peisthetairos himself had not spoken of such an advantage. When the birds wonder whether Peisthetairos is not mad, Tereus assures them of his cleverness in terms that remind us of the qualities promised by Socrates to Strepsiades (*Clouds* 260). Thereupon the birds are naturally most eager to hear Peisthetairos' proposal.

They have some lingering doubt whether they can trust Man, that being full of wiles, but they also know that they are rather stupid and might therefore be helped by human advice. They promise Peisthetairos that if anything good comes from his advice, he will share it with them; they are not so stupid as to believe that he is indifferent to his own advantage. They listen to his speech without raising any objection; there is no debate between Peisthetairos and the birds like the debates between Dikaiopolis and the Acharnians, Dikaiopolis and Lamachos, Demosthenes and the sausage seller, the sausage seller and Kleon, Socrates and Strepsiades, or Bdelykleon and Philokleon. Peisthetairos has won his case with the six verses (375–80) by which Tereus has persuaded his fellow birds that it is wise to learn even from the hereditary enemies of one's race. Hence the decisive action is Peisthetairos' persuasion of Tereus. That action took considerably longer (162–93) than the one by which Tereus persuaded the birds, although Tereus is not a mortal enemy of all human beings as the birds are by nature. The birds can hate, fight, kill, and devour, but they can not argue and contradict; they remind us of hoplites (353, 402, 448), but not of members of the Assembly. The closest approximation to Tereus' persuasion of the birds is Trygaios' persuasion of Hermes by means of meat and by the assertion that Sun and Moon conspire against the Greek gods (*Peace* 192, 406–13). In the decisive respect the birds resemble the gods rather than human beings. No wonder that they can take the place of the gods.

In explaining his design to the birds, Peisthetairos proceeds very differently from the way he did when he explained it to Tereus. When explain-

ing it to Tereus he merely said that if the birds settle down and fortify
the region between heaven and earth, they will rule over all men and can
destroy the gods: He did not even attempt to prove that the proposed
action of the birds is just. Tereus did not need such proof; for him Peisthetairos' proposal is evidently just (316). In the case of the birds, Peisthetairos deems it necessary to show that the birds have a just title to
universal rule. Perhaps the birds are more just or more pious than Tereus.
They surely are less intelligent than Tereus. According to what Peisthetairos tells the birds, they were formerly the kings of everything, even of
Zeus, since they are more ancient than even Earth or simply the earth. As
one might say, the mere fact that chaos, the yawning void that separates
heaven and earth, and in which the birds roam, is older than heaven and
earth proves that the birds are older than heaven and earth. The birds'
being unaware of how ancient they are is due to their stupidity, easy-
goingness, and failure to study Esop. Since they are the most ancient beings, kingship belongs rightly to them. There are many proofs that an-
ciently not the gods but the birds ruled men. In the first place, each of the
three leading nations—Persia, Greece, and Egypt (and Phoenicia) [51]—was
ruled by a bird before it was ruled by kings. The original ruler of the
Persians was the cock, still called the Persian bird. As Euelpides observes,
the cock struts like the Persian king (the boaster par excellence); accordingly, as Peisthetairos observes and Euelpides confirms by an experience
of his own, the cock still exercises rule over all men to some extent. Secondly, even at the time when human beings ruled as kings over individual
Greek cities, a bird sat on their scepters and partook of the gifts that the
kings received. Lastly and above all, Zeus, who reigns at present, wears an
eagle above his head, while Athena is accompanied by an owl and Apollon
by a hawk; these birds receive their share in the sacrifices before the gods
do. One might receive the impression that kingship moved from the birds
to the gods via men. Be this as it may, from all that has been said it follows that in the olden times the birds were held by all to be grand and
holy, whereas now they are held to be slaves and fools. No sanctuary pro-
tects them against the bird catchers who sell them for human consumption, especially to gluttons.

The birds are deeply moved by Peisthetairos' account of their former
greatness and therewith of their degradation. They trace their degradation to their fathers' cowardice. It does not occur to them that their
fathers might have succumbed to the gods' wiles. In their gratitude to the
human being who has reminded them of their original grandeur, they

entrust to him as to their savior themselves and their young, thus abandoning their kingship even before they have recovered it. They wish to learn from him how they can recover their former kingship. According to Peisthetairos they must form a single city, then build a brick wall around everything that lies between heaven and earth and thereafter reclaim from Zeus the dominion that he has usurped. If Zeus fails to comply, they must declare a holy war against him and forbid the gods passage through the birds' territory. Without waiting for Zeus' reply, they must tell the human beings henceforth to sacrifice to the birds in the first place and to the gods only afterward. These suggestions fall short of what Peisthetairos had proposed to Tereus. Peisthetairos does not propose to the birds that they starve the gods. It is easy to see why he does not advise them to command men to stop sacrificing to the gods altogether; the change from the present practice would be too great. But what is true of men is likely to be at least as true of birds as well. This would explain why he speaks differently to the birds than he did to Tereus, if Tereus could be presumed to have a reason of his own for hating the gods. By proceeding now in a more conciliatory manner Peisthetairos does not forego the advantages of sterner proceedings; by building a wall around their region the birds become able to inflict on the gods any evil they might like to inflict. Tereus asks Peisthetairos how men will regard the birds as gods, seeing that the birds fly and have wings. Peisthetairos had always spoken of the gods and the birds as two different kinds of beings; he had not treated the birds as gods. According to his proposal the gods will be subject to the birds without the birds becoming gods, so that the highest beings will henceforth be natural beings of a certain kind. Tereus however wants the birds to become gods simply and formally. His question implies that men will not recognize the birds as gods since they are accustomed to understand by gods only beings like the Olympian gods (603, 606); he raises without knowing it the question as to what is a god. Peisthetairos replies to Tereus' explicit question with the remark that many gods fly and have wings. This leads, however, to a new difficulty. If the Olympian gods are winged in one way or another—for instance, Zeus' lightning bolts are winged—men might think that the gods, having all powers of the birds and in addition other powers, are superior to the birds and hence might continue to recognize and worship only the Olympian gods. In that case, Peisthetairos declares, the birds must starve men in order to convince them of the birds' power and the gods' lack of power. He thus appeals to the birds' ancestral hostility to the human race; he foreshadows Alkibiades' betraying Athens to Sparta. Yet he continues in a different vein. The birds must not leave matters at inflicting on men such harm as the gods can not repair; men will regard the birds as gods, as life, only if they see that by doing so they will get all good things; gods must be philanthropic. Consider wealth first. Wealth is not on Olympus, but the birds can procure it. As it is, men consult the birds in order to prosper; they have only to come to know that the birds never deceive them, and they will regard the birds as gods. The prospect of a thoroughly reliable divination is so appealing that even Euelpides is no longer willing to live with the birds, but eager to live again with men. Health and a long life are indeed on Olympus, but being well off includes being well; and the birds are so long-lived that they can easily give a part of their life span to men. The human being Euelpides, who should know, is satisfied that human beings will be much better off under the kingship of the birds than they are under the kingship of Zeus. Peisthetairos adds as a final recommendation that in the new era men will no longer be compelled to build expensive temples, or to journey to Delphi and to Ammon, or to bring expensive sacrifices. He thus revokes his temporary concession that men shall continue to bring sacrifices to the gods, although only after having sacrificed to the birds. The birds are now entirely willing to march with Peisthetairos against the gods: They will supply the strength; he must supply the wisdom. It goes without saying, for it has been shown by deed, that both the birds and Peisthetairos possess the required courage: They will not throw away their shields in heaven (cf. *Wasps* 22–23). The kingship of the birds will be the kingship of Peisthetairos. One must wonder whether the divinity of the birds is also the divinity of Peisthetairos. His mortality can surely no longer be an objection to his divinity.

With the birds' entire acceptance of Peisthetairos' proposal the Assembly has come to an end. In the opinion of Tereus they must now act without delay. He asks the two men to come with him into his nest and to tell him their names. We thus learn that Euelpides happens to belong not indeed to the same deme but to the same phyle as Socrates.[52] Before going in, Peisthetairos asks Tereus how he and Euelpides can live with the birds although they can not fly. Tereus knows of a root by the eating of which one becomes winged; although he knew of the birds' enmity to his human guests, it had not occurred to him to think of that root. There might be some overcrowding in the nest but for the fact that the leader of the chorus asks Tereus to send his wife, the nightingale, out so that the other birds can play with her. The two Athenians support that wish,

Peisthetairos because he is eager to preserve the birds' good will, Euelpides because he is eager to gaze on the beautiful female. Both are enraptured by her beauty, but only Euelpides desires to embrace her.

While Tereus and his guests partake of food and the majority of the birds amuse themselves with the nightingale and begin with the building of the wall, the parabasis takes place. The sole subject of the parabasis is the birds—their being the most ancient gods and what it means for men to live with the birds or to live like birds. The birds neither praise nor blame Athens, and they say nothing about the poet. Hence the parabasis of the *Birds* can be said to stand at the opposite pole from the parabasis of the *Peace*, the sole theme of which is the poet himself. The *Peace* and the *Birds* are the only plays hitherto discussed that present actions against Zeus. But while the action of the *Peace* is only an *ad hoc* revolt, the action of the *Birds* aims at the complete and permanent change of the government of the world. The revolt presented in the *Peace* is the work of the comic poet: The revolt presented in the *Birds* is not the work of the comic poet; Peisthetairos is not the comic poet. As we have learned from the *Clouds*, Aristophanes' innovation would not go beyond enlarging the traditional pantheon.

Since the (first) parabasis of the *Birds* is altogether silent about the poet, it can be entirely a part of the action of the play as no (first) parabasis of the previously discussed plays is.[53] In the parabasis the birds attempt to win over the human race to their cause. It is only an inevitable accident that as the chorus of an Aristophanean comedy they can not reach the whole human race, but only the Athenians. The case of the Clouds is different; in their parabasis they address the Athenians alone because they desire to be recognized as goddesses by the city of Athens in particular; they are less ambitious than the birds. While one can not compare the birds to the Clouds in cleverness, one must admit that the birds do not proceed without guile: In their solemn address to the human race they at most allude to the imminent revolt against the gods and men's participation in it.

In the parabasis in the narrow sense, the birds develop fully the theme that the Orpheuslike Peisthetairos had developed in his speech to the birds as distinguished from his private conversation with Tereus: The birds, being older than the earth and the gods, are the most ancient beings. They say many things that Peisthetairos had not said. In order to appreciate properly their theology, one must keep in mind the difference between them and Peisthetairos: They are less intelligent than their savior, but better singers than he; their account of the origins reminds us of Hesiod's. They now regard themselves entirely as gods; they describe themselves as deathless, being always, ethereal, ageless, and minding the imperishable. They teach the ephemeral mortals who live in darkness the truth about the things aloft, since they know the birth of the birds and the coming into being of gods, rivers, Erebos, and Chaos. Their teaching expels that of Prodikos. Prodikos had been mentioned by the Clouds together with Socrates as one of their favorites. He apparently was as much a "Melian" as the Aristophanean Socrates.[54] Like Strepsiades, the birds and Peisthetairos do not deny that the gods are, but assert only that they can lose their kingship or power. Socrates' denial of Zeus' being the cause of lightning, for instance, is implicitly rejected by Peisthetairos (576 ff.).

According to the birds, there were four things in the beginning, not of course the four elements, but Chaos, Night, Erebos, and Tartaros; earth, air, and heaven, to say nothing of gods and rivers, came later. Without impregnation, black-winged Night laid an egg in the infinite womb of Erebos; out of that egg came gold-winged Eros, who resembles rotations of windlike swiftness. Mating with winged Chaos in vast Tartaros by night, Eros generated the birds; the birds are the first things brought to light—by Eros or anything. When Eros had mixed everything with everything else—presumably Chaos, Night, Erebos, and Tartaros—there came into being heaven, ocean, earth, and the indestructible gods. The birds say nothing here about the genesis of air. While it is easy for anyone trained by Peisthetairos to see that there could be birds while there was no earth (469–74), it is hard to see how there could be birds—ethereal beings (689) —prior to ether or air. Surely one of the darkest points in the birds' dark account of the origins is the status of air, of the principle par excellence according to Socrates' account.[55] No less dark is the status of Eros: Is Eros, who antedates the birds and still more all other gods, himself a god? Is not a god necessarily a descendant of gods, and hence a first generator of gods not himself a god, just as an Athenian being the son of an Athenian father and an Athenian mother, the first Athenian cannot have been an Athenian?[56] The darkness regarding Eros is connected with the darkness regarding the birds: Does the generating of the birds by Eros precede Eros' mixing of everything with everything, i.e., are the ingredients of the birds (if one can speak of ingredients in their case) radically different from those of all other beings? The birds' account has two foci, the air and Eros. The birds are silent as to the air, the Socratic principle, and they speak very emphatically, not to say clearly, about Eros: They replace air (or ether) by Eros (cf. 574–75). Surely according to their account Eros is the first of all bright or shining beings and the origin of all others, and the birds are Eros' firstlings, hence the most ancient of all gods, living with the lovers, especially with homosexual ones. Since they are the most ancient gods, they are the most beneficent ones. By their seasonal arrivals and departures they indicate to the mortals the seasons and hence the different kinds of work to be done in different seasons by just and unjust men alike. By what they do unpredictably, they guide men as oracles, so much so that every omen is called a bird; they render unnecessary recourse to Apollon and the divinatory Muses. Since they procure for mortals every kind of happiness, not the least of which is wealth, they admonish them to treat them as gods. They go so far as to contrast their nearness to men with the remoteness of Zeus who, affecting stateliness, resides above the clouds: They do not speak of a revolt against Zeus' rule. The strophe of the parabasis, which calls on the woodland Muse, ends with a praise of the ancient tragic poet Phrynichos, the favorite of the Wasps; the antistrophe praises the effect of the swans' praising Apollon on the whole Olympus and the Lords dwelling there. The birds seem to be as pious as the Clouds, to say nothing of the knights.[57] Yet we must remember that Tereus had called on the nightingale to sing sacred hymns that would arouse the response of Apollon and of the choruses of the gods (209–22); in the parabasis there is no longer any reference to such response.

The birds go beyond making a general promise of happiness. In the epirrhema they exhort those spectators who wish to live pleasantly to join them, without making it a condition that those spectators regard the birds as gods. In their way they rejoin Euelpides as distinguished from Peisthetairos. They give this reason: Whatever is "by law" degrading "here" is noble or fine "there," with the birds; the life of the birds or with the birds is the life according to nature. In the first place, father-beating is base by law, but not with the birds. Besides, among the birds there is no distinction between citizens and foreigners, and between freemen and slaves; the birds' society is egalitarian and universal. In the antepirrhema they praise to the spectators the advantages and pleasures deriving from being winged. If a man is hungry while listening to a boring tragic chorus he can, if winged, fly home for lunch and then fly back to us, i.e., to the comic chorus, which will not bore him. Similarly, adultery is much safer for winged men than for unwinged ones. The birds' doctrine of the origins leads to the recommendations set forth by the Unjust Speech, just as the rejected Socratic doctrine leads to the demands for extreme continence and endurance. Socrates asserts the primacy of air or ether; the birds assert for all practical purposes the primacy of Eros. Socrates is led to debunking the things aloft; if we disregard, as we must, his provisional or outdoor teaching regarding the Clouds, we see that he does not leave room for any things by nature beautiful or noble. The birds however, by asserting the primacy of Eros, assign an unassailable place to the naturally festive and golden. As a consequence of this, Aristophanes is more tolerant of Zeus and the other gods than is his Socrates. Socrates' doctrine is radically a-Music because it has no place for Eros; his being unerotic reflects, or corresponds to, the fact that his doctrine is silent on Eros. But the birds' doctrine is erotic and therefore Music. If Aristophanes had been compelled to choose between Socrates' doctrine and the birds' doctrine, he would have chosen the birds' doctrine, a doctrine that, with the help of Parmenides and Empedocles, could easily have been stated in philosophic terms. This entitles us perhaps to say that Aristophanes is not opposed to philosophy simply, but only to a philosophy that, disregarding Eros, has no link with poetry. This would help us to understand the fitness of Plato's reply to Aristophanes: The only Platonic dialogue in which Aristophanes occurs as a character or in which Socrates is presented as conversing with poets is devoted to Eros, and Socrates' doctrine is shown therein to be more profoundly erotic than Aristophanes' or any other poet's. If someone wishes, he might even say that Socrates' ascribing his doctrine to Diotima indicates that in an earlier stage of his life he did not properly appreciate Eros. Be this as it may, by stressing the opposition between Socrates' doctrine and the birds' doctrine, we do not intend to deny or even to conceal the important agreement between the two doctrines: Both doctrines transcend the sphere of *nomos*, of the city or of justice; both doctrines permit father-beating.

Peisthetairos and Euelpides reappear; in the meantime they have grown wings. Euelpides is somewhat more sensitive than his companion to the laughable character of their looks. In Peisthetairos' view the next two things to do are to find a name for the city of the birds and to sacrifice to the gods. Following a suggestion of Euelpides, Peisthetairos hits on the name of Cloudcuckootown. The name is meant to be suggestive of human and divine boasting; Peisthetairos is a boaster. After having made clear that in the new city the birds take the place of the old gods, Peisthetairos commands Euelpides to help the birds in the building of the wall and to send one herald to the gods above and another to the human beings below. He then turns to sacrificing to the new gods. Euelpides leaves with a mild curse on Peisthetairos and never returns. He uses the first decent occasion to disappear. He had wished to live quietly in a quiet city; it would have suited him very well to live with the birds as much as possible like a bird, i.e., to follow the exhortations that the birds address to the spectators in the parabasis; but the complete revolution of bird life that is being brought about by his formidable companion destroys his hope. Peisthetairos' grand design is not to his taste, although he is much too easygoing to work against it. When Peisthetairos proposed his design to Tereus, Euelpides greeted it with silence; when Peisthetairos presented it to the birds, Euelpides did not oppose it because acceptance of the plan by the birds was the only way out of mortal danger. The comments with which he accompanied Peisthetairos' speech to the birds were useless for persuading the birds, if amusing to the audience. Euelpides' absence from the second half of the *Birds* is no less important for the meaning of that play than Demosthenes' absence from the second half of the *Knights* is for the meaning of the *Knights*. There is, however, this difference between the two similar cases: While both Demosthenes and the sausage seller are political men, Euelpides as distinguished from the political Peisthetairos is an unpolitical man.

The sacrifice to the new gods (848, 862) causes some difficulty, since the action might mean that the birds sacrifice to the birds (cf. 853–54). Or must we understand by the new gods the Olympian gods? For the time being the difficulty is solved by Peisthetairos' calling in of a human priest, who prays to the Olympian birds to give their blessings to the Cloud-cuckootownians. But the priest's invocations are much too broad in the view of Peisthetairos, who has no use for birds of prey in particular, given the scantiness of the sacrificial meat. He therefore tells the priest to go away and makes ready to bring the sacrifice himself. At this moment there arrives a poor, shivering poet who has made poems of various kinds for Cloudcuckootown and begs its founder both poetically and shamelessly for gifts. Peisthetairos gives him some warm clothes that he takes away from the priest. The poet leaves, reciting the beginning of another poem on the new city. Peisthetairos is not too pleased with the poet's visit, but his chief reaction to it is amazement about the speed with which the news of the foundation of the new city has reached the poet. Although nothing is impossible for this man, he has still preserved a sense for the difference between what is easy and what is not; in his dealing with the poet he acts on the maxim that one must help the poets. Before he can return to the sacrifice, he is again interrupted, this time by a soothsayer

who comes with an oracle of Bakis concerning the new city. He asserts
that according to the oracle Peisthetairos will not become an eagle in the
clouds unless he makes him considerable gifts. Peisthetairos replies to him
by reciting an Apollonian oracle that refers to the soothsayer as a boaster
who ought to be spanked; the visitor barely escapes being spanked by running away. Before Peisthetairos can even think of returning to the sacrifice, he is bothered by a third visitor, the central visitor—for there are
altogether five of them, the priest not being a visitor—the only one who
is mentioned by name: Meton, the famous geometer and astronomer. He
has come in order to "geometrize" the air with the help of a compass and
thus to lay out the plan of the new city. According to him, the air as a
whole is shaped very much like a stove. He wishes the market place of the
new city to resemble a star. When Peisthetairos hears these things, he
admires Meton in almost the same manner as Strepsiades admired Socrates
when he heard from the pupil how Socrates procured a dinner for his
group with the help of a compass (*Clouds* 175–80, 95–96). Meton comes
closer to Socrates (and his pupils) than any other Aristophanean character. In contradistinction to the poet and the soothsayer who preceded
him, he never mentions any divine beings, not even the Muses; nor does
he demand any gifts. Peisthetairos tells him that he loves him but, differing strikingly from Strepsiades, he has no use for him; there would be
too strong an opposition to him on the part of the citizens, who are violently opposed to all boasters. Peisthetairos did not refer to such an opposition when he dealt with the poet and the soothsayer. When Meton hears
of the danger threatening him, he is eager to leave; but before he can,
Peisthetairos beats him. However much he might love or admire Meton,
he is the founder of a city; and the city has no use for subtleties, at least
not for subtleties of the kind that Meton has to offer,[58] as distinguished
from the subtleties of poets and soothsayers. Let us not forget what we
learned in reading the *Knights*, namely, that the natural ruler is not in
need of any education. We can not help wondering how Euelpides would
have reacted to Meton. What had happened to Perikles on account of his
connection with Anaxagoras can not happen to Peisthetairos. It is obvious
that the principle underlying Peisthetairos' implicit rejection of "Socrates"
differs radically from that underlying the birds' implicit rejection of
"Socrates": The birds were not concerned with what the city needs. The
two visitors succeeding Meton are necessary so that Meton will occupy
the center of the visitors' scene; this is not to deny, of course, that they
are helpful in producing laughter. The first of them is a supervisor sent

by the city of Athens, which intends to treat Cloudcuckootown like any other of its dependencies. The second is a seller of decrees who wishes to sell Peisthetairos new laws—the democracy does not make a clear distinction between decrees and laws; those laws are of course Athenian. Both men, representing Athenian imperialism, are naturally thrown out by the embodiment of a much more lofty and comprehensive imperialism and properly spanked by him. He has long since thrown off the authority of the city of Athens.

The five-visitors' scene is immediately succeeded by the second parabasis. In the *Peace* the first parabasis was devoted exclusively to the poet and the second parabasis exclusively to the farmers. Since the first parabasis of the *Birds* was exclusively devoted to the birds and what we may call for once "birdism," the need for a second parabasis devoted to Athens on the one hand and to the poet on the other would seem to be evident. After the first parabasis Peisthetairos had said that the two things to do next were to give a name to the new city and to sacrifice to the gods. Although the good city is the city par excellence, the city according to nature, it is in need of conventional things. The city was given a name, but the sacrifice was not performed; the expected sacrifice scene became the five-visitors' scene. Given the central position of the Meton incident, we are tempted to say that the expulsion of Meton takes the place of the sacrifice or is interchangeable with the sacrifice. Needless to say, the sacrifice is not simply abandoned; it is performed "indoors" during the second parabasis. We are reminded of the *Clouds*, where the second parabasis concealed Pheidippides' indoor instruction.

In the strophe of the second parabasis the birds present themselves as the successors of Zeus: They see everything and rule everything, and to them all mortals turn with sacrifices and prayers. They tacitly admit that they do not see everything, but only everything on earth: They do not rise as high as the comic poet's dung beetle. Similarly, the only benefit that they claim to procure to the mortals is that they kill insects and other pests. They no longer raise the claims that they had raised in the first parabasis; somehow they seem to have become aware of their limitations. In the epirrhema, taking as their model the Athenians' persecution of the atheist Diagoras of Melos and of the tyrants, they announce grave penalties for bird catchers and the like; they are more punitive than even the Athenians, perhaps because bird catchers are more dangerous to birds than even atheists and tyrants are to human beings. Surely as we have partly learned from the Meton scene, impiety and high treason are as criminal in the new city as they were in the old cities. In the antistrophe the birds praise their felicity by showing how they spend the different seasons; we are gladdened to learn that the birds have no objections to nymphs and the Graces. In the antepirrhema, which reminds us of the second parabasis of the *Clouds*, they speak no longer as birds simply, but as the chorus of the *Birds;* hence the two strophes and the epirrhema belong together and form a whole, the center of which is of course the epirrhema. That whole is as much a part of the action of the play as the whole first parabasis. In the antepirrhema the birds tell the judges which benefits they will bestow on each of them, whether just or unjust, if they award the prize to the chorus, and which punishments they can expect if they fail to do so. Our expectation that the second parabasis will be devoted to Athens and in particular to the poet is then somewhat disappointed, especially if we consider the fact that even the antepirrhema is wholly silent about the virtues of the *Birds*. Aristophanes is then silent about himself in both parabaseis of the *Birds*. This silence is most fitting, given the fact that the play presents a successful rebellion against all gods worshiped by the city or against all old gods, or the success of an Athenian who simultaneously turned his back on the city of Athens and on the gods. This silence of the poet is closely related to Euelpides' disappearance. It is hardly necessary to stress the fact that the second parabasis no longer contains even an allusion to the exhortations addressed to men to live with the birds or to live like birds.

Peisthetairos reappears after having successfully completed his sacrifice indoors. He has barely expressed his surprise about not having had news about the progress of the building of the wall when a messenger arrives. He greets Peisthetairos as the ruler: The birds' having become aware of their being subject to a ruler who is not a bird explains why they have become aware of the limitations of their power. The messenger informs the ruler that the wall—a most beautiful and magnificent work, surpassing by far the wall of Babylon, to say nothing of the walls protecting Athens—has been completed by the birds and only by the birds: Euelpides, we surmise, has gone home, perhaps after having communicated to the birds Peisthetairos' commands (cf. 1160–61 with 841–42). Although Peisthetairos was the one who proposed to the birds that they build a wall surrounding the whole air, he is overwhelmed by the execution of his proposal: "In truth these things appear to me like lies." Following a suggestion of the chorus, we believe that it was less the execution of the plan than the quickness of the execution that appeared to Peisthetairos to border on the impossible. Surely the amazing feat of the birds does not endanger his rulership, for who does not know that the builders, however competent and quick, of walls however high and broad are subject to the political rulers? The birds are not only subject to Peisthetairos; they even work for him without pay. The birds' quick building of the wall appears in a new light during the next scene, which is opened by the arrival of another messenger, who is much too excited to greet Peisthetairos as a ruler. He announces that one of the gods connected with Zeus has entered the new city, i.e., the air, unobserved by the guards. The only thing known about this god is that he is winged; the birds of prey have been ordered to find and to arrest him. Peisthetairos gives out a general call to arms and puts on arms himself. Here is a situation that the birds by themselves could not handle; the birds, as distinguished from their human ruler, are powerless against the gods. As the chorus states, an unsayable war between the birds and the gods begins; the irruption of any further god into the air that separates heaven from earth must be prevented at all costs. At this moment the god who has already entered the air comes to sight: Iris. Neither her looks nor her name prove her divinity. She is wholly unaware of the situation; apparently the birds were unable to ascend to heaven in order to warn the gods with regard to the wall. The winged Peisthetairos commands that the winged goddess be arrested. The birds do not obey his command: Are they confused by the goddess' being winged? Peisthetairos is compelled to engage in a verbal contest with Iris in order to keep the birds in line (cf. 1211). It appears that Iris has entered the new city without having been impeded by any wall or by any birds doing guard duty, i.e., that Peisthetairos can not trust the birds. He tries to save the cause by saying that Iris has committed a capital crime; but Iris defeats him easily by replying that, being an immortal, she can not well be executed. Yet Peisthetairos, undeterred by any impossibility, refuses to grant the conclusion of Iris' unimpeachable syllogism. In the situation in which he finds himself, Socrates or Diagoras would be of no help to him: What is the use of denying that the gods are if one is confronted by a god that is? In this situation one can act only on Strepsiades' premise according to which the gods are, but may lose their power. Peisthetairos saves his cause by turning for the time being from the immortality of the gods to a fact unknown to Iris: We, the birds, are now the rulers and you gods, regardless of whether you can be killed or not, must now obey us. Even if the gods can not be killed, they can be seriously harmed, for, as we have seen, by admitting the possibility of the

impossible, Aristophanean characters are not forced to deny the difference between what is easily and quickly accomplishable and what can
only be accomplished with difficulty and in a long time. As a matter of
fact, the gods are in need of sacrifices: Iris entered the air on her way
from the gods to men in order to tell men that they should sacrifice to the
Olympian gods, the gods in heaven. Peisthetairos now makes the issue
entirely clear by denying that the Olympian gods are still gods; for to be
a god means to be a god for men, but the birds are now the gods for men.
One might say that just as there can be no men without gods, there can
be no gods without men. The fact that Kleon, who pretends to be Zeuslike, absolutely depends on the *demos*[59] throws light on the status of
Zeus himself. Peisthetairos silently replaces the view that it is of the
essence of the gods to be immortal by the view that it is of the essence of
the gods to be gods for men. To understand his silence, one has only to
recall that the birds qua gods claim to be immortal (688), although they
are still afraid of bird catchers. The birds might have mistaken the immortality of their races for the immortality of the individual birds;
similarly it would be a mistake to infer from the immortality of the species
Iris (rainbow) the immortality of the individual Iris with whom Peisthetairos is confronted. Iris has only contempt for Peisthetairos' folly: Peisthetairos and his race will be destroyed by Dike using Zeus' lightning. It
is this threat that completely restores Peisthetairos' ascendancy, an ascendancy temporarily lost through the fault of the birds. He is not for one
moment frightened by Iris' threat of Zeus' power, without of course
doubting for one moment Zeus' existence; for he who after all is not a
barbaric slave knows somehow that Zeus can not kill him by lightning or
any other means. Zeus can annoy him, but he can annoy Zeus too by
sending the right kinds of birds into heaven to cause all sorts of ravages
there. Although we must not be too squeamish regarding what is possible
or not, it is not improper to note that we do not know whether Peisthetairos' birds will ever reach heaven, whereas we do know that the dung
beetle did. As for Iris herself, Peisthetairos threatens to do great violence
to her, despite his old age (and his homosexual preference). She leaves
him with a threat that her father, Zeus, will stop his *hybris*. The birds are
satisfied with the result of the exchange between their ruler and Iris. Having realized that the gods have not heard of the prohibition against entering the air—the herald sent to the gods may not have succeeded in
entering heaven—they publicly announce that prohibition, as well as the
prohibition addressed to men against sacrificing to the gods. As for us, we

have seen that, granted the possibility of the impossible, the revolt against the gods is not possible without the co-operation of Peisthetairos and the birds: Only by speaking as a bird and for the birds could Peisthetairos overcome a difficulty that Socrates would be unable to overcome. It is perhaps not too trivial to note that the Aristophanean comedy would not be possible if the distinction between the possible and the impossible were not maintained within it to a considerable extent: Strepsiades could not possibly become Socrates and vice versa.

One may doubt whether after the scene with Iris Peisthetairos still considers himself as a mortal. He wonders whether the herald sent to the mortals will ever return. At the very moment that he thinks of him for the first time, the herald returns: Everything succeeds for him according to wish (cf. 1119–21 with 1269 ff.). The herald praises above all Peisthetairos' blessedness and wisdom, and he presents to him a golden crown with which all men honor him because of his wisdom. Peisthetairos accepts the crown—he knows that he deserves it for his wisdom—but he wishes to know which work or facet of his wisdom induced the human race to award the unusual honor. He learns from the herald that he is honored so greatly because by founding the ethereal city he has given human life an entirely new and most gratifying direction. Previously all men were madly in love with the city of Sparta—Euelpides was not (125–26, 813–16), whereas Socrates, owing to his extreme continence and endurance, appeared to be a Laconizer (1282)—now they are all madly in love with living like birds. They were madly in love with Sparta because of their love of law; they ceased to be in love with Sparta and fell in love with the birds' life when they understood the superiority of nature to law. While the herald suggests this thought, he retracts it; for what he—a bird or a citizen of the birds' city—interprets as an imitation of the birds' life is in fact the ordinary life of the Athenians; he is a superpatriotic bird. Still, he only exaggerates; ornithomania is rampant in Athens, as he shows by examples that are perfectly cogent. Thousands of men are now eager to come to the birds, desiring to receive wings and crooked talons. The herald warns Peisthetairos silently to supply them only with wings, for how can men be expected to remain subject to the birds if they are given the weapons of birds? Peisthetairos of course silently agrees. He prepares the proper reception of the immigrants by asking his servants to bring him as many wings as they can. While he waits impatiently for the wings, the birds give vent to their pleasure about the spreading love for their city, its widening fame, and its imminent growth. They are not surprised by mankind's response to the new city in which everything beautiful is to be found; the gods mentioned as dwelling in the birds' city are all "personifications" (cf. 1320–21 with *Peace* 456). Not the least of them is Hesychia (Rest). The birds' praise of rest contrasts sharply with Peisthetairos' restlessness. As was made abundantly clear by the herald's report, the practically universal longing for the birds' city derives from Euelpides', not from Peisthetairos', sentiments, from birdism not from titanism. Yet the birds do not possess the inner strength to resist Peisthetairos; they become infected with his impatience and hurry; their settling down has not deprived them of their flightiness.

Since the prospective immigrants belong to different kinds of men, they must be given different kinds of wings, as the birds point out to Peisthetairos. According to them, one must distinguish three kinds of wings: wings of Music birds, of prophetic birds, and of sea birds. The birds prophesy well, inasmuch as three immigrants of different kinds successively appear. The first one is a youth bent on killing his father. He wishes to become an eagle, i.e., a prophetic bird. He seems to be less concerned with becoming winged than with living with the birds or according to the birds' laws. Peisthetairos asks him, "Which laws, for many are the birds' laws." The young man, who thus proves to be less thoughtful than Strepsiades (cf. *Clouds* 1430–31), replies that he likes all the birds' laws, but above all that law according to which it is noble for the birds to bite and kill their fathers. Swearing by Zeus and speaking as a bird, Peisthetairos admits that at any rate father-beating is regarded by the birds as noble. The youth does not see the nice distinction between father-beating and father-killing; father-beating would be of no use to him; he must kill his father in order to get his father's property. He obviously does not wish to live with the birds or as a bird; he wishes to combine the advantages of birds with those of human beings in a doubly impossible way. For, as Peisthetairos tells him, "we birds" have an ancient law according to which the young storks –the storks are the guardians of the wall of Cloudcuckootown—must take care of their old father in compensation for his having reared them. Under this law the would-be parricide, as he sees immediately, would be worse off with the birds than where he came from. Thereupon Peisthetairos supplies him with a wing, a spur, and a cock's comb; since he is so eager to beat or to fight, he should become a soldier and go to war. Swearing by Dionysos, the youth agrees and leaves. Whatever may be the laws according to which the birds act, men are to act as the bird Peisthetairos tells them to, not as the birds act, just as under

Zeus' rule men were not supposed to imitate Zeus' fettering of his father, Kronos. In the new order men will be as little permitted to beat their fathers, to say nothing of committing incest, as in the old. Peisthetairos knows what he owes to himself as the founder of a city, and in particular of the city that will be the city comprising all gods and men. Or, since Peisthetairos speaks as a bird, beings very different from the Olympians may be gods, but no being can be a god unless it fulfills certain conditions; in particular it must not permit men to beat their fathers and the like: A god must be in harmony with the fundamental requirements of the city. It is then for the same reason that he expelled the astronomer Meton that he forbids father-beating; the connection between astronomy and father-beating has become sufficiently clear from the *Clouds*. He is kinder to the would-be parricide than to Meton. In the first place, the youth is easily induced by him to abandon his wicked design, while Meton could not possibly be induced to cease being an astronomer. Besides, the youth did not beat or kill his father in the old city where actions of this kind are forbidden: His coming to the birds in order to be able to kill his father legally shows his concern with legality and therefore in a sense his fundamental justice. Lastly, he swears by Dionysos, the god who has reared Aristophanes, the generator of Peisthetairos. We must not forget the salutary father-beating presented in the *Wasps*. In other words, the Unjust Speech is a father beater (*Clouds* 904–6, 911), but not an astronomer.

The second would-be immigrant is the poet Kinesias. He reveals himself by the song that he recites as a lover of Eros (schol. on 1372). He wishes to become a nightingale. To speak less poetically or more truthfully, he wishes to become winged in order to be able to take novel lyrical preludes from the clouds. The souls of dithyrambic poets seen by Trygaios as he descended from heaven were collecting lyrical preludes, but apparently not from the clouds (*Peace* 827–31). In Kinesias' view, however, the craft of the dithyrambic poets depends entirely on the clouds; for their poems must not only be lofty but cloudy as well. With a view to what we have learned from the *Clouds* (350) we must say that dithyrambic poems, as distinguished from comedies, are glaringly dark. Kinesias was in the odor of being most impious.[60] Peisthetairos refuses to supply him with wings and even spanks him with wings. He asks him however to stay with the birds and to teach choruses of birds. Yet Kinesias wishes as little as the parricide to stay with the birds; he only wishes to acquire certain virtues of the birds. He therefore dismisses Peisthetairos' suggestion as an attempt to ridicule him. The suggestion is no doubt ridiculous, but the line between the ridiculous and the serious is not always easy to draw in an Aristophanean comedy. Surely Peisthetairos does not say as Trygaios does on a certain occasion (*Peace* 173) that he is joking.

The third and last visitor is a sycophant. His character is sufficiently revealed by the fact that he is struck as much by the birds' being penniless as by their being winged. From the very beginning he does not leave the slightest doubt that he has come for no other purpose than to become winged. He needs the wings of sea birds, since he is an informer on the islanders. Peisthetairos does not approve of his life and his profession; he tries to convert him to a just way of earning his livelihood. But the young man refuses to listen to that counsel; he repeats his request for wings. Thereupon Peisthetairos gives him wings by speaking to him: All men become winged, elevated by speeches; by decent speeches—for there are also unjust ones, as no one knows better than the sycophant—men are turned to lawful work. The sycophant refuses to be cured. The theme is so thoroughly Athenian that both men forget where they are and speak as if they were in Athens. Since the incorrigible scoundrel can not be winged by speeches, the founder Peisthetairos, acting as a just man on behalf of justice, wings him with a whip and chases him away. There is no place in his realm for father-beating or any other kind of injustice.

Contrary to the herald's sanguine or boastful announcement, no would-be immigrant has come. As far as we know, there is not a single human being (with the exception of Euelpides) who wishes to live with the birds or like a bird. The three men who did show up merely wished to become winged in order to combine the powers of men with those of birds. The one who occupies the central place within that group is the poet Kinesias, the only one of the three who is called by his name; just as the central figure in the group of five that had delayed the sacrifice and the only one among them called by his name was the astronomer Meton. Poetry and astronomy belong together as being lofty, hard to understand, and boastful. They are also opposed to each other, as appears from the different treatment accorded by the founder par excellence to the poet on the one hand and to the astronomer on the other. Let us remember that the poet was the only one within the first group of visitors who received gifts from Peisthetairos. The founder simply expelled Meton, but he tried to keep Kinesias, however unsatisfactory his poetry might be. He has some fear of the poets (931–32); Meton has no power whatever. Aristophanes only restates the lesson conveyed by Hesiod's tale of the birds—of the hawk and the nightingale, i.e., of the king and the singer—which must be read in the light of the conflict between the poet's unjust brother, Perses, and the poet himself: The king can easily kill the singer, but he can not kill the truth proclaimed by the singer. Peisthetairos is wiser than Hesiod's hawk. This is connected with the fact that, as we have seen, he is on the side of Right. He defends Right against his three visitors, who are anxious to become winged in order to acquire more than human power; the wings are meant to do for them what the cap of Hades is supposed to do (cf. 793–97). The wings that he does give them are speeches; instead of giving them superhuman power, he gives them the advice to be just. This, however, means that the only human being who is winged is Peisthetairos. Does this mean that he reserves for himself alone the power to act unjustly with impunity? The answer to this question depends on what one thinks of his attempt to deprive the gods (the old gods) of their power. It is, after all, not implausible to say that reverence for those gods is essential to justice. Nor is it implausible to say that the supreme guarantor of Right can not be simply subject to Right, but must have his hands free.[61]

After Peisthetairos has left the stage, the chorus of birds gravely expresses its amazement about Kleonymos, who is both an informer and a coward, and about the robber Orestes. The utterance has no relation to the action of the play or to the concern of the chorus as chorus. This is the first time that we are confronted by an utterance of this kind. The only case that has some resemblance to the present one occurred in the *Acharnians* (1150–73), but there the chorus' blaming and cursing Antimachos, who had left them without dinner, is obviously related to the action of the play: to Dikaiopolis' selfish concern with nothing but his own pleasure. The birds do sing now of things or men that only birds could have seen on their flights; and their blaming Kleonymos as an informer has a faint connection with the preceding scene in which Peisthetairos dealt justly with the sycophant. Yet there is a deeper connection of the whole song of the birds with the three preceding scenes in which Peisthetairos dealt successively with the three alleged immigrants, as can be seen precisely if one remembers the occurrence in the *Acharnians* to which we have referred: The birds are as disappointed with Peisthetairos as the Acharnians were with Dikaiopolis; they are indignant about Peisthetairos' usurpation of monarchic rule or his tacit exclusion of the birds from participation in the rule of the birds' city. They can not act against him, since they owe it to him that they will no longer be caught or killed by human beings; being therefore aware of Peisthetairos' power, they dare not go beyond blaming injustice in general by speaking of other unjust men, or rather unjust Athenians.

Another visitor arrives, eager to speak to Peisthetairos. His face is concealed, and since he fears to be seen by the gods from above, he carries an umbrella. When he learns from Peisthetairos that Zeus is gathering clouds, he is not frightened of Zeus' lightning, but rather relieved: Zeus can not see him through the clouds (cf. 1608–9). He therefore uncovers his head; Peisthetairos immediately recognizes Prometheus, the great lover of men and hater of gods. Prometheus beseeches him not to shout or mention his name, for he is still afraid of Zeus. But, as he tells his ally, Zeus is ruined; owing to the foundation of the city in the air, men no longer sacrifice to the gods, who are therefore starved. The barbaric gods who dwell above the Olympian gods threaten Zeus with war if he does not take care that they are provided with victuals. The barbaric gods who threaten the Olympians for the benefit of Peisthetairos are of course not the gods worshiped by the barbarians, i.e., Sun and Moon, with whom Trygaios had threatened the Olympians (*Peace* 406–13), although the divinity of the birds and of nothing but the birds excludes the divinity of Sun and Moon as well as of the barbaric gods and of the Olympians. Could there be a connection between Peisthetairos' expulsion of Meton and his failure to appeal from the Olympian gods to Sun and Moon? The barbaric gods are the Triballians (a Thracian nation) in heaven, just as the Olympian gods are the Greeks in heaven. Prometheus tells Peisthetairos that Zeus and the Triballians on high are going to send ambassadors in order to bring about a reconciliation between the gods and the birds, and he urges him to demand that Zeus restore the scepter to the birds and give Basileia (Kingship) to Peisthetairos as wife. Originally it was understood that the birds themselves would reclaim their kingship for themselves (549–50); Prometheus changes this intention in favor of Peisthetairos. Basileia is a most beautiful girl who is in charge of Zeus' lightning and all other means or sources of power; through possessing Basileia, Peisthetairos will be the possessor of everything. Prometheus gives his advice to Peisthetairos because of his well-known benevolence to human beings: He is not concerned with transferring Zeus' power to the birds. Prometheus, who is himself a god, hates all the gods and hence also himself; he is thus prevented from acting in his own interest. If he were not a god he would resemble the pious Nikias. He tacitly admits that the man Peisthetairos is superior to all the gods.

The conversation between Peisthetairos and Prometheus can not but have aggravated the birds' impotent indignation. Prometheus, who by nature loves man and hates the gods, must have reminded the birds of the fact that they by nature hate man but not the gods, and hence of the unnatural character of their alliance with Peisthetairos against the gods—an alliance from which they can no longer escape. Besides, as the philanthropic inventor of all arts, Prometheus was also the inventor of the arts of catching, killing, and cooking birds. Finally, since he admittedly hates all gods, he has no use for the birds as gods. It is therefore not altogether surprising that after he leaves, the birds devote a song to two men who are much more profoundly unjust than the two unjust men with whom they dealt in the song preceding the Prometheus scene: to the Melian Socrates and his companion Chairephon who, as it were, surround the orator Peisandros. Peisandros, who reminds us by his name of Peisthetairos, reminds the birds somehow of Odysseus. Immediately after this song the ambassadors from heaven arrive; their conversation with Peisthetairos does nothing to appease the birds. After the ambassadors have left, the birds utter their third and last song, which apparently has no connection with the action of the play or with the concern of the chorus as chorus. That song lampoons the crookedness of Gorgias and his Athenian pupil Philippos; Philippos had been the victim of the righteous indignation of the Wasps (*Wasps* 421). Surveying the three kindred songs, we observe that of the seven unjust men described therein at least three (Socrates, Chairephon, and Gorgias) are men who combine rhetoric and *physiologia*. The birds' posture toward Socrates (and therefore also toward Chairephon) is not at all surprising; the birds' teaching regarding the origins was meant to expel Prodikos' teaching. Peisthetairos' action—which by now has proved to be directed not only against the old gods but against the new gods as well, and to aim at the universal rule, hence at the divinization, of a human being—not unnaturally reminds the birds of Socrates; for how could birds be expected to understand the unpolitical character of Socrates' intention? We must also note that among the seven men in question there is not a single poet; the birds, being singers, have no objection to poets. In this respect at any rate the birds agree with Peisthetairos: The city, and a fortiori the city according to nature, is compatible with poetry and even calls for poetry, while it can not tolerate astronomy and *physiologia*. Finally we note that songs of the kind in question are appropriate in the *Birds*, as distinguished from the other plays hitherto discussed, for only in the *Birds* is there such a conflict between the hero and the chorus after the hero has won the decisive battle as concerns rule (the corresponding conflict in the *Acharnians* did not concern rule) and as arises from the hero's having deceived the chorus (the sausage seller did not deceive the knights or Demosthenes).

The embassy from heaven consists of three gods, Poseidon, Herakles, and a Triballian. The Triballian, the most barbaric of all gods, would never have been sent as an ambassador if the gods did not now live democratically, as the aristocratic Poseidon explains. Herakles is full of rage against the man who has blockaded the gods by the wall and wishes to strangle him; Poseidon must remind him of the fact that they have been sent to negotiate peace with that very man; the birds are not supposed to play any role in the transaction. Yet precisely Herakles, owing to his voracity, proves to be the most accommodating of the three gods; he gives in to Peisthetairos as he gave in to Trygaios. (Kinesias swore only by Herakles, 1391.) Herakles is therefore the only god of whom Peisthetairos takes notice to begin with. For when the gods arrive, he is busy preparing his meal. The meat is of birds: Some aristocratic (hence rich, fat, or juicy) birds have been condemned to death by the democrats among the birds. Just as the Olympian gods were always Greeks and hence became democratic when the Greeks became democratic, the birds, the new gods, also have become, if not Greeks, at least democrats. Yet the birds' regime is a democracy only in name; in fact it is the rule of the first man, or rather of the only man, among the birds, who is so firmly in the saddle that he does not have to forgo the eating of well-cooked and well-seasoned, if well-sentenced and well-executed, birds. A strict man might say that Peisthetairos' action is worse than cannibalism, for the birds are now his gods. Poseidon starts the negotiations by stating that peace is to be restored between the gods and the birds. Peisthetairos agrees: We (we birds) are willing to make a just peace, and justice requires that Zeus restore the scepter to the birds. For the time being he does not go beyond the demand that he himself had advised the birds to raise (554); he does not yet act on Prometheus' advice. He goes beyond the original demand only by promising the divine ambassadors a meal if they accept that demand. To Poseidon's disgust Herakles accepts the demand immediately; as Poseidon tells him, he is prepared to deprive his father, Zeus, of his royalty for the sake of a meal. Since this argument has some weight, Peisthetairos is compelled to show the lasting advantage that the peace settlement would have for Zeus and his kin: The gods' strength will be increased if the birds rule below, or if the gods have the birds as allies; since the gods dwell above the clouds, they can not observe men perjuring themselves, while the birds can observe them and hence punish them. The gods wish to punish the perjurers but are unable to do it; the birds are able to do it but hitherto did not wish to do it. Peisthetairos agrees then with

Socrates in asserting that the gods do not punish the perjurers; but whereas Socrates traces this fact to the nonexistence of the gods, Peisthetairos traces it to their deficient power. Poseidon sees Peisthetairos' point immediately: The gods can only gain if the birds use their powers, both natural and acquired, for the extension of the gods' power. Yet, since the birds do not need the alliance with the gods, while the gods need the alliance with the birds—for the gods are anxious to punish men, but the birds are not—and since the birds will therefore determine the purpose for which the alliance will be used, Peisthetairos' proposal is tantamount to demanding that the gods hand over the scepter to the birds. Outwitted by Peisthetairos and pressed by Herakles, the two other divine ambassadors accept that demand. Only after he has achieved this victory does Peisthetairos act on Prometheus' advice; he outwits Prometheus too. Knowing that a peace treaty ought to look like a compromise between the warring parties, he consents to leaving Hera to Zeus, but demands Basileia for himself. Poseidon rejects that demand outright. Peisthetairos, pretending not to be interested in a peace treaty or in fact not being interested in it, returns to the preparation of his meal, in which the divine ambassadors will of course have no share. This is too much for Herakles. Dropping all pretenses to divinity, describing even Poseidon as a human being, he refuses to continue the war for the sake of one woman: He will not make the mistake of the Greeks in the Trojan War or of the Athenians in the Peloponnesian War (cf. *Acharnians* 524–27). Poseidon is amazed by Herakles' folly. Forgetting what he himself has already granted to Peisthetairos, he tells Herakles that if kingly rule is handed over to the birds, Herakles will be poor and powerless after the death of Zeus. The deathlessness of the gods, which was questioned by Peisthetairos earlier (1224), is now denied by the gods themselves: The gods are at most human beings. Peisthetairos refutes Poseidon's argument by telling Herakles that according to the laws Herakles, not being a legitimate son of Zeus, has no claim to Zeus' possessions anyway. The gods, being Greeks, are subject to Greek laws; the only legitimate heir of Zeus is Athena, perhaps because of the incestuous character of Zeus' marriage. Herakles then loses nothing by granting Peisthetairos' demand for Basileia. On the contrary, as Peisthetairos tells him, if he joins the birds, Peisthetairos will make him king. Thereupon Herakles votes in favor of Basileia being given to Peisthetairos, while Poseidon still votes against it. The Triballian's decision, being entirely unintelligible, is interpreted with Peisthetairos' help as agreeing with Herakles' decision; Poseidon is compelled to cede to the will of the majority.

Herakles proposes that Peisthetairos go with "us" to heaven, there to receive Basileia "and everything." He has then no doubt that Peisthetairos can rise as high as Trygaios without needing a dung beetle; he surely rises higher than the birds. But we are not permitted to see Peisthetairos in heaven as we were permitted to see Trygaios in heaven. Owing to Aristophanes' sense of propriety, we do not even hear anything as to whether Peisthetairos ever met his predecessor Zeus, or as to how Zeus took his deposition. Herakles made his proposal in order to have the promised meal entirely for himself; he did not intend to return to heaven. But Peisthetairos holds him strictly to the letter of the proposal: You will go to heaven with "us." Herakles does not even get the meal for the sake of which he made concessions of a magnitude never equaled before or after by anyone.

A messenger announces to the birds, that thrice-blessed race, the coming of their ruler: No star has ever shone forth with such brilliance as Peisthetairos, who comes holding in one hand the hand of his unsayably beautiful bride and with the other wielding Zeus' lightning. Peisthetairos surpasses in splendor both the Olympian and the cosmic gods. The messenger calls on the birds to intone a reverent song inspired by the divine Muse. However disappointed the birds may have been by the bargain that Peisthetairos drove with them, they can not withstand the overwhelming impression of their senses, especially of their sight and smell, to say nothing of the fact that as subjects of Peisthetairos and Basileia they partake in a manner of that couple's splendor, and to say still less of the birds' flightiness. It is after all the birds' city that triumphs in the wedding of Peisthetairos and Basileia; and the triumph of their city, as they never for a moment forget, is due to "that man." Extraordinary successes in foreign policy more than compensate for the loss of freedom at home. Accordingly they comply with the messenger's call. They compare the wedding of Peisthetairos and Basileia to that of Zeus and Hera. The comparison may not be appropriate in every respect, but it can not be blamed as boastful. Peisthetairos enjoys the birds' noble song with great dignity, but he feels that they should also sing something of his now possessing the powers hitherto possessed by Zeus. They nobly comply with his nobly uttered wish, making clear in the process that Basileia has taken the place of Dike. Regardless of whether or not he has fetched Basileia from heaven, he will now ascend to heaven with her to celebrate his wedding. The birds' last words—the last words of the play—are their greeting of Peisthetairos as the highest of the gods.

Of all the plays hitherto discussed, the *Birds* is the most shocking. A speech or action is shocking if it runs counter to authoritative opinions or, more particularly, to the opinion of the gods, of the orators and tragic poets, and of the majority.[62] The *Birds* celebrates the success of an Athenian citizen who, after having turned his back on his fatherland (35), deprives Zeus and the other gods of their power and makes himself the highest god, the successor to Zeus. Peisthetairos' action reminds us of the action of Socrates; like Socrates, Peisthetairos shows no concern for his fatherland and acts against the gods. One could even say that Peisthetairos' action is more shocking than that of Socrates, for Socrates' action proceeds from the utterly incredible assumption that the gods do not even exist and is therefore doomed to total failure, while the action of Peisthetairos, who starts from the contradictory assumption, issues in the most glorious triumph. The action of the *Peace* is much less shocking than that of the *Birds:* Trygaios' transgression of Zeus' explicit prohibition is justified before the tribunal of opinion by the fact that his goal is public peace, whereas Peisthetairos' action has no publicly defensible ground. The shocking character of the *Birds* is underlined by the fact that Peisthetairos is closer to the poet himself than either is to Socrates: Peisthetairos firmly rejects both father-beating and astronomy; his Music birds that develop his Orphic theogony are at the opposite pole from the un-Music Socrates. This state of things is obviously in agreement with the complete silence of the poet regarding himself in the two parabaseis of the play.

Let us consider the reason that induced Peisthetairos to undertake this revolution, while we remember the preferences of Aristophanes as they have come to sight hitherto. Peisthetairos' primary design was to find a place free from that busybodyness that annoyed him so much in Athens, especially when it took the form of eagerness to judge or to condemn. This design does not explain his revolutionary action, unless one assumes that there is a connection between the passion to condemn and the power of the gods. Such a connection was suggested in the *Wasps:* Philokleon was eager to condemn because he believed that he would be punished by the gods if he failed to condemn. Peisthetairos does not explain why he abandons his primary design in favor of the design to dethrone the gods. Perhaps there is the following connection between the two designs: A city can not be at rest if it is not left at rest by its neighbors; only a city without neighbors, a city comprising all men, could be at rest. But such a city must have gods as its rulers; the Olympian gods have never tried to establish such a city; as we know from the *Peace*, the Olympian gods are not even unqualifiedly in favor of peace among the Greeks. Those gods themselves are not at peace with the gods worshiped by the barbarians or with the barbarian gods; it is Peisthetairos' action that brings the Olympian gods and the barbarian gods together; there can not be a city at rest if the gods are not subjected to rule by a man. Yet Peisthetairos knows that there can not be a city without gods. Thus he needs new gods. His choice of the birds is no doubt due to accident, but this does not explain the choice of Aristophanes, who chose that accident. Gods are thought to form a species of beings different from the human species; yet the gods are not sufficiently different from men: They have sexual intercourse with human beings and offspring through it (cf. 557–60), while birds do not even desire sexual intercourse with human beings. Gods are beings to which men look up; they dwell on high; yet the old gods dwell too high, while the birds, which roam higher than any other beings apart from the old gods, are nevertheless near to men (726–29). The birds hate man, but so do the old gods, as is shown by Nikias' demonstration of the existence of the gods in the *Knights* and by the mere presence of the philanthropic Prometheus in the *Birds*; yet the birds are also afraid of man. It is true that the birds' lack of intelligence forces or enables Peisthetairos to make himself the ruler of the birds and therewith the highest god, the ruler of all gods and all men, but he is not simply a human being: He is winged.

The shocking character of the *Birds* may be said to have been sufficiently counteracted in the eyes of the Athenian public by the fact that the deed celebrated in the play—a deed surpassing in sheer greatness all earlier and later deeds—is performed by an Athenian; the play redounds therefore to the glory of Athens even more than the deed of the Athenian Trygaios in the *Peace*.[63] We may use this occasion for remarking that while the Aristophanean comedy holds a mirror to the Athenian vices, it is as such a praise of Athens because it shows what wonderful things might be done by Athenians, even to the gods, as distinguished from what the gods have in fact done for Athens. Those things are done by Athenian private men on their own, not commissioned or even authorized by the laws or by the city; thanks to some of her citizens, Athens possesses within herself the remedy for the not inconsiderable ills from which she suffers. Is justice in every politically relevant sense threatened by Socrates? Strepsiades disposes of this threat singlehanded without needing the help of the laws or of magistrates. Strepsiades is indeed an outstanding man only because he is a man between the two classes to which every other Athenian unqualifiedly belongs. Peisthetairos however may be described as a man surpassing even Alkibiades; he successfully combines the striving for universal rule with extreme impiety, while Alkibiades combined these two things and failed. Alkibiades' design failed, but it was not contemptible like Kleon's; it could not possibly succeed because he had to use Athens as his base, whereas Peisthetairos could use a different base: Comedy presents the impossible as possible. The *Birds* would then hold a mirror to the Athens of 415 by showing that the policy actually pursued by Athens—expanding in a western direction [64] while prosecuting Alkibiades for impiety—is impossible and at the same time lacks grandeur.

One can easily go further and say that the *Birds* can not be shocking because the ridiculous can not be shocking, and Peisthetairos' deed is ridiculous because it is manifestly impossible. Not only will Zeus on Olympos laugh at Peisthetairos' boasts; everyone knows that one can not build a city in the air and starve the gods. Just as the *Peace* conveyed the suggestion that the present peace would be succeeded sooner or later by war, the *Birds* may be said to convey the suggestion that the present dethronement of Zeus would be succeeded sooner rather than later by his restoration: If kingship migrated originally from the birds via men to the gods and within the play from the gods via the birds to man, it stands to reason that it will migrate after the play from man to the gods. Everyone knows that Zeus can not be dethroned. Still, Zeus himself feared that he might be dethroned.[65] Furthermore, while "everyone" also knows that Zeus exists, Socrates did not know it, and his denial of Zeus' being was not merely ridiculous, but also shocking. Yet Socrates' action forms part of a larger whole for which Strepsiades is responsible; Strepsiades' action however is not shocking, for he attempts a crime by means that are singularly inept. What is true of Strepsiades' action is still truer of Peisthetairos' action. If a poet were to present a society that denies the existence of all gods and permits father-beating and incest and yet is happy, he would shock everyone; but if he showed at the same time that that society also requires the fulfillment of impossible conditions (say, the abolition of poverty, of war, and of disease, or that every member of the society be very beautiful and very intelligent), he would shock much less. He would shock to some extent because the message that his play would convey would be ambiguous. He would indeed suggest that the abolition of the gods is as impossible as the abolition of poverty and so on; but he would also suggest that the abolition of the gods is as desirable as the abolition of poverty or, in other words, that the gods are an evil, if a necessary evil. This would reduce piety to "bearing the divine things as a matter of necessity"; it would not be compatible with loving the gods.[66]

We wondered whether Aristophanes approves of the designs that he presents as successful whereas he disapproves of those that he presents as failures. If Peisthetairos' triumph is merely amusing, Socrates' ruin is also merely amusing. Could a triumph of Socrates not be as amusing as his ruin? Why then did Aristophanes choose ruin in the case of Socrates and triumph in the case of Peisthetairos? One can not answer this question without having recourse to the poet's claim that his works are meant not merely to amuse but also to teach the just things. This is the reason why no Aristophanean comedy can be simply shocking and therefore why both Socrates' ruin and Peisthetairos' triumph are edifying. Socrates' ruin is edifying because his action is simply shocking or unbearable and therefore disapproved by Aristophanes in particular. The difference between Socrates' action and Peisthetairos' action will then throw light on the difference between Socrates and Aristophanes. Peisthetairos' action is not simply shocking because of the manifest impossibility of building a city in the air and such like things; Socrates' denial of the existence of the gods can be simply shocking because that denial is manifestly possible. Peisthetairos' action presupposes not only the existence of the Olympian gods but the necessity of the city looking up to gods. It is true that he goes beyond enlarging the recognized pantheon and replaces the recognized pantheon by a new one; yet, on the other hand, he opposes father-beating and expels the astronomer; radically differing from Socrates, Peisthetairos acts in accordance with the fundamental requirements of the city. It is for this reason that Aristophanes teaches the just things through that hero's triumph. In other words, that impossibility which Aristophanes in general respects is the impossibility of successfully denying the fundamental requirements of the city.

Are we then entitled to assert that the happy or unhappy outcome of a play reveals to us the poet's judgment on the design that triggered the action of the play? The assertion is sound provided it is properly understood. The unhappy outcome of the *Clouds* reveals the poet's disapproval not only of Strepsiades' design but also of Socrates' conduct toward Strepsiades. The happy ending of the *Knights* reveals the poet's approval of Demosthenes' design insofar as only that design could have led to the coming to power of the sausage seller, but by this very fact it implies an important criticism of Demosthenes himself. The outcome of the *Wasps* is not simply in agreement with Bdelykleon's design, inasmuch as he succeeds indeed in curing his father of the desire to sit in judgment, but fails to make him a gentleman; yet this failure of Bdelykleon is not simply a failure according to Aristophanes. One can not judge properly on the outcome of the *Birds* without considering the difference between Peisthetairos and Euelpides. Euelpides is no more attached to the Olympian gods than is Peisthetairos. He is even greatly attracted or amused by Peisthetairos' design to replace the rule of the Olympian gods by that of the birds. Yet in contradistinction to his glorious companion he remains an *apragmon*, easygoing and a lover of a quiet, retired life in a private station. He is in no way a boaster; he prefers without any hesitation living with the birds and like the birds to ruling over the birds and through the birds over gods and men; he is a rustic; [67] in a word, he is closer to Aristophanes than is Peisthetairos. Through the fact that Euelpides disappears in the middle of the play, the poet unobtrusively expresses his disagreement with Peisthetairos—a disagreement not based on considerations of justice. Yet one must also say that the *Birds* does not present the feasibility of Euelpides' design, while it shows the feasibility of Peisthetairos' design: Euelpides is in his way as blind to the need for political life as Socrates. The difference between the two heroes of the *Birds* corresponds to the difference between the poet and his role as citizen, between wisdom and the city.

6 *The Lysistrate*

![decorative drop-cap ornament] This is the only play whose title designates a human individual. It is the only play whose title designates the chief character or the human being responsible for the design that is executed in the play. The title comes closest to that of the *Peace* (Eirene); the end pursued in both plays is public peace. Yet while the goddess Eirene is hardly distinguishable from a statue, Lysistrate is a human woman; the *Lysistrate* is altogether a human drama.

The complaining with which the play opens is done by the heroine. Lysistrate is annoyed because she has to wait for the other women whom she has called together. But she does not have to wait as long as Dikaiopolis or Strepsiades; Kalonike arrives almost at once. The *Lysistrate* is the only play that begins with a very brief soliloquy. Kalonike's arrival does not visibly improve Lysistrate's mood. For apart from the fact that she still has to wait for the other women, she can now vent her annoyance on her gentle friend: The women who keep her waiting confirm the bad opinion men have of women; instead of coming to a deliberation about a matter of some importance, they prefer to stay at home in bed. Kalonike admits that the bad reputation of women is deserved, yet defends the members of her sex against Lysistrate's particular complaints: It is not easy for women to leave home, for they have to take care of their husbands, their servants, and, above all, their babies. One wonders whether Lysistrate has children. She surely feels that at the moment caring for babies is not the most urgent thing; those women would not have hesitated to neglect their babies in order to have intercourse with men. Granted that a woman's place is in the home, the home is now threatened by the city; the women must now take care of the city in the first place. Lysistrate had not told the other women what business she plans to submit to their deliberation. Nor does she tell it now to Kalonike. She merely tells her that the salvation of the

195

whole of Greece now depends on the women; therefore she has called together not only the women of Athens but those of Sparta and Boiotia as well: The notorious levity of women is the only hope for Greece, for only by means of that levity can one hope to put an end to the present war.

Myrrhine and the other Athenian women arrive; Lysistrate's reception of them is not too friendly. Very different is her reception of the Spartan Lampito, who arrives as the leader of the women from the enemy camp. The Athenian women are impressed by the beauty of Lampito and other women from the enemy cities—by the beauty of their bodies rather than of their souls, and of parts other than the heads rather than of the heads; they view beauty in the perspective of the Aristophanean comedy, from below. Urged by the others, Lysistrate begins to disclose her design by asking them whether they do not long for the fathers of their children, for she knows that the husbands of all of them are away on military service; she says nothing about her own husband. She appeals to them primarily as mothers. They reply that their husbands are away on military service for many months or at home only for very short periods. She thereupon asks them whether they would not be willing to join her in putting an end to the war if she found a way for achieving this result. They heartily reply in the affirmative. The primary motive prompting the women seems to be maternal care. Yet Lysistrate deems it necessary to mention the fact that not only their husbands but also other sources of sexual satisfaction are unavailable to them as a consequence of the war; here she speaks of "we women"; she appeals to their sexual desire at least as much as to their maternal care. This then is Lysistrate's simple design: If the women desire to enjoy their husbands' love, they must force them to make peace, and the only way in which they can exert that compulsion consists in refusing to have sexual intercourse with them; only by forgoing the present enjoyment of a good can they enjoy the same good securely and always in the future. This design is to begin with entirely unacceptable to the women: Every other evil is preferable to sexual abstention. They speak no longer of their maternal concern. Accordingly, Lysistrate does not even attempt to remind them of that concern. She has only one resource left: example. The only woman who did not openly reject her proposal was Lampito; when Lysistrate addresses her alone, Lampito with some hesitation agrees to the proposal. Thereupon Kalonike, speaking for the other women, is prepared to reconsider her refusal, provided Lysistrate can show that the abstention demanded of them will in fact lead to peace. Lysistrate performs this task with ease: The husbands will make peace when they see that making peace is the necessary and sufficient condition for satisfying their sexual desire; each woman must arouse her husband's desire to its highest pitch while herself remaining immune to desire. Kalonike no longer replies that what is required of the women might be beyond their power. She replies that the husbands might turn their backs on their wives, i.e., that the husbands might find other ways of satisfying their desire; yet she is forced by Lysistrate to admit that the alternatives are less attractive to the husbands. Still, there remains an obvious difficulty: There is no reason to assume that women have greater self-control than men or that women are in this respect superior to men and hence have power over them. In Sparta the women have greater power than the men but, Lampito wonders, is the same true of Athens? The Athenian men can wage war, regardless of what the Athenian women do, because of the navy and the war treasure. Lysistrate reassures her by telling her that the old women of Athens have been ordered to seize the akropolis, where the treasure is kept, while the young women deliberate; she implies that the navy will be of no use without the treasure. After all objections to her design have been disposed of, Lysistrate persuades the women to confirm their agreement at once by a solemn oath. According to Lysistrate's suggestion they would have sworn by Ares,[68] for while their goal is peace, they must wage war against the enemies of peace, i.e., the men: The way to peace is war. Still, a warlike oath is felt to be inappropriate in the situation; accordingly the liquid that the women use for the solemnity is not blood, but unmixed wine: The commitment to extreme continence is made firm by an act of incontinence. Lysistrate calls on the Lady Persuasion; she or another woman swears by Aphrodite. The solemn vow formulated by Lysistrate opens with the women's promise to refuse themselves to all men, not only to their husbands, but to their lovers as well; for it is obvious that if the men can have recourse to women who are not their wives, they can not be starved into submission. In the sequel however the vow speaks only of the husbands: Lovers are a marginal case, which can be disregarded.

In the *Lysistrate* the design antedates the play (26–27) as in the *Wasps* and the *Peace;* but the former design, as distinguished from the designs animating these two other plays, requires for its execution the co-operation of free people as distinguished from slaves. Hence the private deliberation that led to the design must be followed up by a common deliberation (14) that leads to the common adoption of the same design; while the original deliberation precedes the play, the play begins with a repetition of that deliberation. As a consequence, there is no need for anyone to address the audience about the reasons of the design, and hence in particular there is no room for anyone to act as a spokesman for the poet. For the same reason there is no room in the *Lysistrate* for an opening soliloquy like those opening the *Acharnians* and the *Clouds*. Generally stated, in the *Lysistrate*, as distinguished from the plays hitherto discussed, there is no room for a Euripidean prologue. We have no way of knowing whether Lysistrate's private reasons are identical with her publicly stated reason.

According to Lysistrate's design, the women will excite the men's sexual desire to the highest degree and then frustrate it. As a consequence, the *Lysistrate* is Aristophanes' most indecent play. Yet the end that is therein pursued by these indecent means is most decent, most just. Besides, it is understood that the proceedings will take place between lawfully wedded people. While the *Lysistrate* may shock decency by the public exhibition of strictly private things, it does not shock justice or piety. It may suffice here to remind readers of the designs of the heroes of the two other plays devoted to peace, the *Acharnians* and the *Peace*. The *Lysistrate* is at the same time the most indecent and the most moral (most harmless or least revolutionary) of Aristophanes' plays. Perhaps this fact accounts for its singular popularity.

Before the solemn oath-taking is properly completed, i.e., before the large majority of the women have been able to partake of the wine, their attention is distracted by the clamor of the old women who have seized the akropolis. Lysistrate sends Lampito away to Sparta there to take care of their common affairs, while she keeps the other women from the enemy cities in Athens as hostages. The Athenian young women, led by Lysistrate, will join the old ones in securing the treasure against the expected counterattack by the Athenian men, i.e., the old men, for the men in their prime are away from Athens. The chorus of old men enters. They hasten to the akropolis to take it away from the women. They are prepared for a regular battle; they view the seizure of the akropolis by the women as if it were the action of a foreign enemy. Precisely the old men who seem to be beyond the reach of Lysistrate's weapon appear to endanger her whole enterprise. They are prepared if need be to burn the women to death. They particularly hate one woman, the wife of Lykon (270). It is not clear whether that woman is the leader of the old women or of the whole women's conspiracy (i.e., Lysistrate), or whether she is hated on different grounds; yet the mere fact that this is a question shows how little we know of Lysistrate, of her husband or children, her way of life, her position in society, and so on: While the whole action of the play, which is instigated by Lysistrate, turns on the relations of husbands and wives, we hear nothing definite about Lysistrate's own husband. Is her husband by any chance old and impotent, and is she driven to her extraordinary action by the absence on military service of her lover or lovers, whom she can not get back except by the return of peace, and is not the only way in which she can bring back peace to induce all other women in their prime to refuse themselves to their husbands in their prime? In that case the act of supreme continence demanded of the women would be less of a sacrifice for Lysistrate than for any other woman. The only other leading character in the comedies about whom we know as little as we do about Lysistrate is Peisthetairos. Lysistrate would deserve to be called Peisthetaira. Is Lysistrate meant to be the female counterpart of Peisthetairos? While Peisthetairos starves the gods into submission, Lysistrate starves the men into submission. Is she the superwoman as Peisthetairos is the superman? While Peisthetairos becomes the successor of Zeus, Lysistrate does not even dream of acting against the gods. While Lysistrate tries to follow Aeschylus, her male opponents (differing profoundly from their contemporary Strepsiades) take the side of Euripides (188–89, 283, 368).

The chorus of women enters. They have supplied themselves with water in order to fight the fire brought by the old men, or, more precisely, in order to extinguish the fire with which the old men threaten to smoke out or to burn the old women who have occupied the sacred building. While the men had called the women "hated by Euripides and by the gods" and had come to the help of Athena, the women call on Athena to help them and call the men impious; in contradistinction to the men, they call only on Athena. When the two choruses become aware of each other, they hurl threats, insults, and provocations at each other. But the women and their water prove to be superior to the men and their fire; the men are defeated by being drenched. At this point, a proboulos (a high magistrate) appears with a police detachment. He had come to take money for the navy out of the treasure, but was refused entrance by the women within; he is therefore as indignant as the drenched old men. He sees in what happens another sign of that female license which shows itself especially in the strange cults favored by women; in his view the men are ultimately responsible for the women's license, since they unwittingly encourage their wives' adultery. The present situation reminds him of what happened at the time when the Athenians made the disastrous decision to undertake the Sicilian expedition; at that time a woman's lamenting of Adonis was a bad omen for the expedition.[69] This fact seems to prove that the Athenians would have been wise to listen to the woman's voice. But since this would justify the women's present action, the dignitary tries to make the women's license responsible for the Sicilian disaster in order to exculpate his sex. He thus reveals from the beginning the weakness of the position of the Athenian men as against that of the Athenian women and therewith unwittingly prophesies the women's victory. Be this as it may, he orders the archers under his command to open the gates by force.

Before they can obey him Lysistrate comes out: It is neither necessary nor wise to use force if one has to do with a sensible human being like Lysistrate; sense, persuasion, and mind should be used. She hopes to win without fighting. The dignitary disagrees with her view that what is needed is sense and not force; he commands that she be arrested. Lysistrate is forced to threaten that she will use force against force. The archer recoils. When the dignitary commands two archers to fetter her, other women come to her help; the archers recoil before the threats of the women, who swear by female gods. The dignitary prepares an attack in form. Lysistrate warns him that a large force of fighting women who are heavily armed is standing by indoors. When he does not relent, she calls out her fellow fighters, who rout the archers with ease. Since the women desire peace they must prepare for war and even wage war; they must become wasps; it is their good fortune that the men with whom they have to do battle are only decrepit citizens and barbarian slaves. The women claim to have acted only on the defensive; after all, they only defended their conquest. The defeat of the dignitary and his detachment restores the self-respect of the previously defeated old men, who have much less dignity to lose. They delicately describe the dignitary's defeat as a mistaken attempt to argue with brutes. Accordingly they advise him to join them in trying to find out from the women why they have seized the akropolis: His dignity will be preserved if he pretends to act as prosecutor. He is shrewd enough to act on this advice. He learns from Lysistrate —sense and composure incarnate—that the women have seized the akropolis in order to lay their hands on the money so that it will no longer be used for the war; the women who administer the things belonging to the household well enough for the men will henceforth administer the public treasure too. The public treasure is to be used for the war, without which Athens can not be saved? The women, not war, will save Athens. War and peace are not the business of women? Look at the mess that men have made of the war. At first the women, with their usual modesty, said nothing, although they were quite aware of the blunders that the men committed. Then, suffering in their hearts, they laughingly asked their husbands about the decisions of the *demos;* Lysistrate's husband told her that this was none of her business and that she should keep silent; fearing or respecting her husband more than other wives did theirs, she kept silent. But male imbecility increased as the war went on. The women could not help becoming outspoken in their dissatisfaction; their husbands' sole reply was to threaten to silence them by force and to quote Homer, or Hektor, against them: "Let war be the business of the men." Yet the men themselves have come to admit that there is not a single man in the country. When the women heard this, they assembled at once and decided that they must save Greece: Now the time has come for the men to listen and to be silent. The sex that is capable of acting, i.e., acting quickly, claims rule over the sex that has proved to be incapable of acting. This claim—this reversal of the order of nature, as the old fashioned might say —is of course altogether unbearable to the dignitary. He does not give in even when confronted with the fact that "let war be the business of the women" is in Greek metrically as perfect as Homer's "let war be the business of the men." While the metrical equivalence shows that the new order is no less beautiful to the ear than the old, it brings out the extreme character of the change: Lysistrate's design for the time being requires an upheaval, not only within the household, but in the city as well; it is not sufficient that the men be deprived of sexual enjoyment; they must also abdicate politically. The emphasis is now entirely on the political change proper. While in addressing the women Lysistrate appealed to the needs of the women, in addressing the men she must appeal to the needs of the city as a whole. The chorus of women shows a good understanding of the situation by claiming for the women all virtues that could be regarded as titles to rule; female modesty or continence is not among them. They seem to be in danger of forgetting the goal that their temporary seizure of power is meant to achieve and, above all, the means on which they must chiefly rely: the sexual desire that animates them first and then affects the men (553). Lysistrate reminds them of these things in a manner intelligible to them but not to the dignitary. She seems to feel that her great design will be spoiled if it becomes known too early. Perhaps she apprehends that if the men away on military service become aware of their wives' strike, they will not be eager to come home or, in other words, she believes that the wives' abstention must come entirely as a surprise to the husbands. The dignitary understands only that the women mean to put an end to the war, but he has no inkling of how they mean to do it. He does not deny that the women might put a stop to the ridiculous conduct of armed men buying figs or olives from old women in the market, but he denies that they could put a stop to the many great disorders from which the city suffers. Lysistrate, anticipating the Eleatic stranger in Plato's *Statesman*, tells him that the women's work in handling wool is a perfect model for bringing order into the disordered affairs of the city, for restoring peace and the political greatness of Athens; it teaches among other things the wisdom of a liberal policy toward the metics. The dignitary does not pause to consider Lysistrate's comparison of the political art with the arts of wool carding and weaving; he dismisses the women's claim on the simple ground that they understand nothing of the war or, as he puts it, that they do not have the smallest share in the war. This immense stupidity leads immediately to his downfall. As Lysistrate tells him, women suffer more from war than men: The mothers must send their sons into battle; the young wives can not enjoy the best time of their lives since they must sleep alone; the young girls can not marry and become old maids. The dignitary can not contest what Lysistrate said about the mothers and the young wives; he merely asserts that the men too get old during the war. Yet, as Lysistrate replies, the women's season is shorter than that of the men; an oldish man coming home from the war can still marry a young girl, while young men will not marry old girls. The dignitary tries to maintain the equality of suffering of the two sexes against this cogent reasoning by trying to point out that the old maids might marry still older men; but he is rudely silenced by Lysistrate, who tells him that he at any rate is no longer fit for marriage, but only for the grave. Accordingly she and the other women treat him as if he were already a corpse and chase him away with utter contempt.

What Lysistrate indicates about those sufferings that women undergo as a consequence of war approaches the limits of what can be properly mentioned in a comedy. She surely does not speak—or is not permitted by the dignitary to speak (590)—of the misery of the mother (or father) who lost her (or his) son or sons in battle. Yet the transcomical character of the theme is not the only reason why the climactic exchange between Lysistrate and the dignitary is so elliptical. Lysistrate distinguishes between three kinds of women; only the second kind have husbands in the war and are therefore the only ones on which the success of her design depends: They are the women in their prime who as a rule have small children (18–19, 99–100), whereas the women of the first kind already have sons of military age. When Lysistrate speaks of the first kind, she alludes to their fallen sons; when she speaks of the central kind, she does not allude to their fallen husbands. She thus indicates the basic flaw of her design or the impossibility on which her design is based. She abstracts from the widows of the fallen soldiers, the war widows. Those widows can not co-operate with Lysistrate, for no refusal on their part will bring back or contribute toward bringing back their husbands. Besides, the husbands turned away by their wives will not necessarily be turned away by the widows, who also are women in their prime and who may very well believe that they fulfill a patriotic duty by breaking the wives' strike. Lysistrate's design can be imagined as a way out only if one abstracts from the war widows, what one might call the reserve army that every war necessarily produces. The *Lysistrate* is based on the absurd disregard of the fact that war increases the demand of women for men because it decreases the supply of men. The abstraction from the war widows, i.e., of the fallen husbands or, generally stated, of death, is compensated for in a manner befitting comedy by the women's treating the dignitary as a corpse.

The silencing and disgracing of the dignitary is immediately followed by the parabasis. Since Lysistrate's goal is peace—peace also between men and women—and the conflict between the men and the women is still in full force, or rather since the plot calls for two antagonistic choruses, the parabasis of the play differs from the parabaseis of all plays hitherto discussed: There can not be a parabasis proper in which a single chorus addresses the audience; this fact alone would explain why the parabasis of the *Lysistrate* is silent about the poet. Since the plot requires two choruses, the title could not well be taken from the chorus. The parabasis of the *Lysistrate* is altogether a part of the action of the play, as is the parabasis of the *Birds*, which is also silent about the poet. Yet, as we recall, the *Lysistrate* differs from all other plays hitherto discussed by the fact that it lacks a Euripidean prologue and in particular a spokesman for the poet: The poet is more absent from the *Lysistrate* than from the other plays hitherto discussed. The *Lysistrate* and the *Birds* also have in common that each points to two radically different actions. In the *Birds* there is the divergence between the action aiming at the universal rule of the birds as gods or at the dethronement of Zeus, which culminates in Peisthetairos' becoming the successor of Zeus, and the action aiming at men living like birds and with the birds; the parabasis speaks of these two actions, although or because one of them is closer to the spirit of the poet than the other. In the *Lysistrate* there is at least the difference between the domestic action of the women (the wives' strike) and their political action (the change from rule by men to rule by women); the parabasis is silent about the former. There seems to be no reason to suppose that one of these two actions is closer to the spirit of the poet than the other. When the women compare themselves to the dung beetle (695), they may remind us of that animal's helpfulness in obtaining peace (in the *Peace*); there is no reason why they should remind us of the comic poet's art.

The parabasis shows that the women have been victorious—to the extent that they were victorious—only by deed; the men are entirely unconvinced. The chorus of old men draws the only conclusion that anyone not initiated into the women's secret could draw from the women's conduct. They take it for granted that the women are bent on political change, on the establishment of tyranny, and they suspect strongly that the women are conspiring with the Spartans: How else could one explain their desire for peace with utterly untrustworthy Sparta? But the old men will not bow to tyranny; they will follow the model of the Athenian tyrannicides and hit the women hard. The women reply to this threat with a threat of their own. Addressing the audience, they speak of their credentials; they have completed the *cursus honorum* of Athenian girls, which consisted in serving Artemis and Athena; as mature women they have borne warriors to the city. Although they are women, they are entitled to give the city good advice, especially since no one else does. Yet they do not give the city any advice, good or bad: The men would not listen to their speeches but only to their deeds. Besides, the design animating the *Lysistrate* is very broad; hence there is no advice that they might give to the city that is not put into effect by the women in the course of the play itself. The women do not deny that they intend to set up tyranny. No wonder that the old men, who have experiences of their own and who remember the Amazones, expect the gravest danger from the women's political and military action; they prepare for another fight. So do the women, who now almost allude to their negotiations with the enemy and to their resolve to put an end to the democracy and to its ruling by decrees.

The threatened fight does not occur because a crisis has arisen in the other sphere. The women's attention is diverted from their decrepit male opponents to their vigorous female leader. Lysistrate appears again, this time utterly discouraged. The women desert her; they are overcome by desire; she is unable to keep them away from their men; they are eager to go home. She speaks of four cases of attempted desertion that she has discovered just in time. We see on the stage five more such cases. It is in this context that Lysistrate swears perhaps for the first time by Aphrodite: The very goddess on whose power she counts for the success of her design threatens her design. Yet she succeeds in making the women accept their hard lot by assuring them that their husbands suffer no less than they do, and above all by citing to them an oracle that promises them everything they may desire if they stay on the akropolis and do not go home. While she did not need an oracle for initiating her action, at least her public action, she needs one for its completion. It is perhaps more important to note that through an act that is likewise not merely human, the women's husbands, who at the beginning were away from home on military service while their wives were at home, are now at home while their wives are away from home, on the akropolis, on military service. Without this change, which is no less marvelous than Amphitheos' journeying to Sparta and back, Lysistrate's design would have been doomed to failure. In the situation as it was at the beginning, the wives' abstinence would have been easy, but for this very reason wholly ineffectual. Only in the situation as it is now can the wives' abstinence be effectual; but it is also much harder now, in particular since it now lacks its primary incentive, which is the desire to bring their husbands home. Still, thanks to Lysistrate's vigorous leadership her design may well succeed, provided the wives are more continent than their husbands. One may say that the husbands' return, which endangers the wives' resolution, may fortify that resolution.

Lysistrate has succeeded in preventing her army from melting away. Hence the politico-military situation seems to be the same as it was at the end of the parabasis: The chorus of the old men and the chorus of the old women oppose each other. Yet the intervening scene has had a subtle effect; the two sexes are no longer bent on fighting each other. The old men praise a young bachelor of antiquity who hated women and therefore lived on mountains, never going home: If men are married and at home, as at least some of the Athenian warriors are now, everything is lost; the old men do not hope to receive help against women from men in their prime. The women praise Timon who hated, not all human beings, or even all men, but all wicked men, whereas he loved women; the chorus of women is less hostile to the opposite sex than the chorus of men: The women know and admit that they have allies among the men. Still, the men too have become somewhat friendlier to the women than they were before. The present exchange is more obscene than the one that constituted the parabasis. The increase in obscenity is matched by a decrease in political fervor: Not even the men refer any longer to the danger of tyranny. The success of the wives' strike makes unnecessary any change of regime. Hence the old men begin to soften.

The success of the wives' strike depends on their being more continent than the men. The exemplary test takes place in the next scene. Lysistrate calls the women to her; she has seen a man approaching who is visibly in a state of high sexual excitation: Aphrodite has done her work on him. Lysistrate has prevented the wives from going home; now the husbands come to the akropolis. The man in question is Kinesias, the husband of Myrrhine. Lysistrate reminds her of her oath and asks her and the other women to leave. Kinesias enters, followed by a slave who carries a male child of his master and mistress. (We remember Trygaios' two daughters.) We learn immediately why the women are bound to defeat the men: the bodily sign of sexual excitement is much harder to bear or is a much more visible handicap in the case of men than in the case of women; by disregarding everything else the poet proves that continence is harder for men than for women. Lysistrate does everything she can do within the limits of propriety to aggravate Kinesias' condition. She tells him how highly his wife thinks of him. For Kinesias this is only an additional reason why Lysistrate should reunite him with his wife; she promises to send Myrrhine to him. There is no suggestion that Kinesias ever was away from home. Myrrhine appears on high but refuses to descend to Kinesias, even when on his command her child calls her; she only changes her mind when she learns that during the six days she has been with Lysistrate, the child was neither bathed nor given suck. She at least pretends to regard having children as a mere burden and to be utterly indifferent to what happens to her household. While she kisses the child, she forbids her husband to touch her. He now learns for the first time the cause of his wife's strange conduct; Myrrhine tells him that her conduct will not change until the men put an end to the war. He does not show the slightest surprise; in the condition in which he finds himself, he is only concerned with doing whatever his wife demands so that he can enjoy her. He therefore promises that among any other things the women might demand the men will also end the war; she should only lie down with him. Myrrhine finds one excuse after another for refusing, and then, when she can no longer avoid promising to accede, for delaying the performance of the promise; after having kept him in suspense for an eternity, she finally runs away. Earlier in the scene she had extorted from him another promise regarding the peace; but toward its end he promises no more than that he will deliberate about the peace: The wives' refusal may still backfire; even Kinesias, who prefers his wife to all other women, begins to ask himself whether he should not turn toward a second-best solution. The success of the wives' strike is then not yet assured. This makes one wonder again whether the women could not succeed in ending the war by effecting a change of regime in Athens. The chorus of old men is outraged by Myrrhine's trifling with Kinesias and full of compassion for him. While their hatred of women had weakened as a consequence of the women's longing for their husbands, it has regained something of its former strength owing to Myrrhine's intransigence. And, what is at least as important, the old men do not appear at all to have grasped Lysistrate's grand design.

All uncertainties are removed by the arrival of a herald from Sparta. He has been sent by the Spartan authorities to learn from the Athenian authorities whether they are prepared to treat about peace. While in Athens the conflict between the peace party (the women) and the war party (the men) has not yet been settled in favor of the former, the strike of the Spartan wives led by Lampito has been entirely successful. As Lampito had indicated at the beginning (168–71), the power of the Spartan wives over their husbands was much greater than the power of the Athenian women over the Athenian *demos*; [70] in Sparta the victory of the peace party did not require even the semblance of a threat of a change of regime. Or, if you wish, Sparta was already a gynaecocracy. It is the change of mind of the Spartans and nothing else that tips the scale in favor of peace. Things had not been going too well for Athens and hence rather well for Sparta; in that situation it would have been most impolitic for the Athenians to take the initiative for peace. The only hope for peace consisted in the Spartans taking that initiative. Lysistrate's master stroke consisted in hitting on the only thing that could induce the Spartans not only to become willing to make peace but even to sue for it. The Athenian men understand Lysistrate's design only at the moment that design has succeeded, and even then only partly; the arrival of the Spartan herald makes them realize for the first time that the conspiracy under foot is not directed toward the establishment of tyranny (1008). The situation is now so clear and simple that the Athenian magistrate who talks to the Spartan herald can tell him without having been authorized by the Council that the Spartans should at once send ambassadors with full powers to Athens in order to discuss peace, while he will tell the Athenian Council to elect ambassadors for the same purpose: In the given situation there is not the slightest doubt that Athens will make peace, since the Spartans have taken the initiative.

After the herald has left for Sparta, i.e., after the Athenian women have won their fight for peace without having been compelled to change the regime, the time has come for the reconciliation between the two choruses. The defeated old men still give vent to feelings as misogynic as those animating Euripides' Hippolytos. Yet a few deft moves of the old women suffice to break down what is left of the old men's dislike. Moved to tears, they grant grumpily that the little services the women render them are not entirely unwelcome. Addressing the audience for the first time jointly, the two choruses communicate a spirit of good feeling and benevolence to the city as a whole by not saying, as they state explicitly, a single bad thing about anyone and by quasi-promising money and a hearty dinner to everyone. Here would have been the place for a second parabasis if the purport of the play had permitted a second parabasis.

The ambassadors from Sparta arrive, most anxious for peace at any price because their wives' strike is still in force. The Athenians are as paralyzed by the women's strike as the Spartans. It is therefore indispensable for the men from both camps to have recourse to Lysistrate for the making of peace. Lysistrate appears uncalled. She is told that since the first of the Greeks have made her their arbiter—she is of course not a ruler, not even of the Athenians—she must combine now seemingly incompatible qualities, in a word, she must be both good and bad.[71] She asks Diallagē (Reconciliation), a companion of Aphrodite and the Graces, a silent being although obviously not a statue, to bring to her first the Spartans and then the Athenians; by giving orders to Diallagē she makes it quite clear that the peace is of purely human origin. She treats the Spartans with special courtesy. Her credentials are her native wit and her having heard many speeches from her father and men of age (she does not owe any of her wisdom to her husband); she is aware of the inferiority of women. She blames both the Spartans and the Athenians for destroying each other despite their common cults and the presence of their common enemy, the barbarians. She blames each side for being oblivious of the benefits that the other side has conferred upon it. In accordance with their having made the first step toward peace, the Spartans admit their guilt. Agreement between the two hitherto warring cities is rendered both easy and difficult by the fact that both the Spartans and the Athenians are filled with intense desire for the feminine charms of the beautiful girl Diallagē or of Lysistrate herself—a desire that in their present condition they can hardly distinguish from their desire for strategically valuable places still occupied by the opposed party. Fortunately the present needs of their bodies are stronger than all political considerations. At Lysistrate's suggestion the women will dine the men from the two cities on the akropolis, where the solemn conclusion of the peace will take place; thereafter everyone will leave, taking his wife with him. There is no suggestion that Lysistrate's husband will be among the men to be dined by the women.

The chorus expresses its satisfaction with the reconciliation by making another quasi-promise of gifts to all; being concerned with peace it again does not speak evil of any citizen, yet given the poverty caused by the war it can not make genuine promises. There follows an obscure scene; threats of violence are uttered against people who prevent the egress of the Spartans from the dinner. Are these people the unreconstructed war party? It appears that a brawl would be welcome to the audience, but no brawl takes place: Aristophanes here tacitly refuses to employ devices of vulgar comedy; in the *Lysistrate* the poet speaks only inaudibly about himself. The peace banquet proves to have been most satisfactory; both the Spartans and the Athenians were at their best; according to an Athenian the Spartans were charming, while the wine-drinking Athenians were most wise banqueteers. The chorus draws the conclusion that henceforth all Athenian ambassadors to Sparta must do their work in a state of drunkenness, i.e., of benevolence. The work begun by Aphrodite must be completed by Dionysos, in the Athenian manner.[72] A Spartan proposes that they dance and sing in order to gratify both the Athenians and the Spartans; his proposal is of course gladly received. He praises the exploit of the Athenians at Artemision and the exploit of the Spartans at Thermopylai. He is silent on their joint exploit at Plataiai; and he calls on the divine virgin, the huntress Artemis, to help in keeping the peace between Athens and Sparta for a long time: There is no prospect of everlasting peace between the two cities. Thereafter Lysistrate unites the Spartan wives, whom she has kept as hostages, with their husbands; the reunion of the husbands and the wives—of the members of the war party and those of the peace party—naturally follows from the reunion of Sparta and Athens. She counsels the husbands to stay with their wives and the wives to stay with their husbands; her last words in the play are "Let us beware of making the same mistakes again." She means, of course, the mistakes of the Spartans and the Athenians, but the context suggests also the errings of husbands and wives. The chorus of Athenians calls on Artemis, Apollon, Dionysos, Zeus, and Hera, and then on the divinities who are witnesses to that sweet rest which is the work of Aphrodite; it is silent about Athena as well as Athens. At the request of an Athenian, a Spartan sings a novel song; in that song, which concludes the play, the Spartan glorifies Apollon, Athena, and the Dioskuroi and then celebrates Sparta, especially her maidens, whose choruses are led by the chaste Helen: The Spartan maidens shall glorify Athena, the utterly warlike. The play celebrating peace ends with a praise of the warrior goddess (cf. *Clouds* 967). As we have learned from the *Peace*, there is no peace that is not followed sooner or later by war, be it only a war against barbarians, or that can be preserved without the threat of war. The *Lysistrate* does not end with a joint song of the Spartans and the Athenians. As is indicated by the final Athenian and Spartan songs, the reconciliation between the two cities requires that the differences between them be not obliterated: The peace was initiated by the Athenian Lysistrate, who trusted in the power of Aphrodite in Sparta, and Lysistrate's conceit originated in Aristophanes, who had been brought up by Dionysos. Only the Spartans praise Athena in the final songs.

At first glance the *Lysistrate* differs from the two other peace plays by the fact that in the *Acharnians* and the *Peace* peace is brought about by the action, either helped or hindered by the gods, of the comic poet, whereas in the *Lysistrate* peace is brought about by the action, neither helped nor hindered by the gods, of the women: Diallagē acts under Lysistrate's orders after the decisive action has already been completed. Yet, quite apart from Diallagē, the gods are not simply absent from the *Lysistrate:* The peace is the work of Aphrodite (1289–90). As for the poet's absence, we must remember that Dikaiopolis gave a share in his private peace only to a lovesick woman from compassion with her; such compassion animates the *Lysistrate*, in which the women favor peace while the men—with the tacit exception of the poet—favor war: The women take the place of the poet. The poet as poet is less present in the *Lysistrate* than in any of the other plays hitherto discussed: No character of the play represents the poet or swears by Dionysos or acts as spokesman for the poet, and there occurs no questioning of the fundamental requirements of the city (Lysistrate does not even question the essential inferiority of women). If war is the business of men, it seems to follow that peace is the business of women and that the peace-loving poet must take the side of the women. This difference of the sexes is reflected in the theology of the *Peace*, in the opposition of Eirene (and her female companions) and Polemos (and his male companion). Yet precisely in the *Peace* Polemos' being alive was clearer than Eirene's being alive. A similar obscurity may be observed in the *Lysistrate*. Peace seems to be the work of Aphrodite, but Aphrodite is not simply a goddess of peace. Since the poet does not act within the *Lysistrate*, the women must act; they must act like men (war must become the business of women). They must fight like Amazones, and at the same time they must refuse themselves to their husbands and cease to take care of their children: They must destroy life rather than perpetuate it. They bring about peace, not by doing "the golden deeds" of Aphrodite, but by imitating the virgin goddesses Artemis and Athena; these two goddesses are more powerfully present (also through oaths and invocations) in the *Lysistrate* than in any other play. Yet the huntress Artemis and the utterly warlike Athena are even less goddesses of peace than Aphrodite. The ending of the play puts the emphasis altogether on Athena, the warlike goddess who not only does not give birth but was herself not born, not generated by a father and a mother, the embodied denial of life. If we can trust Peisthetairos, she is the only legitimate heir of Zeus (*Birds* 1652–54), who would be the most lawful successor of Zeus but for Peisthetairos' becoming the successor of Zeus.

Peace is brought about not by Aphrodite but by Lysistrate, by the effect of the wives' strike, instigated by Lysistrate, on the husbands. The strike could not be effective if the husbands were not at home, but the wives adopt Lysistrate's design on the ground that the husbands are not at home. Apart from this, the strike could not be effective if the wives did not have greater self-control than the husbands. This assumption is supported by what is expected of women as well as by the existence of such female gods as Artemis and Athena. Finally and above all, the strike could be effective only if there were not the reserve army of war widows, i.e., if contrary to nature the husbands in the armed forces were not killable or, generally stated, if there were no possibility of sexual gratification except through intercourse between lawfully wedded husbands and wives, or if the pleasure of sexual gratification were possible only in and through marriage: Husbands (wives) must have no opportunity for that gratification when away from their wives (when their husbands are in the field).[73] Lysistrate's design presupposes that unnatural coincidence of *physis* and *nomos* according to which war would be against nature because it condemns men and women to sexual starvation or prevents the generation of offspring whereas, to say nothing of other things, a small number of men can fertilize a large number of women: There is no fundamental disharmony between war and nature or between Ares and Aphrodite. Lysistrate tries to overcome this fundamental harmony by assimilating herself and the other wives to the virgin goddesses; those goddesses are accordingly supposed to bring about the coincidence of *physis* and *nomos*. The *Lysistrate* may therefore be said to present the victory of *nomos* and in this respect to resemble the *Clouds* as distinguished from the other plays hitherto discussed, all of which celebrate the defeat of *nomos;* both plays celebrate the victory of beings hated by Euripides (or by Socrates). In both plays the victorious cause owes its victory not to speech but to deed. In accordance with all this the *Lysistrate* answers the question of the godness of the gods poetically by pointing to Athena.

Peace is brought about by the effect of the wives' strike on the Spartan husbands. In Athens the sex strike is not sufficient, given the small power of the Athenian women over the Athenian *demos:* The politically active *demos* is the citizens at home, i.e., the old men, who can not be reduced to submission by sexual starvation; the old men are to be fought in the first place by the old women, who seize the treasure. Yet this action is only preparatory to the women's seizing political power. Lysistrate's design requires the change of regime in addition to the sex strike. One might say that the sex strike is the action of the young women (wives) against the young men (husbands), while the political action is primarily the action of the old women against the old men; there is no suggestion that the political action is the action of wives against their husbands. Prior to the arrival of the herald from Sparta, it was, to say the least, uncertain whether the Athenian women would succeed in inducing the Athenian men to make peace, i.e., whether the Athenians would make peace without a previous change of regime. Both the wives' strike and the women's coming to power are impossible. Yet in the *Lysistrate* the women are the peace party and the men are the war party. Let us assume that the women stand for the men favoring peace, and the men stand for the men favoring war. In that case the play would show that the only possible way to obtain peace in the circumstances is by a change of regime in Athens, the coming to power of the kind of men who would need the support of Sparta to control the *demos* and for this reason will already have made contacts with Sparta, just as Lysistrate does. Such a policy would require the utmost secrecy and therefore an ostensible policy concealing the preparation for the change of regime. The action of the *Lysistrate* reflects this state of things in a laughable manner, inasmuch as the peace party treats the sex strike as a strict secret, while it does not counteract the impression that it aims at political subversion, the setting up of "tyranny." The laughable character of the action of the play is limited entirely to the sex strike. One wonders whether the change of regime—as distinguished from that change of regime which was effected by Peisthetairos—is not the poet's serious proposal. In that case the *Lysistrate* would come closer to suggesting a serious political proposal than any other play. For, to speak only of the most political play, in the *Knights* the poet may be said to propose seriously the ouster of Kleon, but he does not show seriously how this ouster could be achieved. Yet is a serious proposal compatible with the total comedy? Would Athens informed by a regime dependent on Spartan support not be an Athens deprived of its virility? Through the actions of women Aristophanes speaks of the actions of higher or more dangerous beings. He explicitly claims that he does not treat comically mere "human beings" and in particular women.[74] Whatever might be true of the two other women's plays, the *Lysistrate* surely does not contradict that claim.

7 *The Thesmophoriazusai*

This play begins like the *Birds* with a dialogue between two Athenian citizens, but one of these citizens is Euripides. Accordingly, whereas in the *Birds* there could be some doubt as to which of the two Athenians was responsible for the design leading to the action of that play, there can be no doubt that in the present play the design stems from the clever poet. At the beginning Mnesilochos, a kinsman of Euripides by marriage, complains to the poet about being dragged around by him since the early morning without ever being told their destination. The first words of the play remind us of the beginning of the *Clouds*, but the *Thesmophoriazusai* is the only play that literally begins with "O Zeus." Euripides refuses to tell his companion where he is leading him: There is no need for him to hear what he is about to see. The kinsman takes Euripides to mean that there is no need of his hearing anything; he understands as meant absolutely what was meant qualifiedly. The wise man has in mind the natural difference between the sphere within which seeing with one's own eyes is properly supreme and listening to tradition is more or less out of place, and the sphere within which listening to tradition is just because seeing with one's own eyes is impossible—a distinction that is founded on the natural difference between seeing simply and hearing simply. Although or because the kinsman is aware of Euripides' speaking cleverly, he understands him to mean that he should neither hear nor see on the ground that the nature of not hearing differs from that of not seeing. Euripides does not even try to contest the kinsman's conclusion—perhaps there are people who should not or can not see or hear—but he answers his question as to how the nature of not hearing differs from that of not seeing by tracing that difference to Ether's devising. The kinsman is again unable to understand, and his lack of understanding again does not prevent him from being filled with admiration for Euripides' wisdom; he thus for-

214

gets again for a while his becoming lame through being dragged around by the wise man. Fortunately, with a few more steps the two men arrive at their destination. Euripides shows his kinsman a small door (24–25; cf. *Clouds* 91–92) so that he does not have to hear about it any more, but can gaze at it silently. Yet since the meaning of the small door is not visible, he is still in need of hearing; he must therefore be silent and hear, i.e., see and hear. He hears from Euripides that the door belongs to the house of the tragic poet Agathon. The kinsman, to the best of his knowledge, has never seen that Agathon, but Euripides is certain that the kinsman has had sexual relations with that notorious pathic homosexual. A servant of Agathon emerges through the door with fire and myrtles in order to sacrifice, as Euripides surmises, for the success of Agathon's poetic activity. Euripides and the kinsman hide in order to observe the doings of the servant, who solemnly calls for reverent silence, not only of human beings, but of the ether, the sea, the birds, and the savage beasts as well, because Agathon is about to begin a drama; the immense solemnity of the reverent silence is called for by the immense artfulness or artificiality of Agathon's poetry. The kinsman, who is heard and not seen, accompanies the solemn utterance with expressions of disgust about the bombast or the boasting. When the servant becomes fully aware of the presence of someone uninitiated, first the kinsman and then Euripides comes out of hiding. A hostile exchange between the servant and the kinsman is stopped authoritatively by Euripides, who commands the servant to call out Agathon. The servant, who knows what he owes to his master's dignity and hence his own, regards the command as a supplication and replies that Agathon will soon come out uncalled because since it is winter the poet needs the warmth of the sun in order to make his poems properly flexible. Euripides is greatly annoyed at the short delay thus imposed on him. The kinsman does not understand that impatience because he does not know why Euripides is eager to see Agathon, i.e., why the poet has dragged him around since the early morning: The great man is in the habit of giving commands without giving explanations; he is in the habit of concealing his intentions. He now tells his kinsman that on this day his very life is at stake; the women assembled for the Thesmophoria will pass judgment on his criminal offense, which consists in his treating them tragically and speaking ill of them. He wishes to persuade the tragic poet Agathon to go to the women's assembly disguised as a woman in order to defend him if necessary. The kinsman is impressed by Euripides' clever conceit: In contradistinction to the womanish Agathon, who is notorious for his womanish sexuality, Euripides is too much of a man to play a woman.

The theme of the play is then the persecution of a poet. We witnessed the persecution of a poet in the *Acharnians;* but in that play the persecuted man was not persecuted as a poet. He was a comic poet; he was in danger of being put to death immediately without the benefit of a trial; and he escaped persecution by making some borrowings from the tragic poet Euripides. Now Euripides himself is persecuted on account of his poetry; and he can not escape persecution with the means at his disposal, but must have recourse to the help of another tragic poet. Euripides has much in common with Socrates. We witnessed the persecution of Socrates in the *Clouds*, but Socrates was not politically or judicially persecuted because he had offended only one man, and his rhetoric made him immune to judicial persecution; Euripides, however, has offended the whole womanhood (of Athens), and his rhetoric can not be of any use to him since his case will be decided in an assembly in which he can not lawfully appear. In the *Clouds* we were made witnesses to Socrates' crimes because these crimes were not generally known; Euripides' crimes, committed through his tragedies, were generally known. The exchange between Euripides and his kinsman reminds us of the exchange between Socrates and Strepsiades; all the more striking are the differences between the two pairs. Socrates was not responsible for the design that led to the action of the *Clouds*, and he was quite helpless in the face of Strepsiades' action against him; Euripides, however, is alone responsible for the design that leads to the action of the *Thesmophoriazusai*. While there can be some doubt as to whether Socrates or Strepsiades is the chief character of the *Clouds*, and hence some doubt as to the degree of Socrates' guilt, there can be no doubt that Euripides is the chief character of the *Thesmophoriazusai*. Euripides is persecuted because he treats the women tragically and speaks evil of them. Treating someone tragically is of course no offense, but treating someone comically is about the same as speaking evil of him; Aristophanes was accused by his enemies and especially by Kleon of having treated comically the city and the *demos;* [75] the ground of Euripides' persecution will appear to be less grave or more proper to comedy than the ground of Aristophanes' persecution, to say nothing here of Socrates' persecution.

Agathon appears in a surprising manner. It had been announced twice (66, 70) that he would come out. In fact, he is wheeled out by means of a theatrical machine. He becomes visible in the same manner in which Euripides himself had become visible in the *Acharnians* (408–9), yet it was not necessary to knock at his door as it had been to knock at the door of Euripides and at the door of Socrates; in contradistinction to Euripides and Socrates, Agathon appears uncalled. He looks almost altogether like a spoiled and lascivious woman. Working on a tragedy, he sings a hymn partly in the character of a chorus of maidens who as such are easily persuaded to revere the gods, but do not know which gods they should praise; they are told to praise Apollon, Artemis, and Leto in honor of the two goddesses (Demeter and Persephone) celebrated on the Thesmophoria. Euripides is silent about the song. His kinsman tells Agathon that the song is of womanish and lascivious sweetness and that it arouses in him the kind of sexual desire for which Agathon is notorious, although he himself is quite old, but that the poet is for him a complete riddle: There are some obvious signs that he is a young man, while there are other equally obvious signs that he is a woman; is one reduced to determining Agathon's sex on the basis of his song? In addressing his question to Agathon he makes explicit use of some Aeschylean verses, verses that in Aeschylus' drama had been addressed to Dionysos. Agathon is therefore not offended. He replies in effect that his sex can not be discerned from his song, since the poet always adapts himself to his subject. His garb and manner is feminine, i.e., he imitates women, when he composes women's dramas; if he were to compose men's dramas, his body would supply him with the fundamental characteristic. Since he abhors everything rude and crude, he would never compose a satyr play. What is important for the poet is not that he is very masculine but that he is beautiful by nature: A beautiful poet will produce beautiful dramas whether the subjects are men or women, provided he takes care of his natural beauty by adorning himself appropriately through manners and garb. Agathon justifies the extremely artificial character of his poetry by tracing it to his nature; he has as beautiful a nature as any other poet, but he differs from the other poets because his nature is not very masculine, not to say that it is hermaphroditic; yet precisely this fact links him with the god of the theater himself.

Euripides listened to the exchange between his kinsman and Agathon in silence. We take it that he would not have praised Agathon's performance, least of all in the present situation where praise would appear to be mercenary, to say nothing of the fact that a man like Euripides is thrifty with his praise in any circumstances. The kinsman's open blame of Agathon can not have been altogether to Euripides' liking, since he is in need of Agathon's help, but Agathon's deft handling of the kinsman augured well for his hoped-for handling of the women; his self-justification amounted to the ablest and highest self-praise. Thus the exchange between the kinsman and Agathon is from Euripides' point of view better than Euripides' praise of Agathon's performance would have been. Yet now he can not wait any longer. He puts a stop to the exchange between the two others by saying that Agathon's manner of being is of the same kind as his own had been at the beginning of his career as a poet: He does not say a word about Agathon's song. He frankly states that he has come to Agathon as a supplicant since the women are about to destroy him because he speaks evil of them; Agathon alone can save him by attending the women's assembly in the guise of a woman and by speaking there on his behalf: Agathon alone would speak in a manner worthy of Euripides. To Agathon's question why he does not defend himself in the women's assembly, he replies that in the first place he is well known and that secondly, being an old and bearded man, he does not have the looks or the voice of a woman as Agathon has. Agathon simply refuses to comply with Euripides' request because of the danger that he would incur; he bases his refusal on Euripides' own prudent or lifesaving teaching; Euripides should risk his own hide. The kinsman is indignant about the pathic Agathon's refusal, but Euripides refrains from antagonizing Agathon; he merely claims to be in a state of despair. He thus arouses the compassion of his kinsman, who has probably never seen or heard the wise man despairing and who asks him therefore to use him in any way he likes. Euripides accepts the offer without a second's hesitation and with alacrity: The kinsman will have to take the place originally assigned to Agathon in the women's assembly. But the kinsman looks perhaps even less like a woman than Euripides. This does not induce Euripides for a moment to consider that he himself might go to the women's assembly disguised as a woman. He therefore turns to Agathon with the request that he lend him the utensils with whose help the kinsman could be made to look like a woman. Agathon is as obliging to Euripides as Euripides himself was to Dikaiopolis. Euripides shaves and singes the kinsman with Agathon's razor and torch. The poor old man suffers considerable discomfort, but he bears it quite well. Thereafter Euripides asks Agathon for various pieces of women's clothing, adding the words "Of these things at any rate you will not say they are not." (251) Agathon, whom we have seen and heard composing a hymn to certain gods while he was assimilating himself to pious maidens, never swears by any gods, like Euripides in the corresponding scene of the *Acharnians*. Agathon of course obliges Euripides, who clothes the kinsman as a woman with the utmost care; while he is being dressed, the kinsman develops a womanish concern with his looks. As soon as Agathon has supplied Euripides with the last piece of the clothing needed, he has himself wheeled in. The only things that remain to be done by Euripides are to warn his kinsman to imitate a woman's voice and, on the kinsman's request, to swear that he will save him by all means if some evil should befall him. At first Euripides swears not by Zeus but by ether, the dwelling of Zeus, and when the kinsman finds that a mere dwelling is nothing to swear by, he swears by all gods. The kinsman is not altogether assured because of Euripides' alleged justification of perjury in his *Hippolytos*. Still, he obeys Euripides' order to hurry to the assembly of the women. Euripides himself goes home.

It was a piece of good luck for Euripides that he had his kinsman with him when his hope that Agathon would come to his rescue was dashed. In other words, it could seem that Aristophanes has provided for a way out, which Euripides himself had not provided for, or that Aristophanes claims to be cleverer than the clever Euripides. In a sense this is precisely Aristophanes' claim, as appears from the *Frogs*, but one must not underestimate Aristophanes' respect for Euripides' cleverness. We have no right to disregard the possibility that Euripides took his kinsman with him because he reckoned with the possibility that Agathon might not comply with his supplication. The womanish and clever Agathon, who obviously was not the target of the women's persecution, would have been the most desirable defender of Euripides; but Agathon could not be expected to have a sufficiently strong motive of friendship to endanger himself for the sake of his overpowering rival. The kinsman, on the other hand, despite his twofold defect, has the strong motive of kinship—be it only kinship by marriage—to come to Euripides' aid (210). The demonstration *ad oculos* of Agathon's refusal will make it unnecessary for Euripides to supplicate or to command his kinsman to come to his help; the kinsman sees with his own eyes that Euripides would never have inconvenienced him or exposed him to danger if there had been an alternative. This is to say nothing of the fact that Euripides would under any circumstances have needed access to articles of feminine toilet belonging to a man, since no woman must know of the presence of a man in the women's assembly: Agathon's house is the best place where the kinsman can be dressed as a woman. We may also note here that Euripides, as distinguished from Socrates, has a kinsman who offers to help him against his persecutors: Socrates' constant companion Chairephon could not be of any help to Socrates, since he was implicated in the same accusation as his revered master (*Clouds* 1505–7). Euripides' guilt may be more notorious than Socrates', and the poet may therefore be in greater danger than Socrates; but on the other hand the poet is not as isolated as the man whose chief concern is to think or to worry about the things aloft.

The kinsman enters the temple in which the women are assembling. Acting as a woman, he pretends to sacrifice to Demeter and Persephone and prays to them at least to grant him escape from detection today and to grant his (her) daughter a most desirable husband, a man both rich and stupid. A woman acting as a herald calls on the women assembled to pray to Demeter, Persephone, and five other gods or groups of gods that the present assembly may be beneficial to the city of Athens and to the women of Athens, and that the view of that woman be victorious who in deed and speech deserves the best of the *demos* of the Athenians and the *demos* of the women; the herald also asks the women to pray each for her own well-being. The chorus of women then invokes gods not mentioned by the herald (Zeus, Apollon, Athena, Artemis, Poseidon, the Nereids, and the Oreads). The herald next calls on the women to pray to all gods and curses all those who plot against the *demos* of women, who negotiate with Euripides and the Persians to the detriment of the women, who denounce an adulterous wife to her husband, or who harm any woman in any way. The chorus of women then joins in this prayer, omitting in particular the curse of Euripides, but adding that those who reveal secrets to the enemies act impiously and commit an unjust act against the city. Finally, the herald announces in due form that the chief subject on the agenda of today's assembly is what punishment is to be inflicted on Euripides, his guilt being admitted by all women. The solemnity of the proceedings in the women's assembly brings out the sacrilege committed by Euripides' kinsman at Euripides' instigation. The sacrilegious character of Euripides' act is as much underlined as made light of by the fact that those proceedings ridiculously imitate the pious solemnities that opened the assemblies of the Athenian people. The sacrilege is committed by Aristophanes, rather than by Euripides.

The first speaker shows how many bad things Euripides says about the women. She enumerates seven epithets or calumnies with which the poet has insulted her sex in his tragedies. She goes on to say that his words have led to deeds. By presenting the women's ways in the theater, he has made it impossible or very difficult for the women to continue in these ways (for instance, in adultery and the supposition of infants). He has made the men thoroughly suspicious of the women; he has taught the husbands to use precautions regarding their wives that had never occurred to them before. It goes without saying that they no longer trust their wives' fidelity; they do not even any longer trust their wives' honesty in administering the household. Let Euripides, that teacher of evil, that destroyer of households, be condemned to death by poison or in any other way. Other charges against him that are not fit to be publicly pronounced will be deposited by the speaker in writing with the recorder. The chorus is altogether pleased with her speech; the women never heard a better woman speaker. The praise is surprising: The first accuser did not question the truth of Euripides' denunciations of the women. The second speaker says that she will add only a few points to the others so well stated by the first speaker. Yet, although she does not say it and perhaps does not even know it, her accusation of Euripides is much graver than that made by her predecessor. She does not make the poet responsible for the women's loss of illicit pleasures or gains. She—the poor mother of five small children, whose husband perished on a large island [76]—has lost more than half of her income, barely sufficient at the outset, through Euripides: She makes her living by selling wreaths, and Euripides has persuaded the men that there are no gods; therefore the men no longer buy wreaths to be used in the worship of the gods. She urges all her fellow women to punish Euripides; she does not demand that he be punished capitally. Her speech is very short; she has to hurry to the market in order to take care of what is left of her business. The chorus proves to be more intelligent than the simple-minded florist; it finds her speech more intelligent than the first speech: She has set Euripides' *hybris* beyond any doubt. The second speech is superior to the first speech because it sets forth charges that can be stated publicly, while the first speaker's charges are utterable only behind the backs of the men, of the *demos*, or the city. The florist urges the women to punish Euripides "for many reasons": She does not add, as Hermes added at the end of the *Clouds*, "But chiefly since you know that he acted unjustly against the gods." [77] Euripides' atheism is of interest to her only because of its ruinous effect on her livelihood. Needless to say, this does not mean that she is indifferent as to whether the gods are: Euripides did not persuade the women that there are no gods. It means that Euripides' denial is wholly incomprehensible to her, even more incomprehensible, if this is possible, than Socrates' denial was to Strepsiades. She does not stoop to accuse Euripides of impiety because the poet's manifestly absurd contention can not be taken seriously in itself, but only with a view to its adverse effect on her livelihood; the poor woman is not aware, as Strepsiades is at the end of the *Clouds*, that the denial of the gods has had or could have an adverse effect on everybody or on the whole city. Nothing would have been easier for the poet than to present the compassion-arousing war widow accusing Euripides of atheism in order to arouse the greatest ire against him, so that he would be completely ruined for having half-ruined her; nothing would have been easier for the poet than to present religious persecution as rooted in economic interest; he failed to do so. The superior woman's leaving at once by itself makes it almost certain that Euripides' denial of the existence of the gods will not play a role in the rest of the play.

The two accusers are answered by the kinsman, whose defense of the poet is quite clever. He is completely silent on the subject of Euripides' teaching atheism; he replies only to the first accuser. He says that it is not surprising that the women are very angry at Euripides, since he has given them such a bad reputation; he himself (she herself) hates him on that score. Yet, he goes on, making explicit what the first accuser had almost implied, Euripides' crime is attenuated by the fact that what he said about the women is the truth, in fact only a small part of the truth, as women among themselves may admit. He (she) tells the story of his (her) own adultery in all its details as an example of the kind of things that Euripides never made public, and then mentions four other womanly misdeeds of the same description, the central one being connected with their acts of adultery committed while their husbands are away from home on military service. The kinsman may be said to have defended Euripides in this manner: Granted that the poet has spoken ill of the women and hence harmed them; yet he could have harmed them much more than he has done; hence he is not the women's enemy. But in order to make this point, the kinsman had to be extraordinarily frank. No wonder that the chorus is shocked by his daring; it would not have believed that a woman would speak so shamelessly in the women's assembly but—come to think of it— only a woman can surpass in evil the women who are by nature shameless. The chorus surely does not deny the truth of the kinsman's (or Euripides') accusations of the women. Apparently it is paralyzed to act against the kinsman (and Euripides) by its awareness of that truth. Only one woman is not bewitched by the kinsman's speech, but insists not indeed that the proceedings against Euripides be continued but that the defender of Euripides be fittingly punished as a traitor to her sex. The punishment proposed would accidentally reveal the defender's sex and therefore be fatal to Euripides' design. The kinsman therefore protests against being punished for justly defending Euripides. The only woman who has not succumbed to the kinsman's rhetoric replies that Euripides' defender is the only woman who has dared to defend the man who has done the women the greatest harm by presenting in his plays only bad women and never decent women like Penelope: Far from having said the truth about women, he has most unjustly suppressed the truth about them; Euripides' defender deserves unusual punishment because she has defended a grave injustice in an unusually unjust manner. The kinsman, who knows that the best defense may be an attack, defends Euripides by attacking all present-day women, i.e., by acting on the premise that the good is the old: There are no longer any women like Penelope. When this contention is indignantly denied by his sole opponent, he begins to recite another list of misdeeds of contemporary women. His opponent can only curse him and start a fight with him. If the fight were allowed to continue, the kinsman would have won it. At any rate, the solemn accusation brought by all Athenian women against Euripides leads to nothing more serious than a brawl between two women. Euripides' design has been entirely successful despite the fact, which he did not foresee, that the subject of his atheism (and even of his publicly teaching atheism) came up in the women's assembly. He owed his success ultimately to his ability—an ability that Socrates lacks—to imitate women or to make others imitate women, to his being a (dramatic) poet.[78] Accepting his kinsman's offer to defend him in the women's assembly has proved to be a wise action: Agathon could not have done better. But if this is so, why did he make the vain attempt to persuade Agathon to defend him?

The single combat between the kinsman and the woman is stopped by the chorus, which sees another woman running toward the assembly in great haste. That woman proves to be the notorious homosexual Kleisthenes, a woman of a man, who loves the women because his manner is akin to theirs. He has come to warn them of a grave matter of which he has just heard in the market place. The chorus, moved by his concern for the women and desirous to protect sweet little Kleisthenes against the evil consequences of his appearing in the women's assembly in which no man is permitted, calls him a child. Kleisthenes reports that, as people say, Euripides has sent a kinsman, an old man, into the women's assembly, after having singed him and dressed him as a woman, in order to spy on their speeches. The kinsman vainly tries to dismiss the rumor as absurd; Kleisthenes assures the women that he has heard the story from people in the know. We are not told how the secret leaked out. We hesitate to leave it at saying that every secret of this kind can leak out and therefore the manner of its leaking out is unimportant. Kleisthenes is a pathic homosexual, like Agathon (206, *Lysistrate* 1092). Would the secret have leaked out if Euripides had succeeded in persuading Agathon to defend him in the women's assembly? In that case Agathon would have had the greatest interest in keeping the secret. But what interest does he have in keeping the secret after Euripides' kinsman has taken the place originally assigned to him? Who does not like to tell a funny story, especially to intimates, without necessarily inquiring very deeply whether every intimate favors as much as he does the fobber rather than the fobbed? We conclude that Euripides acted wisely in attempting to persuade Agathon to defend him.

When the women hear that there is a man among them, they cease to be paralyzed; they turn with vigor to the search for him and ask Kleisthenes to join them in the search. This request is wise, for the women have to find out whether someone who both appears and claims to be a woman is not in fact a man; but in the circumstances only a man can lawfully or in propriety undress a man, and only a woman can lawfully or in propriety undress a woman. Yet the very fact that seems to call for the co-operation of men and women makes impossible the participation of either men or women in the search: The kinsman's (or Euripides') crime seems to be undetectable, or the transformation of the heard into the seen seems in the present case to be impossible. Kleisthenes tries to overcome the difficulty by a process of exclusion: All women known as women to the other women are not the man in disguise. The kinsman is the only one who fails that test. But obviously an unknown woman is not therefore a man. Yet Euripides' defender is unable to tell the name of her husband and to describe sufficiently the proceedings, known only to women, during the Thesmophoria. There is no longer a doubt that the defender is the man whom the women seek; Kleisthenes must undress him. The kinsman does everything possible to conceal his sex, but all his ingenuity is of no avail. The woman who alone among the others was not bewitched by his speech proclaims that he has been detected and thus solves the riddle of how any woman could have defended Euripides. The kinsman is naturally despondent. He is being watched by the women lest he run away while Kleisthenes informs the authorities. Not only has Euripides' design completely failed, he has now become manifestly guilty of a sacrilege, not only in the eyes of the women, but of the city. The chorus immediately begins to investigate whether there is not some other man who has entered the women's assembly. The kinsman's half-success has obviously alarmed them to the highest degree. While engaged in their search, they are so far from being literally silent as they had intended (660) as to loudly pronounce that if they detect a man who has committed the impious act of listening to the women's proceedings, he will be punished and be an example to the other men of what happens to *hybris*, unjust deeds and godless manners. He will come to state openly that there are gods, and he will teach all human beings to worship divinities and justly to perform pious and lawful acts; if he fails to do so but is caught, both women and mortals will clearly see that a god punishes at once the lawless and impious acts. The chorus does not detect any other man. To some extent the chorus' assertion regarding the punishment of the wicked is borne out by what happened to the kinsman; he surely was not punished for his impious act by any god before he was caught by human beings. On the other hand, there is no sign that the kinsman (or Euripides), after having been detected, will declare that there are gods and will teach men to worship gods. The chorus refrains therefore from referring to the case of the kinsman or generally to the past, but speaks of the punishment of the godless only in the future tense. The always present truth that a god punishes at once the lawless and impious acts will always become manifest by the god's future action, provided those acts are discovered by human beings; the always made assertion always remains in need of future verification. This then is the reason why the women search for a man other than the kinsman who has impiously attended the women's assembly: They must reassert the law of piety. By not finding another man, they show at least that the god's failure to punish that man is in agreement with the law of piety. Be this as it may, while the women were entirely unconcerned with Euripides' atheism, to which the second accuser had drawn their attention in passing, they are now almost concerned with it as a consequence of the detection of the kinsman's impious act, which was instigated by Euripides. The detection of this impious act will lead, as one may hope, to the punishment of the poet by the city, to punishment strictly understood. For, as it seems, the women have in common with the gods that they can not, or do not, inflict punishment strictly understood. Yet how can one expect that the city will punish the poet for his impious act if, as the second accuser asserted, he has persuaded the men by his tragedies that there are no gods? This accusation seems to be borne out by the fact that the women, and not the men, state, however qualifiedly, the belief in divine punishment and hence in the existence of gods, just as the womanish

Agathon, speaking through the mouth of maidens, praised the gods. In other words, if the women lack punitive power strictly speaking, if it is absurd to speak of a *demos* of women distinct from the *demos* proper (306-7, 335-36), why is Euripides afraid of their condemning him?

While the chorus predicts the divine punishment of every man other than the kinsman who commits impious acts, the kinsman tries to protect himself against human punishment. Imitating a move that once had saved Dikaiopolis from the rage of the Acharnians, he takes her baby from the woman who had been his sole opponent and threatens to kill it if the women do not let him escape. The mother and the other women are shocked but helpless; their only comfort is that none of the immortal gods will assist him in his unjust deeds. The kinsman despises their vain talk. In accordance with this the women threaten to burn him alive in order to force him to hand over the baby. He remains firm; he is likely to disarm the women as Dikaiopolis had disarmed the Acharnians. Yet he does better than Dikaiopolis; he undresses the baby (a girl), who proves to be a flask filled with wine; the kinsman's worst enemy is discovered to have committed an impious act by not keeping the day of fasting. Yet this crime is so common among the Athenian women that the kinsman's clever move is of no help to him. Precisely because the women are as bad as Euripides said, they remain victorious. Precisely because Euripides teaches the truth (about the women), he is defeated. His cleverness is inferior to Dikaiopolis'.

The kinsman seems to be lost. Euripides had sworn to him to save him if necessary. Yet how can he let Euripides know of his distress? Fortunately he remembers a device used in a Euripidean tragedy on behalf of Palamedes. In that play the hoped-for savior was informed of Palamedes' need for help by a message written on oar blades that were thrown into the sea. The kinsman, being held far from the sea, in fact in a temple, has no oars but uses votive tablets in their stead—after all, both are of wood; instead of the sea he uses the air as a medium of transmission.

Nothing remains for him to do but to wait for his deliverance by Euripides—a deliverance that seems to be wholly impossible given the nature of the element through which his message is transmitted to the poet. Being kept under guard by the women, the kinsman has no choice but to wait on the stage. The women too wait, but they wait for the coming of the magistrate who is in charge of the kinsman's punishment. The kinsman waits as defeated men wait for the consequence of their defeat, while the women wait as victorious beings wait for the fruit of their victory to ripen. Yet the women owed their victory to their badness. They wisely employ their wait to counteract, by staging the parabasis, the bad impression they have made on the audience. The parabasis of the *Thesmophoriazusai* has no other purpose than to prove that women are good, much better than men. It is wise of them to present this proof in the parabasis as distinguished from a debate: No one can contradict them. As is shown by the *Lysistrate*, women can prove their superiority to men in a debate with men, even with high dignitaries; but to refute Euripides (or his kinsman trained by him) is beyond any woman's power. Accordingly, in the parabasis the women prove their goodness against the charges made by men in general; yet they prove it in the presence of Euripides' kinsman, who is however muted by his defeat (caused by the women's badness) as well as by the absolute impossibility, due to convention, of anyone interrupting the parabasis. The unique features of the parabasis of this play are these: An actor is on the stage during the parabasis; in the scene preceding the parabasis the chorus was successfully debunked by the hero's ally and yet victorious over that ally, and thus the antagonism between the chorus and the hero is still unresolved during the parabasis; the parabasis consists only of the parabasis proper and the epirrhema; the parabasis is devoted to the single theme of the women's goodness. Nothing needs to be said about the chorus' silence in the parabasis as to the comic poet, or about the absence from the parabasis of any invocation of gods, even of the Muses. Its silence as to the sacrilege (to say nothing of the atheism) of the women's enemy is sufficiently explained by the fact that impiety belongs to the tribunal of competent, i.e., male, authority.

The chorus of women defends the female sex against the charge made by all that all evils that afflict human beings—among them civil and foreign war [79]—stem from women. If women are altogether evil, why are men so eager to live with them, to keep them for themselves and close to themselves indoors, and to look even at women who are not their wives? The peculiar character of men's longing for women proves not only that women are not simply bad but that they are, while perhaps not simply good, at least much better than men. Each sex claims to be superior to the other. To settle this controversy with finality, it suffices to compare the names of women with those of men, for the actions agree with the names. The chorus supports this assertion by a number of contemporary examples that must have carried great weight with the audience. It might have referred to the names of Eirene and Theoria on the one hand, of Polemos and Kydoimos on the other. It might have stressed the fact that the names of the virtues are feminine, if the same were not true of the vices. Women hardly steal, for if they do, they steal very little from their husbands, which is not theft strictly speaking, while men steal large amounts from the public treasure and in addition receive public honors as a consequence. Women are inferior to men also regarding the other crimes or vices. Above all, women are much more conservative, much better preservers of the ancestral, than men. For the reason indicated before, the chorus fails to add that since women are so much more trustworthy than men, they are much more likely than men to say the truth about the gods. The chorus does not blame men for being inferior to women. It does not even blame them for claiming to be the rightful rulers of women. Explicitly addressing the city, it merely blames it for not giving some honor to women who have given birth to good citizens, especially to good military commanders, while dishonoring the mothers of bad citizens. One may say that the women prove their superiority most convincingly by accepting the ancestral order of rank among the various kinds of beings,[80] an order not sufficiently indicated by the beauty or lack of beauty of the names of the beings concerned. Although the women's argument seems to be worthless because it is set forth while the other party is prevented from talking back, it ends by granting to the silent opponent what might be thought to be the decisive point and thus paves the way for the eventual reconciliation between them: The beings superior by nature bow to the law proclaiming their inferiority. For however inimical Euripides may be to the *nomos*, he has the *nomos* on his side in asserting the inferiority of the women; he uses indeed this partial agreement with the *nomos* for his radical attack on the *nomos*, i.e., on the gods, for the female sex is by nature more pious than the male. His way of reasoning recalls that used by the Unjust Speech.

Euripides has not responded to his kinsman's message. The kinsman believes that this is because of the poet's being ashamed of the frigid play of his that had suggested to the kinsman the notion of how the message should be sent. He decides therefore to make use of Euripides' recent *Helen* by playing Helen, who waits for her husband Menelaos just as he waits for Euripides, his kinsman by marriage. After all, he has some experience in successfully pretending to be a woman, and he is still dressed as a woman. Undisturbed by the warnings of Kritylla, the woman who acts as his guard, against trying any funny business, he begins to quote from Helen's soliloquy, which opens the *Helen*, and in which the heroine presents herself as waiting for Menelaos. He makes some changes in the

Euripidean text; in particular, he is more hopeful than Euripides' Helen of the speedy arrival of the deliverer. The hope proves to be justified; Euripides keeps his oath; his kinsman's ruin would be his own; he appears in the role of Menelaos. Did he receive his kinsman's message dispatched through the air? This would seem to be the height of impossibility, much more impossible than a *deus ex machina*, for only the gods can do everything, and the gods do not assist men in impious deeds (715–16). Yet Euripides' receiving his kinsman's message is not more impossible than Peisthetairos' founding of Cloudcuckootown. One can not say that Euripides did not receive his kinsman's message on the ground that he arrives only after the kinsman had begun to recite from the *Helen* and responds as Menelaos immediately on his arrival; for the poet would have understood the situation immediately and would act accordingly. The ensuing dialogue between Euripides-Menelaos and the kinsman-Helen culminates in the partial reproduction of the scene in the *Helen* in which Helen recognizes Menelaos, but Menelaos believes that the Helen whom he sees is only a phantom. Yet Menelaos-Euripides recognizes his kinsman-Helen who, differing from Euripides' Helen, urges the kinsman by marriage to take him (her) away with the greatest speed. Kritylla—the wife of Antitheos—who did not recognize Euripides but regarded him in accordance with his quotations from *Helen* as a stranger, had followed the dialogue between the two men without any understanding; nevertheless she is intelligent enough to oppose the kinsman's abduction. Fortunately for her the magistrate, accompanied by a Scythian archer, arrives at this moment and thus prevents the escape of the guilty man. Euripides runs away after having assured his kinsman that he will not let him down as long as he lives, unless his innumerable tricks should fail him. The dialogue between Euripides and the kinsman consists to a considerable extent of quotations from the *Helen;* Euripides uses utterances of Menelaos and once the utterance of another male character, while the kinsman uses utterances of Helen and once the utterance of a nameless old woman. By applying a verse from the *Helen* to his situation, the kinsman calls the altar a grave; he is properly rebuked for this daring act by Kritylla, which does not prevent Euripides from repeating the reprehensible act. Before she noticed the complicity of Euripides, Kritylla rebuked the kinsman for deceiving the apparent stranger; the kinsman had presented himself to Euripides as a wife who has taken refuge at a tomb or altar in order to escape being forced to lie with a tyrant. Kritylla enlightens Euripides by telling him that the would-be woman is a man who has come to the women's assembly in the guise of a woman in order to steal gold from the women; she conceals the kinsman's defense of Euripides, which did not end too well for the women. Even after she has realized that the alleged stranger is an accomplice of the guilty man, Kritylla takes it for granted that the kinsman alone will undergo punishment: The original purpose of the women's assembly is forgotten.

The *Helen* scene is as much a failure as the kinsman's snatching and debunking of the alleged baby. That action of the kinsman had led to the proof by deed of the women's badness, and therewith to the women's admission in the parabasis that despite their alleged superiority they must bow to the *nomos* proclaiming their inferiority. Similarly the *Helen* scene proves the superiority of Euripides; he succeeds perfectly in deceiving Kritylla as to his identity, although she knows that the kinsman had been sent to the women's assembly by Euripides and that the alleged Menelaos is an accomplice of the kinsman. Euripides succeeds perfectly in concealing himself. On a different plane the *Helen* scene constitutes a victory of Euripides, since it refutes completely, if tacitly, the women's charge that Euripides hates women. In the *Helen* Euripides vindicates the chastity of the woman most maligned for her lack of chastity; the only other important female character in the *Helen*, Theonoe, is piety and justice incarnate, while the evil character in the play is a man. The use of the *Helen* thus prepares still further the final reconciliation of Euripides and the women.

The magistrate, acting by the authority of the Council, makes clear at least in the kinsman's view that the poor man will be capitally punished. For the time being he is only disgraced; the magistrate commands the archer to take the kinsman indoors and bind him to a plank, then to expose him outdoors, watching him carefully and using the whip on anyone who might dare to approach him. He is not even granted his wish not to be exposed to the viewers in his ridiculous garb; he is to be held up to laughter before being executed; he has lost all hope of being saved. While he is being bound to the plank indoors, i.e., while he is absent, the chorus chants the praise of some gods (Apollon, Artemis, Hera, Hermes, Pan, the nymphs, Dionysos). It assigns the central place no longer to Artemis, but to Hermes. The chorus explicitly refuses to speak ill of the men: Although the men were taught by Euripides to deny that there are gods, they after all punish the kinsman in deference to the women's wishes. The chorus is silent as to divine punishment. The kinsman seems to be utterly lost, yet the reconciliation between the women and Euripides silently progresses.

The kinsman, bound to the plank and suspended, is brought outdoors by the archer, who treats him cruelly. His situation reminds us of that of Prometheus in Aeschylus' *Prometheus Bound*. Given the fact that the kinsman will soon be liberated by Euripides without any divine help, his resemblance to Prometheus suggests that "the gods and savior Zeus" invoked by the kinsman in his agony (1009) are, to say the least, much less powerful than they are according to Aeschylus. While the archer leaves briefly to attend to his comfort, Euripides signals to the kinsman that he should become Andromeda, who had been bound to a rock by her father in order to be devoured by a monster for the appeasement of Hera and Poseidon, while Euripides himself will be Perseus, who saved Andromeda and married her; the *Andromeda*, like the *Helen*, was a recent work of the poet. Yet, while the conceit to use the *Palamedes* and the *Helen* had been the kinsman's, the conceit to use the *Andromeda* is Euripides'. The kinsman-Andromeda bitterly complains about his (her) lot. Addressing the women, he speaks of his imploring the help of the man who shaved him, dressed him as a woman, and sent him to the temple where the women are. That is to say, for the first time he admits to the women his crime and above all the fact that he is not the chief culprit. One wonders whether he is not trying to achieve his liberation at the expense of Euripides. The poet next turns into the nymph Echo, another character of his *Andromeda:* In order to overcome or win over the women, he himself must become a female being. The voice of Echo that the kinsman hears tells him that she was Euripides' helper last year in the very place where they now are, i.e., in the theater; Euripides destroys the dramatic illusion more than anyone else in the *Thesmophoriazusai*. As Echo he echoes first the pitiable complaints that the kinsman-Andromeda utters at his command in order to arouse the women's compassion; yet the kinsman, annoyed by the echoing, abuses Euripides as "old woman" and curses him. Euripides' echoing of the kinsman proves however to be only preparatory to his echoing of the archer, which begins on the archer's return. The archer is genuinely confused by the voice, whose origin he does not clearly discern; he is led to believe that one of the women is teasing him. While he turns his attention and his rage toward that woman, Euripides appears as Perseus, claiming to approach Andromeda, a virgin as beautiful as a goddess, through the ether; for echoing sounds is not sufficient to loosen fetters. Andromeda beseeches the stranger to free her from her bonds. But however stupid the archer may be, he is not so stupid as to be blind to the difference between a young girl and an old man; even Euripides' speech is powerless against the testimony of the barbarian's eyes in this matter, and this despite the fact that he is willing to grant that Euripides is in love with the being bound to the plank. He surely refuses to permit Euripides to unfetter the kinsman. Euripides leaves with a resolve to use a device fit to persuade a barbarian nature. The *Andromeda* scene ends then, just like the *Helen* scene, in failure. Yet Euripides himself has now for the first time become a female being; he has succeeded in coming near to the kinsman despite the magistrate's strict prohibition and in fact in entering the women's assembly; and he has learned now how he must handle the archer. Above all, since the *Andromeda* scene turns more and more into an exchange between the sophisticated poet and the barbaric archer, the contrast between the two men—between Greek poetry and barbaric jargon—can not but have an effect favorable to Euripides on the Athenian women.

After Euripides has left to figure out how to save the kinsman, the chorus chants another song in praise of some goddesses. In its capacity as the *demos* of women it first calls on Athena, who detests tyrants. It then calls on Demeter and Persephone, whose solemn celebrations may not be viewed by men. This is the first time that the chorus calls solemnly on some gods, and in particular on Demeter and Persephone, in the presence of the kinsman known to the chorus to be a man. It is no longer necessary for the chorus to say as it said in the preceding song that it will not speak evil of men (960–64). It does not even allude to the kinsman's impious act.

After all his failures which, as we have seen, are not simply failures, Euripides no longer delays to offer peace to the women with the promise that he will not speak evil of them in the future. The women do not reject the proposal: They are no longer set on punishing him for the evil that he has done them. They only wish to know what kind of need induces him to make his offer. He tells them that the man bound to the plank is his kinsman; if he sets him free, no evil will be said any more about the women; but if the women do not give in, the poet will tell their husbands after their return from the army what their wives have been doing while they were away.[81] He thus tells the women that his power to harm them is not exhausted by what he has said about them already; he merely restates what the kinsman had told them in his speech defending the poet. The women, who remember the effect of the speech on themselves, as well as the fact that the only woman who was not paralyzed by the kinsman's speech was discredited by the kinsman very soon afterward when her alleged baby proved to be a wine flask, accept Euripides' proposal forthwith. The poet's knowledge of the ways of women, his ability to make these ways publicly known, and his ability to imitate women give him a power over them that saves him. This is not to deny that he proves to be unable to disarm the women without making an important concession to them. Since he has failed to persuade Agathon to defend him in the women's assembly, he is compelled to rest satisfied with the second-best solution to his difficulty. Being compelled to substitute his kinsman for Agathon, he succeeds in preventing his own condemnation only at the price of exposing his kinsman to mortal peril; and he can not save his kinsman without making a grave concession to his persecutors. The women refuse however to free the kinsman from the danger threatening him at the hands of the archer: Euripides must persuade the archer to let his kinsman go. This is the only punishment that the women inflict on him. The poet has anticipated this state of things. He has brought with him a dancing girl and a flute girl, and he presents himself to the archer as an old procuress. The arts of the dancer, who has been well instructed by the poet on the way to the temple, and of the flute player are more than sufficient to arouse the barbarian's desire and thus to make him forget his guard duty. Following instructions, the dancing girl runs away, pursued by the archer. While he is removed from the stage, Euripides unfetters his kinsman and both men escape. The women do not interfere. When the archer returns and sees that he has been fooled, the women misinform him as to which way the kinsmen went and thus contribute their share to Euripides' salvation: Far from being punished by the women, the poet is saved by them. The song with which the chorus ends the play reminds us as much as possible of the ending of the *Clouds*.

In the course of the play the crime of speaking evil of the women for which they persecute Euripides is almost forgotten, and the concern of the women shifts to the sacrilege committed by his kinsman, although or because the kinsman has aggravated the crime of speaking evil of the women by addressing the women in the guise of a woman. Yet Euripides himself is guilty of a much more serious crime than speaking evil of women: He has spoken evil of the gods, for he has taught men that there are no gods. This gravest of all crimes is mentioned only in passing. Furthermore, although Euripides has persuaded the men that there are no gods, the men persecute him or his kinsman for an act of impiety. How can these things be understood? What is the connection between speaking evil of women and speaking evil of the gods? If it is true that the poet has persuaded the men that there are no gods, only the women now believe that there are gods. While there is agreement between Euripides and the men, there is the most profound disagreement between Euripides and the women: He hates the women, he speaks evil of them, and the women respond in kind. Sacrilege is still a punishable offense because the city preserves divine worship, if only for the sake of the women; the gods are indeed by *nomos*, but more particularly by a *nomos* required for the sake of women or produced by virtue of women. This state of things is adumbrated in a manner in the parabasis, in which the women present themselves as by nature superior to men but as bound to the *nomos* that proclaims their inferiority to men: Men, by nature superior to the gods, may bow to the *nomos* that proclaims their inferiority to the gods. The enforcement of the law regarding impiety will then depend to some extent on how much the women insist in a given case on that enforcement. Hence Euripides' power over the women suffices for his escaping persecution by the city.

Yet even if we knew only the *Clouds* we would know that the hypothesis underlying the *Thesmophoriazusai* is impossible: Euripides can not possibly have persuaded the city, the *demos*, that there are no gods; an atheistic city is even more impossible, one might say, than Peisthetairos' becoming the successor of Zeus, to say nothing more of the possibility of a *deus ex machina*, and to say nothing of the impossibility of women having criminal jurisdiction over men speaking evil of them. The utmost that Euripides could have achieved would be to persuade some men of the truth of atheism; his attempt to persuade the city of it would only have led to his ruin, unless he gained the men's favor by making himself the mouthpiece of a sentiment as dear to them as the belief in gods, like hatred of women. We recall the old men in the *Lysistrate* speaking of "the women hated by Euripides and all gods" (283). To speak more seriously, Euripides might have converted a part of the city to his sentiment; like Dikaiopolis he would have saved himself by splitting the city. In the *Lysistrate* the difference between men and women corresponded to the difference between the war party and the peace party. Let us see what follows if one assumes that in the present play the difference between men and women corresponds to the difference between those men who deny and those men who assert that there are gods, as illustrated by the difference between Demosthenes and Nikias in the *Knights*. The "manly" kind of man would of course defer, within reason, to the sentiments of the "womanly" kind and therefore continue to treat impiety as a crime, but punish it only when the latter kind insisted on punishment; one can imagine a situation in which a man guilty of impiety can exert pressure on the part inimical to him so as to bring about his acquittal. At any rate, the *Thesmophoriazusai* does not contradict Aristophanes' claim that he does not treat women comically (cf. p. 213).

The *Thesmophoriazusai*, if contrasted with the *Clouds*, shows the superiority of the poet, at least of the dramatic poet, who is able to appear in various disguises, to the philosopher, to the man who worries so much about the things aloft and therefore lacks that ability. The dramatic poet, who can speak evil (or well) of and hence do evil (or good) to his enemies (or friends), wields power. It is not necessary to repeat what was said when we considered Peisthetairos' treating the poet better than the astronomer. The *Thesmophoriazusai* presents Euripides' success: The concession that he makes to the women fades into insignificance if seen in the light of his escaping capital punishment. His failure is presented in the *Frogs*. It remains to be seen whether that failure throws any light on the relation between tragic and comic poetry.

8 *The Frogs*

The *Frogs* is the only Aristophanean comedy at the beginning of which we see and hear a god. It is the only Aristophanean comedy the action of which proceeds from the design of a god. It differs from all plays hitherto discussed by the fact that it opens with a dialogue between a master and a slave. The master is Dionysos himself, the god of the theater. His slave Xanthias asks him whether he should say one of the things at which the spectators customarily laugh. Dionysos leaves him full freedom except that of using expressions that disgust Dionysos. His prohibition reminds us of the distinction between vulgar and Aristophanean comedy that we know from some of the parabaseis; Dionysos states the preference ordinarily stated by Aristophanes himself. After all, Aristophanes has been bred by Dionysos (*Clouds* 519). The *Frogs* is surely the only comedy that opens with the question, what should a character in the play do with a view to making the audience laugh? This means that the *Frogs* is the only comedy that does not simply open with a complaint or with moaning. Yet Xanthias is eager to make jokes because he wishes relief from the pain caused by the luggage that he is carrying, although he carries the burden while riding on a donkey, whereas his gentle master walks. Xanthias complains about the soreness of his shoulder. It is not necessary for our purpose to follow Dionysos, who wonders how Xanthias can be carrying something since he himself is carried, and, after this difficulty is disposed of, why since Xanthias denies that he derives any help from being carried by the donkey, he does not in his turn carry the donkey. Dionysos is a better arguer than Xanthias, just as he has a better taste than he; he deserves to be the master. It is more important for us to realize that in the beginning of the *Frogs* the complaint is not absent, but as it were subordinated to joking or laughter as the relief for complaint. Laughing presupposes suffering, while the reverse is not true. At any rate

Dionysos, who at the beginning appears to be concerned with the right kind of comedy, soon proves to be concerned above all with the right kind of tragedy.

Dionysos commands Xanthias to get off the donkey, not in order to carry it, but because they have arrived at the god's first destination, the house of Herakles. Dionysos, clothed in a lion's skin and carrying a big club, knocks savagely at the door, which is opened by Herakles himself, who apparently has no servant; in contradistinction to Euripides and to Socrates in the corresponding scenes of the *Acharnians* and the *Clouds* respectively, he surely is not occupied. Contrary to Dionysos' expectation, which is not shared by Xanthias, Herakles is not frightened by his half brother's appearance but only incited by it to unquenchable laughter, for when dressing up for the role of Herakles, Dionysos had forgotten to take off his womanish garments. Dionysos obviously did not come to Herakles, as Dikaiopolis came to Euripides and as Euripides came to Agathon, in order to borrow a disguise; the god of the theater possesses all kinds of disguises. When Herakles asks him where on earth he has traveled in his ridiculous outfit, Dionysos replies that he has taken part in the naval battle of the Arginusai: A man or a god who lays claim to Heraklean prowess must have been able to do what many Athenian citizens and even slaves had done. His pretense to martial glory, as well as some other characteristics that he possesses, foreshadow Falstaff. The god of the theater is at the opposite pole from the fighter Herakles. Although the character responsible for the action of the *Frogs* is a god, he complies with Aristophanes' rule that characters who perform this function in his plays must be Athenian citizens. As he tells Herakles, while he was on a man-of-war on the way to the Arginusai or back, he read Euripides' *Andromeda*, and his heart became filled with an unsayably strong desire for the dead poet: No human being (and in particular not Herakles) can dissuade him from descending to Hades in order to bring Euripides back, for the poets who are still alive are bad. Herakles, for whose understanding Dionysos has a good-natured contempt, does not approve of his brother's liking for Euripides. He asks him why he does not try to bring back Sophocles from Hades rather than Euripides: The bringing back of Aeschylus is not even considered. Dionysos' decisive reason in favor of Euripides and against Sophocles is that one must be a scoundrel like Euripides in order to try to run away from the place where one belongs and, in particular, if one is dead, from Hades, but Sophocles was even-tempered (and hence content and just) here and is even-tempered (and

hence content and just) there. Herakles draws Dionysos' attention to
some other tragic poets; among them is Agathon whom Dionysos, the
admirer of Euripides, also admires, but even he is not comparable in his
view to Euripides. According to Dionysos one can no longer find a
naturally fertile poet who is able to utter risky expressions like "the foot
of time," which Dionysos is crazy about and which Herakles rejects as
altogether bad. One is tempted to think that Herakles, who cuts such a
poor figure in the *Birds*, is sobriety itself when confronted with Dionysos'
infatuation, just as Chairephon appeared to be on the side of law and
order in the *Wasps* when confronted with the final madness of Philokleon.
In Dionysos' view Herakles, being concerned with nothing but food,
understands nothing of poetry. He therefore turns to the purpose of his
visit. Having decided to descend to Hades, he needs Herakles' guidance
because he is wholly unfamiliar with Hades: There is no truth whatsoever
in Heraclitus' saying that Dionysos and Hades are the same.[82] Dionysos
needs Herakles' guidance more particularly because of his softness or love
of comfort; he wishes to know the most pleasant way down as well as
about the hosts in Hades of whom the hero had made use when he had
gone down to fetch Kerberos; he has provided himself with a lion's skin
and a big club in order to be regarded and treated as Herakles while down
there. His softness also explains why he needs the company of Xanthias;
he needs quite a bit of luggage and hence a carrier of it. One wonders
whether it is not his softness that underlies his love of Euripides. Herakles
is shocked by his mad daring, but Dionysos' mind is made up; so great is
his love of the theater that all his cowardice is powerless against it. While
Herakles had gone down to Hades to fetch Kerberos because he was compelled to do so, Dionysos goes down to Hades in order to fetch Euripides
because he loves Euripides' poetry. Dionysos refuses to consider any of
the three kinds of suicide that Herakles proposes to him as ways to Hades,
for he wishes to return. He is eager to learn from Herakles the way by
which he had gone down, because Herakles has come back. Herakles
gives him a gruesome description of the large and abysmally deep lake that
one has to cross on Charon's tiny boat, of the innumerable snakes and
other most terrible beasts, and the mass of foul mire and ever-flowing
sewage in which the most unjust people (among them mother-beaters,
but not Euripides) are thrown. Yet Dionysos is not afraid. Does he not
believe in the terrors of Hades? He surely expects to find every kind of
comfort on his journey. Although Herakles is reticent about the reception that he was given in Hades, he is truthful enough to add that Dionysos

will see, after he has passed the terrors, in a most beautiful light like that of the sun, blessed groups of initiated men and women who will tell him everything he might need to know, for they dwell near the gates of Pluton. After having said this much, Herakles bids Dionysos good-bye without making any further attempt to dissuade him from his journey. He did not ask him why he wished to look like Herakles in Hades. We suggest this explanation of this strange wish. Dionysos does not wish to be recognized in order to be able to see Euripides; he believes that he must steal Euripides just as Herakles had stolen Kerberos, because he expects that the gods below are anxious to keep the best poet; Herakles might be suspected of anything, but surely not of stealing Euripides; the Heraklean appearance is the only one that can not possibly arouse in Hades the suspicion that its wearer is after a poet.

Xanthias was of course excluded from the exchange between Dionysos and Herakles, but he did not accept that exclusion as a matter of course. Three times he complained that no attention was paid to him; after all, his shoulder still aches. He is accustomed to his master's paying attention to him; Dionysos is an easygoing, if not kind master, who lives with his slave on a footing of equality. He accedes at once to Xanthias' request that he leave him on earth and in his stead hire as porter a corpse, which as such is on its way to Hades. Dionysos sensibly refuses to pay the exorbitant sum demanded by the corpse, which is just being carried out, and only then does the sensible Xanthias declare that he is willing to carry the luggage to Hades. The relation of Dionysos and Xanthias resembles that of friends, rather than that of master and slave. Besides, not the terrors of Hades but the soreness of his shoulder had induced Xanthias to consider allowing his master to descend without him.

Dionysos and Xanthias arrive at the lake to be crossed on Charon's boat. Charon does not allow Xanthias on his boat, since he is a slave according to Athenian law, for he did not participate in the naval battle, as he truthfully admits; unlike his master he does not lie. The poor fellow is compelled to walk around the lake while carrying the luggage; it looks as if the difference between free men and slaves will be as important in Hades as it is on earth. At Charon's rude command Dionysos must row, despite his complete lack of naval experience. Charon comforts him by saying that the work will be made easy by a song of the chorus of frogs, which they will soon hear. The frogs sing of the beauty of the song that they chanted in honor of Dionysos on the occasion of the Athenian festival dedicated to that son of Zeus. They are not aware that the god is now listening to their singing; they recognize Dionysos as little as Charon did, but unlike Charon they are concerned with Dionysos. Dionysos loathes the frogs' music but they continue with it, claiming to be beloved by the Muses, Pan, and Apollon. While Dionysos' delicate ears suffer from the frogs' croaking, his delicate hands suffer from the rowing. When the frogs become aware of how much they annoy Dionysos, they annoy him on purpose. Thereupon Dionysos tries to silence them by outcroaking them, in which he succeeds. There is then a contest between the chorus and the individual responsible for the action of the play, a contest that ends with the victory of the "hero," as in the *Acharnians*, the *Wasps*, and the *Birds*. Yet in the *Frogs* the contest is not a contest through speech, nor does it occur in the center of the play. The conflict between the chorus and the hero in the *Frogs* is due merely to the failure of the chorus to recognize the hero. It is impossible to say whether that failure is caused by Dionysos' disguise. One may regard Dionysos' victory in the contest with the frogs as a good omen for his journey, but one must also say that we have only Dionysos' word for it that he defeated the frogs; the moment in which he claims to have defeated the frogs is the moment in which Charon's boat arrives at its destination, i.e., has left the region of the frogs.

When Dionysos and Xanthias meet on the far side of the lake, each claims to have seen the archcriminals of whom Herakles had spoken; but Dionysos at any rate had not given any sign of seeing them while he was rowing over the lake. He is surely uncertain now as to what they should do next. Xanthias suggests that they go on, since the place where they are, according to Herakles, is the region of the monstrous beasts. Yet, according to Herakles the place of the monstrous beasts is reached before the place of the archcriminals. Dionysos is now certain that Herakles has misinformed him about Hades, or more precisely that he has exaggerated the terrors of Hades in order both to frighten him (and thus to dissuade him from bringing back the hated Euripides) and to magnify his own descent to Hades. The only terror of Hades that Dionysos has experienced was the frogs, and those he overcame with ease. Entirely confident now, he is eager to meet a genuine monster of Hades. Xanthias obliges him by claiming to see the Empusa. Dionysos does not see it, either because it does not exist or because he is too frightened to see anything. He is so frightened that he urges his priest, who is sitting in the front row of the theater, to save him. He thus destroys the dramatic illusion without, however, becoming the spokesman for the poet (297; cf. 276). But the terror

—the only terror of Hades that frightened Dionysos—passes soon. The god is free to wonder which god has been trying to ruin him. Xanthias tells him in effect that the god in question is Dionysos' desire for Euripides, or that Euripides is a danger to Dionysos. This suggestion remains ineffectual, for in this moment master and slave hear the playing of flutes and see flaming torches: They have left the region of the terrors and entered the region of the blessed initiated. They step aside in order to watch the procession of the initiated, i.e., of the main chorus of the play. The *Frogs* is the only play that has two choruses, not confronting each other (like the chorus of men and the chorus of women in the *Lysistrate*), but succeeding each other. The play is not called after the main chorus but after the chorus of the frogs, which is never heard of again after its brief contest with Dionysos. The duality of choruses corresponds to the duality of the terrors of Hades and the bliss in Hades. The chorus of frogs takes the place of a possible chorus of the archcriminals of Hades, i.e., of the admirers of Euripides (771–80), which would not have been bearable since it would have been a chorus, a *demos*, of archcriminals that professes the principles of injustice and is not converted by punishment after death. The title of the play draws our attention to this possible impossibility.

The procession of the initiates in Hades, who are of course still Athenians, imitates the procession to Eleusis of the living. They invoke Iakchos, whose relation to Dionysos they leave in the dark, to join them in their sacred and gay dance. They send away the uninitiated, i.e., the a-Music and the politically criminal; in this context they mention Dionysos with reference to comedy; they refer three times to comedy, but never to tragedy. This is in agreement with the festival that they imitate, inasmuch as mockery forms no mean part of it. Yet the initiates are as unaware of the presence of Dionysos (to say nothing of his design) as were the frogs, who also in a manner imitated a celebration in honor of Dionysos. As a rule, the songs and speeches with which the chorus makes its entry in an Aristophanean play are in strict accordance with the dramatic function of the chorus—the chorus of the *Acharnians* acts as the old Acharnians pursuing the traitor Dikaiopolis, etc.—and do not present the chorus as comical chorus. In the *Frogs*, however, the chorus presents itself in the parodos not only as the chorus of Demeter (384–86) but also as the chorus of the play, eager to win in the contest of comedies (392–93). The chorus of the initiates shows tacitly that Dionysos is highly honored in Hades and that he would have been well received there, regardless of whether he is the Dionysos of Aristophanes, who is a civilized Athenian, or the Dionysos of

Euripides' *Bakchai,* who is worshiped above all by the barbarians and belongs together with Demeter (while Aristophanes' Dionysos does not meet Demeter's daughter even when he is in Hades). When Dionysos and Xanthias make their presence, although not their identity, known to the chorus, it asks them whether they do not wish to join in mocking certain Athenian citizens (416 ff.), i.e., in doing the work of Dionysos. Dionysos would not have run any risk in descending to Hades as Dionysos. His disguising himself as Herakles thus appears to be entirely unnecessary. For, assuming that the powers below wish to keep Euripides by all means, he could have made stealthy arrangements with the poet and run away with him at the opportune moment, even if he had appeared as Dionysos.

Immediately after the chorus has lampooned three Athenians, Dionysos asks it for guidance toward the dwelling of Pluton, without referring at all to the themes touched on in the parodos. He learns that he has arrived at the gate of Hades. The chorus continues its celebration of Demeter or Persephone and praises the bliss reserved for those who have been initiated and led a pious life. Being altogether alien to the ways of Hades, Dionysos does not know how he should knock at the gate of Hades. Xanthias advises him to do it along the lines of Herakles, in whose guise he appears. He knocks accordingly at the gate, which is opened by Aiakos, to whom he introduces himself as Herakles. Thereupon Aiakos receives him as Hermes had received Trygaios in the *Peace,* pouring a flood of insults over his ears about his having run away with Kerberos: Now he will pay for it; all the terrors of Hades will be let loose on him. Aiakos mentions the well-known terrors of Hades about which Herakles had remained silent, perhaps because he had escaped them owing to his quick withdrawal. Dionysos is frightened as never before; while despising him as the greatest coward among gods and men, Xanthias comes to his help; Dionysos denies that he is cowardly, but admits that he is less brave than Xanthias, who is as little frightened by Aiakos' threats as he was by the Empusa. Being more quick-witted than his slave, and having realized that his descending to Hades in the guise of Herakles was not only unnecessary but a great blunder, he suggests to Xanthias that they exchange roles; Xanthias will take on the guise of Herakles and he himself that of the slave who carries the luggage. Xanthias, proud of this recognition of his prowess, gladly accepts the suggestion. Since Dionysos is accustomed to living with Xanthias on a footing of equality, the exchange of roles is not too surprising. Immediately thereafter they are confronted not by a terror of Hades but by a maid servant of Persephone, who comes out of the house of the goddess in order to welcome Herakles to a big and delicious meal that Persephone prepared for him as soon as she heard of his return to Hades; the goddess obviously did not resent the theft of Kerberos. A most attractive flute girl and some dancing girls also wait for him indoors. Especially when he hears of the dancing girls Xanthias is highly pleased with this invitation and orders his slave Dionysos to follow him into the house with the luggage. Dionysos of course retracts the change of roles that he had arranged in different circumstances. In order to persuade Xanthias, he is compelled to tell him who solemnly protests that he can not be so insane and foolish as to believe that he, a slave and a mortal, is Herakles. Xanthias obeys. He comforts himself with the thought that Dionysos might live to regret his change of mind and role. The chorus, which still does not know the identity of Dionysos, praises him as a most versatile man (533, 540), a man like Theramenes the turncoat, who in each situation chooses the softer alternative. Dionysos entirely concurs in this praise. This is as it should be: Dionysos admires Euripides, and Theramenes is a disciple of Euripides (967–70). Dionysos is somehow akin to Euripides.

Yet he has not yet encountered the true terrors of Hades. He was saved from the wrath of Aiakos by the intervention of Persephone. Now other low-class inhabitants of Hades take up the business that Aiakos had left unfinished. Two hostesses recognize Dionysos as Herakles, the scoundrel who once upon a time had eaten enormous amounts of food in their establishment and when asked to pay for it had refused to do so and threatened the two women with his sword; now he will pay for his misdeeds; Kleon will be called in, who will bring him to justice this very day. Xanthias is pleased with Dionysos' being so speedily punished for having deprived him of the role of Herakles and confirms the two hostesses in their desire for the punishment of the apparent Herakles. Dionysos, who is again greatly frightened and for this reason, to say nothing of others, does not respond to the women's scolding in kind, is now again most eager to play Xanthias, while he wishes Xanthias again to take on the role of Herakles. Going to the extremes of repentance and self-abasement and swearing most solemnly that he will never again take the role of Herakles from Xanthias, he induces his slave to become Herakles again. The chorus urges Xanthias to act the part of the god Herakles. It sides with Xanthias, or rather with the god against the hostesses. The hostesses' recognizing Dionysos as Herakles has made the chorus certain that Xanthias is not Herakles, although it had ample occasion to observe Dionysos' very un-

Heraklean cowardice; it trusts the hostesses' judgment more than its own eyes, or, if you wish, it is deceived by Dionysos' disguise. It does not praise Xanthias as it had praised Dionysos for his versatility in the parallel strophe; it is aware of Dionysos' superiority.

Dionysos' action seems to be all the wiser since the punishment threatening Herakles proves to be extrajudicial, for Kleon obeys the hostesses' call as little as he had obeyed the call of the wasps. Aiakos appears with some slaves whom he commands to fetter Xanthias-Herakles. Imitating Herakles, Xanthias prepares himself for a fight, but is easily overcome by Aiakos' helpers. Partly from fear and partly from the desire to avenge himself on Xanthias, Dionysos expresses his approval of Xanthias-Herakles' being punished for Herakles' misdeeds. Xanthias in turn avenges himself on Dionysos by denying to Aiakos that he has ever been in Hades before and by asking him to put his slave (Dionysos) to the severest tortures in order to find out the truth. This is too much for Dionysos; he now truthfully declares that he is Dionysos, the son of Zeus, while the alleged Herakles is his slave. Xanthias does not leave matters at denying Dionysos' assertion; he demands that Dionysos be whipped all the more, since if he is a god he will not feel it. Dionysos turns the tables on Xanthias: Since Xanthias too claims to be a god by claiming to be Herakles, he must receive as many beatings as Dionysos himself. Xanthias admits that Dionysos' proposal is fair: By whipping both of them Aiakos will see which of the two is not a god; the one who cries out first when whipped is not a god. Dionysos' proposal is to his interest, since being whipped is preferable to other kinds of torture, and that proposal as restated by Xanthias is acceptable to Xanthias since the hardened slave is likely to be less sensitive to pain than the soft Dionysos. What will be tested in accordance with Xanthias' proposal is not strictly speaking insensitivity to whipping, but the degree of such insensitivity; gods differ from men not in kind but in degree. Sensitivity to pain is akin to vulnerability, which in its turn is related to mortality. We may recall here what happened to the gods' immortality in the *Birds* (see above, p. 188). Aiakos praises Xanthias for his fairness; it is not clear whether he regards him as Herakles; he surely regards him as a mortal (640, 652), i.e., as the one whose fraud will be discovered by the whipping. Seduced by Xanthias, Aiakos assumes that one of the two is a god; he either reasons that if two beings claim to be gods while either of them denies that the other is a god, one of them must be a god, or else he knows that one of the two beings with which he has to deal is Herakles. However this may be, the whipping contest proves to be inconclusive; if not succumbing to pain when whipped is a sign of divinity, Xanthias is at least as much a god as Dionysos. Certainly Aiakos, who prior to the whipping contest was certain that Xanthias is a human being, is no longer certain of it after that contest. He therefore commands the two contestants for divinity to enter the house so that Pluton and Persephone, being gods themselves, can decide which of the two is a god. He acts on the assumption that no being known as a god to other gods can be a mortal in the guise of a god, just as in the *Thesmophoriazusai* the women acted on the assumption that no being known as a woman to the other women can be a man disguised as a woman (see above, p. 224). This could be thought to imply that only gods can know whether a given being is or is not a god, or that human beings as such can not know gods; *deus est quem dei deum esse declarant.* (This obviously leads to the further question of the veracity of the presumed or genuine gods.) Dionysos responds to Aiakos' final command with the remark that Aiakos should have thought of entrusting the decision to Pluton and Persephone before he whipped them. This remark shows not merely that Dionysos was not insensitive to the whipping, but above all that Dionysos himself did not think of the only true touchstone of divinity. One can not say that he was eager to conceal at all costs his being Dionysos, for he had revealed his identity to Aiakos prior to the whipping.

This much is clear: Dionysos lacks forethought. He had shown this sufficiently by his decision to descend to Hades in the guise of Herakles, a decision that led to his being whipped like a slave. This prompts us to wonder whether what induced him to descend at all to Hades—his desire to bring back Euripides—is not a consequence of the same defect: Could the stupid glutton Herakles, who loathes Euripides, be a better judge of tragedies than the god of the theater himself? Is Heraklean prowess, even if accompanied by stupidity and gluttony, not a better guide even regarding Music things than the softness of a playboy, which is characteristic of Dionysos and which underlies in particular his love for the "radical" poet Euripides? In trying to bring back Euripides, the enemy of the gods, he attempted without knowing it to free men from awe of the gods. His favoring of Euripides is about as reasonable as the favoring of the *philosophes* by a part of the French nobility prior to the French Revolution. Dionysos is enabled to indulge his soft habits by what we may call his social position. That position becomes most obviously questioned in the whipping contest, which renders his divinity wholly questionable. Euripides questioned the divinity of all commonly accepted gods (889–94;

Thesmoph. 451). Dionysos receives through his whipping the first inkling of the damage that Euripides' impiety does to his kind and hence to him, and he learns through the inconclusive character of the whipping contest that he depends on his fellow gods for his salvation: He receives a political lesson. We must wonder then whether the troubles that Dionysos gets into on account of his love for Euripides will not cure him of that love. Certain it is that Dionysos' cleverness and rascality is no match for the cleverness and rascality of Euripides as we know it from the *Thesmophoriazusai*. This inferiority must be taken into account when one judges Dionysos' cure of his love for Euripides—a cure that is at least partly the consequence of his foolish decision to descend to Hades in the guise of Herakles.

While the gods pass judgment indoors on the divinity of Dionysos and Xanthias, the chorus stages the parabasis. The parabasis of the *Frogs*, as distinguished from the parabaseis of the other plays, consists of all parts of the normal parabasis except the parabasis proper. The parabasis proper is the customary place in which the chorus speaks to the audience about the poet. The parabasis of the *Frogs* is as silent about the poet as the parabaseis of the three preceding plays. It differs from the parabaseis of all other plays by being silent about the chorus, i.e., about the initiates as such. While it begins with an invocation of the Muse, it is silent not only about the other gods but about the things of the Muses. The parabasis of the *Frogs* is strictly political; the chorus calls itself sacred (675, 686). This peculiarity of the parabasis of the play must be seen in the light of the unique emphasis in the parodos of the *Frogs* on things Music. The chorus imitates or anticipates the movement that takes place in the soul of Dionysos. In studying the *Lysistrate* and the *Thesmophoriazusai* one can observe a kind of atrophy of the parabaseis accompanying an atrophy of the need for a spokesman of the poet. This phenomenon has different reasons in the two plays: The *Lysistrate* is extraordinarily political and the *Thesmophoriazusai* is extraordinarily transpolitical; it remains to be seen what the reason is for the relative atrophy of the parabasis in the *Frogs*. The chorus, which as a matter of course has taken the side of the alleged Herakles against the two hostesses, advises the city to practice equality and hence in particular to be generous toward those who were involved in oligarchic errings, as well as toward all those who have fought in the navy for Athens. It blames the city for its unjust treatment of the gentlemen— the well-born, moderate, and just who were bred in palaestras, choruses, and music—the ancient coin as well as the new gold, which the city does not use, while it uses the bad copper coins struck lately, i.e., strangers and low-class men descended from low-class men. Yet it explicitly refrains from promising success to the city if the city were to make use of the right sort of people.

We hear of the outcome of the important action that took place indoors during the parabasis through a conversation between Aiakos and Xanthias. Yet what we hear about that event is as insufficient as what we hear about the corresponding indoor events in the *Clouds*. Let us note here that the *Clouds* and the *Frogs* are the only plays in which the design that triggers the action remains wholly unfulfilled: Dionysos does not bring back Euripides, just as Strepsiades does not get rid of his debts. We learn from the conversation between Aiakos and Xanthias that Xanthias is now known to be a slave, but this does not necessarily mean that Dionysos has become known to be a god: Aiakos speaks of Dionysos as "a noble man" (737), i.e., applies to Dionysos an expression that he had applied to Xanthias prior to the whipping contest (640). Aiakos has come to admire Dionysos for his easygoing or kind treatment of his slave. It goes without saying that he and Xanthias look at Dionysos and masters in general from the point of view of slaves. We must not be too much impressed by Aiakos' failure to speak of Dionysos as a god; slaves may be the worst judges of divinity. Yet precisely if this is so, they are likely to be the worst judges of other kinds of excellence as well. Xanthias becomes aware of noisy railing indoors. He learns from Aiakos that it is Aeschylus and Euripides who are abusing each other. The reason is this: According to a law of Hades, the best craftsman in any of the grand and clever crafts is seated on a throne near to the throne of Pluton. In Hades, as distinguished from Athens, the highest goal of ambition is then pre-eminence in arts like tragedy. This is all the more remarkable since the rulers in Hades admittedly understand nothing of these arts (cf. 810–11). The throne of tragedy was hitherto occupied by Aeschylus, but when Euripides came down he showed off his tricks to the multitude of criminals who became enamored of him; puffed up with that applause he laid claim to the tragic throne. The *demos* in Hades shouted for a judgment as to which of the two tragedians is wiser in regard to their art. Aeschylus' partisans however are few, since the decent people are few, "just as here," as Aiakos says, destroying the dramatic illusion. Still, the *demos*, i.e., the scoundrels (779, 781), is not altogether depraved, since it is entirely willing to abide by the judgment of an arbiter. Yet the two slaves do not pay attention to such niceties; they detest the rabble as much as the gentlemen do (cf. also 768), just as they have a Heraklean dislike for Euripides. Fortunately Hades is not a democracy; what will be done in regard to the tragic throne depends on Pluton; Pluton has decided that there will be a contest at once between the two tragedians. (Pluton's rulership may explain why the highest ambition in Hades is not political, or why there are no political contests there.) Since there is in Hades an authority independent of both the gentlemen and the *demos*, Xanthias reasonably wonders why the contest is limited to the favorite of the gentlemen on the one hand and the favorite of the *demos* on the other: Why did Sophocles not raise a claim to the tragic throne? He learns from Aiakos that when Sophocles came down to Hades, he accepted Aeschylus' supremacy gladly: He accepted his place in Hades with the same equanimity with which he accepted his being in Hades (80–82). Only if Aeschylus should lose the contest will Sophocles take up the fight against Euripides. Sophocles' posture toward Aeschylus resembles that of Xanthias toward Aiakos (cf. 788–89 with 754–55). Since Sophocles does not participate in the contest, he is not a character in the *Frogs*. Are we entitled to say that Sophocles is not fit to be a character in a comedy, whereas Aeschylus and Euripides are, since Aeschylus and Euripides stand for extremes that as such call for exaggerating imitation or for comical presentation, whereas Sophocles stands for the mean? Is tragedy in its highest form not subject to comical treatment, whereas comedy in its highest form is because of its essential extremism? Be this as it may, Euripides is at the opposite pole from Sophocles as far as self-assertion is concerned; he, and not Aeschylus, is responsible for the form that the contest of the tragedies will take, namely, the precise measuring and weighing of the tragedies of the two competing poets. The only difficulty is who should be the judge, for, as Aeschylus and Euripides agree, only few men are wise. By a stroke of good luck Dionysos has come down to Hades; both poets accept him as judge because of his experience in their art.

The contest of the tragedians is meant to decide "which of the two is wiser in regard to the art" (780). The whipping contest was meant to decide "which of the two is a god" (664). Just as the tragedies of Aeschylus and Euripides will be put to the test (802), Dionysos and Xanthias have been put to the test (642). Just as the impending contest will decide which of the two contestants is superior to the other in their art, the whipping contest was meant to decide which of the two contestants is superior to the other in insensitivity to pain. In trying to understand the later contest we must not forget the earlier one. We must also not forget that the whipping contest was preceded by the contest between Dionysos and the frogs. Only in the central contest is Dionysos' identity—who he is and what he is—the theme, while in the first contest his identity is not even in question, and in the third contest it is known. Perhaps the first contest, but surely the second contest was inconclusive. By mentioning the first contest again we do not mean to ascribe to it an importance comparable to that of the two other contests. It is essential to the *Frogs* that it successively present a whipping contest and a music contest, just as it has two successive choruses.

The chorus describes the imminent fight between the two poets by contrasting in grand language the gigantic grandeur and fury of Aeschylus and the subtle sharp-tonguedness and envy of Euripides. On a loftier plane it puts forth the same preference as Herakles and the two slaves. Dionysos is the only character of the play (apart from Euripides himself) who prefers Euripides. Yet, as seems to be shown by the fact that Dionysos was acceptable as judge to the two poets, the god's point of view is not identical with that of the gentlemen, who unambiguously prefer Aeschylus, or with that of the rabble, who unambiguously prefer Euripides. Furthermore, as we ought not to forget, Dionysos had to pay dearly for his longing for Euripides. Finally, Dionysos was originally concerned not so much simply with the best tragic poet as with the best tragic poet who would be prepared to run away from Hades; this consideration excluded Sophocles, while Aeschylus was not even thought of. Sophocles was excluded from consideration because of his being even-tempered; yet Aeschylus is the opposite of even-tempered (cf. *Wasps* 883–84) and might therefore be perfectly willing to leave Hades. At any rate Dionysos is now compelled to make a choice between Aeschylus and Euripides regarding tragic excellence, wholly independently of whether Aeschylus is willing to return to the living. When he appears in the company of the two poets, he has just advised Euripides to abandon his claim to the tragic throne. In order to see why he did this, we must consider that he had explained to Pluton why he had come to Hades and that he had solemnly promised Euripides to bring him back to Athens (1411–14, 1469–70). Pluton could have regarded Dionysos' action as god-sent: Euripides' disappearance would put an end to the riotous propaganda against the established order, i.e., Aeschylus' supremacy. Yet Pluton was already committed to the contest between the two poets. He could escape his commitment without being charged with injustice by his noisy *demos* only if Euripides publicly withdrew from the contest. Thus he may have asked Dionysos to persuade Euripides to abandon his claim. Yet this would have meant that Euripides tacitly recognized Aeschylus' pre-eminence, and this would have been unbearable for a man of Euripides' desire for distinction: There is no honor for tragedians in Athens that can be compared to the honor that may be awarded to them in Hades. It was entirely possible for Euripides to desire both to return to Athens and to be declared worthy of the tragic throne in Hades, for he knew that he would have to return to Hades sooner or later.

Aeschylus listens to Euripides' refusal to abandon his claim in contemptuous silence, which Euripides traces to his competitor's well-known pomposity. Euripides' insults eventually succeed in inducing Aeschylus to reply in kind. To Euripides' charge that his characters are savages, Aeschylus replies that Euripides' characters are beggars and cripples, not to say incestuous. Dionysos warns Euripides of Aeschylus' terrible rage (the god has compassion for Euripides), and he urges Aeschylus (whom he addresses as if he were a god) to control his anger: Poets must not behave like fishwives. Euripides declares himself willing to be the first to have his tragedies examined, however severely. Aeschylus, however, dislikes to compete with Euripides in Hades: His poetry is still alive among the living, while Euripides' poetry has gone down to Hades with him; yet in deference to the god he accepts Euripides' challenge. Dionysos thereupon commands the chorus to sing to the Muses because he wishes to pray that he may be able to judge of the contest in the most Music manner. The chorus naturally obeys, invoking the divine Muses to watch the coming contest regarding wisdom—a contest that will be conducted on both sides with the greatest power and cunning. Praying at the command of the judge, the chorus is now entirely impartial—as impartial as the Clouds were before the contest between the Just Speech and the Unjust Speech (*Clouds* 952–56).

Dionysos next commands the two poets to pray. Aeschylus obeys this command at once. He prays to Demeter, who has bred his mind, that he be worthy of her mysteries. Demeter is the goddess to which the chorus belongs. Euripides' hesitation to obey Dionysos' command is owing to the fact that he prays to "other gods," to gods of a different kind from those to whom Aeschylus and all others pray (with the exception of Socrates and his like), to gods peculiar to him; he prays to Ether, which nourishes him and which is the pivot of the tongue, as well as to Intelligence and Flair, that he may correctly refute the speeches with which he will have to take issue. Euripides' gods are not local or national, but universal or cosmic. His innovation regarding the gods does not induce the chorus to abandon its impartiality. After all, what is expected of poets is innovation or originality.

Without being asked to do so, Euripides opens the debate. Aeschylus is now silent like his Achilles and his Niobe (832, 911–13), whereas when the poets were asked to pray, Aeschylus was the first to speak without being asked to begin. Furthermore, Euripides opens the debate because he does not intend to argue, as the Unjust Speech did (*Clouds* 940–44), from the premises of his opponent. There is no common ground between him, the worshiper of Ether, and Aeschylus, the worshiper of Demeter. The fact that the disagreement between the two poets regarding the gods comes into the open during the prayer scene explains sufficiently why Euripides does not limit himself, as he originally intended (862–64), to discussing the poetic and technical qualities of the two poets' tragedies. Aeschylus is in his view a boaster, aiming at overawing his simple-minded audience by deliberate obscurity—for instance, by the protracted silences of his heroes and the use of novel and obscure words of oxlike size. Euripides, whose critique of Aeschylus reminds us of Pheidippides' critique of that poet (*Clouds* 1366–67), stands for clarity, straightforwardness, and rationality. Hence his use of the prologue and the democratic character of his plays.[83] When Dionysos advises him, the teacher of Theramenes, not to make too much of his democratism, the poet refers to the fact that he has taught the audience—the audience of the *Frogs* (954, 972)—to talk, to think, to see, to long and desire, to understand, to argue, and to be suspicious by bringing in domestic subjects with which men are familiar and that they understand, so that they can judge of the wisdom of what the poet does (cf. *Wasps* 1179–80): He broke with Aeschylus' habit of stupefying the audience by bringing in subjects beyond its experience. He made the Athenians acquire the habits of thinking, distinguishing, and raising questions, especially regarding affairs of the household.[84] The justice of this claim is strongly confirmed by Dionysos: Euripides has made the Athenians intelligent or intellectual; the god has been wholly convinced of Euripides' superiority to Aeschylus.

The chorus too is impressed by the powerful character of Euripides' attack. It does not fear that Aeschylus will disdain to reply. It fears that he will be unable to control his immense anger and indignation. Yet Aeschylus opens his reply in the most rational manner. Euripides had spoken only of the difference between himself and Aeschylus—of the opposition between his clarity, which made the Athenians more intelligent, and

Aeschylus' obscurantist obscurity. Aeschylus does not quarrel with Euripides' view of the opposition between the two poets or with his claim to have made the Athenians more intelligent. He merely begs Euripides to consider what is implied in his claim to be admirable as a poet; he reminds him in other words of the ground common to both, which is more fundamental than their difference. Euripides replies that the admirable poet makes the human beings in the cities better: Whether making men more intelligent, as Euripides did, is good depends on the answer to the question whether the intelligent man is necessarily a good citizen. Euripides and Aeschylus (to say nothing of Aristophanes) agree as to the highest criterion with a view to which poets must be judged. Euripides had been silent about that criterion: He had been silent about the political function of poetry, just as Socrates was entirely unconcerned with the city. Yet what Socrates could afford to do, if at his own peril, the poet who addresses the city can not. Aeschylus goes on to ask Euripides what he deserves to suffer if, far from making the citizens better, he has changed decent and noble men into altogether bad ones. Dionysos, who does not expect or wish Euripides to pronounce his own capital condemnation, answers the question for Euripides: The proper penalty for such a poet is death. It is hard to see how Euripides could have avoided giving the same answer. Yet it is also not easy to see how Dionysos, the soft and cowardly Dionysos, could give that answer unless we remember that in Hades he has undergone some rudimentary training in political responsibility. While he agrees with the two poets regarding the standard of poetic excellence, he has some doubts whether even Aeschylus has entirely lived up to it. Aeschylus rests his claim on the warlike and patriotic character of his plays, while admitting as a matter of course that noble poets may also teach mystic rites, abstention from bloodshed, the healing of diseases, oracles, the working of the fields, the seasons of harvesting, and the seed times; still, the divine Homer stands out for having taught orders of battle, deeds of bravery, and the arming of men. The outstanding example of what the Homeric-Aeschylean poetry achieved is Lamachos, whom we remember from the *Acharnians* and the *Peace* as the antagonist of our comic poet himself. By presenting lion-spirited warriors Aeschylus bred such warriors, whereas Euripides by presenting debased women filled women with unlawful desires. Euripides does not deny the charge that he failed to breed warriors. In order to deny the charge that he debased the audience, he refers to the goddess who inspired him and who admittedly is wholly alien to Aeschylus: Aphrodite, who belongs together with Peace

(*Acharnians* 989), the blessing that Dikaiopolis secured for himself with the help of Euripides, and who, together with Dionysos, is the sole concern of Aristophanes (Plato, *Symposion* 177ᵉ1–2). Yet it is not sufficient to oppose the divinity of *eros* to the claims of the city. Euripides can not deny that by presenting the power of Aphrodite he has weakened the resistance of noble women to unlawful love. Like all other poets, and not only poets, confronted with this kind of attack, he is compelled to have recourse to the fact that in presenting the overwhelming power of Aphrodite he merely stated the truth. Aeschylus, speaking on behalf of the city, flatly denies that this is a valid defense: It is the poet's duty to conceal evil; by presenting the bad in its glamour, he teaches evil, for he is the teacher of youth; the poets must say only decent things. Euripides is unable to contradict Aeschylus on this decisive point. He evades the issue by denying that Aeschylean grandiloquence is the proper way of teaching the decent things. Aeschylus reasonably replies that grand resolves and thoughts call for grand words and a grand appearance; Euripides has used low words and low appearances in order to arouse compassion for the tragic heroes. But in Euripides' view the arousing of compassion is a good thing. Just as Euripides evaded the question of whether it is not the poet's duty to conceal evil, Aeschylus evades the question of whether it is not the tragic poet's duty to arouse compassion. He goes on to show that Euripides has debased tragedy and therewith the Athenian citizenry; Aeschylus accuses Euripides of the same crime of which the Just Speech accused the Unjust Speech: He has made the citizens more concerned with speaking than with gymnastics and thus also destroyed the deference of the populace to their betters. Dionysos, however, is not so sure that the change for which Aeschylus makes Euripides responsible is altogether a change for the worse. This doubt only induces Aeschylus to make Euripides responsible for all evils that afflict present-day Athens. The Herakles-like Dionysos gladly grants that Athenian athletes are no longer what they were. He may have become doubtful of Euripides' superiority to Aeschylus; he surely has not become convinced of Aeschylus' superiority to Euripides. As for the chorus, there can be no doubt at all that it regards the contest as entirely undecided; in its view the decision will depend altogether on the second half of the contest, i.e., on the half in which will be discussed not the purpose of tragedy but its execution, the poetic or technical virtues and vices of the works of the two poets. That discussion can not be understood by an audience that is not highly sophisticated. The chorus assures the two poets that the Athenians, who always possess excellent natures, are now also no longer untrained or unsophisticated. The chorus thus brings out the fact that the audience is Euripidean, rather than Aeschylean (cf. 954–59, 1069–76).

Hitherto, to repeat, the contest between the two poets has remained inconclusive, as inconclusive as the whipping contest. Aeschylus, who takes the side of the city, Ares, and anger ("waspishness"), has not been refuted by Euripides, who takes the side of the household, Aphrodite, and compassion. Nor has Euripides been refuted by Aeschylus. This ought not to shock anyone, for, to say nothing of the fact that we have not yet reached the end of the contest, in the contest between the two Speeches in the *Clouds*, which has some resemblance to the contest between the two poets, the Unjust Speech was even victorious. These two contests belong together; they differ from all other contests of this kind since their theme transcends the political issues proper, even those involved in the foundation of Cloudcuckootown or in the prosecution of Euripides. The contest between the two Speeches is misunderstood if it is not realized that the position taken by Socrates differs profoundly from the positions taken by the two Speeches. One thus begins to wonder whether the position of Aristophanes—or of Dionysos, Aristophanes' teacher, who had originally not even thought of Aeschylus—does not differ from the positions of Aeschylus on the one hand and of Euripides on the other. The mere fact that Dionysos is a spectator of the verbal contest, rather than a participant in it, could induce one to raise that question. Certain it is that neither of the two poets is simply refuted by the other. The position of each has its strong and its weak sides. Aeschylus does not give their due to Aphrodite and to compassion; Euripides does not give their due to the city or warlike patriotism and to the need for concealing the unwholesome truth. Perhaps in Aristophanes' view there are two kinds of heterogeneous needs that must be satisfied by tragedy but that can not be satisfied except by two different kinds of tragedy. The fact that the kind of need fulfilled by Aeschylus is primary does not by itself prove that the kind of need fulfilled by Euripides is of lower rank. This would mean that Aristophanes is as little a partisan of Aeschylus as is his Dionysos. Aeschylus, full of wrath and given to indignation, fosters warlike patriotism and conceals the glamour of unlawful *eros*. No one can seriously doubt that warlike patriotism and stern self-control, to say nothing here of the worship of the ancestral gods, are the pillars of the city. Yet, as we have seen in the *Wasps* and elsewhere, waspishness becomes a danger if not to the citizen then surely to man; that which edifies the city is in need of a corrective.

The waspish jurymen are appeased by compassion and by laughter (see above, p. 120). Aeschylean tragedy needs as its supplement both Euripidean tragedy and Aristophanean comedy. Jocularly expressed, Aristophanes competes with Euripides but not with Aeschylus, or Aristophanes is an enemy of Euripides. The fact that Euripides and Aristophanes belong together over against Aeschylus is obviously compatible with the possibility that Aristophanes regarded Aeschylus as a greater poet than Euripides; whether he in fact did so can become clear only from the second half of the poets' contest. Nor can we exclude the possibility that the statement of the fundamental problem that is suggested by the first half of that contest is provisional, i.e., that what Aristophanes has in mind is the heterogeneity of the two functions of dramatic poetry, rather than the impossibility of fulfilling these functions by a single dramatist or in a single drama. After all, he himself claims that his dramas fulfill both functions, the edifying as well as the corrective one. Perhaps all good dramatists fulfill both functions, if each in his own way. One may wonder whether the silence on Sophocles is not a pointer in this direction. Let us also not forget the bond that links Ares and Aphrodite.

Euripides turns at once to the examination of Aeschylus' prologues, which he blames for their obscurity. That obscurity, he contends, is partly due to tautology, i.e., to bombast. He discusses one example consisting of three verses at fairly great length. Although he asserts that each of these verses contains many mistakes, he does not discuss at all the central verse, which is recited twice. Aeschylus' justification of the first verse implies in Dionysos' view a blasphemy. His justification of the third verse satisfies Dionysos, but the god is no less impressed by Euripides' rebuttal despite the fact that, as he admits, he does not understand it. There follows a very brief discussion of a second example that in Euripides' view suffers likewise from tautology, but this criticism is refuted by the consideration that Euripides did not take into account the difficulty of talking to the dead. This victory of Aeschylus induces him to turn to the examination of Euripides' prologues. Euripides had claimed that he does not make the mistake of repeating himself or of padding. Aeschylus tacitly confirms the justice of his claim (cf. 1184–85). After having made one successful attempt to apply Euripides' micrologism to Euripides' own prologues, he shows with the gods' help that Euripides' manner of building his sentences permits one to complete those sentences easily with such phrases as "he lost his flask." More generally stated, he shows that while Aeschylus' prologues may be obscure, Euripides' clear prologues suffer from monotony. After Aeschylus has succeeded to Dionysos' dismay in three cases, Euripides does not give up the fight, but swears for the first time by Demeter. Aeschylus succeeds three more times. Up to this point Aeschylus has examined altogether seven Euripidean passages; one might find that the fourth of these passages (1217–19) contains Euripides' reply to Aeschylus' criticism of the first (1182). When Euripides recites a verse of his that Aeschylus can not complete with "he lost his flask," Dionysos from whim or conviction conceals the defeat of Euripides in this part of the contest and asks him to turn to the examination of Aeschylus' songs. Aeschylus could seem to have had a slight edge as regards the prologues.

Euripides declares that he will show Aeschylus to be a bad lyrical poet. The chorus wonders how Euripides can succeed in proving his point, given the manifest supremacy of Aeschylus in this respect; it did not express the same feelings regarding the prologues. Furthermore, owing to Euripides' eagerness to win, Aeschylus has the last word in the section devoted to the songs, just as he had the last word regarding the prologues; as a matter of fact, Aeschylus has the last word in all parts of the contest. All the more striking is Dionysos' failure to proclaim Aeschylus as the victor; in fact he fails to pass judgment on the superiority of either poet. He abruptly commands both poets to stop the songs. Aeschylus too has had enough of the songs, for he wishes to lead Euripides to the scales on which the two poets' verses are to be weighed: This weighing alone can decide the contest between them. This is the first time in the second half of the contest that Aeschylus determines the subject of a part of the contest. The weighing of the tragedies was indeed provided for from the beginning (796–802). Yet Euripides claimed that he had changed the character of tragedy as he had taken it over from Aeschylus by reducing its weight or heaviness (939–41). Aeschylus draws the conclusion that the weighing of the two poets' verses will settle the contest in his favor: Even Dionysos must see that Aeschylus' verses press down the scale. Dionysos accepts the proposal. The chorus is amazed by the novel conceit of deciding a contest between poets by comparing the weight of their verses: No one else—except Aeschylus? except Aristophanes?—would have thought of it; surely clever men go to all kinds of toil. As in the preceding parts of the contest, Euripides speaks first. In this final part of the contest a decision is quickly reached; three times each poet puts one of his verses on the scales, and three times Aeschylus wins. It may suffice to mention the second example. Euripides' verse declares that Persuasion—the goddess of Lysistrate (*Lysistrate* 203)—has no other temple than Speech, but in

Dionysos' view Persuasion is something light and lacks intelligence; Aeschylus' verse however declares that Death is the only god who does not long for presents but, as even Euripides can not deny, Death is the heaviest evil. One might find that Euripides was bound to lose once heaviness became the standard of excellence, for he worships Ether above all (cf. 1352–53). Aeschylus is at least as certain of having been victorious as he ever was before. In the only part of the contest that leads to a clear decision intelligible to the meanest capacity, Aeschylus undoubtedly wins. He proves to be the weightier of the two poets on the lightest or flimsiest ground—on a ground that he had wisely chosen. Yet the chorus remains silent. Dionysos, however, can not remain silent. Aristophanes pays him a great compliment by making him refuse to decide the contest in favor of Aeschylus, for even assuming that the god had become wholly bewildered by the bulk of the poets' exchange, it required a considerable effort to remember that bewilderment after the wholly unbewildering outcome of the final and utterly simple part of the contest. Dionysos refuses to decide the contest on the ground that he wishes to remain on friendly terms with both poets, for he regards the one as wise and the other as enjoyable. In order to remain on friendly terms with both poets, the god leaves it open which of the two predicates he assigns to which of the two poets. While a case can be made for either view (cf. 916–18), we are inclined to believe that Dionysos regards Aeschylus as wiser than Euripides, but Euripides as more enjoyable than Aeschylus. For, to say no more of the difference between the edifying and the corrective, Aeschylus proved to be clearly superior to Euripides in weightiness, and weightiness as such is not pleasant, as is sufficiently shown by the example of death. Besides, we find in both the *Frogs* and the *Thesmophoriazusai* sufficient proof of the imperfect character of Euripides' wisdom. Lastly, to say that Euripides is superior in wisdom to Aeschylus would amount to denying that the gods are (cf. *Thesmoph.* 450–51). However this may be, it is wisest to leave the matter at saying that the contest between the two poets remains undecided, as undecided as the whipping contest between Dionysos and Xanthias.

The contest for divinity, which could not be settled by whipping, was settled by recourse to Pluton. Similarly, the contest for supremacy in tragedy, which could not be settled by examination of the tragedies of the two poets or by Dionysos, is settled thanks to the intervention of Pluton. If Pluton had not intervened, the natural conclusion from the contest between the poets would have been that Aeschylus should remain in possession of the tragic throne; this would have been in perfect harmony with Dionysos' desire to bring Euripides back to the living. It is this simple solution that is prevented by Pluton's intervention. Pluton makes the fulfillment of Dionysos' desire to bring back a tragic poet dependent on his deciding the contest between the two tragic poets. He says that Dionysos will have descended to Hades in vain if he does not pronounce in favor of one of the two poets: To bring back, say, Euripides means to pronounce in favor of Euripides or to declare him, and not Aeschylus, worthy of the tragic throne. Pluton in effect declares that Dionysos can not choose one of the two poets according to his mere whim or pleasure; he must act responsibly. Yet Dionysos proved unable to prefer either poet on grounds of poetic excellence. He begins to overcome his predicament by explaining the purpose of his descent to Hades to the two poets in the following manner: He came down, he now declares, so that the city, having been saved, could conduct its choruses; accordingly he will take back to Athens that one of the two poets who can give the city good advice, i.e., who can bring about the salvation of the city and thus secure the external conditions for Athens' theatrical excellence. This means that Dionysos will pronounce his judgment not on poetic but on political grounds. He had not thought of the city when he went down in the guise of Herakles in order to steal Euripides. Yet he was compelled to reveal his identity and his design to Pluton in order to put an end to his being whipped; he realized his dependence on the community to which he belongs, the community of the gods, and thus acquired some gravity; there was no longer any question of running away stealthily from Hades with Euripides. Furthermore, Pluton compels him to act as arbiter, i.e., impartially, in the poets' contest and thus to pay attention to Euripides' defects —in particular his defects as an educator of human beings in the cities; he surely realized that he could not bring back Euripides without giving an account of his choice of Euripides, an account that would have to be politically defensible. Having learned through the whipping contest the importance of the community, he eventually considers the community in trying to decide the poets' contest. Precisely in Hades, where poetry is honored more highly than in Athens, Dionysos realizes what is meant by the city being the condition of poetry.

The contest for divinity is not decided as long as it is to be decided with a view to the primary criterion (insensitivity to pain), but it is decided as soon as another criterion is applied (recognition of a god by a fellow god). Similarly, the contest for supremacy in tragic poetry is not decided as long as it is to be decided with a view to the primary criterion (poetic excellence), but it is decided as soon as another criterion is applied (goodness in giving political advice). Furthermore, the contest for divinity called for a change of arbiters; the second arbiter (Pluton) settled the contest because he, in contradistinction to the first, had the required competence. In the case of the contest of the poets, however, no change of arbiters takes place; it is somehow taken for granted that just as Dionysos is competent to judge who is the best tragic poet, he is also competent to judge political wisdom. Besides, one must wonder whether one tragic poet is necessarily preferable to another because he is better at giving political advice; if this doubt is justified, the contest of the poets remains undecided; the analogon in the contest for divinity would be that one does not know whether Dionysos or Xanthias is a god. Lastly, the comparison of the two contests induces one to suggest that the contest for divinity is decided on the ground that Dionysos is more useful to the city than Xanthias.

Dionysos asks the two poets in the first place what they think about Alkibiades, for the city has difficulty in reaching a decision about him. Aeschylus wishes first to know what the city thinks about Alkibiades; he seems to think that one can not give advice to the city if one does not know what the city wishes. Dionysos tells him that the city longs for Alkibiades, hates him, and wishes to have him. Thereafter Euripides speaks out clearly against Alkibiades: Alkibiades may be helpful to the fatherland in the long run, but he will first do it great harm; he is good at taking care of himself, but for the city he is ineffective. Dionysos praises his answer and then asks Aeschylus for his view. Aeschylus speaks out in favor of Alkibiades: It is best not to rear a lion in the city, but once one has been reared, one must be subservient to its manners. Dionysos does not praise Aeschylus' answer, which is more in accordance with the wishes of the city than Euripides'. Nevertheless he is again unable to decide: One of the poets has spoken wisely, the other clearly. This result is not surprising; Dionysos from the beginning regarded the question about Alkibiades as only his first question. He now addresses his last question to the poets. Since it has remained uncertain whether Alkibiades can save the city, he asks the poets of what ways of saving the city they dispose. Euripides, who seems to regard Dionysos' expectation as preposterous, reveals a preposterous way, befitting a comedian, of winning a naval battle. Thereupon Aeschylus intervenes, saying that he knows a way and wishes to state it. Euripides is thus compelled to give a serious answer: We must distrust the citizens whom we now trust and entrust the affairs of the city to those to whom we do not now entrust them, for since the present policy has led to disaster, it stands to reason that the opposite policy will lead to salvation. His proposal recalls the one made by the chorus in the parabasis (717–37). Dionysos is greatly pleased with it and only wonders whether it is Euripides' own; the poet assures him that it is his own, while the laughable proposal that he had stated first stemmed from his collaborator or servant Kephisophon; he thus disowns the laughable proposal that he stated before Aeschylus' intervention put him under pressure. Dionysos then asks Aeschylus for his opinion. Aeschylus asks again for some information: Does the city at present entrust its affairs to decent men? When he learns that it does not, while it also dislikes being ruled by bad men, he sees no way of saving it. Dionysos urges him to find a way of saving the city if he wishes to return to the living. Aeschylus, who is obviously anxious to return to the living, replies that he will give his advice "there," but refuses to give it in Hades. On Dionysos' insistence, however, he gives his advice in Hades: The Athenians must regard the land of their enemies as their own and their own land as their enemies', their navy as their wealth and their wealth as their handicap. He advises the Athenians to return to the policy of Perikles or of Themistokles. Each poet thus gave two different answers to Dionysos' final question, but while Euripides' first answer was laughable, Aeschylus' first answer was openly despondent; each poet gave his second answer, which is compatible with action, when he was put under some pressure. Dionysos has some doubt whether the policy recommended by Aeschylus is feasible under the circumstances. He surely does not praise Aeschylus' advice as he praised Euripides' advice. Pluton urges him to make his decision. Dionysos declares that he will choose that poet whom his soul prefers. While everyone waits silently in the highest tension for the god's verdict, Euripides, driven by his eagerness to win and to return to the living, can not remain silent. He tells the god as it were that he has no freedom to choose, but is bound to choose him: In making his choice Dionysos must remember the gods by whom he has sworn to bring Euripides home. This is too much for Dionysos. Euripides is the last man who can demand that Dionysos, or any other god or man, keep his oath. The god quotes from a verse of Euripides that says, "the tongue has sworn but not the mind," and declares that he chooses Aeschylus or judges him to be the victor. To Euripides' outbursts about the god's base action he replies with other apposite quotations, more or less literal, from the poet's works. Euripides has been beaten with his own weapons. At first glance it might seem that Dionysos simply could not withstand the temptation to outsmart the smart Euripides, or that his decision is due to a mere whim. Yet the decision in the poets' contest is as little merely whimsical as the decision in the whipping contest. What was at stake in the whipping contest was the difference between gods and men; gods must be essentially different from men for the sake of the sacredness of oaths (cf. *Clouds* 395–97). Euripides can not have it both ways: denying the gods that avenge perjury (or denying that perjury is sinful) and expecting that others keep their sworn promises to him. Dionysos justly punishes Euripides for his denial of the gods by awarding the prize to Aeschylus. This is not to deny that the god punishes the poet for destroying the basis of the sacredness of oaths by himself committing an act of perjury: He acts wickedly indeed, but justly like the Clouds (*Clouds* 1462). The irresponsible playboy has become altogether edifying. One might question the justice of Dionysos' action on the ground that one can not hold a poet responsible for the utterances of his characters: To hold Euripides responsible for his Hippolytos' saying "the tongue has sworn but not the mind," without even considering the context of the utterance, is about as fair as asserting that according to Aristophanes Zeus does not even exist, since he makes his Socrates say it. Nor must we forget that Dionysos has broken a solemn promise before (526–29, 586–89, 591–601).

After Dionysos has annihilated Euripides, Pluton invites Dionysos and Aeschylus to take a meal in his house before they depart. In their absence the chorus, which never speaks for Aristophanes, sums up the result of the contest by contrasting the perfectly sensible man who is blessed and goes home again for the benefit of his fellow citizens and his kinsmen and friends with the insane man who, sitting with Socrates, engages in vain talk, having discarded music and forsaken the highest part of the tragic art. In order not to misunderstand this song entirely, i.e., in order not to mistake this utterance of the chorus for an utterance of Aristophanes himself, we must remind ourselves that it was not Socrates from whom Euripides learned to uphold the claims of Aphrodite, and that it was not Aeschylus as he presents himself in the *Frogs* from whom Aristophanes learned to be a champion of peace. The view expressed by the chorus and conveyed in a manner by the play as a whole is the Aeschylean or chthonic view, a partial view and in fact a low view: the view belonging to Hades. One must not forget the high or heavenly view as presented especially in the *Peace*. Then one will realize how strongly the case for corrective, as distinguished from edifying, tragedy is stated even in Hades.

Pluton, Dionysos, and Aeschylus reappear. Pluton bids farewell to Aeschylus and urges him to save "our city" with good counsels and to tell some obnoxious Athenians to come quickly to him by committing suicide if they do not wish to be brought down by Pluton's violent action: Hades is the right place for undesirable people. Aeschylus replies that he will do what Pluton told him to do and urges the god in his turn to give Aeschylus' throne to Sophocles, who is second only to Aeschylus, and to keep it for him if he should ever return: Aeschylus hopes never to return to Hades. He goes on to urge Pluton to prevent the scoundrel, liar, and buffoon, i.e., Euripides, from ever occupying the tragic throne. We note that Aeschylus does not call Euripides a boaster (cf. 909). The last word on Euripides is entirely Aeschylus': Not only does Pluton not promise Aeschylus that he will execute his last will and testament; Dionysos himself is altogether silent in this last scene. Euripides is sufficiently punished by being left in Hades to which Aeschylus, despite his hope, will have to return sooner or later: He will have to die a second time.[85] Given the fact that Euripides is already dead, one may find that his punishment is less severe than Socrates'; no one will interfere with his exhibiting his extraordinary conceits to the large multitude of his admirers. We have seen why it is just that his punishment should be less severe than Socrates'. Pluton consoles Aeschylus for his silence about the poet's last word by asking the chorus to send him forth with his own songs. Nothing is said of the whereabouts of Xanthias, who may be left behind in Hades as the dung beetle was left behind in heaven, or about who is to carry Dionysos' luggage. The chorus prays to the nether gods to grant a good journey to Aeschylus and good thoughts of great goods to the city, and it intimates its hope for peace.

The *Frogs* presents the education of Aristophanes' educator from an unqualified admiration for Euripides to a preference for Aeschylus. This education takes place in Hades. Dionysos' not altogether successful descent to a quite Athenian Hades contrasts with Trygaios' altogether successful ascent to heaven, an ascent that is successful because of the conflict between the Greek gods and the cosmic gods. Dionysos' conversion is decisively prepared by his blunder of having descended to Hades in the guise of Herakles, for that blunder leads to the whipping contest that is so similar and so dissimilar to the contest regarding wisdom between Aeschylus and Euripides.

9 *The Assembly of Women*

This play begins like the *Acharnians* and the *Clouds* with a soliloquy by the character who is responsible for the design that issues in the action of the play. Yet Praxagora is more unambiguously the initiator than Dikaiopolis and Strepsiades, for Dikaiopolis' design presupposes Amphitheos' intervention, and Strepsiades' design is not achieved without the intervention of the Clouds. Praxagora reminds us of Lysistrate, who also opens the play whose heroine she is with a soliloquy, but Lysistrate's soliloquy is unusually brief. Like Lysistrate, Praxagora waits for her fellow women, but her opening utterance rises more above her situation than do the opening utterances of any other characters. She invokes a lamp that she carries and that is to give signals to her fellows: The light of the lamp is the only light that shines on the women's secrets, their secret pleasures —their intimacies as well as their thefts—on secrets that must be concealed from the sun; the man-made lamp sees what neither the sun nor the moon sees. Praxagora as it were calls on the art that corrects the law. The lamp will also be witness to the execution of the designs that the women have decided on some time ago. The women decided to assemble at night in order to occupy, disguised as men, the seats of the Assembly before day breaks. Praxagora has been waiting for her friends, but unlike Lysistrate she is not annoyed by their keeping her waiting because she knows how difficult it is for them to leave their houses at night without their husbands knowing it; since there is now peace, their husbands are not away on military service. The other women (all of them married and townspeople) appear in groups or by themselves. When they are all assembled, Praxagora asks them to sit down so that she can find out from them whether they have prepared themselves in accordance with the decision of the preceding women's assembly, so that they will look in today's Assembly altogether like men. They do not yet look entirely like men—for instance,

263

they have not yet put on the beards that they brought with them—for otherwise they might have difficulty in recognizing one another. After they have passed the examination satisfactorily, Praxagora turns to the business that they must transact before the Assembly opens at daybreak. They must again face the enormity of the action that they have decided to perform today: to take over the affairs of the city in the interest of the city. In order to succeed, they must rehearse what they are going to do and say in the Assembly. The rehearsal is necessary since, with the exception of Praxagora, the women lack experience in how to behave in the Assembly (242–44). As the women make mistakes, i.e., reveal their being women, in particular by swearing by goddesses by whom only women swear, Praxagora gives them a specimen of how one must speak in the Assembly on behalf of the women. After having prayed to the gods that they prosper the decisions of the Assembly, she speaks of the poor quality of the rulers of the city, a defect owing to the poor quality of the *demos:* The city was better off during the period when there were no Assemblies. Everyone thinks only of his own interest, no one of the common good. The city can still be saved if the Assembly hands over the city to the women, who administer the households well enough. The women are of better character than the men: They follow in every respect the ancient law and ancient practice, whereas the men—at least the Athenian men—are eager to innovate even if the present practice is perfectly sound. Accordingly Praxagora urges the Athenian men to hand the city over to the women, without asking the women what they will do after they have come to power. Their qualities as mothers and administrators of the households give a sufficient guarantee. In particular they are so good at cheating that they can not be cheated. (How good they are at cheating they show by their present action.) The good rulers, as Praxagora conceives of them, follow the ancient law and are benevolent deceivers. After having answered some questions regarding her and the other women's conduct in the Assembly, Praxagora orders them all to put on garb of men and march like men to the Assembly in a hurry: If they do not arrive in time, they will not get the assemblymen's pay. Since the women must act like men, they must become concerned like men with private gain (cf. 205–7).

There is a certain similarity between Praxagora's proposal and Lysistrate's proposal (*Lysistrate* 493–95), but what Lysistrate tried to achieve by force, Praxagora, true to her name, tries to achieve by talking or by fraud. Above all, Lysistrate's objective is much more limited than Praxagora's. Lysistrate wishes to bring about peace; Praxagora wishes to bring about an unheard-of change of regime. What is true of Lysistrate's design is true of the designs that animate the actions of all the other plays hitherto discussed, with the exception of the *Birds;* all those designs lack the breadth of Praxagora's design. The breadth of Praxagora's design is reflected in the breadth of the observation with which she opens the play.

With the exception of Praxagora and two others, the women form themselves into a chorus before our eyes, just as in the *Birds* the chorus formed itself on the stage. After they have been reminded of the risk they run if they are found out, one half of the chorus sings as if it consisted of men marching to the Assembly, eager to receive the pay. The women relapse once into revealing that they are women. The second half of the chorus, pretending to consist of men from the countryside, praises the good old times when the pay was small and citizens did not perform their civic duties for the sake of the pay. Neither half of the chorus complains about old age: They may succeed in playing men, but they will not succeed in playing old men.

After the women have left the place in front of Praxagora's house where they had assembled, Blepyros, Praxagora's husband, appears. He is bewildered by the absence of his wife, for it is almost dawn. He noticed his wife's absence because he needed his shoes and his cloak, and he needed these things because he is under urgent pressure to ease himself. He has no choice but to put on his wife's dress and her slippers. His wife's voluntary disguise forces him into an involuntary disguise. He is not worried about how he looks, for it is still dark; therefore he can also sit down anywhere. Reflecting in a manner reminiscent of Strepsiades on the root of his discomfort, he curses himself for having taken a wife when already being an old man; she is likely to have gone out on an amorous adventure. His moanings awaken a neighbor. Thus his disgraceful discomfort will not even remain secret. Fortunately for him the neighbor suffers from the same discomfort as he, at least to the extent that his wife too has disappeared, taking with her his cloak and shoes. The neighbor consoles himself or Blepyros with the thought that his wife may have been invited to breakfast by one of her women friends. Both men are eager to go to the Assembly, but they are prevented from doing so, the neighbor because he possesses only a single cloak and Blepyros because he suffers from constipation, which delays his easing himself. Despairing of all human help he prays to the goddess who assists women in childbirth that she prevent his becoming a nightstool belonging in comedy. His circumstances compel him to give much more thought to his digestion than to his wife. He has barely succeeded with infinite ado in getting rid of his trouble and is about to rise again when Chremes appears, returning from the Assembly, which has ended. Blepyros' session has lasted as long as the session of the Assembly. While Praxagora, as we shall soon see, has reached the highest height to which human beings in cities can rise, her husband has reached the lowest low. What is united in the dung beetle is divided between Praxagora and Blepyros in such a way that Blepyros comes closer to the goal of its lowest aspiration than Praxagora comes to the goal of its highest aspiration. Blepyros' is the most ridiculous situation in which we find any Aristophanean character, as appears with perfect clarity if we look at it, as we must, in the light of the contemporary situation of his wife. The ridiculous par excellence, we suggested, is pretense or boasting. Blepyros reminds us in the most drastic manner that there is a kind of the ridiculous that has no relation whatever to boasting, unless one finds that his having married a young wife constituted an act of boasting. This other kind of the ridiculous is present in all comedies and in particular in most, if not all, heroes or heroines. Surely neither Dikaiopolis, nor the sausage seller, nor Euelpides, nor Lysistrate is a boaster. Blepyros—an old man who spends on the toilet seat the time during which his young wife becomes the ruler of the city, and therewith also his ruler—is ridiculous because he suffers from a kind of helplessness or ineptitude that does not arouse compassion. He is aware of the ridiculous character of the situation: He fears that he will become an object belonging in comedy (371). While he knows that he is ridiculous he does not, like Trygaios, joke about himself. He is the only character of the play who swears "by Dionysos" (344, 357, 422). What connects Blepyros, in contradistinction to Praxagora in particular, with the comic poet is the fact that the comic poet too can not help becoming a laughingstock: In reading the plays we laugh not only with Aristophanes and through his agency but also at him; the inventor of the mad conceits of Strepsiades and all the rest must partake of their madness to some extent. Everyone can see what protection this inevitable concomitant of comedy affords to its author.

Chremes is as surprised as the neighbor was by Blepyros' having put on his wife's dress; Blepyros tells him that he put it on by accident in the dark; he obviously does not wish to be laughed at. He prevents further embarrassing questions by asking Chremes where he was coming from and learns from him that he came from the Assembly. Chremes tells him that today's Assembly was attended by more human beings than any other. The citizens assembled looked like shoemakers, since they were pale-faced. In addition, they had assembled at an unusually early hour so that those who came later could not be admitted. Chremes traces this feature of today's Assembly to the fact that the subject of deliberation was the salvation of the city. The Assembly shouted down the first speaker because he could not save himself, let alone the city. The second speaker—a needy fellow with a threadbare cloak—made the democratic proposal that the fullers and tanners be compelled to supply the needy with warm robes and warm lodging places. Blepyros suggests that a similar obligation might usefully be imposed on the dealers in grouts. In other words, it would be fair to impose the care of the needy on those who supply men's most urgent needs. It is obvious that the second speaker's proposal for the salvation of the city was dictated by his own inability to save himself. Entirely different was the case of the third and last speaker, a handsome youth with a pale complexion. He proposed that one ought to hand over the city to the women. The proposal was greeted with applause by the multitude of shoemakers, but booed by the rural population; yet the shoemakers were in the majority. Blepyros agrees with the rural opposition. We see that Praxagora was entirely successful. The only failure that one might discern is that the women looked pale despite all their efforts to become tanned (59–64). The third speaker justified his proposal by speaking of the vices of men and the virtues of women. He praised the women for their ability to keep secrets, an ability so strikingly demonstrated today, and for their reliability and honesty in their dealings with one another. Praxagora is silent about that virtue of women on which she had laid the greatest stress in her rehearsal speech, viz., their adherence to the ancient or their conservatism. In fact, the chief reason why her proposal was accepted in the Assembly was that rule of women is the only thing that never existed in the city. There are various ways in which one can reconcile this contradiction between the rehearsal speech and the Assembly speech. Since Praxagora knew that her proposal would be adopted by an overwhelming majority, she did not care particularly whether her conclusion agreed with her premise, especially in a rehearsal. Besides, the entirely new order as the most reasonable order is the order according to nature, but nature is more ancient than any human contrivance. Finally, if adherence to ancient law and ancient practice is the greatest virtue, and if women surpass men in this respect, the ancient law contradicts itself by subordinating the women to the men. Chremes is quite satisfied with the new order. Blepyros, who approves of all innovations that increase his comfort, has only one objection: If the women rule, they can coerce their husbands into fulfilling their marital duties, and compulsory cohabitation belongs among the most terrible things. Chremes leaves Blepyros with the observation that if such cohabitation is useful to the city, every man must practice it. Perhaps Chremes is not quite as old and decrepit as Blepyros.

The chorus, i.e., the women, return from the Assembly. They are still disguised as men and still exert themselves to march like men; the success of this morning's action depends on its being believed that the gynaecocracy was voted in by the male citizens. The chorus stops in front of the house of Praxagora, *the* she-general. Partly spontaneously and partly at the behest of Praxagora, who comes home shortly after them, they get rid of as much as possible of their disguise. Praxagora is eager to enter her house and to return her husband's things before he sees them. The women regard themselves entirely as the subjects of Praxagora, the cleverest woman they have ever seen. Praxagora in her turn assures them that she will make use of all of them as her councilors.

When about to enter her house, Praxagora is met by her husband, who asks her whence she comes. In the ensuing conversation Praxagora is still dressed as a man and her husband as a woman. She replies, "What difference does it make to you?", i.e., she replies foolishly, as Blepyros tells her. For, granted that in her new position she no longer owes him any account of her goings and comings, she can not yet know of her new position unless she has attended the Assembly, and she can not admit that she did that. Blepyros thinks of course that she might have been with a lover. Praxagora refutes this suspicion by an observation that implies that Blepyros is not too familiar with her amorous habits. She explains her stealthy disappearance with his things by a brazen lie that could easily have been found out. Blepyros knows from his neighbor that Praxagora is not the only woman who left her house with her husband's things, and he knows from Chremes that most of the citizens in today's Assembly were strikingly pale-faced. However this may be, he acts as if he did not think it profitable to probe into his wife's secret too deeply. He points out to her that through her fault he has been unable to attend the Assembly and tells her that the Assembly has decided to hand over the city to the women. Praxagora is only moderately surprised. Her response to the amazing news is that "by Aphrodite" the city will be blessed from now on. When Blepyros asks her for her reason, he gives her an opportunity to state how the women, or rather she herself, will use the newly acquired power.

Praxagora no longer speaks about women's superior goodness. We recall that the denial of women's goodness, or at least the assertion that women are inferior to men, was a most important link between Euripides and the ancient law.[86] By asserting the superiority of women, Praxagora had tacitly turned not only against the ancient law but against Euripides as well. Women's superiority supplied them with their title to rule. What is important now is that by virtue of their goodness they will establish an order in which everyone will be good. For instance, there will no longer be sycophants. Blepyros, who hitherto lived from sycophancy, regards this as a calamity. Above all, in the new order no one will envy his neighbor, for no one will be poor. Chremes approves entirely of Praxagora's goal, but is doubtful whether it can be achieved. Praxagora is sure that she can show its feasibility so that Chremes will be satisfied and her husband will be silenced. The chorus encourages her to use her powers in defense of women by proving the beneficence of the entirely novel scheme—novel not only in deed but in speech as well. It reminds her that the spectators love novelty as well as quickness; they detest the old and the slow, i.e., they detest moderation. Thereupon Praxagora discloses that this precisely is her greatest fear: The spectators may be averse to her scheme because of their too strong adherence to the ancient. (This fear had induced her earlier to recommend the rule of women on the ground that women adhere more to the ancient than men do.) Blepyros assures her that she has no reason to be downhearted on that score: Precisely the contempt of the ancient is the sole starting point of Athenian deliberations. The starting point of the new order is the simple rejection of the equation of the good with the ancient. Praxagora goes much beyond Peisthetairos, who at least ostensibly tried to restore the most ancient order and who, besides, did not bring about his radical change in Athens. In her way Praxagora is as radical as the Unjust Speech, but since she intends a change beneficial to the city, a political change, she is inspired by justice.

The novel scheme that Praxagora presents in the exchange with Blepyros and Chremes is altogether her own; it has been thought out without the benefit of counsel from the other women. Praxagora talks as if she were the sole ruler or legislator of Athens (594, 597, 673 ff.) and she is so in fact: Her official status as general reveals even less of her position than that status did in the case of Perikles. Her novel scheme is entirely lawful since the Assembly, which was lawfully assembled and lawfully consisted of male citizens only, entrusted the rule over the city to the women and elected Praxagora general; and the women in their turn acquiesce and more than acquiesce in Praxagora's supremacy. According to Praxagora, the women in their goodness will make the men good, not by their example, but by abolishing the causes for badness. All possessions will be in common among the citizens: There will no longer be poor and rich; there will be one way of life for all. From this common property the women, famous for their thrifty and sound administration of the households, will supply the men with food and everything else they need: There will be no motive or opportunity for stealing or cheating. This change seems indeed to follow necessarily from the gynaecocracy: Since the women are henceforth to take care of the city, they can no longer take care of individual households. They can not impose on the men the duties formerly fulfilled by the women without having to fear instant revolt; there is no way but to transform the city into a single household. The community of goods or the abolition of private households demands a no less profound change regarding sexual relations. There must be community of women as well. In this sphere however a difficulty arises that did not arise in regard to property: Equality of women as objects of men's desires is not possible, given the inequality of women in beauty. For this reason and related ones the discussion of the community of women is about twice as long as the discussion of the community of property. Praxagora overcomes the difficulty caused by the natural inequality of women by a law that makes all women equal through giving a priority to the ugly ones: No man can enjoy a beautiful woman before he has cohabited with an ugly one. Praxagora, one might say, replaces natural inequality by legal equality.[87] Yet, Blepyros objects, this arrangement so fair to ugly and old women is unfair to old men, whose fate will at any rate be worse in the new order in which they will have no money to buy girls' favors. Praxagora silences her husband by laying down the law that women may not sleep with beautiful (and young) men before they have gratified the ugly (and old) ones. She points out that this arrangement is democratic, for it makes ridiculous the stately or pompous. This remark is helpful for a better understanding of her whole scheme. Gynaecocracy itself is a consequence of the democratic premise when qualified by the further premise that the two sexes are unequal; these two premises lead to the question of which sex is the most egalitarian and therefore deserves to rule, a question that can not but be answered in favor of the female sex: Every woman competes in a way with every other woman, but not every man competes with every other man. Blepyros sees yet another difficulty: Under the new order how can one know one's children? (Nothing is known of Blepyros' and Praxagora's having children.) Praxagora leaves no doubt that the community of women requires community of children: The younger generation will regard all men of the older generation as their fathers. There is no reason to fear that this will lead to widespread father-beating and father-killing: Everyone seeing an older man beaten by a younger man will come to the older man's help for fear that it may be his own father who is being beaten. Praxagora may thus supply a sufficient protection against father-beating; she surely does not supply a sufficient protection against incest becoming customary in the new order. On the contrary, since in the new order children and parents do not know each other, and the younger people are compelled by law to cohabit with the older ones, incest between parents and children becomes undetectable and lawful (cf. 1041–42). The prohibition against incest being one of the fundamental requirements of the city, Praxagora effects a change that is much more radical than the change effected by Peisthetairos. The fact that Blepyros and Chremes do not become concerned with the issue of incest does not prove that the author of the *Clouds* was not aware of it. The order established by Praxagora is a city without households or families. Blepyros, who for all we know may not be concerned with the issue of incest because he has no children, is concerned with the question of the production or reproduction of the wealth that the citizens are to enjoy in common; after all, in the old order the poor, who are much more numerous than the rich, are sufficiently induced by their needs to work hard for their living, and this inducement is about to disappear with the abolition of poverty. This question is discussed in the central and shortest section (four verses) of the exchange between Praxagora and Blepyros on the new order. Praxagora's decision is to the effect that the land will be cultivated by the slaves and the women will weave the clothing; men will have nothing to do but to enjoy the fruits of the slaves' and the women's labors. Blepyros has one more question: Since no one will have money of his own, how can he pay the fines to which he may be condemned by the magistrates? Praxagora replies that there will no longer be any lawsuits. She reminds her listeners that there can no longer be lawsuits of any sort regarding property. As for lawsuits arising from assault, the punishment will consist in the deprivation of food. When she shows that owing to the abolition of private property there will no longer be gambling, Blepyros is induced to bring up still another subject, the last subject of the exchange: the new way of life as a whole. Praxagora declares that she will turn the town into a single household by abolishing all privacy, and that she will transform the courts of justice into dining halls and the tribune into a place to put drinking bowls of wine and water pots; and the list of citizens from which hitherto jurors were selected by lot will be used for allotting seats in the dining halls. That is to say, the institutions peculiar to democracy will be abolished: The democracy will be abolished (cf. 229–32). Everyone will have food aplenty, and after dinner the old men will enjoy the most attractive girls. Blepyros is now altogether satisfied; Chremes is silent. Praxagora must leave for the market place in order to accept the movable property that the citizens are to surrender to the city and to take care of the first common meal to be supplied this very day. She will also put an end to prostitution so that the youths will gratify respectable women, like those forming the chorus; she thus makes clear that in the new order there is no longer a prohibition against adultery. For the same reason she must prevent the cohabitation of freemen and slave girls. Blepyros follows her in order to be admired as the she-general's husband.

Praxagora breaks with the ancient much more radically and openly than any other Aristophanean character who is concerned with the city or with ruling. There is one link between her novel order and the order preceding it: egalitarianism. Taught by the *Clouds*, we regard as the gravest of her innovations her tacit legitimation of incest between parents and children. This innovation follows from the co-operation of two premises: the transformation of the city into a single household and the substitution of conventional equality for the natural inequality in regard to age and beauty; that equality is in fact an inequality in favor of a higher right of the old and ugly. As a rule, the old cherish the ancient to a higher degree than do the young. The egalitarian premise from which Praxagora starts counteracts to some extent her willingness to go to any length in getting rid of the ancient. We must now turn to the question of what Aristophanes thinks of Praxagora's scheme.

Praxagora had spoken of the new order in the future tense. Yet, since her word is law and there is no trace of resistance to her word, the new order has now come into being or her design has been realized. Accordingly one would expect the parabasis to take place. But there is no parabasis in the *Assembly of Women*. There is also no parabasis in the only later play, the *Plutos*. It is possible that the absence of parabaseis from the only two plays that date from after Athens' defeat in the Peloponnesian War is due to reasons external to Aristophanes' intention and to no other reasons. In considering this question, one must however pay attention to the changes that the parabasis underwent on the way from the *Acharnians* to the *Frogs*. In the first five plays Aristophanes himself was an important subject of the parabasis. The parabaseis of the four following plays are silent about the poet. If the most important function of the parabasis is to enable the poet to speak about himself or his work, the silence about him in the parabaseis of the later plays amounts to an atrophy of the parabasis, and its atrophy would naturally lead to its disappearance. We have indicated how the poet's silence about himself in the *Birds* and in the *Lysistrate* is connected with the themes of these plays; [88] as for the *Thesmophoriazusai* and the *Frogs*, it is relevant that they are the only plays obviously dealing with the fate of poets. Be this as it may, the *Assembly of Women* differs from all earlier plays not only by the disappearance of the parabasis; it also differs from all other plays by the disappearance of the character responsible for the design after what one may call with some exaggeration the middle of the play. One can not explain Praxagora's disappearance by saying that she is no longer needed since her design has been realized. The design of Dikaiopolis, for instance, is also realized in the middle of the *Acharnians*, and he is present till the end of that play. One could say that Dikaiopolis must act till the end of the *Acharnians*, since otherwise one could not know what use he will make of his private peace; yet given the unqualified public-spiritedness of Praxagora, the only question is what use the city will make of her new order.

After Praxagora and Blepyros have left, honest Chremes prepares the surrender of his movable property to the city; his slaves carry the various pieces from his house and put them on the street, where he arranges them for their transportation as if they were to march in a procession in honor of Athena. Whether Blepyros will comply with the new law we can not find out, since he is occupied with accompanying his wife. While Chremes obeys the law, another citizen appears who takes the opposite view: It is foolish to give away the fruit of one's sweat and thrift without knowing first what the whole thing means. He first refuses to believe that Chremes is set to give away his property and then denies Chremes' contention that one must obey the laws; only a fool would obey a law before he has seen whether that law is obeyed by the bulk of the citizens. Chremes can not imagine that the bulk of the citizens are not law-abiding. The dishonest man disagrees on the ground that the new law runs counter to ancestral custom, which favors taking from the city rather than giving to it. It also runs counter to the practice of the gods, or their statues, who also take rather than give. Chremes does not meet the objection that the old order is in agreement with the gods; he surely can not deny that the new law demands a complete break with age-old custom, but he acts on the view that the law is the present law and that men are not entitled to imitate the gods' actions. His opponent draws his attention to the further facts that even according to law men are not always obliged to obey the law and, above all, that the Athenians may repeal the law establishing community of property as they have repealed so many other laws shortly after having enacted them. Chremes replies that things have changed from top to bottom: Now the women rule. He believes that the citizens will obey the new law, but must admit that if the majority refuse to hand their property over to the city, they can not be coerced into doing so. The argument of the two men is interrupted by the appearance of a herald who calls all townsmen to hurry to Praxagora, who will assign everyone by lot to a seat in one of the dining halls; all sorts of delicacies and delights for all senses await them. Chremes does not respond, but his opponent is eager to do his civic duty by complying with this command of the city. He no longer refuses to surrender his property to the city, for the refusal would cost him a splendid dinner with all its accompaniments, but he postpones that surrender. Since he thus tacitly admits his obligation to obey the law, Chremes permits him to follow his procession, but he does not permit his opponent to help carry Chremes' movables, since he might claim that he is bringing in his own property. When the scene ends, he has not yet found a device for reconciling participation in common dinners with keeping his property, but this does not prevent him from participating in the imminent common dinner. We are left wondering whether the new order regarding property will work. Chremes' compliance with the law does not guarantee general compliance. If we disregard the facts that the new law has been enacted altogether illegally and that Praxagora has provided only for tilling of the soil and weaving, and not for the other ways of producing wealth, we might expect that the majority, who hitherto had to work hard for their living, will comply with the new law and force the rest to comply; but honest Chremes surely has no interest in not working or in living at the expense of the city. He obeys the new law because he believes that it is beneficial to the city (471–72), since it promises to do away with all crime, vice, and misery (560–68). Yet it can not keep its promise if the majority does not obey it, and he does not know that the majority will obey it. Accordingly, in defending his complying with the new law against his opponent, he does not say a word to the effect that the law is in fact beneficial. His sole motive for obeying it is his belief that it is good and right to obey the law, i.e., any law, regardless of whether it is good or bad and whether the other citizens do the same or not. He is the incarnation or the dupe of unqualified law-abidingness. His exchange with his opponent reminds us of the exchange between the Just Speech and the Unjust Speech, but Chremes' justice and his opponent's injustice are presented in complete abstraction from the questions regarding the gods as well as the virtues of the ancient; the law to which Chremes is unqualifiedly loyal is of merely human origin, and it is altogether novel. This does not do away with the fact that his opponent is altogether unjust: Even the foolishly just man is superior to the unjust one.

After the poet has given us an inkling of the difficulties that beset the transformation of private property into community of goods, we expect him to show how the transformation of marriage into community of men and women works. Instead he shows how the community of men and women affects people who are not yet or no longer married. More precisely, he shows how the community not of women but of men works. We suggest this explanation. Praxagora is no longer seen, and we hear only of her public activity, but apart from being the ruler of the city, she is still a woman; we can not help wondering what her fate as a woman is in her new order.

The next scene—the center of the part following Praxagora's disappearance—opens with an exchange between an old woman and a young girl. They are waiting for men, the girl for her lover and the old woman for any man. The old woman's beauty is entirely artificial, the girl's beauty is natural. Since the old woman is about to try to attract some man or draw his attention to her by singing, the girl threatens her with a countersong. She knows that while this exchange will annoy the spectators, annoyances of this kind are also amusing and fit for comedy. She appeals to the audience's delight in the amusing, as Praxagora had appealed to its delight in political innovation as such (581–87). The exuberance coming from her youth and beauty, as well as from her expectation of her lover, culminates in laughter and therefore also in her being willing to contribute her part to a laughable situation; she knows that not she but the old woman will become ridiculous. Blepyros, we recall, was afraid of becoming an object fit for comedy, for he was at that time in a most ridiculous situation (371). He has long ago ceased to be in such a situation, but the girl will soon find herself in one. From this we may infer that the new order is good for old men, and more particularly for that old man who is Praxagora's husband, and bad for young girls. Closer inspection will show that thanks to the new order Blepyros is perfectly ridiculous and perfectly happy, while the girl is perfectly unhappy and not simply ridiculous, but rather an object of compassion to such an extent that the new order, responsible for this state of things, becomes an object of indignation.

The old woman sings to the accompaniment of a flute. She praises the wisdom of old age and experience in matters of sex as well as the constancy of the old: The old are naturally superior to the young even as regards love. Replying to her in the same manner, the girl praises the more obvious advantages of youth in the decisive respect and warns her antagonist not to be envious of young girls: Despite the new order, which was supposed to abolish envy (565), envy still persists. She reminds the old woman of the kinship between youth and life on the one hand, and old age and death on the other; the hag's sole response consists in cursing the girl. Certain that no curses can destroy her youthful bloom, the girl is more worried by her lover's delay than by the hag's curse. When a young man appears, the old woman pretends that he is her lover and that she was waiting for him, rather than for a man in general. The girl withdraws in order to show her opponent that he is her lover and is coming to her as a matter of course. The old woman has no choice but to withdraw too. The youth knows that his desire for the girl is thwarted by the new law, which compels him first to sleep with an older woman; he finds this state of things unbearable for a free man. For the old woman, however, the new law is precisely in perfect agreement with freedom, since it is in agreement with democracy, i.e., with the regime in which the free as free rule as equals, and the equality of all is brought about by a law privileging the naturally inferior at the expense of the naturally superior; or, if you wish, the requirements of freedom may have to give way to those of equality. The girl, who believes that she has fooled the older woman into staying indoors, calls on the youth to join her, which he is only too eager to do. Both pray to Eros for his help, in addition to praying to each other. While the youth is at the girl's door, the old woman reappears and makes her claim on him in accordance with the new law; the law that obliges him to satisfy her is only the reverse side of the law that entitled him to a free dinner. She quotes to him the text of the new law, according to which the old women may use force against a youth who is recalcitrant; the text as quoted by her is silent about the rights of old men; there is no way out for the youth that is not clearly against the laws, the women's laws. When he is about to give in, the girl, who is as dissatisfied with the women's laws as the youth, succeeds in freeing him from the hag's clutches by pointing out to her that she is old enough to be his mother and that the new law leads to incest between mothers and sons, i.e., is manifestly invalid. But this victory of the girl—in the new order only females can be victorious—is of very short duration. A second hag appears, older and uglier and therefore still more privileged by the new law than the first, too old to be the mother of the youth and therefore beyond the girl's ultimate appeal; she raises her claim on the youth and drags him away. She does not play the loving woman like the first hag, who had sworn three times by Aphrodite, but merely refers to the law. At that moment a third hag, still older and uglier and therefore still more privileged than even the second, lays hold on him with the result that he is in danger of being torn to pieces by the two. The oldest hag wins out. The girl's misery is beyond words. The youth's misery is so threefold that he fears—quite wrongly, we believe—that he is by law obliged to satisfy the second hag also before he can enjoy his girl. He is not comforted by the thought that however terrible compulsory cohabitation may be, it may be of benefit to the city (cf. 471–72). In the new order Eros does not listen to the prayers of lovers. Death and decay triumph over life and bloom.

In the second scene there was complete silence about Praxagora: Does she approve of the atrocities committed or threatened by the hags? The silence of the heroine is in a way continued till the end of the play. The chief character in the last scene is a tipsy maidservant who was never before as happy as she is now. She speaks of her mistress as most blessed: Could her mistress be Praxagora? Her mistress has sent her to bring her mistress' husband to the dinner; when she meets him, she greets him as blessed and thrice happy. Blepyros could be called thrice happy, since he is the husband of the ruler of the city. Yet the maid calls him thrice happy not for this reason but because he is the only citizen who has not yet had his dinner: He is the only one who has something marvelous to look forward to. We thus learn incidentally that the community of men and women has not yet become actual: The maid's mistress and master are still husband and wife; the friendship between husbands and wives still persists. The maid also invites to the dinner the benevolent among the spectators and in particular among the judges. Her master tells her to enlarge the invitation still further and to invite the whole population to dine at home, while he will go to the public dinner. The women of the chorus too have not yet had their dinner and are therefore to come together with the mistress' husband. Perhaps what is true of these women is true also of the rest of the Athenian women who, for all we know, were busy preparing the dinner and, if the condition of the maid is a clue, drinking wine. The promised dinner is a dish of unbelievable and even unsayable richness and variety—a manifest boast that no one believes. We are at a loss to say whether Praxagora's scheme has made the Athenians happy, if only to the extent that thanks to that scheme the whole citizenry once got a dinner at the expense of the city. The only people of whose happiness we can be certain are a slave girl and the oldest hag. The chorus owes its happiness not to Praxagora's scheme but to the anticipation of victory in the contest of comedies.

The ending of the play is unsatisfactory. We do not see whether the community of property and women works. We do not see whether Praxagora made the city as a whole happy or unhappy. In all other plays we see at the end whether the character responsible for the design that animates the action has succeeded or failed or partly succeeded, and therewith whether and to what extent the poet approves of the design; at any rate in this sense the endings of all the other plays are satisfactory. In all the other plays we see the victory of human beings who deserve to win or of a worthy design, or the defeat of human beings who deserve to lose or of an unworthy design; or if the victory or defeat is only partial, we see to what extent they win or lose, i.e., deserve to win or lose. Bdelykleon succeeds in curing his father of his obsession with condemning men judicially, but he fails to make a gentleman out of him; Euripides fails to be completely acquitted by the women, but he succeeds in being conditionally acquitted; Dionysos fails to bring back Euripides from Hades, but he succeeds in bringing back another tragic poet. By making us see in this simple way the difference between worthy and unworthy designs, the poet teaches the just things. Yet since the designs—as distinguished from the ends by themselves, like peace—are in all cases laughable, he teaches us the just things by making us laugh. The designs are laughable because they are (more or less obviously) impossible; by making a part of the audience think about why a given design is impossible, the poet addresses the wise as distinguished from the laughters (1155–56).

Someone might say that the ending of the *Assembly of Women* is as satisfactory in the sense defined as the ending of any other comedy, since the poet has revealed his judgment on Praxagora's scheme through the most elaborate scene that he devoted to the new order in action, the scene showing the conflict between the old women and the young lovers. The scene shows that Praxagora made happy not indeed the whole city but the old women, and she made unhappy not indeed the whole city but the young lovers. In other words, she brought about, as every revolutionary does, not the abolition of misery but a redistribution of misery and happiness. In the old order the hags were miserable, since they suffered from a deprivation that, if they wanted, would remain private or secret and hence decent; in the new order the hags' happiness is necessarily public and not only indecent but repulsive: Those who deserve to lose triumph. This shocking fact is only slightly concealed by the superficially exhilarating character of the final scene. The ending of the *Assembly of Women* is unsatisfactory in the sense that it is repulsive or nauseating, while the endings of all the other plays are exhilarating. It is not sufficient to say that the *Assembly of Women* is the ugliest comedy; it is *the* ugly comedy. In the *Lysistrate* the women bring the men to their senses; they cure them of a folly indeed, but not of a degrading folly. In the *Assembly of Women* the women induce or compel the men, and not the least the young men, to sacrifice all concern with the noble or beautiful for the prospect of being lavishly fed and otherwise taken care of by the women: The women's action deprives life of all beauty. One does not see how Praxagora's action can redound to the glory of Athens. The *Assembly of Women* is the only play where no significant resistance is offered by men or elements to the design informing the action; surely the beauty of victory in an open and fair fight is lacking, unless one is willing to call the quasi-arrest of the youth by the hags a victory in an open and fair fight.

One may question the premise of the preceding argument according to which in the Aristophanean comedy the character or cause that triumphs deserves to triumph and vice versa: If the hags' triumph does not mean that they deserve to triumph, it is surely less revolting than if the opposite is true. What then do victories and defeats in the Aristophanean comedies mean? Do the hags triumph merely because their triumph is more laughable than their defeat would be? Is Socrates defeated merely because his defeat is more laughable than his triumph would be? Are the lovers of peace victorious merely because their victory is funnier than their defeat would be? It is more reasonable to understand the unique character of the ending of the *Assembly of Women* in the light of the unique character of its obvious theme. The *Assembly of Women* is the only play in which the poet attacks not democratic institutions like the jury system, or policies like the war against Sparta, or demagogues like Kleon, but the very principle of democracy, egalitarianism. It is for this reason that the poet proceeds in this play, as distinguished from the plays hitherto discussed, ironically, i.e., he pretends to accept the premise that he rejects and hence presents a most objectionable consequence of extreme egalitarianism as if it were entirely unobjectionable and deserved to triumph: Under no circumstances must the enemies of equality be allowed to triumph. He shows the consequences of egalitarianism without showing the collapse of egalitarianism. Egalitarianism calls for the abolition of all inequalities and therefore for absolute communism (communism regarding property, women, and children); yet, since the most important inequalities are ineradicable, egalitarianism requires that the inferior be given privileges in order to compensate them for their defects; their envy must be appeased. The absurdity of egalitarianism is not as palpable in the case of property as in the case of sex, since whether men are rich or poor depends as much on chance as on natural inequality. This explains why the scene between the hags and the young lovers is both so important and so unambiguous. The triumph of the hags reflects the triumph of Praxagora. It is the triumph of art over nature: Not the sun, but the lamp is Praxagora's emblem. It is because Praxagora's scheme in a sense follows from the egalitarian principle that it meets no resistance to speak of in Athens. It is because Praxagora, who has no equal in either sex, is the living refutation of egalitarianism pure and simple that she is not seen and barely heard of in the second half of the play.

Yet we must not forget that although she is an outstanding human being, Praxagora is a woman. She is much younger than her old and erotically repulsive husband. Since her new laws are meant for the sexual gratification of free women (718–20), they take care of hers too. In her new order adultery can no longer be prohibited. As we have seen, in the transitional stage between the old order and the new, the friendship between husband and wife still persists: Praxagora can always claim, if her husband agrees, that she has fulfilled her onerous duty and is therefore always free to cohabit with young men. She is much better off in the new order than before. The new order then brings about the happiness not only of repulsive hags but also of pretty young wives who are married to old men. The privilege of the hags is a kind of equivalent for what adultery was in the old order: A privilege that is admittedly unattractive takes the place of a crime; no wonder that Chremes, the champion of law-abidingness at any price, has no objection to the new order (cf. 471–72). Praxagora then has a powerful private incentive for her revolution, which necessarily, if accidentally, bestows such great privileges on old women. From what we know of Blepyros, we are entitled to assume that he in his way is as satisfied with the new order as his wife is in her way. This is not to deny that if the hags' interpretation of the new law were correct, Praxagora must gratify another old man before she can enjoy a young one; but who can doubt that this interpretation will have to give way to the interpretation that is both fairer and more acceptable to the ruler of the city? The strange ending of the *Assembly of Women* conceals from us the private triumph of Praxagora, who surpasses by far all men and women, i.e., a deserved triumph.

Yet this deserved and exhilarating triumph is not presented, whereas the shocking triumph of the hags is presented. One may even say that since the former triumph is not seen, we can not even be certain of it. Surely, Praxagora's conjectured triumph is inexorably linked to the hags' manifest triumph. We thus become inclined to return to the view that Praxagora deserves to lose, or perhaps that while she may deserve to triumph, her scheme deserves to lose: Everything might have gone well if she had sought only her own happiness, as Dikaiopolis had done. The strange ending of the *Assembly of Women* conceals the defeat of Praxagora's scheme. Why does Aristophanes conceal that defeat? Her scheme is of incredible boldness. It is comparable in this respect to Peisthetairos' scheme. It surpasses Peisthetairos' scheme in boldness above all by what it implicitly provides in regard to incest, i.e., by not respecting a fundamental requirement of the city, while in other regards it falls short of Peisthetairos' scheme. It is surely the boldest scheme conceived by a woman. In order to see what this means in an Aristophanean context, we must pay attention to a difference, which we hitherto had no occasion to consider, between his women-plays and his men-plays. In the men-plays gods and divine things (like the divine intervention through Amphitheos, the oracles of Kleon, and the oracle given to Philokleon) are important, if not decisive, for the formation of the original or final design informing the action. Gods and divine things play no such role in the women-plays. We may also recall the women's unconcern with Euripides' atheism in the *Thesmophoriazusai*, as well as the peculiar identification of nature and law that underlies Lysistrate's scheme. However bold Praxagora may be, no one can accuse her of acting against the gods. Prometheus is a man. Crudely speaking, a higher degree of moderation (*sophrosyne*) is demanded of women than of men,[89] while the opposite is true of manliness. Let us never forget the great virgin goddesses, Artemis and Athena. By concealing the failure of the boldest scheme conceived by the most outstanding woman, Aristophanes conceals the failure of Woman, the limitation of Woman: he spares Woman. He does not need the lesson that his Euripides needed. Exaggerating grossly for the purpose of clarity, we may say that the ugliness of the *Assembly of Women* reflects the ugliness of moderation. We do not refrain from using this harsh expression, since it is helpful for rethinking the thought to which Plato's *Phaedrus* is devoted: the praise of *mania*. Certain it is that Socrates' correction of Praxagora's scheme, which we find in the *Republic*, is not properly understood if one does not consider—against the letter of the *Republic* [90]—the difference of sex between Socrates and even the wisest woman; the scheme presented in the *Republic* is altogether of male origin.

10 *The Plutos*

This play is the only one that begins with a soliloquy of a slave. The soliloquy of the slave Karion takes place in the presence of his master, Chremylos, but without the master's hearing it or listening to it. Reminding us of one of the slaves in the *Peace*, Karion complains about his lot by complaining about the folly of his master; for the lot of a slave, i.e., of a human being whose body is under the control not of the body's (natural) ruler but of him who bought the body or the slave is bearable if the master is sensible. If the title of the play were not *Plutos* (Wealth), we would not say that the slave is a part of the master's wealth. As we learn from Karion's soliloquy, Chremylos' folly or madness is a consequence of an Apollonian oracle (like Philokleon's madness). Having gone to Delphi in order to consult the god and having received the god's answer, Chremylos has been following a blind man without ever answering Karion's questions as to why he does this strange thing. Judging from the maddening effect of the oracle, Karion has become doubtful whether Apollon is truly the wise physician and diviner people say he is. There is no doubt that his patience with his master is now exhausted: Chremylos must tell him now and here why he is following the blind man and forces Karion too to follow him; he must tell him who the blind man is. After a slight hesitation owing to his sense of being the master, Chremylos explains to Karion his seemingly mad behavior. He is a pious and just man but poor, while impious and unjust men are rich. He thus has come to believe that impiety and injustice are the way to prosperity. Yet in a matter of such gravity he did not wish to rely on his own judgment. He therefore went to Apollon out of concern not for himself, whose life is spent, but for his only son: Should his son change his manner of life and become unjust? The god replied clearly that Chremylos should cling to whomever he met first on leaving the temple and should persuade him to come home with him: The blind man whom he has followed from Delphi to Athens is the first man he met on leaving the temple. Chremylos like Strepsiades [91] has only one son; but while the unjust Strepsiades turned to Socrates, the just Chremylos turns to Apollon.

Karion is dumbfounded by the stupid literalism with which his master understood the oracle: The god had said in the clearest manner that Chremylos should make his son's conduct follow that of the first man he met, i.e., the common practice of the country at the present time. This reply is so palpably sensible that the god can not have meant anything else; Apollon is after all the wise god people say he is. In other words, Apollon said that the son should obey the custom or *nomos*, i.e., the ancestral custom; but the corrupt slave argues that following the ancestral custom is meant to be salutary, and it is patently not salutary in an age of corruption; hence the god must have meant that the son should follow the corrupt practice of the age. We shall not neglect the fact that Apollon did not clearly and distinctly advise Chremylos to continue in the ways of justice. At any rate, as we learned when considering Strepsiades' reaction to Socrates' teaching, literalism is not always stupid. Chremylos refuses to believe in Karion's interpretation of the oracle. Not only can Apollon not have recommended the practice of injustice; the mere fact that the first man whom Chremylos met on leaving the temple, despite his blindness, went by himself to Athens, to the place in front of Chremylos' house, proves that the oracle must be literally understood and has a higher meaning than Karion imagines. To discover that meaning, one must know who the blind man is and why he led Chremylos and Karion to where they would have gone without obeying the letter of the oracle. Karion rudely asks the blind man who he is and receives a rude reply; yet Chremylos, who asks him gently, does not fare better. Only when master and slave threaten him with extinction does he say that even when they know who he is they will harm him and will not let him go. Still, when they comply with his wish at least to take their hands off him, he tells them that he is Plutos.

Nothing could be more surprising to Chremylos than this disclosure, especially since Plutos does not look at all like Plutos, but is in very poor shape and extremely dirty. Plutos traces his condition to Zeus' envy of men. When Plutos was still young, he threatened to go only to the just, the wise, and the decent; to prevent him from doing so, Zeus blinded him so that he should be unable to discern the worthy: so envious is Zeus of the worthy. Chremylos finds this action of Zeus very strange, since Zeus is honored solely on account of the worthy, perhaps because the experience of human virtue is the seminary of divine worship. Now he must become reconciled to the fact that he learned from Plutos that Zeus is envious, not of the rich and mighty, but of the just, the wise, and the decent, i.e., of those whom men genuinely honor. Plutos admits to Chremylos that if he could see again, he would avoid the bad men and go to the just ones. He has now satisfied Chremylos' and Karion's curiosity regarding his identity; their surprise is so great that they forget to ask him why he went from Delphi to Athens, although Chremylos at any rate knows that he must learn that reason in order to understand Apollon's oracle (53–55). As his reward for satisfying their curiosity Plutos asks the two men to let him go. Yet after Chremylos knows who the blind man is, he is even less willing to release him than before, when he wanted Plutos to stay with him merely because the oracle literally understood had told him to take into his house the first man he met on leaving the temple. He beseeches Plutos, who longs for the company of the good, to stay with him who belongs to the best that are. Plutos refuses to do so; for, while not questioning Chremylos' justice, he believes to know from experience that his presence, through which people become rich, makes them therefore exceedingly bad. He thus unwittingly vindicates Zeus' conduct toward him: If wealth corrupts absolutely, Plutos must by all means be kept away from the good for whose company he longs; Zeus blinded him, not from envy of the worthy or from injustice, but from love of the worthy or from justice. Chremylos denies Plutos'—or Zeus'—premise: Not all wealthy beings are bad; but this denial does not make any impression on Plutos. Chremylos next tries to persuade him to stay with him by appealing not to his love of justice but to his self-interest; he expresses the hope that, the gods willing, he might cure Plutos of his blindness. Plutos, however, who does not deny that he might be cured, does not wish to be cured. Karion thereupon calls him such a human being as is by nature miserable: By nature Plutos seems to prefer the bad things to the good ones, or nature seems to be his enemy; it is for this reason that he believes that wealth corrupts absolutely or, more generally stated, that all men are bad. Yet Karion is twice wrong. The enemy of Plutos is Zeus: Zeus will destroy him if he hears of Chremylos' design to restore his sight. Yet, as Chremylos points out to him, Zeus is already acting as Plutos' enemy. Plutos does not dare to admit this: so great is his fear of Zeus. Chremylos for his part is entirely free from that fear. He was a pious man who went piously to Delphi and understood the oracle in the most pious manner. His change can only be due to what he learned from the god Plutos about Zeus: He worshiped Zeus because he believed in Zeus' justice. He therefore accuses Plutos now of being the most cowardly of all divinities: Since Zeus lacks the power stemming from justice, he possesses only the power stemming from Plutos; he will lose that power once Plutos sees again, once justice and only justice leads to wealth. Plutos fears Zeus so much that he refuses to listen to Chremylos. Yet Chremylos, swearing "by heaven" and using Karion as his witness, demonstrates to him that Plutos surpasses Zeus in power: Men sacrifice to Zeus and pray to him only for the sake of Plutos, and they sacrifice to Zeus only through Plutos; through wealth, if not for the sake of wealth, whatever is resplendent and fine or graceful accrues to men. In fact, wealth alone is the sole cause of whatever men do and of how they fare. Of everything else men can get too much, but of wealth never. Plutos, who was wholly unaware of his power and to begin with saddened to hear of men's love for him, gradually realizes that wealth has not only a bad effect or that men are not simply bad. Eventually he has only one fear: He does not see how he can become the master of the power that, according to Chremylos and Karion, he possesses. Since wealth does not corrupt all men, he can fulfill his longing to stay with the just; he has been cured of the belief that Zeus' keeping him away from the just by blinding him agreed with the interest of justice. Yet he still fears Zeus, or at least despairs of success in acting against Zeus' will. In Chremylos' view this merely proves the truth of what everyone says, viz., that wealth, i.e., the wealthy, is cowardly in the extreme. The impossibility on which the *Plutos* is based is the fact that *plutos* is both wealth pure and simple, a quality or appurtenance of human beings, and a god, a self-subsisting being, or, if you wish, a being that literally talks.[92] Chremylos assures Plutos that if he only becomes an eager and willing man, his sight will be restored by Chremylos. Plutos' doubt that Chremylos, being only a mortal, will be able to achieve this feat, is quenched by Chremylos' assertion that Apollon approves of the plan. Yet Chremylos also spontaneously refers to the multitude of human allies whom they will have in their fight against Zeus' will: the many just men who are poor and who will become powerful by becoming rich or by the prospect of becoming rich. Without waiting for Plutos' assent, Chremylos orders his slave to call his fellow peasants, who are probably now working hard in the fields—for they are the many just men who are now poor—to join him in partaking of Plutos. He asks Plutos, whom he now addresses as the supreme deity, to enter his house, which Plutos must make rich today by fair means or foul. This remark understandably reawakens Plutos' old belief in the badness of all men. Yet Chremylos sets his mind at rest by presenting himself to his divine guest as a man who does not go in for extremes and by making it clear to him that everyone tells the truth to Plutos. Far from making men simply unjust by his presence, Plutos makes them just at least to some extent: Everyone is sincere in telling Plutos that he loves him above everything else. Even Zeus told Plutos the true reason why he blinded him. As for Chremylos, he does not go to the extreme of telling the truth to everyone; he is of moderate or average justice.

Chremylos has done literally what Apollon had told him to do. He refused to understand the oracle cleverly; that clever understanding would have led straightway into rank injustice. Through his literal understanding he is eventually led to bring about the restoration of Plutos' sight, i.e., the practice of justice becomes rewarding as it never was before; the seemingly most stupid or absurd interpretation of the oracle proves to be the true interpretation. By inducing Chremylos to follow Plutos, Apollon seems to assure him that he will help him in restoring Plutos' sight (210–14). The oracle as Chremylos understands it is much more worthy of a god than as Karion understands it. Yet Plutos' sight can not be restored without acting against Zeus' will—just as in the *Peace* peace could not be restored without acting against Zeus' will—and, as the sequel shows, without depriving all gods except Plutos of their power. Surely this outcome can not have been intended by Apollon. We must conclude that it was a mere accident, not foreseen by Apollon, that Plutos was the first one whom Chremylos met when leaving Apollon's temple, and that Plutos in his aimless roamings just happened to walk from Delphi to Athens (cf. 121). The blindness of Plutos reminds us of the blindness of Chance. (One may therefore say that by restoring Plutos' sight Chremylos abolishes chance.) In other words, Plutos' walking from Delphi to Athens would lend itself to being understood as a miracle, but for its consequences. This does not necessarily mean that Karion's interpretation of the oracle was correct; Apollon might not have known of the corruption of the age, or the age is perhaps not as corrupt as Karion thinks. Yet it surely means that Apollon did not reckon with Chremylos' stupid or literal understanding of the oracle, with his simplicity or simple piety. More generally stated, the downfall of the gods in the *Plutos*, as distinguished from the downfall of the gods in the *Birds*, is ultimately due to an improvident act of one of the gods. Apollon's action may therefore be compared to Dionysos' going down to Hades in the garb of Herakles. While Karion's frivolous interpretation of the oracle would lead only to trivial consequences, Chremylos' pious interpretation leads in a manner to the destruction of piety.

Let us not be rash. We do not know that Apollon did not foresee that the first one whom Chremylos would meet on leaving the temple would be Plutos and that Plutos would walk to Athens; in that case the god's oracle would have meant that what Chremylos needs in order to remain just is wealth. What the god did not foresee is that Plutos would be forced by Chremylos to tell his story and that this would have the effect it had. In other words, the god's knowledge of Chremylos was insufficient. Chremylos is not wrong in regarding himself and his fellow rustics as just. Farmers are generally loved and respected because they are supposed to be just, since they live from their work and not on others.[93] How much Aristophanes defers to this supposition one sees from a number of his plays. The farmers' justice is what Plato would call vulgar justice, justice of a crude kind, by no means immune to great temptations. Chremylos would not have gone to Delphi if he had not become doubtful as to whether it was wise to bring up his son in the ways of justice and whether the gods are firmly opposed to the practice of injustice. Plutos, we take it, has a stricter view of justice; accordingly he arrives at the conclusion that all men are bad or, as one might also say, that nature is inimical to justice and hence to Plutos, the lover of justice. Chremylos tacitly denies the necessity of making strict demands on men. He learns from Plutos that Zeus is envious of the just, hence inimical to them, and therefore makes it practically impossible for men of even ordinary justice to become rich: Zeus is not even of ordinary justice. Zeus is envious of the just because he wishes to be just but knows that he can not be just. What Plutos says about Zeus is more credible than what he says about all men, since when he observed Zeus' envy of the just he was still seeing, while his view that all men are bad arose when he was already blind. Yet Chremylos is just enough not to infer from what he learned about Zeus that he should become, or make his son become, downright unjust. The only alternative left to him is no longer to honor Zeus, but to throw off Zeus' rule. He is just and wishes to be rich; he learns from Plutos that this wish is in agreement with Plutos' original intention; the only thing for him to do is to restore that original intention by restoring the god's sight.

Karion returns with the chorus consisting of old peasants who are supposed to protect the god and the man against Zeus' wrath. Karion, who was in a great hurry, had only told them to come to his master as quickly as they could; they were panting after him as if they were pursuing a runaway slave. Now they want to know why they have been called. Karion tells them that they who are lovers of toil will live to their pleasure in freedom from that hardship. It takes some time until the old men, who are somewhat hard of hearing, hear from the slave who, being overjoyed, enjoys teasing them, that Chremylos has brought Plutos home with him to make them rich. For a moment they doubt whether the good tiding is true, but a single oath of the slave almost reassures them. In their exuberance Karion and the chorus engage in a lyrical exchange of an explicitly mocking character: Karion explicitly assumes that he will imitate the Kyklops calling his sheep and goats, and Kirke, who transformed her followers into swine; the chorus, thus treated as actual sheep and goats and as potential swine, explicitly announces that it will imitate Odysseus. Nothing of this kind ever occurred in the parodos of any other play, for in the parodos of the *Assembly of Women* the women only tacitly pretended to be men. The chorus' tacit reference to Odysseus' blinding of the Kyklops reads like a sort of divination of the imminent reparation of Zeus' blinding of Plutos, just as the tacit reference to Odysseus' salvation from Kirke through Hermes reads like a sort of divination of Hermes' action in the play. The peasants and Odysseus have in common that they defeat superhuman beings with the help of superhuman beings. Besides, we should recall Philokleon's imitation of Odysseus' escape from the Kyklops' cave in the *Wasps:* Just as Philokleon did, the chorus of the *Plutos* acts, albeit unknowingly, in obedience to an oracle.

Karion enters his master's house in order to steal some food for his immediate consumption. Chremylos comes out and greets his fellow peasants with a novel expression that corresponds to the novelty of their situation: They are now the saviors of the god. Accordingly they take on a warlike posture toward the god's enemy whose identity, however, they do not know. They have an implicit faith in Chremylos; there is no need and no possibility of their engaging in a debate with him, or for that matter for their accompanying the action of the play with any comments. The situation changes when Blepsidemos arrives. He too arrives in a hurry; he has obviously heard that something big has happened. He has heard the rumor that Chremylos has suddenly become rich. All the greater is his surprise that Chremylos is calling for his friends; ordinarily people call for their friends only when they need them. Chremylos explains to him that he is not yet rich and that there is still some grave danger: Chremylos is still in need of his friends. Blepsidemos suspects that his friend may have stolen gold or silver from Apollon's temple or committed some other lucrative crime short of murder and is now afraid of being found out. The more Chremylos protests with many oaths, the more Blepsidemos is confirmed in his suspicion. He is sure that Chremylos, who was formerly so honest, has become dishonest; he now believes that all men are bad, i.e., that they give in to gain. Thereupon Chremylos suspects that Blepsidemos is eager to partake of the ill-gotten wealth. His suspicion is confirmed when Blepsidemos declares himself willing to protect Chremylos against punishment by bribing possible accusers, provided he receives a cut. Chremylos believes that he can convince Blepsidemos of his honesty by telling him that he is going to make only decent people rich, but this proves to Blepsidemos only that his friend must have stolen a lot. Yet, as this reply shows, Chremylos' argument was not entirely ineffective: By his reply Blepsidemos tacitly admits that there are many decent people, i.e., he tacitly retracts his earlier assertion that all men are bad. By retracting this assertion Blepsidemos makes it easier for us to believe that he too is in a manner just. In other words, since Chremylos desires both to enrich his friends and to enrich decent men, he seems to suggest to us that his friends are decent men. At any rate, for the first time Blepsidemos gives his friend the opportunity to tell him that he has Plutos in his house and that the two friends must restore the god's sight in order to derive benefit from him. Blepsidemos' trust in Chremylos' honesty is now completely restored. Without having seen Plutos, Blepsidemos believes Chremylos on his word when he says that Plutos is in his house. This is preferable to saying that statements regarding gods do not depend for their credibility on the honesty of the speaker, for Chremylos believed in the divinity of Plutos without testing it, on the ground of Plutos' manifest justice. On the other hand, however, he continued to believe in Zeus' divinity although he had ceased to believe in Zeus' justice. Blepsidemos proposes that they call a physician, yet he does not know of a single one who is at present available in Athens. Chremylos tells him that the best thing to do is to make Plutos lie in the temple of Asklepios, as he had planned all along. He had said to Blepsidemos shortly before that Plutos' sight would be restored if the gods willed it: He did not tell him that the restoration of Plutos' sight is an action against the will of Zeus. Blepsidemos' distrust of Chremylos' justice did not go far or deep enough. He is, as his name indicates, a man who looks toward the *demos*.

Hitherto everything has gone tolerably well. Chremylos, urged on by Blepsidemos, is about to hurry Plutos to Asklepios' temple. At this moment the two friends visibly meet the more-than-human obstacle to their enterprise of which Chremylos has been aware and afraid all the time. Now his chief ally sees with his own eyes how justified Chremylos' apprehension was. They are opposed not indeed by Zeus or his lightning but by Penia (Poverty), Plutos' female counterpart. The two men, familiar enough with poverty, do not know Penia. Her appearance is as repulsive as that of the blind Plutos. She reminds Blepsidemos vaguely of an Erinnys, a terrible goddess. In a repulsive voice she accuses the friends' design of impiety and illegality: They dare to do what no god or man ever dared to do—we wonder whether their daring surpasses that of Peisthetairos— accordingly she threatens to destroy them this very day. There is no reason to assume that Zeus has sent her, but she surely acts on behalf of Zeus. Just as Plutos is the accuser of Zeus, Penia is his defender. Yet Penia, as distinguished from Plutos, is silent about any punishment to be expected at the hands of Zeus. Accordingly, the more the two men see of her and the more she talks, the more their courage returns. They regard her as a spiteful and vulgar woman who shouts shrilly at people who have not wronged her a bit. She replies that they do wrong her grievously by trying to expel her from every place where she might happen to be and in particular from Athens, for she is Poverty who has been dwelling with them for many years. When Blepsidemos hears who she is, he wishes to run away. Chremylos however now shows that he surpasses his friend in courage as he has already proved to surpass him in justice: They, two men, can not leave Plutos in the lurch out of fear of a single woman. In fairness to Blepsidemos one must say that Chremylos was better prepared than his friend to stand up to Penia, owing to his success in standing up to Plutos; besides, he knows that if any danger threatens them at all, it comes from Zeus and not from Penia.

Chremylos restores Blepsidemos' courage by reminding him of the power of Plutos. Penia, who had silently listened while Chremylos was preoccupied with his ally's fear, i.e., who had not attempted to increase that fear, repeats her charge that the two men wrong her by trying to restore Plutos' sight. Chremylos does not see how they can wrong her by procuring a great blessing for all human beings: A being that stands in the way of universal happiness only gets what it deserves if it is expelled in the first place from Greece and then from the whole earth. In other words, Penia acts unjustly, regardless of whether she is a human being or a superhuman being; an action benefiting all human beings (or all human beings except one) but injurious to gods is just. If a god acts as an enemy of the human race, he is justly treated as an enemy. Penia thereupon contends that she alone is responsible for all good things that men have, i.e., that Chremylos wrongs her, because he as well as the other human beings have always been benefited by her. She goes much beyond Plutos' contention that poverty is the indispensable condition of worthiness; while Plutos' contention is attractive only to worthy men, Penia's contention is attractive, or can be made attractive, to unworthy ones as well. Besides, her view is more reasonable than Plutos', who both wished and did not wish that the just be wealthy; therefore she could be thought to be more formidable than Plutos. Penia also disagrees with Chremylos' contention that wealth, or the desire for wealth, is the sole cause of all good and bad things (182–83). The desire for wealth animates first the poor proper but also the rich, who strive for further wealth and hence regard themselves as not rich enough, i.e., as in a manner poor; Chremylos may therefore be said to contend that poverty is the sole cause of all good and bad things. Accordingly, Penia's contention is more attractive also than Chremylos'. Yet however attractive her contention may be, she herself is repulsive. She is willing to hazard her fate on her success in proving her contention. She treats the desire to make all men rich and the desire to make only the just rich as equivalent, rightly implying that from the moment when justice begins to be visibly rewarded, all men will be just. Her promise to enlighten the two men, her appeal to reason, is received by them with scorn. Still, the two parties reach an agreement to the effect that the side that loses will die more than one death. Whatever the outcome of the debate may be, we must not forget that the proposal to settle the issue by argument and not by force was made by Penia. This is not to deny that Penia is compelled to have recourse to argument since her curses failed to impress Chremylos. The outcome of the most daring action ever undertaken by gods or men depends not on force (and in particular not on the force possessed by Zeus) but on argument.

The chorus briefly encourages its two friends to defeat Penia in the debate. Chremylos begins it by justifying his and his friend's daring on the ground, evident to him, that it is just that honest men do well while bad and godless ones fare ill; if Plutos sees again, eventually all men will be honest and revere the things divine, and this is obviously the best thing for the human race. As it is, insanity or rather the rule of an evil demon seems to obtain: Many wicked men are rich, and many honest men are poor. Chremylos does not present himself as a man of extraordinary daring; he traces the design to restore Plutos' sight to "us," i.e., at least to Blepsidemos and himself. Nor can he be accused of dissimulation on account of his praising piety, for he knows better than anyone else that the bliss for which he longs will be due to the god Plutos. Penia does not for a moment doubt that Chremylos and his ally can restore Plutos' sight and thus make all men rich. Nor does she yet take issue with Chremylos' premise, according to which the just ought to be well off and the unjust live in misery. Above all, as little as Plutos does she question Chremylos' justice except as regards his attempt to restore Plutos' sight.

Penia opens her counterattack by vigorously denying that the state for which her opponents long will be good for them: If Plutos could see again, i.e., if all men were rich, no one would pursue any art or any kind of wisdom. When Chremylos retorts that slaves will exercise the arts, Penia tells him that if all men will be rich there will no longer be any slave traders, and that in addition to the work he is doing now, Chremylos will have to do all the work now done by slaves. Besides, the cessation of the arts means of course the disappearance of the products of the arts, i.e., of all amenities, whereas as things still are, those amenities abound, for Penia compels the artisan through his need to produce them. Chremylos himself had stated in his exchange with Plutos that all arts and clever inventions are due to Plutos, i.e., to the desire for wealth, which means to the absence of wealth (160 ff.). He is unable to deny Penia's contention that wealth is due to human work, which in its turn is due to human need or to poverty. Yet he denies that the amenities which the poor, compelled by need, produce, are enjoyed by the poor; the life of the poor is repulsive, hard, and filthy. Penia replies that he mistakes poverty for beggary: To lead a beggar's life means to live without possessing anything, but to lead a poor man's life means to live with thrift and work, neither to get rich nor to be destitute. Chremylos has no use for this distinction; he treats it as if it were a subject fit for comedy. Still, Penia's argument suffers from an obvious defect: To prove that poverty is preferable to beggary is not to prove that poverty is preferable to wealth. It should be mentioned that while Penia includes tilling the soil among the arts, she puts the emphasis on the arts other than farming (cf. also 617–18); if the poor man par excellence is the artisan as distinguished from the farmer, it becomes quite clear that the poor work for others, rather than for themselves.

Penia tries to remedy the defect of her first argument in what proves to be the central part of the debate. While she could not deny that the rich live better than the poor, she now asserts that she makes better men—better in mind and in looks—than Plutos. This argument could be expected to appeal to Chremylos, who is proud of his and his friends' justice. Penia claims that she makes men wasplike, i.e., good fighters for their city, and moderate or decent, whereas wealth brings out the opposite qualities. She repeats in effect Plutos' assertion according to which all rich men are bad. She does not at first mention justice among her effects. Chremylos reminds her of some kinds of crime that are more likely to be committed by the poor than by the rich. Here we may recall Blepsidemos' suspicions of his friend Chremylos. Penia replies that orators, while they are poor, are just in regard to the *demos* and the city; but when they have enriched themselves from the public revenue they act unjustly, conspiring against the multitude and waging war on the *demos*. This is the only argument advanced by Penia with which Chremylos agrees, but it is obviously not decisive: The orators turn to unjust gain while they are still poor. Penia does not make clear whether the virtue that she praises is the outcome of need (534), just as the arts or their exercise are; it is surely not the kind of virtue that results from good breeding, like the virtue of the knights for instance. In other words, she as well as Chremylos abstract entirely from that class of men who are neither rich nor poor, the middle class, which could be thought to be better fitted for virtue than either the rich or the poor.[94] Chremylos says that if Penia were right, one could not understand the fact that all men flee her. Yet according to her this very fact proves her contention that she makes men better: Men run away from her as children run away from their fathers. Chremylos fails to reply to this argument. Thus it looks as if Penia has proven that she is more conducive to virtue than Plutos.

Yet Chremylos is not silenced. He was accustomed to hold that Zeus is just without being compelled to be just by need or poverty. Through what he has learned from Plutos he has ceased to believe in Zeus' justice, but he still believes in Zeus' being wealthy or still being wealthy (130–31, 140–42). Hence he counters Penia's assertion according to which poverty is better than wealth by saying that if she were right, Zeus would lack judgment, for he possesses wealth. Penia has only contempt for this old-fashioned view: Zeus is poor. We have reached a point where the vindication of Zeus' wisdom or justice calls for a far-reaching innovation in theology: Zeus belongs with the poor and not with the rich.[95] Penia does not go so far, however, as to say that Zeus is in need, and that it is his need that makes him just, humane, and wise; what she means, we might suspect, is that he is just and wise because he is not in need, which amounts to meaning that he is not poor.[96] Yet, if he is poor, as Penia contends, he is not likely to be very powerful, and this conclusion is confirmed by the fact that Plutos' cure can be prevented, if at all, only by Penia's speech.

Penia does not of course attempt to prove Zeus' poverty by his lack of power; she proves it by the fact that the prizes awarded at the Olympian games are according to Zeus' decree very inexpensive. Chremylos thinks, not without justice, that this fact by itself does not prove that Zeus is poor, but could be the consequence of Zeus' stinginess. Penia can only reply that calling Zeus stingy is a much greater insult or blasphemy than calling him poor. Since one does not refute a thesis by proving that it is blasphemous, the exchange regarding Zeus ends in a draw. Remembering her apparent success in the first two parts of the debate, Penia repeats her contention that we owe all good things to poverty. Chremylos now tries to refute her simply by referring to the deed or speech of another god (Hekate). Without giving Penia a chance to retort, he chases her away with gross insults. Penia, who at no point concedes that she has been defeated, no longer claims however that Chremylos will be punished today (433). She now merely claims that he will call her back at some time. But the further action of the play shows that her curses or terrors are of the same character as the terrors of Hades in the *Frogs*.

If one considers only that part of the debate about which ordinary human beings can judge competently, one can say with some plausibility that Penia, defeated in deed, defeats Chremylos in speech. One may go a step further and say that her argument is the comical equivalent of the rational argument: Who can doubt that wealth does not come into being without human work, which comes forth under the spur of necessity? All the more striking is the fact that Chremylos' irrational design will prove to be entirely victorious in the end. The *Plutos* is the only play in which the design meets a firm opposition that is more reasonable than the design and is not overcome by speech, and yet is unambiguously victorious. If one considers the fact that Penia sings the praise of honest work, one will be inclined to compare her thesis to that of the Just Speech; the Just Speech too is defeated by speech, but his defeat is avenged by the outcome of the *Clouds*, while Penia's defeat is upheld by the outcome of the *Plutos*. As for the *Birds*, it suffices to say that Peisthetairos' design meets no reasonable opposition. In all comedies other than the *Plutos* the victorious causes are the causes that deserve to be victorious; if a cause does not simply deserve to be victorious, as in the *Assembly of Women* and to some extent in the *Wasps*, it is not simply or unambiguously victorious. Penia's defeat taken by itself is as shocking as the victory of the hags over the young couple in the *Assembly of Women*. One is therefore tempted to say that the *Plutos* is in its way as ugly as the *Assembly of Women*.

Yet however reasonable Penia may be, she is repulsive. Why is she repulsive? To exaggerate for the purpose of clarity, why is Good Sense repulsive? Why is she defeated in deed despite her being victorious in speech? What is it that makes Reason Unreason? The strongest point of her argument, which Chremylos could not question, was that wealth is due to human work. Yet this truth is contradicted by the fundamental premise of the play, according to which wealth is a god whose mere staying with a man makes that man wealthy, or that there is a god Plutos who does not need Penia as his basis, so that his restoration to his pristine state coincides with the complete disappearance of Penia. Her reasonable thesis is rendered manifestly absurd by the mere existence of Plutos. She is repulsive in the light of Plutos. In other words, by asserting that poverty is preferable to wealth, Penia in effect says that everything is good as it is; Chremylos' design implies that human life as it is now is very imperfect and therefore in need of a radical change; this imperfection is rendered manifest by the fact that there are gods.

Plutos is a god unlike all other gods. While Zeus is envious of the just, Plutos loves them. When Plutos learns that through the restoration of his sight he will bring it about that all men will be just (and in addition learns that he has many good allies), he overcomes his fear of Zeus. Other gods too fulfill the desires or wishes that men could not fulfill by their work. But what the other gods do from time to time, Plutos (once his sight is restored) does always: He makes human work altogether superfluous, and by this very fact makes all men just. As things are now, the production of wealth requires the exercise of the arts, but the exercise of the arts is only the necessary condition of wealth. Human well-being needs good luck in addition to human work; it requires therefore divination, sacrifices, and prayers in addition to the arts.[97] While the helpfulness of the other gods reminds us of the random character of chance, Plutos' helpfulness is universal and necessary. Men can not be blamed therefore for worshiping Plutos as the sole god, or at least as the highest god, once they have become aware of his power. Plutos, we may say, differs from all other gods because he alone is helpfulness itself, goodness that can not help communicating itself universally. This is not to deny that in contradistinction to the other gods, he is in need of man, of human help, in order to come into his own or to be himself. In a way he is divinity itself—that which makes a god a god. If this is so, Penia as the defender of Zeus is compelled to show that Plutos—the only god still worshiped by Chremylos—is not a god, i.e., "does not even exist." Far from attempting to prove this, she does not even attempt to prove that Plutos' sight can not be restored. Her disgraceful failure even to attempt to perform her most important task may be said to be the secret of her repulsiveness.

This much seems to be clear: If there were no Plutos, Penia would not appear to be repulsive. Yet this statement needs a qualification. Penia claims to be the sole cause of all good things that men have (470–72). This does not necessarily mean that men owe nothing good to the gods; they surely owe to Zeus' blinding of Plutos the presence or efficacy of Penia. Penia is the need that gives rise to the arts or that calls for the arts. This implies that need by itself, need without the arts, is bad or constitutes deprivation, i.e., is repulsive. Let us tentatively say that Penia is human nature without the arts, but indeed pointing to the arts. Human nature by itself is bad, but it becomes good or is relieved through art and law.[98] If law is a burden,[99] nature is also a burden. The gods however are thought to be free from all burdens. Whatever may be true of the other gods, Plutos makes the arts superfluous; he takes the place of the arts. Under his altogether benign rule, needs will be satisfied without any effort so that all men will in fact be just. No violence will be done to nature. Thanks to Plutos, nature will not be an enemy, not even a conquered enemy.

Yet we are still very far from this happy consummation: Plutos is still blind. The success of Chremylos' design requires, in addition to his victory in speech over Penia, a deed that he is unable to perform. He is still in need of an art, the art of medicine. By a strange coincidence no practitioners of that art are available at present (406–9). Plutos' sight must therefore be restored miraculously by the god Asklepios: The gods make the arts unnecessary. With the help of Karion, Chremylos and Blepsidemos rush Plutos to Asklepios' temple to sleep there for the whole night; in this matter they can not help complying with the *nomos*. Blepsidemos is still afraid that "someone"—someone other than Penia—might interfere with their action. His fear of Zeus proves to be wholly unfounded.

What takes place in Asklepios' temple is decisive for the success or failure of Chremylos' design. Of these proceedings we can not be eyewitnesses; we know of them only through a report given the next morning by Karion, who is the first to return from the temple. He congratulates the hitherto poor but worthy farmers and their like on their bliss: Thanks to the healing Asklepios, Plutos' sight has been restored. The chorus shouts Asklepios' praise. Chremylos' wife, who has been waiting indoors for the outcome, is induced by the shouting to come out; she learns from the slave first the good news in general and then all the details of the proceedings in the temple. Perhaps because they are so deeply impressed by the divinity of Asklepios, but surely also because of Plutos' looks and demeanor, which are so little godlike (cf. 78, 118), both Karion and his mistress speak of Plutos as a mere human being. As Karion reports, the proceedings in the temple took place in the greatest possible darkness and silence, or, to be somewhat more precise, under conditions more favorable to observation through hearing than through seeing. All patients and their companions lay down, and most of them fell asleep. Karion was kept awake by his hunger. He observed Asklepios' priest appropriating to himself the edible offerings to the god that had been put down on altars or sacred tables. Having earlier observed a pot of porridge standing near the head of an old woman, Karion felt justified by the priest's action in himself appropriating the contents of the pot. He feared not the god but that the god might get hold of the pot first; he succeeded by making the woman believe that he was one of Asklepios' serpents. When Asklepios himself appeared, Karion observed his doings stealthily. The god first treated a more or less blind thief and sycophant; he made him still more blind, while inflicting on him the utmost pain in order to punish him for his wickedness. Then he turned to Plutos, whom he treated with the help of one of his daughters and two immense serpents; in an incredibly short time the god Asklepios healed the god Plutos, whereupon Asklepios and his serpents immediately vanished from sight, and Karion awakened Chremylos. Apparently Asklepios cured Plutos without knowing whom he cured; the actions of the gods are not co-ordinated. On the other hand, Plutos and Asklepios belong together; Asklepios' conduct toward the sycophant shows clearly that a god other than Plutos is just and helpful. Asklepios may even be said to be superior to Plutos. Not only is health a greater good than wealth (633–36); Asklepios, as distinguished from Plutos, to say nothing of Apollon (11), is wise. The *Plutos* is silent on the relation between Asklepios and Apollon.

Asklepios had cured Plutos early in the night. Those lying near Plutos were awakened and, filled with joy about the cure, stayed awake through the rest of the night. Plutos could not leave as early in the morning as Karion, since in their joy a large crowd consisting of men who hitherto were poor and just kept him back. Those who hitherto were rich through injustice were of course greatly worried. Nothing is said as to how those who were rich not through injustice responded to Plutos' cure; but it is implied that there are such men (cf. 110). At present Plutos and those whom he made happy are on their way to Chremylos' house. Plutos comes to sight first. He bows reverently, first to the sun and then, not indeed to

Athena,[100] but to her land. We note here that the oath "by the heaven" occurs more frequently in the *Plutos* than in all other plays taken together.[101] Plutos is ashamed of his former misfortunes and mistakes, of his living together with the unworthy and avoiding the worthy; he is now cured of his ignorance; he will change his life from top to bottom. Chremylos arrives somewhat later; being well known to many, he was besieged by a still larger crowd than Plutos. Chremylos' wife is eager to welcome Plutos with figs and other desserts, as one welcomes newly bought slaves, but Plutos thinks it is unseemly for him to receive gifts rather than to give them. It would be particularly unseemly to receive the gifts outdoors, i.e., on the stage, where he would be practically compelled to throw them to the spectators and thus to force them to laugh. In his view this would be unworthy of Aristophanes: The seeing Plutos acts as a spokesman for the poet. Like the poet, Plutos makes men better or just,[102] and like the poet he can not help sharing the good things that he enjoys, possesses, or is with those tolerably just men with whom he comes into contact, or can not help making them laugh (758).

The four verses in which Plutos speaks on behalf of the poet may be said to take the place of the parabasis in this play. They surely occur in the situation in which the parabasis occurred in some plays, i.e., after the hero has become completely victorious, and before the fruits of his victory are presented. After the other characters have entered Chremylos' house, Karion comes out and expresses the pleasure that he feels as a member of the household to which he belongs: We have become rich without having invested anything or without having committed any unjust act; to be rich in this manner is a pleasant thing. Even Karion has become just. As he tells us, the house is filled not only with excellent food and drink but with gold, silver, and ivory as well. The wealth is fully shared by the slaves. Apparently their legal status is unchanged, but actually they are at least as well off as their masters: While Chremylos slaughters sacrificial animals on the largest scale and together with his wife prepares a splendid meal, the delicate Karion leaves the house in order to escape the smoke to which his master and mistress patiently submit.

The first visitor of Plutos is a just man who thanks to the god has become rich and is eager to pray to him. As he tells Karion, he had inherited a sufficient fortune from his father, but lost it by helping needy friends, thinking that such acts of friendship are useful for life. As things were then, he became poor and was deserted and despised by those whom he regarded as his friends. He apparently did not, like Chremylos, begin to wonder whether injustice might not be more useful for life than justice. He lived for thirteen years in great poverty without rebelling against his fate. Surely the kind of justice that the first visitor practiced or expected —helping friends or gratitude—will be unnecessary and even impossible in the new order. While Karion and the just man converse, the second visitor arrives. He is a sycophant who, thanks to Plutos, has been ruined. He is indignant because Plutos had promised to make "all of us" rich at once if his sight were restored and has ruined him alone of all just people. The sycophant regards himself as a just man whose property has been unjustly appropriated by the just man and Karion; in accordance with his usual practice he threatens them with criminal proceedings. They only laugh at him. He regards himself as just because he devotes his life to coming to the assistance of the established laws by accusing transgressors, for according to law everyone who wishes may act as accuser; he claims to live altogether for the city. Since he was well off under the old order, he may be said to imply that under the old order the just, i.e., the public-spirited, were rewarded by the law. The just man however holds that just men earn their livelihood not through political action but through farming, commerce, or the arts; they are not busybodies. The sycophant has only contempt for the private life that reminds him of the life of sheep; even if he were given Plutos himself he would not abandon his life devoted to accusation. Apart from Penia, he is the only one in the play who rejects the new order or the idle life (921–23) simply. Since under Plutos' reign all men will be just, i.e., lead a private life or mind their own business, there will no longer be law courts and hence no sycophants; the sycophants belong altogether to the age of Zeus. In the period of transition they as well as the other unjust men are still punished. To some extent the sycophant was punished by Plutos himself, who deprived him of his property. But this informal act does not suffice. Accordingly he is formally punished by Karion, who now usurps the role played by the sycophant in the old order (928–29; cf. 918–19); with the entire approval of the just man, he takes away the sycophant's good coat and shoes and forces on him the worn-out things belonging to the just man. The sycophant is too weak to offer resistance, but he does not give up; realizing that Karion is only an agent acting on behalf of Plutos, he threatens that if he finds a helper "that strong god" will be punished on this very day for single-handedly dissolving the democracy. The point is well taken; if all men are just, there will no longer be a need for laws and hence for a legislative body. The sycophant's threat is of course altogether ineffectual. Owing to

Plutos' revolution the sycophant will change places with the just man, as
in the *Knights* Kleon changed places with the sausage seller, it being understood that thanks to Plutos' presence there is no longer a need for a
human ruler. One sees at once how mild the new order is when one compares the sycophant's punishment by Karion with the punishment of another sycophant by Asklepios (716–26). After the sycophant has fled,
Karion and the just man enter the house so that the just man can pray to
Plutos.

The third visitor is an old woman who tries to behave like a kittenish
young girl. She tells Chremylos, who welcomes her, that since Plutos has
begun to see, she has suffered a terrible injustice that makes life unbearable
for her. She had a poor but handsome boyfriend who fulfilled her every
want, while she took care of all his needs. He needed small amounts of
money in order to buy things for himself, his sisters, and his mother.
Apparently he was the only man in his family, so that his aged girlfriend
had to "keep" the whole family in order to keep him. He surely convinced
her entirely of his unselfish and undying love for her. Now he has completely changed. Not having been wicked and therefore now having become well-to-do, he returned her gift of sweets with a somewhat nasty
remark about her age. The contrast between the way in which he treated
her before and the way in which he treats her now is shocking and might
make one wonder whether he deserved to be enriched by Plutos. The hag
is certain that he did not. Chremylos, vindicating the cause of the god,
assures her that her just grievance will be redressed. She demands that her
former lover be compelled to pay his debts to her. Chremylos replies that
the young man has paid his debts by living with her hitherto. Yet he had
promised not to leave her as long as she lived. While Chremylos tries to
find a way out of this difficulty, the boyfriend himself appears. He adds
insult to the injury that he has done to his former love; Chremylos not
only approves of this but joins in it. Yet however much he is amused by
the ridiculous hag, his sense of justice does not permit him to forget her
just claims: Since the youth has drunk the wine, he must drink the dregs
too. The youth refuses to listen and, but for respect for Chremylos' age,
might have beaten him. He asks the youth, who had come to pay homage
to Plutos, to enter the house. When the hag says that she too wishes to talk
to the god, the youth is eager to leave, but Chremylos assures him that no
compulsion will be exerted against him. He may have to compensate the
hag for his breach of promise, but the compensation, we may be sure, will
not be too hard on him. His case is obviously more complicated than that

of the sycophant; hence it is more helpful for understanding the transition period than is the latter. His obligation to the hag was a consequence of his former poverty, but he can not get rid of the obligation by the payment of money, which he now has in abundance. Since the fulfillment of the obligation is beyond the endurance of a man who is not in very great need, some arbitration by a man like Chremylos is necessary. The scene with the youth and the hag reminds us of the scene in the *Assembly of Women* in which the hags lay their hands on the youth enamored of the girl. If we contrast the victory of the hags in the *Assembly of Women* with the pitiable situation to which the hag is reduced in the *Plutos*, we see how inferior Praxagora's scheme is to that of Plutos or of Chremylos. While Praxagora ruthlessly sacrifices natural inequality to legal equality (or natural superiority to legal superiority of the naturally inferior), Plutos abolishes conventional inequality and thus restores natural inequality to its full sway; for whatever compensation may have to be awarded to the hag for her boyfriend's breach of promise, henceforth no youth will ever be compelled by poverty to do what he did. Both Praxagora and Plutos free *eros* from servitude to wealth; yet while Praxagora achieves this by doing greater violence to *eros* than wealth ever did, Plutos liberates *eros* from servitude to wealth without subjecting it to any other servitude. By putting an end to the perversion of *eros* through wealth or law, he brings it about that *eros* comes into its own, just as he brings it about that wealth no longer has to be calumniated as corrupting. This may be said to constitute Plutos' reply to Penia, whose repulsiveness reminds us of that of the hag: The inequality among men regarding wealth or poverty does disturb the natural order. The doubt that may have been cast on nature through the figure of Penia is removed by Plutos: Penia is—or is concerned with—need, but *eros* is not simply need; the arts may be the children of Penia, but *eros* is not. In the words of Diotima, Eros stems from the mating of Poverty and Wealth.

The fifth visitor is Hermes. He wishes to talk to Chremylos and his whole family, not to Plutos. He never speaks of Plutos as a god. He fails to talk to Chremylos (and his family) since he is met at the door by Karion, and his conversation with Karion renders his talking to Chremylos unnecessary. His intention was to tell Chremylos that Zeus would like to punish Chremylos and his family (and, I suppose, his friends, not to say all just men) for their impiety, for since Plutos' sight has been restored, no one brings sacrifices to the gods. Karion replies that the stoppage of the sacrifices is final and moreover just, since the gods did not take care of men: They were as unjust as the friends of the just man, i.e., they were more unjust than anyone appearing in the play. Hermes does not contradict him; he does not even repeat Zeus' threat. He has only one concern: He is starved to death. In Karion's view Hermes deserves his fate on account of his injustice. Yet the somewhat thievish slave has compassion for the god of thievery, who has acted as Karion's friend more than once. He is therefore prepared to help the god in his straits to the best of his power. Hermes wishes to live with men and more particularly to be a member of Chremylos' household. As he admits without blushing, he is deserting his fellow beings, his fatherland as it were, since the true fatherland is the place where one does well. If justice is minding one's own business and nothing else, Hermes is just. But as his fate under Plutos' reign shows, he is as little truly just as the other gods. Therefore he can not partake of the wealth that henceforth is reserved for the just; he must work for his livelihood. He proposes various kinds of employment, but all of them prove to be no longer needed. He finally proposes to become president of the games both musical and gymnastic: Owing to the universal leisure brought about by Plutos' reign, the need for such games is greater than it ever was. Karion accepts this proposal, while leaving no doubt that Hermes will earn his livelihood by acting as a servant of human beings. The mere fact that a slave can take care of Zeus' threat and Hermes' grievance or request shows abundantly how much the reign of Plutos is the reign of man. In the new order of the *Plutos*, Plutos occupies the place that the birds occupy in the new order of the *Birds*.

The last visitor is a priest of Zeus the Savior. He too looks for Chremylos and not for Plutos. He too never speaks of Plutos as a god. He too is starved to death because men no longer bring sacrifices, since now they are all rich; the temples are deserted and held in contempt. He too is anxious to desert the gods and to stay with Chremylos. Chremylos has no objection provided the god wills it, for, as he puts it, Zeus the Savior has come here on his own initiative: The true Zeus the Savior is Plutos. Priests will be needed in the new order, as well as a president of the games. The time has now come to establish Plutos where he was established formerly, in the good old times, namely as the guardian of the *opisthodomos* of Athena, where Athens' treasure is kept. Chremylos arranges the procession. He assigns functions in the procession to Zeus' priest and to the hag. The hag learns from Chremylos that her boyfriend will visit her that evening; we are permitted to hope that this will be his final visit. Plutos, who is in a way the most important personage in the procession, is completely silent.

The relation of the youth to his repulsive girlfriend reminds us of the relation of Chremylos to Penia and therewith to the age of Zeus. It is in accordance with this that of the six visitors of Plutos only the hag and the former priest of Zeus are mentioned in connection with the final procession. Thanks to Chremylos' initiative, a disgraceful dependence based on compulsion and pleasurable only to one side gives way to the dependence on Plutos, who can not help being altogether kind—a dependence that is in fact the use of Plutos or the control of him by man. One must also not forget the parallel between the youth's deserting the hag and the priest's deserting Zeus.

The *Plutos* celebrates the wished-for recovery of Athens from her present decline and the wished-for restoration of her former wealth (1191–93) by presenting that recovery as having taken place in a miraculous, impossible, or laughable manner. What is true of the *Plutos* is true of all the other comedies with the exception of the *Assembly of Women:* They all celebrate a wished-for blessing for Athens or for an Athenian by presenting that blessing as having come about in a miraculous, impossible, or laughable manner; the burning down of Socrates' think-tank is meant to be a blessing for Athens. The present from which the *Plutos* starts is low, not only when compared with the past in which Athens was at her peak—before her defeat in the Peloponnesian war or before that war—but also through belonging to the age of Zeus as compared with the age of Kronos, or rather with the age when Plutos was still young and seeing (88–89, 95, 221, 581). The *Plutos* presents the dethronement of Zeus as necessary for justice to be rewarded with wealth and hence for all men to be just. Aristophanes' approval of Chremylos' design is not surprising: The poet means well by justice. The end of Zeus' rule is not the end of divine rule, for Plutos takes the place of Zeus. It almost goes without saying that the two other fundamental requirements of the city—the prohibitions against father-killing and incest—are, to say the least, left intact by the transition from the rule of Zeus to the rule of Plutos.

The dethronement of Zeus is also celebrated in the *Birds*, in which the three fundamental requirements of the city are likewise respected. Yet in the *Birds* the man responsible for the design himself becomes the successor of Zeus, whereas in the *Plutos* not the man responsible for the design but the god Plutos becomes the successor of Zeus. In the *Birds* the initiative is altogether with Peisthetairos; in the *Plutos* the initiative is with Apollon's oracle literally understood and literally obeyed by the pious Chremylos. One may therefore say that in the *Plutos* the undoing of the Olympian gods is caused by these gods themselves, by their ineptitude rather than by the Promethean action of a human being. One must also not forget the decisive and unwitting contribution of the god Asklepios to the outcome of the play: Asklepios never dreamed, during the many centuries during which Plutos was blind, of restoring Plutos' sight, and it is more than doubtful whether he knew that the blind being whom he cured was Plutos. Peisthetairos, that super-Alkibiades, is concerned with becoming the sole ruler of all gods and men. Chremylos, a crudely just peasant, is concerned with his justice and the justice of his likes being rewarded with wealth. The change effected by Chremylos takes place in Athens; the change effected by Peisthetairos obviously affects all men. Chremylos is the most humdrum hero whom Aristophanes has created. In accordance with this, the *Plutos* is his most humdrum play. It lacks the luster that the other plays possess, if to different degrees, thanks to the presence in them of natural rulers male or female, Socrates, Euripides, and the comic poet himself. It is altogether an old men's play: Chremylos' son never appears; the youth is necessary only for the sake of the hag; no beautiful female appears on stage and thus embellishes the play. We hear much of Plutos' having become seeing again; we hear nothing of his having become young and beautiful again. The *Plutos* does not end with a wedding as the *Birds* does. What is true of Chremylos and Plutos is true of the new order that they bring about. In the new order all men will be wealthy and hence just: There is no place in it for education toward justice and gentlemanship. This is the reason why Chremylos' son never appears: It was the concern with his upbringing that induced Chremylos to consult the Delphic oracle. There is no place in the new order for the arts or crafts. Old age, death, and disease will remain; since there will no longer be physicians, men will need more than ever before the help of the good god Asklepios. There will no longer be human government, and hence the desire to rule will wither away. Yet crimes are committed not only from desire for wealth and for rule. Crimes are also committed from *eros*. Incest is such a crime. Ought one to say that in the new order incest will not be regarded as a crime? The fact that slavery is preserved would seem to indicate that the family is also preserved. It is therefore better to say that in the *Plutos eros* is disregarded and at most only alluded to by the presence of the hag, the only character in the play who swears by Aphrodite (1069–70). In the new order no one will commit any crimes from *eros* or any other motive, since every crime will be punished instantly with poverty. This is not to deny that in the new order *eros* will no longer be perverted through wealth, but this is only the inevitable and unintended consequence of the abolition of poverty. Considering the relation between *eros* and music, or wisdom in general, one may indeed describe the new order by saying that there is no place in it for the vulgar crafts or for government, but all the more for *eros* and wisdom. Yet one must add at once that the *Plutos* does not celebrate the new order on this ground: The survival of old age (and death) and of simplicity is more visible than the survival of *eros* and of wisdom. Plutos can speak on behalf of the poet (796–99) because the play celebrates the rule of wealth as distinguished from that of Aphrodite. The humdrum character of the *Plutos* can not be traced to the dethronement of Zeus, as is proven abundantly by the *Birds*.

Zeus is much less powerful than Plutos when guided by Chremylos, just as he is much less powerful than the birds openly ruled by Peisthetairos. Chremylos' action on behalf of Plutos reminds us not only of Peisthetairos' action on behalf of the birds but also of Trygaios' action on behalf of Eirene. Plutos contributes as little or almost as little to his victory as Eirene does to hers. While there can be no doubt about Plutos' being alive and capable of walking and talking, he lacks Eirene's beauty. In different ways Plutos and Eirene are each severally divinity itself. Once Plutos' sight is restored, he becomes necessarily and universally helpful by taking the place hitherto occupied by the arts, *nomos*, and chance, or by being as it were the unity of the arts, *nomos*, and chance.[103] This means however that Plutos is only one ingredient of the divine. Just as Eirene's liberation is opposed by Polemos, Plutos' liberation is opposed by Penia. Polemos and Penia act on behalf of Zeus or in accordance with Zeus' will, explicit or implicit. While Eirene and Plutos are attractive or gracious, Polemos and Penia inspire fear (438, 575). Polemos and Penia are easily thwarted. The undefeated opposite of that ingredient of the divine, the comical equivalent of which is Plutos rather than Eirene, is Athena *pammachos*, who is celebrated at the end of the *Lysistrate*, rather than Polemos. Through observing the correspondence between Penia and Polemos we become aware that the open praise of poverty as such is not matched anywhere in the plays by an open praise of war as such.

The *Plutos* celebrates the replacement of Zeus' rule by Plutos' rule: With the cessation of Zeus' rule, injustice among men ceases. The example of Hermes would seem to show that in the new order the gods too will have no choice but to be just. At the beginning of the play Plutos was more than half convinced of Zeus' wisdom in blinding him, for he was convinced that wealth corrupts absolutely. Yet he also believed that Zeus is unjust, for he traced Zeus' blinding him to his envy of the just. Penia vindicates Zeus' justice by inferring from the corrupting character of wealth that Zeus is poor and hence just. Above all, if wealth absolutely corrupts, Plutos himself must be absolutely unjust. Surely if wealth corrupts absolutely, all men are bad. Yet the play shows that this sad view of man (and of Plutos) is not true: If justice is manifestly rewarded, or if there is no opportunity for injustice—in other words, if justice is the necessary and sufficient condition of wealth—all men will be just. Plutos' justice is proven by the fact that his victory is the victory of the just and the defeat of the unjust. Plutos' rule is the perfectly just order; it achieves completely what the law merely wishes to achieve, namely, the reward of the just and the punishment of the unjust; therefore it renders the law superfluous. The *Plutos* may then be said to celebrate the victory of the spirit of the law. The law does not expect men to do what is right merely because it is right and to avoid the wrong merely because it is wrong, for it relies on rewards and punishments. Accordingly, the order established by Plutos or Chremylos is based on the premise that what all men by nature seek is not law-abidingness or justice but wealth, and hence that the desire for wealth, not to say the love of gain, is not as such bad. The *Plutos* vindicates the dethronement of Zeus through vindicating the love of wealth, rather than the love of justice. Under Plutos' reign justice is secure because it is manifestly necessary; justice is more "necessary" than ever before, for since all men are rich the danger of *hybris* is greater than ever before, and injustice is instantly punished by poverty. Justice is necessary, i.e., it is not desirable for its own sake; men's enjoyment of life derives less from their awareness of their justice than from *eros*, music, and the like. The *Plutos* presents the comic equivalent of this view of justice by presenting that view in the perspective of old and poor peasants of crude justice. As Aristophanes' comedies show, this view of justice is perfectly compatible with the most earnest desire to teach the just things in all seriousness.

IV · Conclusion

We turned from the *Clouds* to the other comedies because we were unable to learn from the *Clouds* to what extent Aristophanes had considered the implications of his judgment on Socrates, i.e., on Socrates' thought or teaching, and in particular on his thought or teaching regarding the gods. We never expected that the poet's judgment on Socrates would be identical with his judgment on sophists or philosophers in general. Aristophanes put himself under the law that demanded that he choose an Athenian sophist-philosopher, and among the Athenian sophists-philosophers Socrates was the most outstanding; Socrates had traits of body and soul that distinguished him from other sophists-philosophers, Athenians or strangers, for instance from Prodikos. Despite or because of this, Aristophanes' presentation of Socrates is the most important document available to us on the ancient disagreement and opposition between poetry and philosophy as such [1]—between the two forms of wisdom, each of which claims supremacy—as this feud appears from the side of poetry.

The other comedies confirmed the view that Aristophanes regards himself as superior to his greatest antagonist on account of his self-knowledge and prudence (*phronesis*): Whereas Socrates is wholly indifferent to the city that feeds him, Aristophanes is greatly concerned with the city; whereas Socrates does not respect, or comply with, the fundamental requirements of the city, Aristophanes does. The kind of wisdom that exhausts itself in the self-forgotten study of the things aloft and in its corollaries is unable to protect itself against its enemies because it is unable to act on the city or to humanize it by counteracting the waspishness of the city, and it is unable to do this because it does not in the first place recognize the necessity of that waspishness; the poet however, whether comic or tragic, can protect himself against persecution. Surely in the sense indicated Aristophanes teaches, as he claims to teach, the just things, or all his comedies are the true Just Speech. By seeing the necessity of justice the poet indeed sees its limitations. In other words, he complies with the fundamental requirements of the city without looking at them altogether as the city looks at them. Hence his teaching of the just things is identical with his treating them comically: The just things and the laughable things do not occur in his plays side by side, but they are inextricably interwoven. By presenting as laughable not only the unjust but the just as well, he brings it about that his comedy is total: There is no Aristophanean character of any consequence who does not act laughably, let alone who is good sense incarnate.[2] This does not mean that in his view life as a whole is a comedy; if it were, there would be no need for comic equivalents of noncomical things. The Aristophanean comedy is only a partial mirror of life. Therefore it points to what escapes it or transcends it.[3] With considerable exaggeration one may say that it points to what is the preserve of tragedy; for there is no reason for assuming, for instance, that the indoor instruction given by Socrates to Strepsiades and Pheidippides, which is withheld from the audience because of its noncomical character, is tragic. The Aristophanean comedy certainly presupposes tragedy; it builds on tragedy; in this sense, at any rate, it is higher than tragedy. It conjures up for us, within the limits of that possibility which it must respect, a simply pleasant falsehood: a life without war, law courts, terrors caused by gods and death, poverty, and coercion or restraint or *nomos*. The falsehood points to the truth; the truth is the inevitable suffering, coeval with man, that is caused by both *physis* and *nomos*. That harsh truth is indicated but also obfuscated by what human beings say about the gods; yet the hostile power of the gods—as distinguished from the harshnesses due to *nomos* proper and to *physis*—can be easily overcome, as appears with particular clarity if one compares the *Assembly of Women* on the one hand with the *Peace*, the *Birds*, and the *Plutos* on the other. One could say that both tragedy and comedy present the transgressions of sacred laws, tragedy presenting such transgressions as acts of *hybris*, and comedy presenting them as acts of *alazoneia* (boasting). This does not mean that in a given comedy the most conspicuous character or the character responsible for the design—in the *Knights*, for instance, the sausage seller on the one hand and Demosthenes on the other—is a boaster. Nor are Lysistrate and Chremylos boasters. In the *Acharnians*, not Dikaiopolis but Lamachos is the boaster. In a narrow and vulgar sense—in the perspective of very common people—everyone who excels in any way, who is "something special" and therefore is held to "wish to be something special" is a boaster, and it is of the essence of the Aristophanean comedy to present things to the mere laughers within this perspective. The boaster par excellence, the boaster in a nonvulgar sense, is the comic poet himself, who after all is responsible especially for those successful transgressions of sacred laws that he celebrates in his plays. This is not to deny that he sometimes engages in vulgar boasting (cf. *Acharnians* 646–54). How this judgment must be restated in the light of his suggestions regarding the being of the gods has been stated with utmost clarity in the proper place.

The second trait that, according to Aristophanes, distinguishes Socrates from the poets is his ineptitude in judging human beings and in handling them. The man who above everything else worries about the things aloft has a very inadequate knowledge of the manners and souls of the various kinds of men: From on high one does not see human beings as they are (*Peace* 821–23). Hence not the sophist-philosopher but the poet is able to raise and answer the question that Socrates never raises, let alone answers, as to the godness of the gods. Socrates, one may say, is a leader of souls (or of ghosts—*Birds* 1555) without being a knower of souls. If this is so, the truth discerned by the sophist-philosopher about the things aloft must be integrated into a whole that is the concern of the poet, despite the fact that that whole is a part of the all-comprehensive whole with which the sophist-philosopher is concerned. For we are not entitled to assert, although we are not forbidden to surmise, that there is a connection between the dualism of the two ingredients of the divine and such dualisms as those of Love and Hatred or of Motion and Rest. It suffices here to remind the reader of what was said on the occasion of the birds' theo-cosmogony.

Finally, the Aristophanean Socrates is characterized by being anerotic. This is connected with his being apolitical: The family is the cell of the city. The fact that the family needs the city is in perfect harmony with the tension, not to say disharmony, between the family and the city. The anerotic Socrates is a-Music, or does not love the beautiful in any form, including the beautiful use of the ugly; he is the great debunker. For the same reason he lacks that spiritedness or waspishness that is an indispensable ingredient of the comic poet: Socrates' arrogance and impatience with stupidity can not be mistaken for anger and indignation.[4]

Isocrates addressing the Athenians tells them, "I know that it is hard to oppose your opinions and that, while there is a democracy, there is no freedom to say everything except here [sc., in the Assembly] for those who are most thoughtless and do not care for you at all, and in the theater for the comic poets." ⁵ What Isocrates says about the doubtful character of the freedom to say everything in the Assembly is beautifully confirmed by Diodotos' speech in Thucydides. Isocrates does not question the view that at any rate the comic poets enjoy or use the freedom to say everything. We have seen however that Aristophanes draws a line somewhere, obeying the dictates less, as he claims, of good or gentlemanly taste than those of wisdom. He ridicules Socrates, not for trying to keep his teaching secret from the uninitiated, but for his ineptitude in this respect.

The Xenophontic and Platonic Socrates differs from the Aristophanean Socrates in almost all the aforementioned respects. He is a man of the greatest practical wisdom, or at the very least of the greatest longing for it (*Phaedo* 68ᶜ2); he is the only truly political Athenian; he respects not only the fundamental requirements of the city but all her laws; he is the best of citizens and in particular a model soldier; he is the unrivaled master in judging human beings and in handling them, in knowing souls and in guiding them; he is the erotic man par excellence and a devotee of the Muses, especially of the highest Muse; he is of infinite patience with stupidity and of never-failing urbanity. Accordingly the wisdom of the Platonic Socrates is superior to the wisdom of the poets: The truth discerned by the poets must be integrated into the all-comprehensive truth with which the philosopher is concerned; or the true knowledge of the souls, and hence of the soul, is the core of the cosmology (of the knowledge of the things aloft). One can easily receive the impression that Plato and Xenophon presented their Socrates in conscious contradiction to Aristophanes' presentation. It is certainly impossible to say whether the Platonic-Xenophontic Socrates owes his being as much to poetry as does the Aristophanean Socrates (cf. Plato *Second Letter* 314ᶜ1–4). It is almost equally difficult to say whether the profound differences between the Aristophanean Socrates and the Platonic-Xenophontic Socrates must not be traced to a profound change in Socrates himself: to his conversion from a youthful contempt for the political or moral things, for the human things or human beings, to a mature concern with them. The clearest and most thoughtful exposition of this possibility known to me is to be found in Muhammad b. Zakariyya al-Rāzi's *The Philosophic Way of Life*.⁶

Notes

I *Introduction*

1. *Oeconomicus* 6.12–13, 11.3; *Memorabilia* I 1.11–16. Cf. Burnet on *Apol. Socr.* 21ᶜ5. Cf. *Laches* 186ᵇ8–ᶜ2.
2. *Philebus* 48ᵃ8–50ᵃ10.
3. *Republic* 516ᵉ8–517ᵃ2, 517ᵈ4–6; *Theaetetus* 174ᵃ4–ᵈ1.
4. *Acharnians* 645, 655, 661–62; *Knights* 510; *Frogs* 389–90, 686–87, 1008–12, 1049–57; *Assembly of Women* 1155–57.
5. *Republic* 498ᶜ9–ᵈ1.
6. See especially the account of *The Birth of Tragedy* in *Ecce Homo* and the section entitled "The Problem of Socrates" in the *Dawn of Idols*, but above all *Beyond Good and Evil*.
7. Karl Löwith, *Nietzsches Philosophie der ewigen Wiederkehr des Gleichen* (Stuttgart, 1956), p. 122.
8. *Beyond Good and Evil*, nos. 6 and 211.
9. Xenophon *Memorabilia* I 4.3.

II *The Clouds*

1. Heine, *Werke*, ed. Elster, V, 283–84. Cf. Friedrich Schlegel, *Wissenschaft der europäischen Literatur*, ed. Ernst Behler, pp. 88 ff., and Hegel, *Aesthetik* (Werke, ed. Glockner, XIV, 560–61).
2. In the conversation between Strepsiades and the pupil prior to Strepsiades' becoming aware of Socrates, nine subjects of inquiry are mentioned, five of them in reply to Strepsiades' questions.
3. Only the last feat serves a practical purpose; two of the three other feats are originated by Socrates and both are failures, through the actions of Strepsiades and of the lizard respectively: The lizard made Socrates the astronomer ridiculous, while Strepsiades will make Socrates the rhetorician ridiculous and not only ridiculous.
4. Cf. Plato *Republic* 596ᵇ12–ᵉ3; *Sophist* 233ᵉ5–234ᵃ6.
5. The context suggests that compared with Socrates Prodikos is rather effeminate; cf. Plato *Protagoras* 315ᵈ4–6.

315

6. Cf. the triad mentioned in 419 with Xenophon *Memorabilia* I 1.19.

7. The Muses go abroad veiled in thick air: Hesiod *Theogony* 9.

8. Plato *Ion* 534 reads as if the Muses were the only gods, if not the only god.

9. Cf. Plato *Republic* 510a1–3, 516a6–7.

10. Xenophon *Memorabilia* IV 3.1–2 and 5.1–2.

11. Cf. Plato *Laws* 945e.

12. Only in the antistrophe are the localities mentioned of the gods there spoken of; it would have been hard to ascribe a locality of this kind to Ether, who is spoken of in the strophe.

13. Cf. Diogenes of Apollonia B 4–5 (Diels-Kranz, 7th ed.); Aristotle *De anima* 404a9–10.

14. Contrast this with what the poet does in the *Knights:* The important action in the Council, which takes place during the parabasis, is duly reported immediately after the parabasis (614, 624 ff.).

15. Empedocles B 43.

16. That Strepsiades' memory is not as bad as it appears when he is under the strain of his threatened expulsion from Socrates' school appears from a comparison of 787–89 with 1248–58.

17. Cf. 1048–49 with 1046 and 1011–19. Thucydides (I 49.1–3) characterizes the old times by "spiritedness and strength" in contradistinction to knowledge or art, characteristic of the present.

18. Cf. Thucydides III 45.

19. Thucydides V 105.2.

20. Proceeding differently than Burnet and A. E. Taylor, I have come to agree with part of their view of the Aristophanean Socrates. My disagreement with them has two different, although not unrelated, reasons. Burnet and Taylor are concerned with the *Clouds* as a source rather than with understanding the play by itself. Above all, their position is what for want of a more convenient term may be called harmonistic. On the historical level that tendency shows itself in Taylor's assertion that the Aristophanean Socrates is both a physiologist along the lines of Diogenes of Apollonia for instance and a thinker concerned with the royal or political art in the sense of Plato (or Xenophon); he does not pay proper attention to the assertion of Plato's *Laws* X, according to which failure to grasp the radical difference between soul and, say, air leads to contempt of the political (or royal) art. Burnet and Taylor are unable even to consider the possibility that the Platonic (or Xenophontic) Socrates is to some extent a reaction or response to the Aristophanean Socrates. To state my criticism of Burnet more simply, one of his two canons for the interpretation of comedy is based on the premise that "statements of facts are not funny" (*Greek Philosophy* sect. 113)—a premise that would be true only if there were never any funny facts.

21. Both Aristophanes and the Unjust Speech, as distinguished from Socrates and the Just Speech, swear by Dionysos. The only other character in the *Clouds* who swears by Dionysos is Pheidippides.

22. Plato *Laws* 671c6–7.

23. Sophocles *Oedipus Rex* 1361, 1403–7.

24. Consider Plato *Clitopho* 410a7–b1 and *Protagoras* 337c7–d4.

25. There are no women in the *Clouds* except such as can not be embraced (257).

26. Cf. Plato *Theaetetus* 173a6–174b6.

27. Cf. *Birds* 1491–95. Cf. Plato *Phaedo* 60c9–61b7.

III *The Other Plays*

1. 493; cf. Plato *Laches* 185ª1–2.
2. *Frogs* 959, 976–77, 1021–27, 1040, 1063–64.
3. Thucydides is silent about Lamachos in his account of the war up to and including the time when the *Acharnians* was first performed.
4. Cf. 87, 109, 135, 373, 605.
5. In the *Acharnians* there is no parallel to the second parabasis of the *Clouds*, in which the chorus reveals the large agreement between the chorus' concern and the poet's concern.
6. Consider the three mentions of *agora* and the three proper names in 836–59.
7. Consider the contrast between 1000–2 and 1003–17 in the light of the sequel. Consider *Frogs* 739–40 in the light of the opposition, crucial for that play, between Dionysos and Herakles.
8. Cf. G. Kaibel, *Comicorum Graecorum Fragmenta*, p. 141b 1.48–50; see *ibid.*, p. 66 1.13: *in tragoedia fugienda vita, in comoedia capessenda exprimitur.*
9. Cf. the silence on the comic poets in *Clouds* 1089–94. Goethe makes on the proper occasion the following remark: "[der Poet und der Prophet] sind von Einem Gott ergriffen und befeuert, der Poet aber vergeudet die ihm verliehene Gabe im Genuss, um Genuss hervorzubringen, Ehre durch das Hervorgebrachte zu erlangen, allenfalls ein bequemes Leben." *Noten und Abhandlungen zum Divan,* "Mahomet."
10. Compare the implication of the speech on wine in the first two books of Plato's *Laws*.
11. Cf. Strauss, *Thoughts on Machiavelli* (Glencoe, Ill.: The Free Press, 1958), 342 n. 181.
12. 875–80; cf. *Clouds* 1089 ff.
13. 1010; cf. 364–65, 962–64, 998, 1056–57, 1242, 1385. Cf. 877–80 and Thucydides III 37.3.
14. 1321; cf. Plato *Second Letter* 314ᶜ4.
15. Cf. 1331 with Thucydides I 6.3.
16. Cf. Plato *Fifth Letter* 322ª8–ᵇ1.
17. Cf. e.g. *Clouds* 547–48, *Wasps* 1044, 1053.
18. Kleon claims to be the father of the *demos* (1037–39), but never to be its child.
19. Cf. Aristotle *Politics* 1291ᵇ15 ff. and 1318ᵇ6 ff.
20. Cf. Aristotle *Constitution of Athens* 16.
21. 134, 948–50, 1229–43.
22. Consider Thucydides I 138.3 and, above all, Xenophon's *Education of Cyrus*.
23. Consider Plato *Laches* 179ᵇ6–ᵈ5.
24. Both Dikaiopolis and the sausage seller are masters of the art of cooking (*Acharnians* 1015–16 and the scholia on the *Knights passim*; cf. Plato's *Gorgias*); but the sausage seller, as distinguished from Dikaiopolis, uses that art for Demos, rather than for himself; there is no emphasis on his supplying Demos with wine (1187).
25. Cf. *Frogs* 727–36 with *Knights* 181, 185–86, 336–37. As Seth Benardete points out to me, the suggestion made in the text may throw light on the end of the second parabasis (1300–15): In the world in which nothing impossible happens, Kleon is likely to be replaced by the lamp seller Hyperbolos; just as

Kleon is stopped by the miracles of Demos having become personified and the unrecognizable natural ruler meeting Demosthenes at the right moment, Hyperbolos could only be stopped by the miracle of the triremes becoming speaking and thinking beings.

26. Xanthias explains to the audience the *logos* (54), Demosthenes the *pragma* (*Knights* 36).

27. 269–70; cf. 220 and 365.

28. Cf. 359–61 with Plato *Republic* 562e3–563a2 and 567e5–7.

29. Diopeithes (381) reminds us of the Athenian who brought in the bill that provided that those who do not believe in the divine things and who teach about the things aloft should be impeached (Plutarch *Pericles* 32.1).

30. Consider the inverse situation as indicated by the change from the singular to the plural in 975–76.

31. Compare the presentation of Laches in Plato's *Laches*.

32. 50 (cf. 44); cf. note 26 above.

33. Schol. on 119. The *Aiolos* is the play from which Pheidippides quotes a passage dealing with incest (schol. on *Clouds* 1371).

34. *Knights* 1013, 1087; *Birds* 514–15.

35. 240–41; cf. *Acharnians* 978–87, 964.

36. Cf. *Wasps* 57.

37. Cf. Thucydides V 75.3 (see *The City and Man* 222).

38. Cf. 267 with 271 and 276–78 with 285; cf. 214 and 218.

39. 269–73, 280–84, 320; cf. *Knights* 1390–93.

40. *Clouds* 225–26, 584–86, 1506–7; *Birds* 1572–73 (cf. Deuteronomy 4:19).

41. Cf. 188; *Knights* 156.

42. Cf. Thucydides VII 14 and 48.4 (cf. *The City and Man* 197–200).

43. Cf. Plutarch *Fabius Maximus* 22 and Thucydides II 13.5 (*The City and Man* 161).

44. Cf. Diels, *Vorsokratiker*, 7th ed., no. 36.

45. See the last word of the *Lysistrate*.

46. Xenophon *Memorabilia* I 1.2.

47. Cf. Aristophanes' speech in Plato's *Symposion* (191e6–192b5) and Xenophon's *Hiero* 1.29–38 and 8.6. Cf. above p. 101 and note 12 above.

48. Cf. 175–77 with *Knights* 173–75.

49. Melos was starved into submission by the Athenians. In *Clouds* 830 Socrates is called the Melian, i.e., the atheist, since Diagoras of Melos was the most notorious atheist; cf. *Birds* 1073.

50. Aeschylus *Agamemnon* 1629–30; Euripides *Iphigenia in Aulis* 1211–14; Simonides fr. 27 Diehl.

51. Cicero *Republic* III 14 (cf. Herodotus).

52. Schol. on 645; Plato *Apology of Socrates* 32b2.

53. This character of the parabasis of the *Birds* is underlined by the fact that the chorus' claim to a prize for the performance of the play occurs not in the parabasis but long before (445–47).

54. *Clouds* 361; cf. Cicero *N.D.* I 118.

55. Cf. schol. on 1218: "Chaos" stands here for air.

56. Cf. Aristotle *Politics* 1275b22–34.

57. See above, p. 127.

58. Aristotle *Politics* 1277a18–20.

59. See above, p. 110.

60. *Lyra Graeca*, ed. J. M. Edmonds, III, 262–64.

61. One may wonder whether the co-ordination of the three kinds of birds (mantic, music, and sea birds—1332–33) with the three visitors (father killer, the poet, and the sycophant) does not point to the following three postures regarding Right: 1) justice identical with legality, 2) justice distinguished from legality, 3) simple rejection of justice.
62. See above, p. 33.
63. Compare the conflict between piety and patriotism (poetry) as indicated in the *Minos* (318e6–319b2, 320e2–321a1).
64. See above, p. 103.
65. Aeschylus *Agamemnon* 170–72, *Prometheus* 755 ff.
66. Cf. Thucydides II 64.2 with Aristotle *Rhetoric* 1391b1–3.
67. 585; cf. 494–96 and 110–11.
68. 188–90; cf. Aeschylus *Seven against Thebes* 43–45.
69. Cf. Plutarch *Nicias* 13.7.
70. Cf. Aristotle *Politics* 1269b12–1270a8.
71. 1109. For the interpretation cf. Xenophon *Memorabilia* II 2.2 and III 1.6 as well as *Cyropaedia* I 6.27.
72. Plato *Laws* 637a–b.
73. 954–58, 1091–92; *Thesmoph.* 491–96.
74. *Wasps* 1029–30, *Peace* 751.
75. 85 and 181–82; cf. *Acharnians* 630–31 and *Wasps* 1284–91.
76. Of course not on Sicily (446); cf. *Lysistrate* 590.
77. 454; *Clouds* 1508–9.
78. *Republic* 396e2.
79. Cf. Dikaiopolis' account of the origin of the Peloponnesian War in *Acharnians* 523–29.
80. Cf. above, p. 208.
81. Cf. above, p. 222.
82. Diels, *Vorsokratiker*, 7th edition, fr. 15.
83. Cf. Plato *Theaetetus* 180c7–d5.
84. Cf. *Thesmoph.* 383–432; Xenophon *Memorabilia* III 4.
85. Cf. Xenophon *Oeconomicus* end.
86. Cf. above, p. 228.
87. Rousseau, *Contrat Social* I 9 end; cf. *Acharnians* 718 and context.
88. Cf. above, pp. 170 and 203.
89. Aristotle *Politics* 1277b20–23.
90. 540c5.
91. According to the fifth *hypothesis* (Hall-Geldart), Chremylos' name is derived from "debt" and "deceiving": "He who deceives his debtors on account of poverty."
92. There is a particularly close connection between Plutos and money (131, 141, 147, 154, 194–96), i.e., the conventional par excellence.
93. Aristotle *Rhetoric* 1381a19–23.
94. Cf. Aristotle *Politics* 1295b1–34.
95. Cf. *Acharnians* 53; cf. Aristotle *Rhetoric* 1391b1–3.
96. Cf. Xenophon *Memorabilia* I 6.10.
97. Cf. Xenophon *Memorabilia* I 1.6–9.
98. Cf. *The City and Man*, 42 and 86.
99. Cf. above, p. 140. Hugo Grotius, *De aequitate* etc. 2.2: *leges omnes, quatenus libertatem impediunt, habent aliquid acerbi, contra iis liberari dulce est.*

100. Cf. above, p. 212.
101. 129, 267, 366, 403, 1043. Cf. *Knights* 705.
102. *Acharnians* 649–51; *Frogs* 1008–10.
103. Cf. above, p. 296.

IV   *Conclusion*

1. Plato *Republic* 607b5–c3 and *Laws* 967c5–d1.
2. Cf. especially Philinte in Molière's *Misanthrope* (and Rousseau's critique of this character in his *Lettre à d'Alembert*).
3. The most striking example is the verse on Sophocles in the *Frogs* (82) and the corresponding absence of Sophocles among the characters of the play.
4. Cf. Aristotle *Rhetoric* 1383b3–8.
5. *On the Peace* 14.
6. See Paul Kraus, "Raziana I," *Orientalia*, 1935, 300–34.

Index